The Writing of History

EUROPEAN PERSPECTIVES: *A Series of the Columbia University Press*

Allegorical etching by Jan Van der Straet for Americae decima pars
by Jean-Théodore de Bry (Oppenheim, 1619)

Michel de Certeau

THE WRITING
OF HISTORY

Translated by Tom Conley

Columbia University Press
NEW YORK

Columbia University Press
New York   Oxford
Copyright © 1988 Columbia University Press
L'écriture de l'histoire copyright © 1975 Editions Gallimard
All rights reserved

Library of Congress Cataloging-in-Publication Data

Certeau, Michel de.
[L'écriture de l'histoire. English]
The writing of history/Michel de Certeau; translated from the French by Tom Conley.
p. cm.—(European perspectives)
Translation of: L'écriture de l'histoire.
Includes bibliographies and index
ISBN 0-231-05574-9
ISBN 0-231-05575-7 (pbk.)
1. Historiography. I. Title. II. Series.
D13.C3413 1988
907'.2—dc19   87-30900
CIP

Book design by Jennifer Dossin

Printed in the United States of America

Hardback editions of Columbia University Press books are Smyth-sewn
and are printed on permanent and durable acid-free paper.

CONTENTS

TRANSLATOR'S INTRODUCTION
For a Literary *Historiography*

OVER the decade between the publication of *L'Ecriture de l'histoire* and his untimely death in 1986, Michel de Certeau came to feel that of all his writings, this book was the most terse, sustained, prismatic, and synthetic. In 1980 he wrote a preface for a revised edition, in which he endorsed further the tenets of its many reflections on historiography and religion. He had been especially eager to see the work appear in English. The Americas figure prominently in his anthropology of belief and ideology in the early period of colonial development. Their allegorical and spatial presence furnishes a geography for the movement of his speculations; the Western hemisphere also figures as one of the panels of the diptych of *The Writing of History*. The American world in fact tests the conclusions of his European historiography, its pragmatic orientation being foreign to his psychoanalytical approach, while its discovery can be seen to mark the beginnings of modern history.

Dividing his labors between the Ecole des Hautes Etudes en Sciences Sociales and the University of California, de Certeau used his travels between France and the Americas to cultivate the art of deracination essential to the historian's craft. Historiography in general, he argued, has arisen from the European encounter with the unknown other. Sometimes this other is fancied as a country of endless vistas; or, as the European first sets foot upon American shores, the New World appears as an exotic maiden, surging up from his own dreams about destiny and travel. The imagination suddenly throws askew a European mind, at that time mired in conflict between belief and fact throughout the Renaissance, that sought to establish a past and order a knowledge within Judeo-Christian tradition. Before it ever took shape, the great Hegelian edifice of absolute history was fissured by the division between the New and Old Worlds.

No doubt Michel de Certeau wished to see how his book would be received when mirrored in English. But now, alas, too late, for the author died prematurely, not long after this translation was undertaken. He was unable to see how his project would stand in the world through which he wandered, from West to East, like Freud's Moses, without patriotic ties. That he wished to see how his writings would move between old and new continents suggests that *The Writing of History* entails careful study of unconscious allegorical tendencies often at the basis of historiography.

Historiographers study the shape of evidence. Often they desire to determine how its form outlines the contour of an absence, a void, or a silence which in turn is assumed to be the ground of history. The writing of history can begin only when a present is divided from a past. An initial act of exclusion separates current time from past time, or the living from the dead. The historian's sense of duration is defined by what is left behind, or registered as past. Once this "other" time is established, interpretation is legitimized, speculation develops, and writing is set in motion. Scholars must draw a line between what is dead and what is not. By inaugurating this difference in their position and method, historians posit death as a total social fact (often without stating or even imagining it as such); but also, in their very act of indication, they deny its presence. A sense of loss is advanced, but its void is immediately filled with the knowledge the historian reaps from his division of past and present. Historians endlessly establish contingent time through archeology; they produce the past by virtue of practicing arcane crafts of resurrection, animation, and even ventriloquism.

The aim of creating worlds of words that convey—and betray—the truth of the past is thus based upon the obsessive relation that the contemporary age holds with death. The historiographer and the analyst virtually generate forms of knowledge from their continued confrontation with death, and only through this relation with death do they begin—

and continue—to write. That very beginning is, quite paradoxically, unendingly present; the past, once it is named as such, establishes the crux of current time. The labor of *writing* is ongoing, perpetually dividing and suturing the past and present. It is seen at once in the dynamics of writers' living relation with death and in the knowledge springing from their dynamic rapport with its presence. This knowledge, inevitably and invariably a form of allegory, gives recognizable contour to evidence or historical fact.

Michel de Certeau suggests that the movement of writing, what indeed motivates figural thinking, also inflects historiography. We glimpse its passage in historians' desire to travel back to foreign lands of times past, but especially in the language that describes their imaginary navigations. As such, metaphor and allegory, determining much of what is expressed in historiography, also play decisive roles in the rapport that the present time holds with death. The tropes of history advance terms both present and absent; they invite their readers to move with the motion of figures articulating their research. Quite often for the contemporary historian, the unyielding stability of facts only grounds perceptions. At best it marks a position from which movement can be traced.

The contemporary historian, mindful of discourse as a force that bears upon the shaping of the past, envisages his or her language as one that yields partial facts as a by-product of motion. The figures of historiography encapsulate the entire design that an author makes of the past, yet by englobing the past within metaphor, historians succeed in fragmenting, isolating, dividing, but also in creating their fields of knowledge. For this reason, when Michel de Certeau locates the labor of historiography in the styles of discourse or arrangements of reported facts, he emphasizes how we can envisage movements of language valorizing our sense of history.

In this respect the archival endeavor is obsessively fragmentary. Local totalities are fashioned from research that remains always intensely specific, partial, and of needs in areas situated between the physical aura of objects and the discourses that name them. Historians work upon the limits that their discipline imposes. From the vicissitudes of methods of inquiry, the historiographer builds "local" representations of the past or solves partial problems. Yet the fragmentary nature of the enterprise implies that totalities may be gleaned from scrutiny of detail. Structures are somehow glimpsed through patterns subtending the contingency or gratuity of events. At any time, de Certeau maintains, only a limited number of representations can be made; these "discursive formations" produce the ideological range of representation, what he calls "the limits of what can be thought" (especially in chapter 2 and the introduction to part II, the "Productions of Time"). They tell us that historians can only imply a sense of totality through the figures that play between interpretation and knowledge. Inquiry into highly specific issues can offer glimpses of unconscious totalities no less effectively than the mythic omniscience that the historian had sought in former times.

Something of the literary or "textual" analyst inspires the historiographer. Both specialists appeal to the rhetoric of the documents they study. They recover how the "speech acts" which seem to be recorded or staged in their evidence betray something *other* that their writing cannot entirely efface. In the movement between the constancy of language that represents events and the contingency of their fabrication, the literary historian and the chronicler work together. They use the notion of the unconscious, likened to a rhetoric, in order to disengage how languages of the past are always in a silent dialogue with unyielding problems of mimesis.

For these reasons, what had been named "invention" in rhetoric, a category synonymous with selection in documentary study, is of common and urgent concern to analyst and historian alike. At issue is what a writer or a document chooses as worthy of discourse; every indexical act entails forces of attention and of oblivion, simultaneously in the past (in what was then included, what excluded) and the present (in the analyst's will to privilege given documents over others). Both the student of rhetoric and the student of history show us that understanding is based on effects of representation. Critics and historians discover that whatever is deemed trivial or worth forgetting may, upon close scrutiny, evince a "strategy" that wills to efface, marginalize, or even repress more complicated and ambivalent designs. For both disciplines, the criteria of selection become the object of study no less than an archive or a literary text. But what produces and perpetuates those criteria? Alert historians address these questions and deal with what de Certeau calls "acquired rationalizations," used to organize the past and present. They must be studied no less pervasively than knowledge or its visible architecture in the heritage of disciplines and their methodologies.

Former totalities of history are studied in terms of the allegorical process that shaped the contour of their evolution. According to the type of historiography that de Certeau advocates, self-enclosing designs that produce an "author," a "period," an "epoch," or even a "generation" or "movement" are worthy subjects of study. Their modes of appropriation are keynote. The latter betray forces of self-legitimation that invariably reflect the investments the current time places in the past for the purpose of its own advancement. A symmetry or grand design—the *telos* or intention that a project or a discipline heralds for itself—partakes of the rapport that allegory holds with the production of information. In prior historiography, the archivist was concerned with designing schemes that would apply to and comprehend a totality. The historian, de Certeau argues, once held a realm or an empire, whereas today students of the past cultivate analytical methods that enable them to discern motivations that change over time. They now practice methods rather than keeping watch over a single area of study. Contemporary historiography deals with unconscious relations that inform objects and practices; it takes up areas formerly consigned to silence or set outside of the frame of given disciplines.

In this way *The Writing of History* implies that the aims of historiography and literature have been converging since the Enlightenment. The task of the archivist involves deciphering hidden relations held in discourses of other times, while the creative writer weaves those same relations, whether with death or posterity, into a fabric of poetry fashioned from contemporary life. Where the historian reveals the ineffable dimensions of social order that the past could not control, the modern artist invests them in conscious designs that are not a product of chance—in webbings of contradiction, ambivalence, and equivocation of language. On many occasions Michel de Certeau suggests that fiction and history are quasi-identical. Historiographers, he notes, have been marginal, even deviant figures in their societies. Their mythic desire to produce totalities of knowledge is sapped by the very methods that are used to bring form and symmetry to knowledge. "The historian is no longer an empire builder. He no longer aims at the paradise of a global history," for nowadays he prefers "to circulate about acquired rationalizations" of the past (chapter 2). The historiographer is a "prowler" who works on the edges of reason. Like the fictioneer who fabricates worlds of words that cannot fit the ends of a practical scheme, the historiographer is a "poet of details" who endlessly "plays on the thousand chords that a rare composition awakens in a network of knowledge."

Indeed, the present state of "literature" or "text," de Certeau notes, stages a perpetual movement of reorganization, or a mortuary circulation that produces knowledge as it concomitantly effaces itself. Where histo-

riography puts its own scientific urgencies into question, literature finds
some of its esthetics in formal modes of inquiry that had been the mark
and even the elegance of history. Historians are now quite skeptical of
the designs or the rhetoric that once made their orders so clear, convincing, or compelling. By elaborating similar networks in entirely illusory areas, so also are creative writers. De Certeau's point is limpidly clear
in the ninth chapter in which, through a close reading of Freud's *Moses
and Monotheism*, he shows how the psychoanalyst makes an ultimately
complex—scientific, autobiographical, mythic—history from the figure
of movement, of writing, of errancy and destiny in unpromised lands.

   The Writing of History works toward the conclusions of its last section
(chapters 8 and 9) through varied speculation on the trajectory that the
West has taken in moving away from faith in its attraction to reason.
Since the advent of Cartesian thinking, reason contends with but even-
tually supersedes a fideistic view of the universe; it makes knowledge and
ratio the evidence of a divine order that must necessarily be taken as invisible, self-evident, and unbendingly true. The historian explains the paradox in two ways. On the one hand, he subscribes to Lucien Goldmann's
figure of the "hidden god" of the seventeenth century, in which the disappearance of what had been a medieval presence (by virtue of its identity
with the languages and forms of matter) is now a sign of emergent capitalism. Gnostic views overtake those of animism.[1] This is the moment
when "state policy" (which translates the French expression *raison d'Etat*)
arrogates religious structures in order to create subjectivity. The laws of
God function within the reach of those who control rational thinking.
Through an optic that is limited to the fortunes of belief, the author
shows how political religion takes root in seventeenth- and eighteenth-
century Europe. He later uses contemporary human sciences to indicate
how their culmination in "enlightenment" has ultimately been severely
questioned. Enlightenment comes of exclusion; what is "repressed" then
surfaces in mystical expression. In the Classical Age, this repressed is the
language of the woman possessed; or it is figured in contorted images
drawn from encounters with the primitive in the New World. As time
proceeds, areas that are associated with folklore—regional hagiographies,
local legend, communal practices that resisted or took place alongside
formal institutions imposed by centralized power from without—become part of a mystical heritage. Although mysticism necessarily pervades
Europe in the fifteenth century—a problem which de Certeau studies at
greater length in his last work, *La Fable mystique* (1982)—its local and

regional manifestation evinces the ways that official rationale, after using a practice of incarceration, develops a reason which, in the guise of "enlightenment," purports to account for mystical expression. Here the author develops analyses of local forms of possession and madness (notably in chapters 6 and 8) whose documentary detail probes many of the suggestive tenets in Michel Foucault's *Madness and Civilization*. Such are the implicit narrative threads linking the chapters of *The Writing of History*, devoted to theory in the first two parts and textual analysis in the third and fourth.

In part I de Certeau begins by studying the present state of historiography. Its development has mirrored other transformations within the human sciences. Moving away from a will for totality (*Geistesgeschichte*), it no longer purports to be an autonomous and self-guaranteeing enterprise. It cannot furnish a model which will account for diversity. In its study of the tactics of expression and the rhetoric of mimesis, historiography appears to resemble the detailed workings of literary analysis. It attends to discourses that test the margins of social cadres; it mixes statement with irony. In part II, de Certeau shows how, in the fortunes of Christendom in the Classical Age, the state fabricates the image of a self-identical nation emerging from the hegemony of Church; the state now assigns rational order to the formerly heterogenous communities that had made up much of the rural medieval world, communities that had been left intact in the realm of religion. Close in orientation to current historical research on questions of centralization and the design of Louis XIV's rise to power,[2] chapters 2 and 3 trace how belief is transformed into moral utility. An ascending political body uses religion to frame social mores according to its intentions. Part III demonstrates how the confusions of belief and social action mark the alterities in early modern Europe. In the work on Jean de Léry and ethnography in the Americas in the fifth chapter (which plays a crucial role in explaining the preface to the second edition and its frontispiece), de Certeau indicates how the European practice of writing in the early years of the printing press takes hold of oral cultures and subjects them to its subliminal control. Similar repression marks the fortunes of the madwomen at Loudun (chapter 6), who shift between madness and "unreason" in the trials that ultimately determine how orders of confinement confirm the ways "state policy" excludes anomaly and difference—whether sexual, religious, or linguistic—from its views about faith. The dissolution of hagiography into a censured discourse is shown (in chapter 7) to be further evidence of the same movement, in which agrarian and oral traditions, celebrating the supple extension of body, space, and language, are marginalized in the eighteenth century.

The fourth part of *The Writing of History* turns upon the other three. Freud's treatment of the past—what he "makes" of history—represents a countermovement turning back upon the Enlightenment. Freud writes protean analyses of origins which are at once science, folklore, riddle, comedy, and structural exegesis. They have no single goal, and their composition embodies movements of displacement and translation. Psychoanalytical history marks the limits of Hegelian projects that aimed to attain absolute knowledge and spirit. Freud's *writing* is seen as a concretely modern and an archaic, mystical activity. It works through a gnostic rationale by the myriad ways that it rides along the paradoxes its expression puts forward as emblems, conundrums, or other shapes of wit. Its formulation is one of a "reasoned rebus," or a combination of rational (vocal, historical, pragmatic, diurnal) process with its own goal, and other (nocturnal, visual, unconscious, polymorphous) designs that critics call a discourse of "ambiguity," of *Bilderschriften* (image-writing or hieroglyphics), of literal dimensions that both ground scientific inquiry and make their resolution baffling.[3] These rich and engaging chapters culminate the volume and establish the importance of de Certeau's identification with simultaneously literary and historiographical strands of Freudian analysis.

All of the major tenets of de Certeau's writings have resonance in *The Writing of History:* the historian's relation with death; the presence of the past as a return of repressed force; the fact that Western historiography cannot fail to stress the crucial importance of religion and community at the center of its discipline; the importance of everyday life in study of times past; the vital role that mysticism plays in the historian's relation with writing; the birth of the modern world when voice, image, or schema become discrete languages. These and other motifs are synthesized in the author's two prefaces before they recur within the analytical texture of the subsequent chapters. The work on possession and errancy appears to mirror de Certeau's transdisciplinary use of the human sciences, European religious history, contemporary literature, and psychoanalysis. Because de Certeau's method is located in his mode of writing, several concepts which inform the *Writing of History* merit review. Their dynamics reveal how and why de Certeau writes in a hermetic but entirely logical and dazzlingly lucid style.

The author uses a psychoanalytic notion of the event (or *événement*) to remind us that every "fact" that has been recorded and is today assumed to be historically valid is shaped from conflicting imaginations, at once past and present. Try as we may to describe an event in order to determine "what happened there," we must realize that events are often our own mental projections bearing strong ideological and even political imprints. De Certeau does not dispute the point that certain events may have occurred. Rather, he emphasizes how events are described, how they are considered meaningful, how they become worthy of record or notice. The eye that recognizes them is necessarily conditioned by the ideologies, assumptions, and dispositions of the observers and scribes from the past, of the chroniclers who have created the modern historian's archives. This background inevitably inflects the ways historians select and interpret events.

In this manner, events can be likened to highly coded tropes that "read" or allegorize the past. The symmetries of their allegory have optical qualities which betray and constitute the verisimilitude of history. Because they are expressed in metaphor, events become fantasies that congeal into images; like illustrations or photographs in history books, they generate affective charge through their stenographic reduction of information. They "freeze" continuous process into emblems. In its highest logical category, the event belongs to the dialectical traditions of historiography and psychoanalysis, in which occurrences are named in imaginary terms that frame other, far more "real" issues or structures—such as language, or death—which not only resist change but also establish the bedrock of present time.

The historian and the artist both fabricate discourses whose meaning is located less in the semantics of speech or grammar than in obsessive knots of half-signs that are grasped syntactically, by interlocutors' distraction or by sudden shifts in perspective or attention. Among literary critics, for whom the "event" is generally a consequence of representation, the process is not unfamiliar. Here Michel de Certeau draws much from practices of textual analysis, for the sake of infusing archival labor with the breadth of the literary imagination. All of his studies display rigor and patience. Unlike many Freudians, he reads and analyzes Freud in German. His bibliographic research is exhaustive and scrupulous. Yet the documentary methods he employs, which had often been used narrowly in positivism, biography, bibliography, or in the study of sources, now provide a fresh, highly material sense of writing. Erudition becomes a field of play rather than a substantiation of fact.

No doubt the historiographer senses the past through the ways that anthropology and psychoanalysis have inflected the fortunes of the human sciences in France. It is worth remembering that in his initial essay of *Structural Anthropology,* devoted to the relation of history to ethnography, Claude Lévi-Strauss noted that the historian and ethnographer share the same "road toward the understanding of man, which goes from the study of conscious content to that of unconscious forms." The ethnographer moves ahead in order to attain more and more of the unconscious through conscious forms, while the historian, "keeping his eyes fixed on concrete and specific activities from which he withdraws only to consider them from a more complete and richer perspective," moves backwards.[4] De Certeau begins from what Lévi-Strauss called the Janus-like solidarity of the two disciplines and follows the very same path through the fortunes of religion from the early modern age into the Enlightenment. In this context ethnographers, historians, and psychoanalysts have begun to question the severe limits that empirical science had drawn around the *événement.* They have reminded us how fluid and legendarily diverse history becomes when figured in the unconscious movements of language and symbolic exchange.

Michel de Certeau's historiography studies how events are handed down to us. They *do* occur, to be sure, but in part according to the conventions dictating how we receive, imagine, and pass them on. They may do no more than mark a position in a movement of forces, or perhaps they are scripted in order to occur. At other times, they cannot fail to transpire. Whether Freudian returns of the repressed, Marxian inversions of tragedy and comedy, or Nietzschean eternal recurrences, their effects anticipate future patterns, since they carry in themselves the residual presence of typologies which dictate our relation with what we construe to be past.[5] *L'Ecriture de l'histoire* ascertains how the same repetitions work in narratives which both mirror and incarnate a sense of historical order.

The *réel,* the term the author uses to situate these tales, accounts, or archeologies, is taken from Lacanian psychoanalysis. By *réel* the author implies a world of unmarked space and time that cannot be mediated by language or signs. The object-universe, like the unconscious dimension of history, is in fact impervious to language. We know that sensorial reality—what we touch, read, see, hear, and smell—exists only insofar as it is coded according to a culture and tradition of philosophical sensibility. Our apprehension of it, then, is strictly filtered through systems of knowledge and belief that are perforce circumstantial and local but continually present and always renewed through representation. Yet the real world is not merely a figment of language. The world of objects is there, terribly "real" in resisting human modification.

For de Certeau, it appears that the *réel*—a primary world of forms resisting intelligible practices which would strive to make them recognizable or reduce them to rational systems (such was the European fantasy of America in the sixteenth century)—is a "nature" always in dynamic relation with "culture," glimpsed in its points of strain, or heard in its silences. The historian apprehends it in the gaps that knowledge cannot rationalize. It appears on the edges of systems of intelligibility or seeps through lapses where discourses from one period cannot be assimilated into those of others. The *réel* jumps forth when Jean de Léry cannot describe what he sees in the clearing in the woods that shroud him; de Certeau likens the moment to a "ravishment" in which the one possessed is unable to break through the aura of a trance. A moment "evading legalities, disciplines of meaning" (as described in chapter 5), the *réel* may involve something of a "cerebral, illegal" pleasure crossing through the subject, who is buoyed in a vision where language and the world intersect and vanish in the body.[6] At that moment, the utter alterity of the subject becomes evident.

On a broader plane, de Certeau implies that the *réel* can be imagined as constitutive of history, because its virtually impossible but necessary condition establishes the discontinuity forming chains or narratives of events. History becomes something *other* that lends contingent shape to the world; it both "approaches" and reflects the *réel*. In contrast, "reality," like the world of moral utility in the period of "state policy," is often what a subject strategically chooses it to be. Derivative of a view *selected* through the historian's imaginary relation with the world, reality emerges as a material dialogue with its other, that is, with language which produces its order.[7] Historians are aware of these paradoxes in their agencies of selection and exclusion; and all the more when they encounter the *réel* through the intransitivity of writing.

Historiography traces an unending drama of encounters with the *réel*. The historian's ever-repeated affrontments recreate the beginnings and continuities of documentary activity. Time and again de Certeau invokes the *réel* to destabilize the statistical or empirical privilege held over divisions of time that are taken as classic, such as the "Age of Reason," the "crisis of conscience" in the eighteenth century, or the "Enlightenment." And by approaching history through theories of religion, he views language and mimesis as forces informing most collective relations. Because modern history cannot fail to study the erosion of the symbolic shapes of religion, it must always return to question the narratives and legends that engender a communally significant past. The *réel* shows us how transitory such meaning really is.

Prevalent throughout the nine chapters is a continuous and tortuous movement to and from *sujet* and *objet*. The author's use of "object" has resonance in the context of historiography, dealing with the unstated intentions of the historian. A surface glittering with the subjective limits and aims of consciousness, the *objet,* because it is part of the *réel,* refuses to absorb or represent the historian's desires which are projected toward it. As a partialized figure of the historian's preoccupations, *objet* acquires the psychoanalytical charge of something akin to a loss. It is what the documentarian attempts to recover, at the very same time that its absence makes it absolutely, maddeningly neutral and thus a shape that spurs historiographic drive. Since the archivist's *objet* is both structural and documentary, it partakes of intense subjective investment.

Better than in any of de Certeau's other works, *L'Ecriture de l'histoire* locates a fissure between symbolic traditions and the "real" in early modern history and literature, running from the incunabulum up to the Enlightenment. As noted, emphasis in the first half of the book falls upon French religious history, especially the ways that the logic of mystical thinking is contained within categories of "unreason" or invisibility that replace what had been accepted as the alterity of the mystic. The author suggests that texts written prior to the age of Louis XIV have to be read multifariously, as complex bodies. Symptoms are scattered over their visible surfaces and through their multiple allegories. These texts summon practices that the reader animates through intellection and the five senses. When, after the Reformation, the past becomes only a sign of that former complexity, texts bear the effects of reason. The relation that mystical thinking holds with the body and with writing falls victim to gnosis and to increased distance between the senses and tactile forms. Associations and analogy, modes that had been a commonplace in archaic areas of religion and literature, find themselves divided and realigned. Alterity is no longer left alone; henceforth, it is studied and contained within reason. By situating such strategies of containment in religious space (in ways not dissimilar to Michel Foucault's emphasis on shifts of epistemology), de Certeau suggests that a religious rationale moves into political spheres during the growth of centralized government.

But where and how do explosions of alterity "erupt" in early modern time? For de Certeau mysticism is hardly an abstraction. It is very material, if not graphic, evidence of a continued historiographical or "scriptural" (*scripturaire*) process engaged in a dialectic of belief, writing, and absence. Mystical texts are the repository of our own unconscious, because their manifest being—including the composite whole of their printed or written characters as well as their semantics—is identical to both their author's bodies and the alterity of their vision. Yet the historiographer reconstitutes the mystical vision for the end of deciphering the alchemical wonder of a body transformed—oxydized as it were—and traced into ink, paper, or vellum. Mystical writing bodies forth the stakes of engagement with death. Not struggling to deny death, the mystic affronts, incorporates, embodies, and scatters it within the shape of its memory left in the rifts between language and writing. In a very compelling and real way de Certeau defines the modern condition of literature, what he esteems to be, since the heritage of Mallarmé, "the scriptural experience unfolding in the relation between the act of moving forward and the mortuary ground on which its travels are traced."[8]

Michel de Certeau's tact in infusing interpretation with archaic vision is proof of another principal concept, *le retour du refoulé*. The French translation of the Freudian phrase, "the return of the repressed," indicates that historiography must exhume what it cannot know, or dig up whatever it can muster, to have a fleeting grasp of the present. The past will always enter the flow of current life because it is an absence on which the visible evidence of truth is based. Most often this return is shaped in what de Certeau terms the "scriptural" basis of writing. Here the repressed is not easily discerned; its language is a graphic presence of bodies conjured up from visions or memories of other worlds. It is heterogenous to the ratio of knowledge or of preestablished chronological time. Like orality thrown into a culture based on writing (one of the topics of chapters 5, 6, and 7), the repressed resurges as something seen as other, and recognizably different from what conveys it. Historiography is constantly being rewritten in the abyss between the idea of the repressed and the fear of its continuous return.

That gap can be treated in another problematic concern of *L'Ecriture de l'histoire,* that of *discours*. Few concepts have been used so pervasively or productively over the last decade as "discourse." Its most carefully crafted and lucid origins are located in Emile Benveniste's *Problems in General Linguistics*.[9] Studying the difference between uses of the first or second persons and uses of the third, the linguist demonstrates that historiography aims at the exclusion of the existential relation with language that would be implied by the seeming presence of an "I" or a "you." Historians have traditionally attempted to transcend the contingency of discursive scenes by establishing "fact" through strategies of self-effacement or omniscience. This is achieved by prevalent use of the third person, the "he" or "she" attached to verbs in the preterite tense. A gloss of truth is obtained when self-effacement legitimizes a subjective ordering of events which discourse designates and arranges. Descartes' hidden performativity in the aptly titled *Discours de la méthode* is pertinent, where the "I" becomes the foundation for a position that will authorize itself later to speak in the third person, in the guise of total objectivity. Contrary to the simulation of living speech conveyed by discourse as it is performed, historical enunciation is possible only in writing.

The power-structure of historiography is underscored, as de Certeau will illustrate through allusion to Machiavelli in the preface to the revised edition, when the historian avers to be, whether in competition for a position under Lorenzo de Medici or for a tenured rank in a university, a courtier. The paradox of "historical discourse" is used to shift back and forth from writing to speech, but its reigning virtue—its ineffable power—depends in part upon the absent presence of the third person. The gap between the first and third persons, or between the voice and its alien other—writing—activates many of de Certeau's analyses. He locates rifts between the historical will-to-truth and the veracity its discourse seems to be producing. It could be implied that he argues for a *discours de l'histoire,* a discourse of history—but not "historical discourse"—written along the interstices of lived, existential relations with language and collective desires wishing to bring living adequacy to inherited symbolic forms.

Yet the book's title is *L'Ecriture de l'histoire:* like most of de Certeau's formulas, the words are not difficult to turn into English, but translated they convey little of the complexity expressed in the French usage. The simple analogue, "the writing of history," does not tell us that *écriture* implies more than verbal discourse: it is a Scripture in secular garb, but it is also literature, "writing," in an imperiously intransitive form. Following in the steps of Freud's Moses, writing sets off in search of its own poetics. *Ecriture* shares much with literary practice, a discipline without *telos* or object in sight. The homologies of literature, Scripture, and history are implied in the French, locating—in the formulation of de Certeau's title—the doubly identical mission of literature as both *écriture* and chronicle. We can assume that his work moves in the direction of a specifically "literary" historiography. With its independently aural and visible "tracks" (as in cinema, a figure de Certeau favors in the fifth chapter with his use of the term "voice-off"), written discourse fashions literature from history. The great historiographers—Machiavelli, Marx, Michelet—are most documentary and most patently *real* for their readers when their historical imagination is seen as identical to the writer's craft. The inscription of movement, of attraction, of fear or belief betrays history enough to assure us of its firm grounding in literature.

L'Ecriture de l'histoire keeps an uncanny and active relation with translation. For if transcription had been one of the tasks of the chronicler, its theory and renewed play are those of the historiographer. The latter always betrays events; he or she turns unfamiliar or repressed figures of meaning into coherent discourse. In a compelling way the very same risks and pleasures of translating *L'Ecriture de l'histoire* begin with a similar relation. It is initiated with the frontispiece. Europe, imagined as Amerigo Vespucci dressed in a tunic hanging over a suit of armor, disembarks from his galleon to behold America, a supine, Rubenesque woman rising from her hammock. Whence de Certeau's legend. A tradition of *writing* faces the desired *image* of the exotic repressed, the other, just as, contrariwise, the initial page of de Certeau's history faces the pictural alterity of the allegorical engraving to its left. One "translates" the other, but is irreducibly different from what it juxtaposes.

The same blindness marks the translation beneath the reader's eyes. It has been written in an effort to be scrupulously faithful to the rhythm and temper of de Certeau's sentences. Now and then the disposition of the author's French approaches the syntax of mystical writing. Like the organization and goal of the book (which is lucidly described in geometrical terms in the two prefaces), the style combines "curial" diction[10] with involutions characteristic of psychoanalytical discourses. The shape of de Certeau's sentence often produces meaning in its balance of paratactically positioned clauses. They are conceived as units cast in spatial disposition, their visual perimeter defined by the left and right ends of the sentence itself. The meaning that develops from the reader's scansion of the sentence (moving from left to right) is contrasted to the visibility of its paratactic order. The author appears to keep the narrative and visual elements in constant dialogue with one another. Occasionally his arguments afford dialogue with meaning in the grammatical field. Hence the arguments have a choppy or "vertical" aspect (as in Stendhal's legalistic, ironic, and lyrical French) because they are mantled into triadic groups.

Shades of numerical allegory infuse the style. Analogical signs sally forth from within the lexical scheme of the expositions. Their clarity therefore blinds; they are thrust ahead by a religious order combining the force of logic with a poet's verbal drive. The often "early modern" design of Michel de Certeau's prose has a Cartesian aspect, but it also functions according to associative patterns common to earlier writing. A medieval, juridical, dialectical style conveys his thinking, but its ubiquitously psychoanalytical cast—borrowed in part from the Mallarmean tradition that he draws from Lacan's *Ecrits*—arches the formulations back over themselves. Direct and indirect objects or relative constructions can refer to different antecedents in both single or contiguous sentences. Within the clarity are cast deep shadows of equivocation.

Frequently Michel de Certeau lets personal pronouns float (in the dative or accusative cases), seemingly in order to modify one or two particles at once. Equivocation yields an analogical sense of infinite extension of reference, but within the order of classical French. Absolute clarity betrays rich ambiguity. Now and again some equivocation has been attenuated for the sake of underscoring his analytical thrust. Where de Certeau strings a concept through a pronoun cast over the length of several sentences, I have occasionally felt it necessary to repeat the initial reference, to suggest how a Proustian undercurrent in his syntax allows rigor and drift to flow together. I have abbreviated his usage of the *colon:* a mark employed more often in dissertative French, but yet part of the literary stenography of the Cartesian heritage, the colon often uses its arrest to produce an effect of truth. The abruptness of its assertion is too convincing. In the original French the author devaluates it through profusion of usage. I have extended some of his sentences that cluster independent clauses to give them a feel of extension. Because the author both summarizes and advances arguments in the cadres of each individual clause, I have attempted to make the visual symmetry of their sequences resemble the meaning held in their grammatical order. His terse, somewhat anti-Ciceronian style tends to impose meditative arrests in the gap between each sentence (as well as the synthetic units of paragraphs or chapters). I have felt the need to respect their pace and rhythm. The tradition reaches back from Descartes to Montaigne, but de Certeau's use of the mode in modern French, akin to the meditative temper of the style of a Roland Barthes or a Jean-Louis Schefer, makes the utter clarity of analysis a form of poetry.

The Writing of History is also a work of erudition. A *speculum* and an encyclopedia, it includes a wealth of documents in its plethora of allusion. Wherever possible I have located available English translations of secondary references. Others I have translated from the original French. In the case of Freud, whom de Certeau translates from the *Gesammelte Werke,* I have used the *Standard Edition* for all quotations in English. If any of the brilliance of Michel de Certeau's style shines through the English, it is thanks to the patient editing of Luce Giard and Ann Miller. Kerry Bruce McIndoo prepared the drafts with consummate expertise. The success of the translation will owe much to these individuals. Any infelicities that remain are my responsibility.

Tom Conley

NOTES

1. As Wlad Godzich notes in his careful review of Michel de Certeau's *Heterologies,* the gnostic viewpoint reigned supreme "with the Cartesian reversal of the relationship of faith to reason in relation to truth: henceforth the belief in God and the truths that he dispenses would be subject to the prior operations of reason." See "The Further Possibility of Knowledge," preface to *Heterologies* (Minneapolis: University of Minnesota Press, 1986), p. xv.

2. Among other studies: Louis Marin, *The Portrait of the King* (Minneapolis: University of Minnesota Press, 1988), and Michel Foucault, *Madness and Civilization* (New York: Pantheon, 1965).

3. Along with de Certeau, studies of this aspect of Freud—that is, his writing which overrides the themes and aims of the psychoanalytical project—are a growing industry. In French, see Patrick Lacoste, *Il écrit* (Paris: Galilée, 1980), and Jean-Michel Rey, *Des mots à l'oeuvre* (Paris: Aubier-Montaigne, 1979). In English, see Samuel Weber, *The Legend of Freud* (Minneapolis: University of Minnesota Press, 1981), and Leo Bersani, *The Freudian Body* (New York: Columbia University Press, 1986).

4. Claude Lévi-Strauss, *Structural Anthropology* (New York: Anchor Books, 1967), 1:24–25.

5. Erich Auerbach's "Figura" outlines the schema of such timeless history; see his *Scenes from the Drama of European Literature* (Minneapolis: University of Minnesota Press, 1984), pp. 11–78. The principle motivates Erwin Panofsky's study of medieval iconography in *Early Netherlandish Painting* (New York: Harper and Row, 1971).

6. "Ravishment" is a charged term in de Certeau's work. It refers to the mystical experience through allusion to Marguerite Duras' postwar novel, *Le Ravissement de Lol V. Stein.* Also the subject of one of Jacques Lacan's most enlightening studies about vision and language—entitled "Le Ravissement de Lol V. Stein de Marguerite Duras," in *Marguerite Duras* (Paris: Albatros, 1980); available in En-

glish in *Marguerite Duras by Marguerite Duras* (San Francisco: City Lights Books, 1987), pp. 122–29—the novel marks a decisive connection between the contemporary experience of the *réel* and de Certeau's historical mapping of its presence as glimpsed in his study of Loudun (chapter 6), in Freud (chapter 8) and, later, in *La Fable mystique* (Paris: Gallimard, 1982; see especially p. 48).

7. In a typically thorny aphorism, Lacan, one of de Certeau's avowed masters, sums up the quintessence of the *réel*: "Cette illusion qui pousse à chercher la réalité au-delà du mur du langage est la même par laquelle le sujet croit que sa vérité nous est déjà donnée, que nous connaissons à l'avance, et c'est aussi bien par là qu'il est béant à notre intervention objectivante," *Ecrits* (Paris: Seuil, 1966), p. 308. "This illusion which drives us to seek reality beyond the wall of language is the same one according to which the subject believes that its truth [that of reality] is pregiven to us, known beforehand; and it is also according to this [illusion] that he [the subject] is void to our objectifying speech" (my translation).

8. Michel de Certeau, *L'Invention du quotidien* (Paris: Union Générale d'Editions, 1975), p. 328. Available in English as *The Practice of Everyday Life* (Berkeley and Los Angeles: University of California Press, 1984).

9. Especially "Les Relations du temps dans le verbe français," in *Problèmes de linguistique générale* (Paris: Gallimard, 1966), 1:231–50. Available in English as *Problems in General Linguistics* (Miami: University of Miami Press, 1971).

10. Secular manifestations of the curial style are explained by Jens Rasmussen in *La Prose narrative en France au quinzième siècle* (Copenhagen: Munksgaard, 1958).

PREFACE

A MERIGO Vespucci the voyager arrives from the sea. A crusader standing erect, his body in armor, he bears the European weapons of meaning. Behind him are the vessels that will bring back to the European West the spoils of a paradise. Before him is the Indian "America," a nude woman reclining in her hammock, an unnamed presence of difference, a body which awakens within a space of exotic fauna and flora (see the frontispiece accompanying the title page). An inaugural scene: after a moment of stupor, on this threshold dotted with colonnades of trees, the conqueror will write the body of the other and trace there his own history. From her he will make a historied body—a blazon—of his labors and phantasms. She will be "Latin" America.

This erotic and warlike scene has an almost mythic value. It represents the beginning of a new function of writing in the West. Jan Van der Straet's staging of the disembarkment surely depicts Vespucci's surprise as he faces this world, the first to grasp clearly that she is a *nuova terra* not yet existing on maps[1]—an unknown body destined to bear the name, Amerigo, of its inventer. But what is really initiated here is a colonization of the body by the discourse of power. This is *writing that conquers*. It will use the New World as if it were a blank, "savage" page on which Western desire will be written. It will transform the space of the other into a field of expansion for a system of production. From the moment of a rupture between a subject and an object of the operation, between a *will to write* and a *written body* (or a body to be written), this writing fabricates Western history. *The Writing of History* is the study of writing as historical practice.

If for the last four centuries all scientific enterprise has included among its traits the production of autonomous linguistic artifacts (its own specific languages and discourses) with an ability to transform the things and bodies from which they had been distinguished (a reformation or revolution of the surrounding world according to textual laws), *the writing of history* refers to a "modern" history of writing. In fact, this book was first conceived as a series of studies intended to mark off some chronological stages of this practice: in the sixteenth century, the "ethnographical" organization of writing in its relation with "primitive," "savage," "traditional," or "popular" orality that it establishes as its other (part III of this book); in the seventeenth and eighteenth centuries, the transformation of Christian Scripture, the legibility of a religious cosmos, into pure "representations" or "superstitions" marginalized by an ethical and technical system of practices capable of building a human history (part II); at the dawn of the twentieth century, the return of repressed alterity, originating in Freud's modes of writing (part IV, chapters 8 and 9); finally, the current system of the historiographical "industry,"[2] which articulates a socioeconomical site of production, the scientific laws of a form of mastery, and the construction of a tale or a text (part I, chapters 1 and 2). Added to these studies is what, at the end of the eighteenth century, takes up the struggle of a scriptural rationality—"enlightened," revolutionary, and Jacobin—against the idiomatic fluctuations of oral forms of dialect.[3]

Instead of proceeding with a chronological reconstruction overly obedient to the fiction of a linearity of time (see chapter 2, third paragraph), it seemed preferable to bring into view the *present* site in which this investigation took its form, the *particularity* of the field, of the matter, and of the processes (those of "modern" historiography) allowing the scriptural operation to be analyzed, and the *methodological deviations* (semiotic, psychoanalytical, etc.) that introduce other theoretical possibilities and practices into the Western function of writing. For this reason the book is a fragmented discourse fashioned from tactical investigations each obeying specific laws: a socioepistemological approach (in part I), a historical approach (in part II), a semiotic approach (in part III), and a psychoanalytical, Freudian approach (in part IV) make up the sum. Refusing the fiction of a metalanguage unifying the whole work clarifies the relation between *limited* scientific procedures and what they miss of the "real" with which they deal. I have avoided the illusion—necessarily dogmatizing—which belongs to discourse claiming to make us believe our words are "adequate" to the real. Such a philosophical illusion lies hidden in the requirements of historiographical work, and Schelling confessed marvelously its tenacious ambition in the remark, "For us the tale of actual facts is doctrine." That tale deceives us because it wishes to establish law in the name of the real.

Historiography (that is, "history" and "writing") bears within its own name the paradox—almost an oxymoron—of a relation established between two antinomic terms, between the real and discourse. Its task is one of connecting them and, at the point where this link cannot be imagined, of working *as if* the two were being joined. This book is born of the relation that discourse keeps with the real that is forever its object.[4] What alliance is there between *writing* and *history*? It was already fundamental to the Judeo-Christian conception of Scripture. Whence the role played by religious archeology within the modern elaboration of historiography, which has transformed the terms and the very nature of this past relation in order to give it the stamp of fabrication, no longer allowing it to seem simply a matter of reading or interpreting. From this standpoint, reexamination of the historiographical operation opens on the one hand onto a political problem (procedures proper to the "making *of* history" refer to a style of "making history") and, on the other, onto the question of the subject (of the body, of enunciative speech), a question repressed in the direction of fiction or of silence through the law of a "scientific" writing.[5]

Michel de Certeau
1980

NOTES

1. See W. E. Washburn, "The Meaning of *Discovery* in the Fifteenth and Sixteenth Centuries," *American Historical Review* (1962), pp. 1ff.; and Urs Bitterli, *Die "Wilden" und die "Zivilisierten": Grundzüge einer Geistes- und Kulturgeschichte der europäisch-überseeischen Begegnung* (Munich: C. H. Beck, 1976), pp. 19–80.

2. The term is Marx's. "Industry is the *real* and historical link between nature and man," and it is the "basis of human sciences." On the historiographical "industry," see my "Ecriture et histoire" in *Politique aujourd'hui* (December 1975), pp. 65–77.

3. See Michel de Certeau, Dominique Julia, and Jacques Revel, *Une politique de la langue: La Révolution française et les patois* (Paris: Gallimard–Bibliothèque des Histoires, 1975).

4. On this point, see Michel de Certeau and Régine Robin, "Le Discours historique et le réel," *Dialectiques* (Summer 1976), no. 14, pp. 41–62.

5. See part IV below, and my *Fable mystique, XVIᵉ–XVIIᵉ siècle* (Paris: Gallimard–Bibliothèque des Histoires, 1982).

The Writing of History

INTRODUCTION
Writings and Histories

S TUDIOUS and charitable, tender as I am for the dead of the world
    . . . thus I roamed, from age to age, always young and never
    tired, for thousands of years." The open road—"my road"—seems
to take hold of the text of this traveler on foot: "I went, I wandered . . .
I ran along my path . . . I went . . . as a bold voyager." Walking and/
or writing is a labor knowing no rest, "by the force of desire, pricked by
an ardent curiosity that nothing could restrain." Michelet multiplies his
meetings, with "indulgence" and "filial fear" in respect to the dead who
are the inheritors of a "strange dialogue," but also with the assurance
"that never could anyone ever stir up again what life has left behind." In
the sepulcher which the historian inhabits, only "emptiness remains."[1]
Hence this "intimacy with the other world poses no threat":[2] "This security made me all the more charitable toward those who were unable
to harm me." Every day he even becomes "younger" by getting acquainted over and over again with this world that is dead, and definitely
other.

After having successfully passed through the *History of France,* the
shadows "have returned less saddened to their tombs."[3] Discourse drives
them back into the dark. It is a deposition. It turns them into *severed
souls.* It honors them with a ritual of which they had been deprived. It

"bemoans" them by fulfilling the duty of filial piety enjoined upon Freud through a dream in which he saw written on the wall of a railway station, "Please close the eyes."[4] Michelet's "tenderness" seeks one after another of the dead in order to insert every one of them into time, "this omnipotent decorator of ruins: O Time beautifying of things!"[5] The dear departed find a haven in the text *because* they can neither speak nor do harm anymore. These ghosts find access through *writing* on the condition that they remain *forever silent*.

Another, graver mourning is added to the first. The People are also the separated. "I was born of the people. I had the people in my heart. . . . But I found their language inaccessible. I was unable to make it speak."[6] It is also silent, in order to become the object of this poem that speaks of it. Surely, only this language "authorizes" the historian's writing, but, for the same reason, it becomes history's absent figure. An *Infans*, this Voice does not speak. It exists only outside of itself, in Michelet's discourse, but it allows him to become a "popular" writer, to "jettison" pride and, becoming "rough and barbaric," to "lose . . . what I had owned of literary subtlety."[7]

The other is the phantasm of historiography, the object that it seeks, honors, and buries. A labor of separation concerning this uncanny and fascinating proximity is effected. Michelet stakes himself at this border where, from Virgil to Dante, *fictions* were erected that were not yet *history*. This place points to the question that scientific practices have been articulating ever since, and that a discipline has assigned itself to solve. Alphonse Dupront has said, "The sole historical quest for 'meaning' remains indeed a quest for the Other,"[8] but, however contradictory it may be, this project aims at "understanding" and, through "meaning," at hiding the alterity of this foreigner; or, in what amounts to the same thing, it aims at calming the dead who still haunt the present, and at offering them scriptural tombs.

The Discourse of Separation: Writing

MODERN Western history essentially begins with differentiation between the *present* and the *past*. In this way it is unlike tradition (religious tradition), though it never succeeds in being entirely dissociated from this archeology, maintaining with it a relation of indebtedness and rejection. This rupture also organizes the content of history within the relations between *labor* and *nature;* and finally, as its third form, it ubiquitously takes for granted a rift between *discourse* and the *body* (the social body). It forces the silent body to speak. It assumes a gap to exist between the silent opacity of the "reality" that it seeks to express and the place where it produces its own speech, protected by the distance established between itself and its object (*Gegen-stand*). The violence of the body reaches the written page only through absence, through the intermediary of documents that the historian has been able to see on the sands from which a presence has since been washed away, and through a murmur that lets us hear—but from afar—the unknown immensity that seduces and menaces our knowledge.

A structure belonging to modern Western culture can doubtless be seen in this historiography: *intelligibility is established through a relation with the other;* it moves (or "progresses") by changing what it makes of its "other"—the Indian, the past, the people, the mad, the child, the Third World. Through these variants that are all heteronomous—ethnology, history, psychiatry, pedagogy, etc.—unfolds a problematic form basing its mastery of expression upon what the other keeps silent, and guaranteeing the interpretive work of a science (a "human" science) by the frontier that separates it from an area awaiting this work in order to be known. Here modern medicine is a decisive figure, from the moment when the body becomes a *legible* picture that can in turn be translated into that which can be *written* within a space of language. Thanks to the unfolding of the body before the doctor's eyes, what is seen and what is known of it can be superimposed or exchanged (be translated from one to the other). The body is a cipher that awaits deciphering. Between the seventeenth and the eighteenth century, what allows the seen body to be converted into the known body, or what turns the spatial organization of the body into a semantic organization of a vocabulary—and vice versa—is the transformation of the body into extension, into open interiority like a book, or like a silent corpse placed under our eyes.[9] An analogous change takes place when tradition, a lived body, is revealed to erudite curiosity through a corpus of texts. Modern medicine and historiography are born almost simultaneously from the rift between a subject that is supposedly literate, and an object that is supposedly written in an unknown language. The latter always remains to be decoded. These two "heterologies" (discourses on the other) are built upon a division between the body of knowledge that utters a discourse and the mute body that nourishes it.

First of all, historiography separates its present time from a past. But everywhere it repeats the initial act of division. Thus its chronology is composed of "periods" (for example, the Middle Ages, modern history, contemporary history) between which, in every instance, is traced the *decision* to become different or no longer to be such as one had been up to that time (the Renaissance, the French Revolution). In their respective turns, each "new" time provides the *place* for a discourse considering whatever preceded it to be "dead," but welcoming a "past" that had already been specified by former ruptures. Breakage is therefore the postulate of interpretation (which is constructed as of the present time) and its object (divisions organizing representations that must be reinterpreted). The labor designated by this breakage is self-motivated. In the past from which it is distinguished, it promotes a selection between what can be *understood* and what must be *forgotten* in order to obtain the representation of a present intelligibility. But whatever this new understanding of the past holds to be irrelevant—shards created by the selection of materials, remainders left aside by an explication—comes back, despite everything, on the edges of discourse or in its rifts and crannies: "resistances," "survivals," or delays discreetly perturb the pretty order of a line of "progress" or a system of interpretation. These are lapses in the syntax constructed by the law of a place. Therein they symbolize a return of the repressed, that is, a return of what, at a given moment, has *become* unthinkable in order for a new identity to *become* thinkable.

Far from being self-evident, this construction is a uniquely Western trait. In India, for example, "new forms never drive the older ones away." Rather, there exists a "stratified stockpiling," Louis Dumont has noted. The march of time no more needs to be certified by distances taken from various "pasts" than a position needs to establish itself by being sectioned off from "heresies." A "process of coexistence and reabsorption" is, on the contrary, the "cardinal fact" of Indian history.[10] And, too, among the Merina of Madagascar, the *tetiarana* (former genealogical lists), then the *tantara* (past history) form a "legacy of ears" (*lovantsofina*) or a "memory by mouth" (*tadidivava*): far from being an "ob-ject" thrown behind so that an autonomous present will be possible, the past is a treasure placed in the *midst* of the society that is its memorial, a food intended to be chewed and memorized. History is the "privilege" (*tantara*) that must be remembered so that one shall not oneself be forgotten. In its own midst it places the people who stretch from a past to a future.[11] Among the Fô of Dahomey, history is *remuho*, "the speech of these past times"— speech (*ho*), or presence, which comes from upriver and carries downstream. It has nothing in common with the conception (apparently close to it, but actually of ethnographical and museological origin) that, in *dissociating* current time from tradition, in thus imposing a break between a present and a past, and in actually upholding the Western relation whose terms it simply reverses, defines identity through a return to a past or marginalized "negritude."[12]

It would be senseless to multiply the examples, beyond our historiography, that bear witness to another relation with time or, in what amounts to the same thing, another relation with death. In the West, the group (or the individual) is legitimized by what it excludes (this is the creation of its own space), and it discovers its faith in the confession that it extracts from a dominated being (thus is established the *knowledge* based upon, or of, the other: human science). It comes of realizing how ephemeral is every victory over death: inevitably, the reaper returns and cuts his swath. Death obsesses the West. In this respect, the discourse of the human sciences is pathological: a discourse of *pathos*—misfortune and passionate action—in a confrontation with this death that our society can no longer conceive of as a way of living one's life. On its own account, historiography takes for granted the fact that it has become impossible to believe in this presence of the dead that has organized (or organizes) the experience of entire civilizations; and the fact too that it is nonetheless impossible "to get over it," to accept the loss of a living solidarity with what is gone, or to confirm an irreducible limit. What is *perishable* is its data; *progress* is its motto. The one is the experience which the other must both compensate for and struggle against. Historiography tends to prove that the site of its production can encompass the past: it is an odd procedure that posits death, a breakage everywhere reiterated in discourse, and that yet denies loss by appropriating to the present the privilege of recapitulating the past as a form of knowledge. A labor of death and a labor against death.

This paradoxical procedure is symbolized and performed in a gesture which has at once the value of myth and of ritual: *writing*. Indeed, writing replaces the traditional representations that gave authority to the present with a representative labor that places both absence and production in the same area. In its most elementary form, writing is equivalent to constructing a sentence by going over an apparently blank surface, a page. But isn't historiography also an activity that recommences from the point of a new time, which is separated from the ancients, and which takes charge of the construction of a rationality within this new time? It appears to me that in the West, for the last four centuries, "the making of history" has referred to writing. Little by little it has replaced the myths of yesterday with a practice of meaning. As a practice (and not by virtue of the discourses that are its result) it symbolizes a society capable of managing the space that it provides for itself, of replacing the obscurity of the lived body with the expression of a "will to know" or a "will to dominate" the body, of changing inherited traditions into a textual product or, in short, of being turned into a blank page that it should itself be able to write. This practice of history is an ambitious, progressive, also utopian practice that is linked to the endless institution of areas "proper," where a will to power can be inscribed in terms of reason. It has the value of a scientific model. It is not content with a hidden "truth" that needs to be discovered; it *produces* a symbol through the very relation between a space newly designated within time and a *modus operandi* that fabricates "scenarios" capable of organizing practices into a currently intelligible discourse—namely, the task of "the making of history." Indissociable from the destiny of writing in the modern and contemporary West until now, historiography nonetheless has the qualities of grasping scriptural invention in its relation with the elements it inherits, of operating right where the *given* must be transformed into a *construct*, of building representations with past materials, of being situated, finally, on this frontier of the present where, simultaneously, a past must be made from a tradition (by exclusion) and where nothing must be lost in the process (exploitation by means of new methods).

History and Politics: A Place

BY taking for granted its distancing from tradition and the social body, in the last resort historiography is based upon a power that in effect distinguishes it from the past and from the whole of society. "The making of history" is buttressed by a political power which creates a space proper (a walled city, a nation, etc.) where a will can and must write (construct) a system (a reason articulating practices). In the sixteenth and seventeenth centuries, by being established spatially and by being distinguished by virtue of an autonomous will, political power also occasions restriction of thought. Two tasks are necessary and especially important from the standpoint of the historiography that they are going to transform through the intermediary of jurists and "politicists." On the one hand, power must be legitimized, it must attribute to its grounding force an authority which in turn makes this very power credible. On the other hand, the relation between a "will to produce history" (a subject of the political operation) and the "environment" (into which is carved a power of decision and action) calls for an analysis of the variables thrown into play through any intervention that might influence this relation of forces—that is, an art of manipulating complexity as a function of objectives, hence a calculus of possible relations between a will (that of the prince) and a set of co-ordinates (the givens of a situation).

These are two features of the "science" constructed between the six-teenth and the eighteenth century by "historiographers." Mostly jurists and magistrates, they were provided by the prince—and in his service—with a privileged "place" whence it was necessary, for the "utility" of the state and "the common good," to bring into accord the truth of the letter and the efficacy of power—"the first dignity of literature" and the ca-pacity of a "man of government."[13] On the one hand, this discourse "leg-itimizes" the force that power exerts; it provides this force with a familial, political, or moral genealogy; it accredits the prince's current "utility" while transforming it into "values" that organize the representation of the past. On the other hand, the picture that is drawn from this past, which is the equivalent of current prospective "scenarios," formulates *praxeological* models and, through a series of situations, a typology of fea-sible relations between a concrete will and conjunctural variants; by ana-lyzing the failures and successes, this discourse sketches a science of the practices of power. In this way, it is not satisfied with historical justifi-cation of the prince through offering him a genealogical blazon. The prince receives a "lesson" provided by a technician of political management.

Since the sixteenth century—or, to take up clearly marked signs, since Machiavelli and Guichardin[14]—historiography has ceased to be the rep-resentation of a providential time, that is, of a history decided by an in-accessible Subject who can be deciphered only in the signs that he gives of his wishes. Historiography takes the position of the subject of action—of the prince, whose objective is to "make history." The historiography gives intelligence the function of mobilizing possible moves between a power and the realities from which it is distinguished. Its very definition is furnished through a policy of the state; in brief, its purpose is to con-struct a coherent discourse that specifies the "shots" that a power is ca-pable of making in relation to given facts, by virtue of an art of dealing with the elements imposed by an environment. This science is strategic because of its object, political history; on other grounds, it is equally strategic through the method it uses in handling given facts, archives, or documents.

It is through a sort of fiction, however, that the historian is accorded this place. In fact, the historians are not the agents of the operation for which they are technicians. They do not make history, they can only engage in the making of histories: the partitive usage indicates the role they play in a position that does not belong to them, but without which a new kind of historiographical analysis would not have been possible.[15] They are solely "around" power. Thus they receive the directives, in more or less explicit form, that in every modern country burden history—from theses to textbooks—with the task of educating and mobilizing. Its discourse will be magisterial without being that of the master, in the same way that historians will be teaching lessons of government without knowing either its responsibilities or its risks. They reflect on the power that they lack. Their analysis is therefore deployed "next to" the present time, in a staging of the past which is analogous to that which, drawn also through a relation to the present, the prospectivist produces in terms of the future.

Thus located in the vicinity of political problems—but not in the place where political power is exercised—historiography is given an ambivalent status which shows forth most visibly in its modern archeology. It is in a strange situation, at once critical and fictive. The fact is evident with particular clarity in Machiavelli's *Discorsi* and *Istorie fiorentine*. When the historian seeks to establish, for the place of power, the rules of political conduct and the best political institutions, he *plays the role* of the prince that he is not; he analyzes what the prince *ought* to do. Such is the fiction that gives his discourse an access to the space in which it is written. Indeed, a fiction, for it is at once the discourse of the master and that of the servant—it is legitimized through power and drawn from it, in a position where, withdrawn from the scene, as a master thinker, the technician can replay the problems facing the prince.[16] The historiographer depends on "the prince in fact," and he produces "the virtual prince."[17] Therefore he must act *as if* effective power fell under the jurisdiction of his teaching even while, against all probability, his teaching expects the prince to insert himself into a democratic organization. In this way his fiction puts in question—and makes chimerical—the possibility that political *analysis* would find its extension in the effective *practice* of power. Never will the "virtual prince," a construct of discourse, be the "prince in fact." Never will the gap separating reality from discourse be filled; to the very degree that this discourse is rigorous, it will be destined for futility.[18]

An originary frustration that will make the effectiveness of political life a fascinating question for historians (just as, inversely, the political man will be led to take the historian's position and to play back what he has done, in order to reflect upon it and accredit it), this fiction is also betrayed in the fact that the historian analyzes *situations* whereas, for a power, it was at the time a question of *objectives* to be sought. The historian receives, as already realized by another, what the political man should do. Here the past is the consequence of a lack of articulation over "making history." The unreal is insinuated into this science of action, with the fiction which consists of acting as if one were the subject of the operation—or with this activity which reproduces politics in laboratory conditions, and substitutes the subject of a historiographical operation for the subject of a historical action. Archives make up the world of this technical game, a world in which complexity is found, but sifted through and miniaturized, therefore made capable of being formalized. A precious space in every sense of the term: I would see in it the professionalized and scriptural equivalent of what games represent in everyone's common experience; that is, practices by which every society makes explicit, puts in miniature, and formalizes its most fundamental strategies, and thus acts itself out without the risks or responsibilities of having to make history.

In the case of historiography, fiction can be found at the end of the process, in the product of the manipulation and the analysis. Its story is given as a staging of the past, and not as the circumscribed area in which is effected an operation characterized by its gap in respect to power. Such was already the case of the *Discorsi:* Machiavelli offers them as a commentary on Livy. In fact, the historical figure is only a dummy. The author knows that the principles in whose name he is erecting the model of Roman institutions "fragment" the tradition and that his enterprise is "without precedent."[19] Roman history, a common reference and an agreeable subject in Florentine discussions, furnishes him with a public arena where he can deal with politics instead of the prince. The past is the area of *interest* and *pleasure* that situates beyond the current problems the prince is facing—within the field of "opinion" or public "curiosity"— the scene where the historian can play his role as the prince's technician-substitute. The gap in respect to present events delimits the space where historiography is manufactured, around the prince and near the public. It plays between what one *does* and what *pleases* the other, yet it can be identified neither with the one nor the other. Thus the past is the fiction of the present. The same holds true for all veritable historiographical labors. The explication of the past endlessly marks distinctions between the analytical apparatus, which is present, and the materials analyzed, the documents concerning curiosities about the dead. A rationalization of practices and the pleasure of telling legends of former days ("the charm of history," Marbeau used to say)[20]—the techniques that allow the complexity of current times to be managed, and the poignant curiosity surrounding the dead members of the "family"—are combined within the same text in order to produce both scientific "reduction" and narrative techniques turning the strategies of power into metaphors belonging to current times.

The real which is written in historiographical discourse originates from the determinations of a place. A *dependency* in respect to a power established from elsewhere, a *mastery* of techniques dealing with social strategies, a *play* with symbols and references that represent public authority: such are the effective relations that appear to characterize this space of writing. Placed next to power, based upon it, yet held at a critical distance; holding in its hands—mimicked by writing itself—the rational instruments of operations modifying the balance of forces in the name of a conquering will; rejoining the masses from afar (from behind political and social separation, which "distinguishes" it from them) by reinterpreting the traditional references that are invested in them: in its near totality, modern French historiography is bourgeois and—not astonishingly—rationalist.[21]

This given situation is written into the text. The more or less discreet dedication (the fiction of the past must be upheld so that the scholarly play of history can "take place") bestows upon discourse its status of being *indebted* in respect to the power that, beforehand, belonged to the prince, and that today, by the way of delegation, characterizes the scientific institution of the state or its eponym, the *patron* (or thesis director). This "envoy" designates the legitimizing place, the referent of an organized force, inside of which and through which analysis has its place. But the *story* itself, a body of fiction, through the methods it uses and the content it takes up, also marks on the one hand a distance in respect to this debt, and on the other, the two foundations that allow for this deviation: through a technical labor and a public interest historians receive from current events the means for their research and the context for their interests.

By virtue of this triangular structuring, historiography therefore cannot be thought of in terms of an opposition or an adequacy between a subject and an object; that is nothing more than the play of the fiction that it constructs. Nor could anyone believe, as much as historiography might tend to have us believe, that a "beginning" situated in a former time might explain the present: each historian situates elsewhere the inaugural rupture, at the point where his or her investigations stop; that is, at the borders demarcating a specialization within the disciplines to which he or she belongs. In fact, historians begin from present determinations. Current events are their real beginning. Lucien Febvre already noted this fact in his own style: "The Past," he wrote, "is a reconstitution of societies and human beings engaged in the network of human realities of today."[22] That this place prohibits the historian from speaking in the name of Man is what Febvre would never have admitted. He felt historical work to be exempt from the law that would submit it to the logic of a *site* of production, and not just to the "mentality" of a period in a "progress" of time (see the last pages of "A Social Place" in chapter 2). But, like all historians, he knew that *to write* is to meet the death that inhabits this site, to make death manifest through a representation of the relations that current time keeps with its other, and to struggle against death through the work of intellectually controlling the connection of a particular will to the forces facing it. Through all of these aspects, historiography stages the conditions of possibility of production, and it is itself the subject on which it endlessly writes.

Production and/or Archeology

PRODUCTION is indeed historiography's quasi-universal principal of explanation, since historical research grasps every document as the symptom of whatever produced it. Clearly, it is not so easy to do as Jean Desanti has said, to "learn from the very product to be deciphered and to read the concatenation of its generative acts."[23] On a first level of analysis, we can state that production names a question that appeared in the West with the mythic practice of writing. Up until then, history was developed by introducing a cleavage everywhere between *materia* (facts, the *simplex historia*) and *ornamentum* (presentation, staging, commentary).[24]

It aimed at recovering a truth of facts under the proliferation of "legends," and in thus instituting a discourse conforming to the "natural order" of things, at the point where mixtures of illusion and truth were proliferating.[25] The problem is no longer advanced in the same way from the time when the "fact" ceases to function as the "sign" of a truth, when "truth" changes its status, slowly ceasing to be what is manifest in order to become what is produced, thereby acquiring a scriptural form. The idea of production transposes the ancient conception of a "causality" and separates two kinds of problems: on the one hand, reference of the "fact" to what *made it possible;* on the other, a *coherence* or a "concatenation" among observed phenomena. The first question is translated in terms of genesis, and endlessly bestows privilege upon what occurs "before"; the second is expressed in the form of series whose makeup calls for an almost obsessive worry on the part of historians over filling lacunae and maintaining, more or less metaphorically, an order of structure. Often reduced to being no more than a filiation and an order, the two elements are combined in the quasi-concept of temporality. In this respect, it is true, as Desanti says, that it is "solely at the time when a specific concept of temporality is at hand and fully elaborated that the problem of *History* can be approached."[26] Meanwhile, temporality can designate the necessary linkage of the two problems, and expose or represent in the same text the ways by which the historian meets the double demand of expressing what existed beforehand and filling lacunae with facts. History furnishes the empty frame of a linear succession which formally answers to questions on *beginnings* and to the need for *order*. It is thus less the result obtained from research than its condition: the web woven a priori by the two threads with which the historical loom moves forward in the single gesture of filling holes. For lack of being able to transform the postulate of their study into its object, historians, Gérard Mairet says, "replace an acquaintance with time with the knowledge of *what* exists within time."[27]

In this respect, historiography would simply be a philosophical discourse that is unaware of itself; it would obfuscate the formidable questions that it bears by replacing them with the infinite labor of doing "as if" it were responding to them. In fact, this repressed dimension returns endlessly in its labors; it can be seen, among other signs, in that which inscribes into it the reference to a "production" and/or in the questioning that can be placed under the sign of an "archeology."

So that, through "production," we will not be limited to naming a necessary but unknown relation among known terms—in other words, to designating what supports historical discourse but which is not the object of analysis—we must recall what Marx noted in his *Theses on Feuerbach,* to the effect that "the thing, reality, sensuousness" must be grasped *"as a human sensuous activity,"* as a *"practice."*[28] A return to fundamentals: "Life involves, before everything else, eating and drinking, habitation, and many other things. The first historical fact [*die erste geschichtliche Tat*] is thus the production [*die Erzeugung*] of the means to satisfy these needs, the production [*die Produktion*] of material life itself. And this is a historical fact [*geschichtliche Tat*], a fundamental condition [*Grundbedingung*] of all history, which today, as thousands of years ago, must daily and hourly be fulfilled."[29] From this base, production diversifies according to needs that are or are not easily satisfied, and according to the conditions under which they are satisfied. Production is everywhere, but *"production in general* is an abstraction": "When we speak of production, we always have in mind production at a definite stage of social development, of the production by individuals in society. . . . For example, no production is possible without an instrument of production . . . It is not possible without past, accumulated labors. . . . Production is always a particular branch of production." "Finally, not only is production particular production, but it is invariably only a definite social corpus, a social subject, that is engaged in a wider or narrower totality of production spheres."[30] Thus the analysis returns to needs, to technical organizations, to social places and institutions in which, as Marx notes of the piano manufacturer, only that labor which produces capital is productive.[31]

I emphasize and underscore these classical texts because they specify the interrogation that I have encountered by beginning from a so-called history of ideas or mentalities: what relation can be established among definite *places* and the *discourses* that are produced therein? Here it has seemed to me that it might be possible to transpose what Marx calls productive labor in the economical sense of the term to the extent that "labor is productive only if it produces its opposite," that is, capital.[32] Discourse is doubtless a form of capital, invested in symbols; it can be transmitted, displaced, accrued, or lost. Clearly this perspective also holds for the historian's "labor" that uses discourse as its tool; and in this respect, historiography also clearly pertains to what it must study: the relation among a *place,* a *labor,* and this "increase of capital" that can constitute *discourse.* That for Marx discourse falls into the category of what is generated by "improductive labor" does not impede us from envisaging the *possibility* of treating in these terms the questions placed before historiography, and the questions posed by it.

Perhaps it is a question of giving a specific content already to the "archeology" that Michel Foucault has surrounded with new prestige. For my part, born as a historian within religious history, and formed by the dialect of that discipline, I asked myself what role religious productions and institutions might have had in the organization of the modern "scriptural" society that has replaced them by transforming them. Archeology was the way by which I sought to specify the return of a repressed, a system of Scriptures which modernity has *made* into an absent body, without being able to eliminate it. This "analysis" allowed me also to recognize in current labors a "past, accumulated" and still-influential labor. In this fashion, which made continuities and distortions appear within systems of *practice,* I was also the subject of my own analysis. That analysis has no autobiographical interest, yet by restoring in a new form the relation of production that a place keeps with a product, it led me to a study of historiography itself. The subject appears within his own text: not with the marvelous liberty that allows Martin Duberman to become in his discourse the interlocutor of his absent characters and to tell of himself by telling of them,[33] but in the manner of an unassailable lacuna that brings to light a lack within the text and ceaselessly moves and misleads him, or indeed *writes.*

This lacuna, a mark of the place within the text and the questioning of the place through the text, ultimately refers to what archeology designates without being able to put in words: the relation of the *logos* to an *archè,* a "principle" or "beginning" which is its other. This other on which it is based, which makes it possible, is what historiography can place always "earlier," go further and further back to, or designate as what it is within the "real" that legitimizes representation but is not identical to it. The *archè* is *nothing* of what can be said. It is only insinuated into the text through the labor of division, or with the evocation of death.

Thus historians can write only by combining within their practice the "other" that moves and misleads them and the real that they can represent only through fiction. They are historiographers. Indebted to the experience I have had of the field, I should like to render homage to this writing of history.

NOTES

1. Jules Michelet, "L'Héroïsme de l'esprit," unpublished project from the preface to *L'Histoire de France,* 1869, in *L'Arc* (1973), no. 52, pp. 7, 5, and 8. [Unless otherwise indicated, all translations from the French are my own.——Tr.]

2. Jules Michelet, *Préface à l'Histoire de France,* Morazé, ed. (Paris: Colin, 1962), p. 175.

3. Michelet, "L'Héroïsme de l'esprit," p. 8.

4. [De Certeau refers to a passage in Freud's *Moses and Monotheism* which is crucial for the relations of historiography and psychoanalysis. See chapter 9 below.——Tr.]

5. Michelet, "L'Héroïsme de l'esprit," p. 8.

6. Michelet, quoted by Roland Barthes in "Aujourd'hui Michelet," *L'Arc* (1973), no. 52, p. 26.

7. Michelet, "L'Héroïsme de l'esprit," pp. 12–13.

8. Alphonse Dupront, "Langage et histoire," in *XIIIe Congrès international des sciences historiques* (Moscow: 1970).

9. See especially Michel Foucault, *Naissance de la clinique* (Paris: PUF, 1963), pp. v–xv. Available in English as *The Birth of the Clinic* (New York: Vintage Books, 1975); see pp. ix–xix.

10. Louis Dumont, "Le Problème de l'histoire," in *La Civilization indienne et nous* (Paris: Colin, Coll. Cahiers des Annales, 1964), pp. 31–54.

11. See Alain Delivré, *Interprétation d'une tradition orale: Histoire des rois d'Imerina* (mimeographed thesis; Sorbonne, Paris, 1967), especially part 2, "Structure de la pensée ancienne et sens de l'histoire," pp. 143–227.

12. On this last point, see Stanislas Adotevi, *Négritude et négrologues* (Paris: Union Générale des Editions, "10/18," 1972), pp. 148–53.

13. To cite but one study, see Dieter Gembicki, "Jacob-Nicolas Moreau et son Mémoire sur les fonctions d'un historiographe de France (1778–1779)," *Dix-huitième siècle* (1972), no. 4, pp. 191–215. The relation between a literature and a "state service" will be central to the historiography of the nineteenth century and the first half of the twentieth.

14. In fact, we must go all the way back to Commynes (1447–1511), to Florentine chroniclers, and ultimately to the slow transformation of history produced toward the end of the Middle Ages by the emancipation of cities, subjects of power, and the autonomy of jurists, technicians, thinkers, and functionaries of this power.

15. [The author distinguishes between *faire de l'histoire,* what is tantamount to the task by which rhetoric is used to make an illusion of posterity, and *faire l'histoire,* the making of a limited number of material effects in a given time.——Tr.]

16. See Claude Lefort, *Le Travail de l'oeuvre Machiavel* (Paris: Gallimard, 1972), pp. 447–49.

17. See *ibid.,* p. 456.

18. In the last resort this futility acquires meaning in the relation between the historian-philosopher and *Fortuna:* the infinite number of relations and inter-

dependencies prohibits man from hypothesizing an ability to control or even influence events. See Felix Gilbert, "Between History and Politics," in *Machiavelli and Guicciardini* (Princeton: Princeton University Press, 1973), pp. 236–70.

19. See Lefort, *Le Travail*, pp. 453–66.

20. Eugène Marbeau, *Le Charme de l'histoire* (Paris: Picard, 1902).

21. See for example Jean-Yves Guiomar's remarks in *L'Idéologie nationale* (Paris: Champ Libre, 1974), pp. 17 and 45–65.

22. Lucien Febvre, preface to Charles Morazé, *Trois essais sur histoire et culture* (Paris: Colin, Coll. Cahiers des Annales, 1948), p. viii.

23. Jean T. Desanti, *Les Idéalités mathématiques* (Paris: Seuil, 1968), p. 8.

24. See for instance Félix Thürlemann, *Der historische Diskurs bei Gregor von Tours. Topoi und Wirklichkeit* (Frankfurt: Peter Lang, 1974), pp. 36–72.

25. In the fifteenth century, Agricola writes, "Historiae, cujus prima laus est *veritas, naturalis* tantum *ordo* convenit, ne si *figmentis* istis aurium gratiam captit, fidem perdat," in *De inventione dilectica libri tres cum scholiis Ioannis Matthaei Phrissemii*, III, VII (Paris: apud Simonem Colinaeum, 1529), p. 387. The italics are mine. The foundation of this historiographical system must also be remarked: the text takes it for granted that truth is credible and consequently that showing what is true is tantamount to producing belief, of producing a *fides* among readers.

26. Desanti, *Les Idéalités mathématiques*, p. 29.

27. Gérard Mairet, *Les Discours et l'historique: Essai sur la représentation historienne du temps* (Paris: Mame, 1974), p. 168.

28. Karl Marx, *Theses on Feuerbach*, Thesis I, in Karl Marx and Friedrich Engels, *Basic Writings on Politics and Philosphy*, L. S. Feuer, ed. (New York: Doubleday, 1959), p. 243. On the same topic, see also "Marginal Gloss to the Program of the German Workers' Party," paragraph 1, Marx and Engels, *Critique of the Gotha Erfurt Program*, in *Basic Writings*, pp. 112–32.

29. Karl Marx and Friedrich Engels, *The German Ideology*, in *Basic Writings*, p. 249; and Karl Marx, *Die Fruhschriften*, S. Landshut, ed. (Stuttgart: A. Kroner, 1853), p. 354.

30. Karl Marx, *Introduction to a Critique of Political Economy*, in *The German Ideology*, C. S. Arthur, ed. (New York: International Publishers, 1978), pp. 125–26.

31. Karl Marx, *Critique of Political Economy*, in *The German Ideology*, pp. 127ff.

32. *Ibid.*

33. See Martin Duberman, *Black Mountain: An Exploration in Community* (New York: Dutton, 1973).

I

Productions of Places

I

Making History

Problems of Method and Problems of Meaning

F IRST of all, religious history is a field of confrontation between historiography and *archeology*, whose place it has taken to some degree. Second, religious history allows us to analyze the relation between history and *ideology*, which it must account for in terms of production. These two questions intersect and can be envisaged together in the narrowly circumscribed sector that is the "treatment" of theology by methods that belong to history. From the outset, historians take theology to be a religious ideology which functions within a broader totality that we assume can explain this ideology. Can theology be reduced to the terms resulting from this operation? No, probably not. But as an object of their discipline, theology is shown to historians under two equally uncertain forms in the field of historiography; it is a religious fact, and it is a fact of doctrine. The aims of this chapter are to study through this particular given case the manner in which historians treat these two types of facts nowadays, and to specify the epistemological problems that are thus broached.

This study was first published in *Recherches de science religieuse* (1970), 58:481–520.

History: A Practice and a Discourse

THIS analysis will obviously be determined by the very circumscribed practice with which I can be credited, that is, through the location of my work—at once in a period (the history called "modern"), as a subject matter (religious history), and in a place (the French scene). These limits are of capital importance. The display of the particularity proper to the location from which I am observing is linked in effect to the subject under study and to the point of view which I must assume in examining it. Three postulates define the subject and the point of view. They must be directly put forward as such (even if they seem to arise quite obviously from current historical practice), since they will not be the object of any proof.

First, underscoring the singularity of each analysis is equivalent to indicting the possibility of an all-encompassing systematic process, and instead, keeping central to the problem the need for discussion proportioned to a plurality of scientific procedures, social functions, and fundamental convictions. In this way we tentatively analyze the function of discourses which can throw light on the question, which are written after or beside many others of the same order: while these discourses speak *of* history, they are already situated *in* history.

Second, these discourses are not bodies floating "within" an all-encompassing whole that can simply be called history (or even a "context"). They are historical because they are bound to operations and are defined by functions. Thus we cannot understand what they say independently of the practice from which they result. In different ways we can probably find here a good definition of contemporary historiography (but also of theology—including, most specifically, its most traditional kind).[1] In any event, both the one and the other will be grasped at this junction between a "content" and an operation. Furthermore, such a perspective characterizes the current scientific process; for example that which, as a function of "models" or in terms of "regularities," can explain phenomena or documents by clarifying rules of production and possibilities of transformation.[2] But more aptly, we shall take seriously all these expressions loaded with meaning—"making history," "making theology"; usually we are all too likely to erase the verb (or their productive act) to give more weight to the complement (the fruits of their labors).

Third, for this reason I mean by "history" this practice (a discipline), its result (a discourse), or the relation of the two in the form of a "production."[3] To be sure, in current usage "history" connotes both a science and that which it studies—the explication which is *stated,* and the reality of *what has taken place* or what takes place. Other disciplines are not burdened with this ambiguity: French does not refer to "physics" and "nature" with the same name. The very term "history" therefore already suggests a situation of particular proximity between the scientific operation and the reality that it analyzes. But the first of these aspects will serve as our entry into the subject at hand, for various reasons: because the breadth and extension of the "real" are forever designated and considered as meaningful solely within the bounds of a discourse; because this restriction in the use of the word "history" gives its correspondent (historical science) over to science, or at least to the particular function which is indeed the field of theology; finally, we have to stay out of the virgin forest of History, a region of "rich fuzziness" in which ideologies proliferate and where we will never find our way. Perhaps, too, by holding to the idea of discourse and to its fabrication, we can better apprehend the nature of the relations that it holds with its other, the real. In this fashion, doesn't language not so much implicate the status of the reality of which it speaks, as posit it as that which is other than itself?

Beginning thus with historiographical practices and discourses, I propose taking up in turn the following points:

1) The treatment of religious ideology by contemporary historiography requires us to recognize the ideologies that are already invested in history itself.

2) There exists a historicity of history, implying the movement which links an interpretive practice to a social praxis.

3) History thus vacillates between two poles. On the one hand, it refers to a practice, hence to a reality; on the other, it is a closed discourse, a text that organizes and concludes a mode of intelligibility.

4) History is probably our myth. It combines what can be thought, the "thinkable," and the origin, in conformity with the way in which a society can understand its own working.

A SIGN: THE TREATMENT OF RELIGIOUS
IDEOLOGY IN HISTORY

THE relation between history and theology is first of all a problem germane to history. What is the *historical* significance of a doctrine within the totality of a period? According to what criteria can it be understood? How can it be explained in relation to terms advanced by the period under study? These questions are difficult and debatable if, on the one hand, we cannot be satisfied with a purely *literary* analysis of the contents or of their organization;[4] and if, on the other, we refuse ourselves the facility of considering ideology solely as a social epiphenomenon, a facility which effaces the specificity of doctrinal affirmations.[5]

For example, what rapport can be established between Jansenist spirituality or theology and the sociocultural structures or social dynamics of the same period? A broad range of answers is offered to us. Thus for Orcibal, a radical experience in its pristine state, in the oldest primary source, must be sought above all. Yet still it is alienated within the constraints of a contemporary language; the history of its diffusion will thus be the history of a progressive degradation. Even by returning endlessly to the oldest primary sources, by scrutinizing the experience that linguistic and historical systems mask as they develop themselves, historians never apprehend origins, but only the successive stages of their loss. In opposition to Orcibal, Lucien Goldmann finds in Jansenist doctrine both the result and the symptom of the economic situation in which a social category is located: losing their power, lawyers turn to the heaven of predestination and the hidden God, and thus betray the new political circumstances which seal off their future from them; here spirituality, a sign of what it does not express, refers back to the analysis of an economic change and to a sociology of failure.[6]

Works on Luther present the same diversity of positions: some authors refer to the events in Luther's youth to find the organizing principle and unspoken secret of his doctrine (Strohl and Febvre for example); others place his thought within the continuum of an intellectual tradition (Grisar, Seeberg, etc.); still others observe in it the effects of a modification in economic structures (Engels, Steinmetz, Stern), or the growing consciousness of sociocultural transformations (Garin, Moeller, etc.), or even the result of a conflict between the adolescent and the society of adults (Erikson). Finally, the Lutheran movement has been considered as an emergence of a religious disquiet which characterizes the period (for example, by Lortz and Delumeau); the end result of a promotion of the laity as opposed to the clerical order (Natalie Z. Davis), an episode belonging to the series of the evangelical reforms which mark the history of the church; or the wave precipitated in the West by the eruption of a truly unique advent (Holl, Bainton, Barth). All of these interpretations have been proposed, and many more can be enumerated.[7]

Clearly, all of the above interpretations are relative to the response that each author proposes for analogous questions located in present times. Although this is a patent truth, we should recall that any reading of the past—however much it is controlled by the analysis of documents—is driven by a reading of current events. Readings of both past and present are effectively organized in relation to problematic issues which a historical situation is imposing. They are haunted by presuppositions, in other words by "models" of interpretation that are invariably linked to a contemporary situation of Christianity.

The "Mystical" Model and the "Folkloric" Model: A Hidden Essence

GLOBALLY and also for France, two tendencies seem to have marked religious history for about three centuries: one, issuing from spiritual currents, directs its attention to an analysis of doctrines; the other, marked by the "Enlightenment," places religion under the sign of "superstition." In sum, we would have on the one hand emergent truths in texts, and on the other "errors," or a folklore abandoned along the roadside of progress.

Without going very far back in time, we can observe that during the first half of the twentieth century religion hardly took advantage of the new trends that mobilized medieval or "modernist" historians, in for example the socioeconomical analysis of Ernest Labrousse (1933–1941). Religion was rather an object of study, disputed among exegetes or historians of Christian origins. When it intervened within the history of mentalities in Lucien Febvre's work (1932–1942), it was as a sign of coherence belonging to a past society (and surpassed, thanks to progress), in a perspective very much inflected by the ethnology of "primitive" societies.

Paradoxically, two names appear to symbolize the more or less explicit place reserved for the analysis of belief between the two world wars, and the slippage produced during that period: Henri Bremond and Arnold Van Gennep. The former, partaking of the tradition of literary history, attests to a loss of confidence in doctrines by referring them to "mystical" meanings, or to a hidden "metaphysics" of saints.[8] The latter, a scrupulous observer of religious folklore, envisions the resurgence of an immemorial element of societies, the return of an irrational cause, of an originary and almost repressed force.[9] Their two positions are not without analogy, even if they are cast in very different methodological terms. Bremond refers the meaning of the literature being studied back to a mystical source of man, to an "essence" which is diffracted, expressed, and found compromised in institutional or doctrinal religious systems. The doctrinal facts are thus isolated from their meaning, which remains forever hidden in depths ultimately foreign to social or intellectual categories. In his fashion, inspired by American or German anthropology (and especially the Jungian school), Van Gennep reveals signs of unconscious archetypes and permanent anthropological structures within religious folklore. Across an always-menaced mysticism (according to Bremond) or a folklore (for Van Gennep), the religious element embodies the figure of a marginal or timeless type; in this way, a profound nature—foreign to history—is combined with what a society throws along the wayside.

Quite visible in these two authors, this model can be located in other forms; for example, in the concepts of the sacred, panic, the collective unconscious, etc. No doubt it can be explained by the position that Christianity had assumed before 1939 in French society, divided between a movement of interiorization—with Maritain's *Primacy of the Spiritual* (1927) or Mounier's *Esprit* (1932)—and a religious positivism among traditionalists. It also explains why religious history had been "hard to think" in a social history and why it remained aberrant in respect to the history that was being fashioned, particularly the socioeconomic history of Henri Sée (1921–1929), of Simiand (1932), of Hamilton (1934–1936), of Marc Bloch (1939–1940), or of Ernest Labrousse. But in turning the research it inspired more and more toward the study of spiritual currents or popular culture, this model directed religious history toward a splendid future. Science would examine a field of pure religious "phenomena" whose meaning was withdrawn into another, hidden order. It would situate them in the direction of ethnology, and link an exoticism of inner man to a lost *essential* part, in the region of the imaginary or of symbolic orders of society. In religion, science could seek the metaphor of a nonhistorical basis of history.

The Sociological Model: Practice and Knowledge

THE importance that the analysis of religious practice takes on with Gabriel Le Bras must be connected with a recent archeology.[10] Linked to the rise of sociology, ethnology, and the study of folklore,[11] this interpretative model represents a French reaction in favor of sociological practices (polls, etc.) as opposed to the theoretical typologies of Troeltsch (1912), Weber (1920), or Wach (1931). But from the standpoint of Christianity, it also presupposes a new situation which dates back to the "modern" period. A past haunts this present.

To be sure, the religious practice probably does not hold the same meaning in the course of different periods of history. In the seventeenth century it acquires a function that it had had to a much lesser degree in the thirteenth or fourteenth century. The crumbling of beliefs within societies that were no longer religiously homogenous makes objective reference all the more necessary: the believer has to be distinguished from the unbeliever—or the Catholic from the Protestant—through his practices. In becoming a social element of religious differentiation, the practice acquires a new religious relevance. Regroupings are made and accounted for according to this criterion.

Today, by keeping practice as the basis of a quantitative measurement of religion, sociology makes manifest a historical organization of Christian conscience (which moreover was not the case for Jansenism). It also accentuates a presupposition which had always been latent in these four-centuries-old origins: that is, of a rift between objective gestures and subjective belief. In the seventeenth century, religious belief had already begun to be dissociated from practice—a phenomenon which, since that time, has never failed to increase. In order to count their followers and to mark ruptures, reformists became suspicious of doctrines and insisted on social acts. Currently, in the works which count visible actions, interest has been drawn to practices precisely because they represent a *social* reality; on its underside this interest bears a scientific devalorization of their *dogmatic* meaning (referred to as "prejudices" demystified by progress, or private convictions which are impossible to introduce into scientific analysis). The logic of a sociology therefore further widens the schism between social religious facts and the doctrines which claim to explain their significance.[12]

In turn, a sociological view has changed beliefs into objective facts. A sociology of religious *knowledge* has developed in proportion to the withdrawal inward of meaning. The same break is thus found in the apparently opposed field of research dedicated to ideology. Furthermore, in our relation as historians to the seventeenth century, we cannot dissociate the knowledge we have of its nature from the influence it still exercises over our methods of inquiry. The sociological view of ideologies and the conceptual tools which organize our cultural analysis (for example, the distinction between the elite and the mass, the use of knowledge versus "ignorance" as criteria for evaluating dechristianization, etc.) are still proof of the social function that knowledge was acquiring in the course of the seventeenth century. When the religious unanimity of Christendom was broken down into the diversity of European states, a knowledge was needed to take up the slack of belief and allow each group or each country to receive a distinctive definition. With the effects of the printing press, of a growing literacy and education, knowledge became a tool of unification and differentiation: a corpus of knowledge or degrees of wisdom sectioned off or isolated social levels, at the same time that illiteracy was associated with delinquency and considered its cause, or with the masses and considered to characterize them. These social divisions are not as new as the fact that it was a shape of knowledge or a doctrine that established the means of putting them into place, of maintaining or changing them. Among churches, too, the differences in knowledge became decisive. The determination of what was known, when one was either Catholic or of Reformed faith, furnished the community with its modes of identity and distinction. Catechisms changed and were refashioned by the urgency of definitions circumscribing at once both intellectual contents and socioinstitutional limits.

Today some very recent work (such as that of René Taveneaux) reconstructs sociocultural networks, outlines mental trajectories, establishes the geography of hidden groups from traces and resurgent points of religious ideas, just as physiological movements can be seen by means of the travels of some visible substance through the dark folds of the body.[13] In sum, this work travels over trails made in the past by the ways in which a society availed itself of its modes of knowledge. In emphasizing the former roles of ideas, by exploiting them in turn as remainders (perhaps the only visible ones, at that) of frontiers between social groups, Taveneaux explains the usefulness that these ideas had already surreptitiously acquired—the service that they rendered to societies which circulated them, but at the cost of the "doctrinal" meaning that contemporary people gave to them or that these ideas can still keep. Since then such drawing and quartering of methods has separated more and more, in every doctrinal work, a sociological "object" at which the historian aims and a theoretical object which seems to be left aside for literary analysis.

A Cultural Model: From Ideas to the "Collective Unconscious"

BACZKO once remarked that the "history of ideas" is born of common reactions, in particular a reaction against the divisions within a particular body of work or period of time that followed in the wake of specialization of disciplines. Thus instead of arbitrarily fragmenting the work of Newton, dividing it among different specialties according to whether he deals with the Apocalypse, calendars, "natural philosophy," or optics, unities and organizing principles are sought.[14] Similarly, there are objections to explaining a body of work in terms of influences, to frittering a corpus away by referring it to the muddle of its primary sources, to instigating, by going endlessly back through the dust of fragments, the disappearance of the totalities of the segments, of the ruptures that constitute history.

But how can this study be furnished with adequate methods? Since the advent in the United States of the *Journal of the History of Ideas* (in 1940 in New York and Lancaster), the first of the reviews dedicated to the topic, its development has been pursued. It lacks a proper name: in Germany, it is called *Geistesgeschichte;* in the United States, it is "intellectual history"; in France, it goes by the term *l'histoire des mentalités;* in the Soviet Union it is the "history of thought," and so on.

Within all of these tendencies, Baczko was able to trace distant, communal, Hegelian origins through the works of Dilthey, Lukács, Weber, Croce, Huizinga, Cassirer, Groethuysen, etc., around the decade between 1920 and 1930. *Ideas* become a mediation between the Spirit (*Geist*) and sociopolitical realities. They presumably form a level where the body of history meets its consciousness—the *Zeitgeist*.[15] But the simplicity of the postulate breaks down under analysis, into complex and apparently insoluble problems. For example, who is the *real* Newton? What is the kind of unity being postulated—that of his work, or perhaps that of a period? What framework furnishes so many different ideas with the unity lent to the "ideas of the time," the "mentality," or the contemporary "collective consciousness?"

This unity—in other words, the scientific object being sought—is worthy of discussion. We should like to go beyond individualist conceptions tending to cut apart and reassemble writings in accord with their "belonging" to a single "author," a move which confers upon biography the power of defining an ideological unity,[16] and which supposes that a thought always corresponds to a man (thus the interpretive architecture reiterating the same singularity in the three parts of the classical model: the man, the work, and the thought). Attempts have been made to identify overall mentalities of periods of history, for example in the *Weltanschauung* in Max Weber (a conception of the universe or a vision of the world), the scientific "paradigm" in Thomas Kuhn's work, the "unit idea" of A. O. Lovejoy,[17] and so on. These standards of measure refer to what Lévi-Strauss called the society that is *thought* in opposition to the society that is *lived*. They tend to make the coherences "sanctioned" by a period spring forth—that is, the received coherences implied by what can be "perceived" or "thought" in a given time, the cultural systems that might provide the basis for periodization or temporal distinction.[18] A classification of raw material operates thus in forming the basis of ideological beginnings and endings, or in establishing what Bachelard has called "epistemological ruptures."[19]

The ambiguities of these modes of interpretation have been vigorously criticized, most vehemently in the work of Michel Foucault.[20] They essentially depend upon the uncertain status, neither fish nor fowl, of "totalities" which are not legible on the surfaces of texts, but which lurk just beneath them, in the fashion of invisible realities that would uphold phenomena. How can we simply assume these unities, and how can they be spotted in the middle depths between consciousness and the economic realm? They assume the place of a "collective spirit" and, as such, retain the trace of ontologism. Their function is soon carried on by the hypothesis of a "collective unconscious." Not being subject to real control, these underlying regions can be extended, stretched, or shrunk at will. They have the breadth of phenomena to be grasped, "understood." Far more than an analytical instrument, in fact they represent the need of historians for such vague notions. They signify a necessity of the scientific operation, but not a reality which can be discerned in its object.

This approach declares that it is impossible to eliminate from the labor of historiography the ideologies that inform it. But in awarding them the place of an object, in isolating them from socioeconomic structures, or in supposing, furthermore, that "ideas" function in the same fashion as these structures, parallel to them and on another level,[21] the "history of ideas" can only find in the form of an "unconscious" this inconsistent reality in which it dreams of discovering an *autonomous* coherence. What it manifests is in fact the unconscious of historians, or rather, that of the group to which they belong. The will to define history ideologically is the concern of a social elite. It is based on a division between ideas and labor. It has been equally usual for this elite to neglect the relation between the sciences and their techniques, between historians' ideologies and their practices, between ideas and their limited fields of applicability or the conditions of their production within the socioeconomic conflicts of a society, and so on. It hardly seems surprising that this division, a resurgence or a reinforcement of an elitism already strongly marked by the end of the eighteenth century (among others, François Furet has often underscored this point), is symbolized by the juxtaposing a "history of ideas" with an "economic history."

The search for a coherence belonging to an ideological level thus refers to the *place* of those who develop it in the twentieth century. Gramsci has probably best indicated its virtual breadth when, in turning over the history of ideas, in its place he substitutes the history of "organic intellectuals," a particular group that he analyzes through the relation between its social position and the discourses it uses.[22]

HISTORICAL PRACTICES AND SOCIAL PRAXIS

THE study of these models (whose listing and analysis could be extended) reveals two related problems: the evanescence of ideology as a reality to be explained, and its reintroduction as a reference in relation to which a historiography is elaborated. As an *object* of study, it seems to be eliminated—or always lacking—in current methods of research. But in contrast, it resurfaces as the *presupposition* of the models that characterize a type of explanation; it is implied by each system of interpretation, by the kinds of relevance it maintains, by the procedures that are proportioned to it, by the technical difficulties met in the process, and by the results obtained. To put it differently, those who *make history* today seem to have lost the means of grasping a statement of meaning as their work's objective, only to discover this statement in the process of their very activity. What disappears from the product appears once again in production.

It could be that the term "ideology" no longer has enough strength to designate the form by which meaning enters into the historian's optic or "viewpoint." The current use of the word dates from the moment when language became objectified; or, reciprocally, when problems of meaning were shunted in the direction of their operation and posed in terms of historical choices folded into the scientific process. This was a fundamental revolution, to be sure, since it replaced the historical *given* by historiographical *process*. It transformed the search for meaning unveiled by observed reality into analysis of the options or organizations of meaning implied by interpretive operations.

This does not mean that history rejects reality and turns in on itself to take pleasure in examining its procedures. Rather, as we shall observe, it is that the *relation* to the real has changed. And if meaning cannot be apprehended in the form of a specific knowledge that would either be drawn from the real or might be added to it, it is because every "historical fact" results from a praxis, because it is already the sign of an act and therefore a statement of meaning. It results from procedures which have allowed a mode of comprehension to be articulated as a discourse of "facts."[23]

Before defining this epistemological situation, which no longer permits meaning to be sought in the form of an ideology or a "given" of history, we would do well to recall the indications in current historiography. It is a matter of taking up the problem formerly posited in Raymond Aron's classical thesis.[24] Yet we cannot be satisfied with historical interpretation, as he was, at the sole level of implicit philosophy common to historians. There we would end with an infinite play of ideas relative to one another, a game reserved for an elite and associated with the protection of an established order. The organization of every historiography as a function of particular and diverse points of view refers to historical *acts*, to what establishes meaning and founds the sciences. In this respect, when history takes "doing" (or "making" history) into consideration, it simultaneously locates its origins in the actions which "produce history." Discourse can be dissociated today neither from the origins of its production nor from the political, economic, or religious praxis that can change societies and, at a given moment, make various kinds of scientific comprehension possible.

From Historical Prejudices to the Situations They Reveal

NOWADAYS the regress of time, and no doubt a greater epistemological reflection, help us discern the prejudices that have constrained much recent religious historiography. These appear in the choice of subjects and in the determination of the given objectives of the study. But in each instance these prejudices are linked to situations which rivet the historian to a particular position in relation to religious realities.

Thus the conflicts between church and state, or the debates concerning the free school or *école libre* and the lay school, the *école laïque*, have had as one of their effects that of favoring those religious phenomena offered in the form of an opposition to orthodoxies, and consequently of favoring the history of "heresies" rather than that of ecclesiastical institutions or of "orthodoxies." Less than personal intentions, sociocultural localizations thus inspire the interest and type of research.

For example, in the study of the beginnings of the sixteenth century, historians adhere to the notion of "pre-Reformation" instead of examining scholastic currents however dominant and equal in importance. "Humanism" is envisaged in terms of a rupture with the Christian tradition, instead of being seen as an extension of patristic thought, or placed among successive reformisms, or within the series of renascences of antiquity throughout the Middle Ages.[25] In the same fashion, the religious stamp of the seventeenth century has been identified with Jansenism, prophetic "rebellion," while this is only one of many phenomena of the period. Many of the elements assumed to be characteristic of Jansenism are found within other spiritual currents.[26] And also, theological or exegetical writings have been virtually erased from the works of the great "savants" of the sixteenth and seventeenth centuries as vestiges of epochs long since over, esteemed as unworthy of interest to a progressive society.[27]

Within the tissue of history, analysis therefore chooses "subjects" conforming to its place of observation. It is hardly surprising that studies aimed at correcting such edited views in order to promote the greater value of the writing of others originate not only from different ideological traditions, but also from *places* juxtaposed and often opposed to the former—for example, ecclesiastical settings or cultural Centers outside

the French university. Thus have arisen the notices of Father Bernard-
Maître and others, running all the way up to Massaut's great book on
conservative theologians at the beginning of the sixteenth century;[28] the
works of Father de Lubac or of Father Bouyer on the repetition of apostolic and patristic exegesis in Erasmian humanism;[29] those of Gilson
on the traditional vocabulary taken up by Descartes;[30] those of Bremond,
and so many since then, on a whole range of mystical currents in which
Jansenism plays a role. The considerable importance of these studies does
not attenuate their more or less discreetly apologetic character. Perhaps
the richness of their content has even been made possible through this
quality of rejoinder or of crusade, which has made them equivalent to a
Trojan horse.

The mark of socioideological compartmentalization is especially visible
in French religious historiography. This compartmentalization is a quality
of French society that is often underlined. Scientific works have consequently shown the university's position on this map. They have favored
the liberal Catholics over the "unbending" Catholics (except in René
Rémond's work, the latter have been studied particularly by the English
or the North Americans, who are not concerned in quite the same way
by French problems);[31] or they have given their preferences to scientific
or social "modernism" rather than to "integrism," the recent doctrine upholding the totality of a system (in which Emile Poulat has just shown
historical interest).[32] Debates inherent to French society have induced
historiographical rigidity and have also long induced the unlimited reproduction of formal distinctions, while at the same time a new erudition
was modifying its content.

This schematism has left as its effect a present reemployment of formerly opposed "sides"—Reform or Catholic, Jansenist or Jesuit, modernist or integrist, etc.—but turned them into partisan banners, less from
personal conviction than for reasons of sociocultural situation. The former polemics unconsciously organized scientific research. The historians,
notes Lucien Febvre, reached the point of "slipping under the cassock,
the frock, or under the robe of their forebears, without noticing that
these were the habits of controversists or of predicators each arguing for
his own cause."[33]

A silence about certain problems remains as a trace of this recent past.
It even seeps into magisterial studies on classical society and thought:
thus Goubert's discretion with regard to theologies,[34] or even to religion[35]
and the absence of reference to religious literature in the interpretation

that Foucault makes of the classical *episteme*.[36] But inversely, there is the silence too of Father Cognet on socioeconomic history in *La Spiritualité moderne*[37] or even, on the opposite side, in numerous works devoted to the temporal affairs of abbey churches, a silence on the social pressure that made so many clerical historians inattentive to the religious life of these abbeys.[38]

The Transformation of Prejudices Into Objects of Study

DETACHED from conflicting situations which are now further and further away from us, we can now more easily discern their presence in these studies. Today we are already elsewhere. As the divisions that formerly organized both a period and its historiography are being eroded, their presence can be analyzed in the very work of their time. The disappearance of the period is the condition for such lucidity, but this seemingly better comprehension that is now ours is due to the fact that we have changed our position: our situation can allow us to be familiar with their situation in ways other than their own ways.

What makes the relativization of these former debates possible—and the recognition of the constraints they placed on scientific discourse—is the new position of religion in our own society. Quite far from being a force, a menace, a totality of constituted bodies and groups as was the case in the past, French Christianity is throwing off its social weight by freeing itself from recent compartmentalizations. It no longer establishes correct, vigorous, but closed categories within the nation. It is becoming a poorly defined and poorly understood region of French culture. A religious historiography is *able* hereafter to treat its subject as a new exoticism, similar to that which once attracted the ethnologist to the "savages" of the forest or to French sorcerers. Christianity had a stronger social existence when it was granted less place in *Le Temps* yesterday than in *Le Monde* today. Either everyone was silent, or people were partial when crucial issues involved partners, adversaries, or groups circumscribed within their own vitality. More is said today, now that Christianity is no longer a force and now that through necessity it has "opened" itself, "adapted," and conformed to a situation in which it becomes the object of an impartial curiosity and a distant sign of "values."[39] The renewal of religious history, therefore, does not mean a resurgence of Christianity, but rather the dilution of its institutions and doctrines within the new structures of the nation—its passage from the state of being a resistant and opaque body to a state of mobility and transparency.

The prejudices of history or of historians disappear when the situation to which they referred is modified. The formerly living organization of a society invested within their point of view is changed into a *past* that can be placed under observation. Its status is transformed: no longer being present within authors as the frame of reference of their thought, it is now situated within the object that we, as new authors, have to render thinkable. As the function of an *other* situation, from now on it is possible to study our predecessors' modes of comprehension as prejudices, or simply as the givens of a period; we can sketch their relations with other elements of the same era, and write their historiography into the history that is the object of our own historiography.[40]

Within this approach, the modes of comprehension that belonged to former historiography are located in the same position held by Christian ideologies or beliefs. The latter simply represent the traversing of a greater distance from the conviction that had furnished a past with its principles of intelligibility, and which today must be understood according to other frames of reference. The gap between these two positions points to the very problem of historiographical work: the relation between the "meaning" which has become an object, and the "meaning" which today allows it to be understood as such.

Now whenever we seek the "historical meaning" of an ideology or of an event, not only do we encounter methods, ideas, or styles of understanding, but also the society to which the definition of what has "meaning" is always referable. If, therefore, we face a historical function specified the ceaseless confrontation between a past and a present—that is, between what had organized life or thought and what allows it to be thought nowadays—there exists an *infinite series of "historical meanings."* Religious belief offers only an extreme case of the relation between two systems of understanding across the passage from a society still religious (that of the sixteenth century, for example) to another society, our own, in which the conditions of thought have become secularized.

HISTORY, DISCOURSE, AND REALITY

Two Positions of the Real

NOW if we recapitulate these givens, the situation of the historiographer makes study of the real appear in two quite different positions within the scientific process: the real insofar as it is the *known* (what the historian studies, understands, or "brings to life" from a past society), and the real insofar as it is entangled within the scientific operations (the present society, to which the historians' problematics, their procedures, modes of comprehension, and finally a practice of meaning are referable). On the one hand, the real is the result of analysis, while on the other, it is its postulate. Neither of these two forms of reality can be eliminated or reduced to the other. Historical science takes hold precisely in their relation to one another, and its proper objective is developing this relation into a discourse.

Certainly, depending upon the periods or the groups, history is mobilized in favor of one over the other of its two focuses. There are in effect two types of history, according to which one of these positions of the real is chosen as the center of attention. Even if hybrids of these two types are more prevalent than the pure cases, the types can be easily recognized. One type of history ponders what is comprehensible and what are the conditions of understanding; the other claims to reencounter lived experience, exhumed by virtue of a knowledge of the past.

The first of these problematics examines history's capacity to render thinkable the documents which the historian inventories. It yields to the necessity of working out models which allow series of documents to be composed and understood: economic models, cultural models, and the like. This perspective—more and more common today—brings historians back to the methodological hypotheses of their work, to their revision by means of pluridisciplinary exchanges, to principles of intelligibility that might produce relevance and even "facts," and finally, back to their epistemological situation, present in all research characteristic of the society in which they are working.[41]

The other tendency valorizes the relation the historian keeps with a lived experience, that is, with the possibility of resuscitating or "reviving" a past. It would like to restore the forgotten and to meet again men of the past amidst the traces they have left. It also implies a particular literary genre, narrative, while the first approach, much less descriptive, prefers to compare series that make different types of methods emerge.

Between these two forms there is tension, but not opposition. Historians are in an unstable position. If they award priority to an "objective" result, if they aim to posit the reality of a former society in their discourse and animate forgotten figures, they nonetheless recognize in their recomposition the orders and effects of their own work. The discourse destined to express what is *other* remains *their* discourse and the mirror of their own labors. Inversely, when they refer to their own practices and examine their postulates in order to innovate, therein historians discover constraints originating well before their own present, dating back to former organizations of which their work is a symptom, not a cause. Just as the "model" of religious sociology implies, among other things, the new status of practice or of knowledge in the seventeenth century, so do current methods—erased as events and transformed into codes or problematic issues of research—bear evidence of former structurings and forgotten histories. Thus founded on the rupture between a past that is its object, and a present that is the place of its practice, history endlessly finds the present in its object and the past in its practice. Inhabited by the uncanniness that it seeks, history imposes its law upon the faraway places that it conquers when it fosters the illusion that it is bringing them back to life.

The In-Between, the Situation of History, and the Problem of the Real

IN the realm of history, an endless labor of differentiation (among events, periods, data or series, and so on) forms the condition of all relating of elements which have been distinguished—and hence of their comprehension. But this labor is based on the difference between a present and a past. Everywhere it presupposes the act advancing an innovation by dissociating itself from a tradition in order to consider this tradition as an object of knowledge. The decisive break in any given science (exclusion is always necessary for rigor to be instituted) assumes in history the form of an originary *limit* which founds a reality as "past." This is clarified in the techniques proportioned to the task of "making history." Now this gap seems to be negated by the operation that establishes it, since this "past" returns in historiographical practice. The dead souls resurge, within the work whose postulate was their disappearance and the possibility of analyzing them as an object of investigation.

The status of this necessary yet denied limit characterizes history as a "human" science. It is human, indeed, not insofar as it declares that man is its object, but because its practice reinvests in the "subject" of science what had been distinguished as its "object." Its functioning refers back and forth, from the one to the other, the two poles of the "real." The productive *activity* and the period *known* distort each other. The gap that had placed between them an urgency inspiring scientific investigation (and the origin of its "objectivity") begins to waver. It is thrown topsy-turvy, it is displaced, it moves forward. This movement is precisely due to the fact that this gap was posited, *and* that now it cannot be maintained.

In the course of the movement displacing the terms of the initial relation, this relation itself becomes the site of the scientific operation. But it is a site whose mutations, like a buoy floating on the sea, follow the more vast movements of societies, their economic and political revolutions, complex networks of influence among generations or classes, and so forth. The scientific relation reproduces the labor which, for some groups, assures domination to the extent of making others the objects they possess; but it also attests to the industry of the dead who, through a sort of kinetic energy, are silently perpetuated through the survival of former structures, "continuing," as Marx says, to live their "vegetative life" (*Fortvegetation*).[42]

Historians escape neither from these latencies nor from the weight of an endlessly present past (an inertia that traditionalists call "continuity" before declaring it to be "truth" of history). And no longer can historians make abstractions out of the distancings and the exclusions that define the period or the social category to which they belong. In their labors, occult carryovers and innovative ruptures are combined. History demonstrates this all the more as it takes for its task the distinguishing of the one from the other.[43] The fragile and necessary boundary between a past object and a current praxis begins to waver, as soon as the fictive postulate of a *given* that is to be understood is replaced by the study of an *operation* always affected by determinisms, always having to be taken up, always depending on the place where it occurs in a society, and specified, however, by a problem, methods, and a function which are its own.

Here, then, history is played along the margins which join a society with its past and with the very act of separating itself from that past. It takes place along these lines which trace the figure of a current time by dividing it from its other, but which the return of the past is continually modifying or blurring. As in the paintings of Miró, the artist's line, which draws differences with contours and makes a writing possible (a discourse and a "historicization"), is crisscrossed by a movement running contrary to it. It is the vibration of limits. The relation that organizes history is a changing rapport, of which neither of its two terms can be the stable point of reference.

The Relation with the Other

THIS fundamental situation is revealed today in many ways which concern the form or content of historiography. For example, the analysis of a brief or long socioeconomic or cultural period is preceded in the works of history by a "preface" in which the historian speaks of the course of his research. The book, made of two uneven but symbolic halves, joins to the history of a past the itinerary of a procedure. Already in 1928 Lucien Febvre inaugurated his study of Luther with the examination of his own situation as historian within the series of previous works dedicated to his object. He was inscribing himself within the evolution of a present history, at the same time that he was placing Luther within an analogous but much older series. Since Febvre, historians not only specify their points of view, but also the movement they have made or the transformation that has been realized in their methods and inquiries. Thus Pierre Vilar and Emmanuel Le Roy Ladurie, whose works dominate current historiography, juxtapose the drawing of a methodological curve of their undertaking with that of the structural transformations of Catalonia or of Languedoc over a period of four centuries.[44] The truth of history resides in this "in-between" on which a work marks its limits, without being able to create an object taking the place of this relation. In the case of Marc Soriano, analysis of Perrault's fairy tales becomes itself the narrative or avowal of an investigation, in such a way that the object of his research—fragmented as it is by diverse methodological inquiries—finds its unity in the operation where the actions of the author and the resistances of the material are being combined endlessly.[45]

With this internal tension that is the mechanism of historical explanation, we must align another no less striking aspect of current research: the confrontation between an interpretive method and its other, or, more precisely, the manifestation of the relation that a mode of comprehension holds with the incomprehensible dimensions that it "brings forth." For example, the immense cultural erudition of Alphonse Dupront always extracts a "panic" from history, a sacred and savage depth. If sometimes this "collective spirit of panic," this originary drive, or this opaque neutral element of a "collective mentality" assumes the shapes of a referent, of a meaning, or of the ground of history, it is by dint of a sort of fiction based on Jung's and Otto's more questionable views. For in reality, this "panic" is the name that prodigiously extensive knowledge assigns to its own limits, to the unknown that it reveals and meets as it advances, to the aporia of knowledge brought out by the progress of a science. A depth of history is therefore designated (and not, as in the case elsewhere, eliminated) but by an "irrational" proportioned to the investigation, which positions itself under the sign of a knowledge of ideas and cultural forms. "The nonhistorical element," notes Dupront, "is indispensable for the historical one."[46]

Pierre Vilar offers an analogous phenomenon: the very existence of his subject matter—Catalonia—is the enigma that is brought forth by his rigorous socioeconomic analysis. How does Catalonia establish itself as a unity in its own right? How does this unity change with the equally problematic manifestation of the "Spanish" unity? With these questions Vilar's remarkable proof—which converts economic theory into historical analysis in order to apprehend a "deep history" from economic variation—meets its other. It opens onto enigmas, such as "the formations of groups with a strong communal conscience" and the nature of "regional" or national "personality" and of a "political will."[47] The rigor of his interpretation reveals, as its remainder or as that which *becomes* incomprehensible, the unity of consciousness whose conditions and functions have nonetheless been so vigorously enlightened.

It is hardly surprising that the problem opened by the *other* erupting into scientific process also appears in its object. Research no longer merely seeks successful comprehension. It returns to things that it cannot understand. It measures what it loses by fortifying its needs and methods. Michel Foucault's *Madness and Civilization* delimits the time when an augmented scientific sensibility was confronted by zones that it left as its remainder or unintelligible underside.[48] As it progresses, the science of history witnesses the enlargement of the silent areas of its lacunae. This occurs at the same moment when other sciences are taking an inventory of the harm born of their success. Michel Foucault's book is a sign of this interrogation. It is expressed through an object *lost* by the work of history, an object that is nonetheless impossible to suppress: namely, madness, as it is constituted by the exclusions of reason. Certainly, after this, the author's attempt to restore to madness its own language can only end in failure and be contradictory; it vacillates between the "redemption" of madness within a new kind of understanding, and the infinite enlargement of the abstract sign—"madness"—fated to designate the empty space that can never be filled through the work of historiography.[49] But there remains this abyss opened before scientific reason in the form of objects that it winds around without reaching. Studies devoted to sorcery, to miracles, to madness, to "primitive" culture, and so forth, have multiplied since the publication of Foucault's work. They designate a face-off whose disquieting uncanniness ethnology and psychoanalysis have allowed history to clarify. Scientific "reason" is indissolubly wedded to the reality that it meets again as its shadow and its other, at the very moment when it is excluding it.

Such a mobilization of historiography on the limits which both specify and furnish its discourse with relativity can also be located in the more epistemological form of works dedicated to the modes of *differentiation* among sciences. Here too, Michel Foucault is eminently important. Taking up former studies, especially those of Canguilhem, he shows how history is classified (and defined) in relation to a synchronic combination of discourses which are mutually contradistinguished and referable to common laws of differentiation.[50] Whatever the author's own position, his work both describes and engenders the movement which leads history to become a *work on the margins:* to situate itself through its relation to other discourses, to place discursivity in its relation to an eliminated other, to measure results in relation to the objects that escape its grasp; but also to establish continuities by isolating series, to analyze methods closely by distinguishing distinct objects which they grasp at once in a single fact, to revise and to compare the different periodizations that various types of analysis bring forth, and so forth. Hereafter the "problem is no longer of tradition and trace, but of delimitation and margins."

We can speak more appropriately of "limit" or of "difference" than of "discontinuity" (a far too ambiguous term, because it seems to postulate evidence of a rift in reality). From now on we must say with Foucault that the limit becomes "at once the instrument and the object of study."[51] As an operative concept of historiographical practice, it is both the working apparatus and the area of methodological investigation.

The Discourse of History

ONE step further, and history will be envisaged as *a text* organizing units of meaning and subjecting them to transformations whose rules can be determined. In effect, if historiography can have recourse to semiotic procedures in order to renew its practices, it likewise offers itself to these procedures as an object of study, inasmuch as it makes up a story or a discourse of its own.

Up to now, it may be that essays written on history from this perspective have not been entirely convincing, to the extent that they have posited the univocality of the genre of the "historical" over the ages. This is the case for Roland Barthes when he wonders whether "the narration of past events submitted to . . . the sanction of historical 'science,' placed under the imperious guarantee of the 'real,' justified by principles of 'rational' exposition . . . truly differs, through indubitable relevance, or through some specific trait, from imaginary narrative such as one finds in the epic, the novel, and the drama."[52] To seek an answer to this question solely through the examination of some "classical" historians—Herodotus, Machiavelli, Bossuet, and Michelet—isn't this to take too quickly for granted the homology among these discourses? To give too easily the examples nearest to narrative but quite distant from current research? To assume the discourse apart from the actions that establish it in a specific relation with the (past) reality from which it is distinguished? And consequently, not to account for successive modes of this relation? And finally, doesn't this deny the current movement that makes of scientific discourse the exposition of the conditions of its production, instead of the "narrative of past events"?

It still happens that throughout these "classic" works, the status of a "historical" writing seems to be defined by a combination of *meanings* articulated and advanced only in the name of *facts*. But indeed for Barthes (if we leave the details of his linguistic argument aside), the "facts" about which history speaks will function as indications. Throughout the relations established among facts, or the elevation of certain of them to the value of symptoms of a whole period, or the "lesson" (moral or political) which organizes the discourse as a whole, in every history a process of meaning can be found which "always aims at 'fulfilling' the meaning of History": "Historians are those who assemble not so much facts as signifiers."[53] They seem to tell of facts while, in effect, they express meanings which moreover refer what is *noted* (what historians hold to be relevant) to a conception of *whatever is notable*. The *signified* of historical discourse is made from ideological or imaginary structures; but they are affected by a referent outside of the discourse that is inaccessible in itself. Barthes labels this artifice proper to historiographical discourse the "realistic effect"; its task is to hide under the fiction of a "realism" a way of positing meaning, necessarily within language. "Historical discourse does not follow the real; rather, it only signifies it, endlessly reiterating that *it happened*, but without having this assertion be anything other than the obvious underside of all historical narrative."[54]

In evoking the "prestige of *it happened*" as regards history, Barthes places it in direct relation with current developments in the realistic novel, in the diary, in bits of news, museums, photography, documentaries, and so on. All of these discourses are actually built over a lost (and past) *real*; inside the closure of a text, in the form of a relic, they reintroduce the real that was exiled from language. It appears that words can no longer be accredited with an effective relation with the things they designate; they are especially adept at formulating meanings, the less they are restricted to adhering to the real. Rather than representing a return to the real, "realism" expresses the release of a population of words that until now had been attached to well-defined facts and that, from this point on, become useful for the production of legends or fictions. The vocabulary of the "real" penetrates all verbal matter that can be organized into a statement concerning what can be thought or what is thought. This vocabulary no longer has the privilege of being the outcrop of facts, of allowing a grounding Reality to emerge through them , or of being sanctified with the power of expressing both the "thing itself" and the Meaning which would infuse it.

From this standpoint it is true to say as Barthes does that "the sign of History has since become less the real than the intelligible."[55] But we are not dealing with just any kind of intelligibility. "This erasure of narrative in current historical science" attests to the priority accorded by this science to the conditions in which it elaborates "what can be thought"— this being the sense of the whole structuralist movement. And in the field of history, this analysis which bears on the methods—that is, on the production of meaning—cannot be dissociated from its site and from an object. Through its procedures, the site is the present act of this very production and the situation that currently makes it possible by virtue of determining it; the object is the set of conditions in which such and such a society could ascribe meaning to itself through a work that has its own determinations. History is not an epistemological criticism. It remains always a narrative. History tells of its own work and, simultaneously, of the work which can be read in a past time. Besides, history understands the latter only as it elucidates its own productive activity, and reciprocally, it understands its own work through the set of productions, and the succession of productions, of which this history is itself an effect.

If therefore the story of "what happened" disappears from scientific history (in order, in contrast, to appear in popular history), or if the narrative of facts takes on the allure of a "fiction" belonging to a given type of discourse, we cannot conclude that the reference to the real is obliterated. This reference has instead been somewhat displaced. It is no longer immediately given by narrated or "reconstituted" objects. It is implied by the creation of "models" (destined to make objects "thinkable") proportioned to practices through their confrontation with what resists them, limits them, and makes appeal to other models; finally, through the clarification of what has made this activity possible, by inserting it within a particular (or historical) economy of social production.

In this respect we can agree with A. J. Greimas, who states that with respect to models that can take cognizance of the functioning of a language, or if one prefers, with respect to the analysis of *possible* combinations in the organization and transformation of a finite number of elements, the historical element appears in the structuralist formulation "as a limitation of the possibilities of its manifestation." "Just as the atomic structure," he remarks, "is conceived easily as a combinatory whose currently manifest universe is only a partial realization, so then the semantic structure, imagined according to a comparable model, remains open and becomes closed only through history."[56]

The *limit* is found in the center of historical science, designating the other of reason, or of the possible. In Greimas' figure the real appears once again within science. It might be, moreover, that the distinction between "exact" and "human" sciences no longer passes through a difference in formalization or in the rigor of proof, but rather tends to separate disciplines according to the place that the one group of sciences accords to the *possible*, and the other accords to the *limit*. In any case there is no doubt that bound to the ethnologist's or the historian's task is a fascination with limits, or what is nearly identical, with the other.

Yet the limit is not only that which historical work constantly con-

fronts, organized as it is by the will to make all things thinkable. It also
keeps in view the fact that every interpretive procedure has had to be
established in order to define the procedures suited to a mode of comprehension. A new determination of "what can be thought" presupposes
those economic or sociocultural situations that are its conditions of possibility. All production of meaning admits to an event that took place
and that permitted it to be accomplished. Even exact sciences are led to
exhume their relation to a history, that is, the problem of the relation
between their discourse and what it implies without stating it—between
a coherence and a genesis. In historical discourse, investigation of the
real therefore comes back, not only with the necessary connections between conditions of possibility and their limitations, or between the uni-
versals of discourse and the particularity attached to facts (whatever their
delimitation may be),[57] but in the form of the *origin postulated* by the
development of a mode of "the thinkable." Scientific practice is based on
a social praxis independent of knowledge. The space of discourse refers
to a temporality different from that which organizes meaning according
to the classifying rules of verb tenses. The activity that produces meaning
and establishes an intelligibility of the past is also the symptom of an
activity *endured,* the result of events and structurings that it changes into
objects capable of being thought, the representation of an evanescent order of genesis.

HISTORY AS MYTH

HISTORY would fall to ruins without the key to the vault of its entire
architecture: that is, without the connection between the act that it promotes and the society that it reflects; the rupture that is constantly debated between a past and a present; the double status of the object that
is a "realistic effect" in the text and the unspoken element implied by the
closure of the discourse. If history leaves its proper place—the *limit* that
it posits and receives—it is broken asunder, to become nothing more
than a fiction (the narrative of what happened) or an epistemological
reflection (the elucidation of its own working laws). But it is neither the
legend to which popularization reduces it, nor the criteriology that would
make of it merely the critical analysis of its procedures. It plays between
them, on the margin that separates these two reductions, like Charlie
Chaplin at the end of *The Pilgrim,* running along the Mexican border

between two countries both chasing him in turn, with his zigzags marking both their difference and the seam joining them.

Also thrown back either toward their present or toward a past, historians experiment with a praxis that is inextricably both theirs and that of the other (another period, or the society that determines them as they are today). They work through the very ambiguity that designates the names of the discipline, *Historie* and *Geschichte,* an ambiguity ultimately laden with meaning. In effect, historical science cannot entirely detach its practice from what it apprehends to be its object. It assumes its endless task to be the refinement of successive styles of this articulation.

This is probably why history has taken up "primitive" myths or ancient theologies ever since Western civilization has become secular and ever since it has defined itself, in a political, social, or scientific mode, by a praxis which engages its relations equally with itself and other societies. The tale of this relation of exclusion and fascination, of domination or of communication with the *other* (a position filled in turn by a neighboring space or by a future) allows our society to tell its own story thanks to history. It functions as foreign civilizations used to, or still do, telling tales of cosmogonic struggles confronting a present time with an origin.

Such localization of myth does not appear merely with the movement that leads sciences, whether "exact" or "human," back to their history (allowing scientists to be situated within a social totality);[58] or with the importance of the vulgarization of history (which makes thinkable the relation of an order with its changes, or which exorcises it in the tone of "things have always been that way"); or yet with the thousand and one resurgences of the genial identification, bound together by Michelet, between the history and the autobiography of a nation, of a people, or of a party. History has become our myth for the more fundamental reasons summarized in the preceding pages.

An Identity Through a Differentiation

HISTORICAL discourse makes a *social identity* explicit, not so much in the way it is "given" or held as stable, as in the ways it is *differentiated* from a former period or another society. It presupposes the rupture that changes a tradition into a past object, in the manner in which the history of the ancien régime implies the Revolution.[59] But this relation with an origin, either near or distant, from which a society separates itself without being able to eliminate it, is what historians analyze. They make this relation the locus of their science. In a text that still has the shape of a narrative, they link the practice of a new intelligibility to the remainders of different pasts (which survive not only in documents but also in the particular "archive" which is the historical work itself).

If, in one respect, the function of history expresses the position of one generation in relation to preceding ones by stating, "I can't be that," it always affects the statement of a no less dangerous complement, forcing a society to confess, "I am other than what I would wish to be, and I am determined by what I deny." It attests to an autonomy and a dependence whose proportions vary according to the social settings and political situations in which they are elaborated. In the form of a "labor" immanent to human development, it occupies the place of the myths by means of which a society has represented its ambiguous relations with its origins and, through a violent history of Beginnings, its relations with itself.

The Origin of Language: The Living and the Dead

DESPITE its introductions or its prefaces in the first person (in *Ichbericht*) which have the value of an introit and put forward an "in those days," thanks to a noted difference from the author's time of writing, history is a *discourse in the third person*. Battles, political struggle, or debates over salary are the subject-object, but, as Roland Barthes has written, "no one is there to assume responsibility for the statement."[60] Discourse about the past has the status of being the discourse of the dead. The object circulating in it is only the absent, while its meaning is to be a language shared by the narrator and his or her readers, in other words, by living beings. Whatever is expressed engages a group's communication with itself through this reference to an absent, third party that constitutes its past. The dead are the objective figure of an exchange among the living. They are the *statement* of the discourse which carries them as an object, but in the guise of an interlocution thrown outside of discourse, in the unsaid.

Through these combinations with an absent term, history becomes the myth of language. It manifests the very condition of discourse: *a death*. It is born in effect from the rupture that constitutes a past distinct from its current enterprise. Its work consists in creating the absent, in making signs scattered over the surface of current times become the traces of "historical" realities, missing indeed because they are other.

But the absent term is also the present form of the origin.[61] Myth exists because, through history, language is confronted with its origins. Certainly in this case the confrontation assumes different poses: it is the relation of historical discourse with whatever period has been favored as an object of study within the linear succession of a chronology; or else it is the movement which refers this period to its more primitive time and endlessly traces it back to its imaginary "beginning," to a fictive but necessary caesura allowing us to travel back through periods of time and classify them, and so on. But a closer and more fundamental rapport is signified by this initial zero-degree, the rapport of every discourse with the death that makes it possible. The origin is inherent to discourse. It is precisely the topic about which nothing can be said. This discourse in its basic definition is *speech* articulated over what else *took place;* its own beginning is one which presupposes a *lost* object; its function is one of being, among human beings, the representation of a primitive scene that is effaced but is still an organizing force. Discourse is incessantly articulated over the death that it presupposes, but that the very practice of history constantly contradicts. For to speak of the dead means to deny death and almost to defy it. Therefore speech is said to "resuscitate" them. Here the word is literally a lure: history does not resuscitate anything. But the word evokes the function allocated to a discipline that deals with death as an object of knowledge and, in doing so, causes the production of an exchange among living souls.

Such is history. A play of life and death is sought in the calm telling of a tale, in the resurgence and denial of the origin, the unfolding of a dead past and result of a present practice. It reiterates, under another rule, the myths built upon a murder of an originary death and fashions out of language the forever-remnant trace of a beginning that is as impossible to recover as to forget.

Saying and Doing

HISTORY finally refers to a "making," a "doing," which is not only its own ("making history"), but also that of the society which specifies a certain scientific production. If it allows a common way of operating to find its own technical language, it refers to this social praxis as what allows a production of texts organized around a new intelligibility of the past.

This relation of discourse to a "doing" is internal to its object, since, in one fashion or another, history always deals with tensions, webbings of conflicts, or plays of force. But it is also external to its object, insofar as modes of comprehension and types of discourse are determined by the greater sociocultural ensemble which defines the particular situation of history. Stable societies allow history to favor continuities and tend to confer the value of a human essence upon a solidly established order. In periods of movement or revolution, ruptures of individual or collective action become the principle of historical intelligibility. Yet this reference to the social organization of history's operating—mobilized by the development of a political order or by the foundation of new regimes— intervenes only indirectly in scientific analysis. It is introduced symbolically through a *topos* of intelligibility: depending upon the periods of historiography, it is the event, or it is the continuous series, which is the point of departure and the definition of the intelligible. A type of society reveals itself also through the mode in which the discursivity of "understanding" and the uncanniness of "what happens" are combined; for example, socioeconomic models will be preferred to biography, or the inverse.

As a mirror of the "doing" which defines a society today, historical discourse is its representation and its underside. It is not the sum—as if knowledge provided reality or made it accede to its highest degree! Such an inflation of knowledge is superannuated. The entire movement of contemporary epistemology in the field of the so-called human sciences contradicts this inflation and humiliates its consciousness. Historiographical discourse is only one more bill in a currency that is being devalued. After all, it is only paper. But it would be erroneous to toss it from an excess of favor into an excess of indignity. The text of history, which must always be taken up over and over again, doubles the doing both as its trace and as its interrogation. Articulated upon what it is not—the "stir and toss" of a society, but also scientific practice itself—the text runs the risk of stating a meaning that is symbolically combined with its doing. History is not a substitute for social praxis, but its fragile witness and necessary critique.

Dethroned from the place to which it had been elevated by philosophy, which in the time of the Enlightenment or of German idealism, had made it the last manifestation of the World Spirit, historiographical discourse probably exchanges the place of the king for that of the child in the tale, pointing to a truth that everyone feigns to overlook. Such also is the position of myth, reserved for the festival which opens within daily labors the parenthesis of a truth. Without withdrawing anything from the functions underlined above, we do not have to neglect that which binds historical *saying* to social *doing*, without identifying the former with the latter: work is so reminded of its relation with death and with meaning; it situates genuine historiography in the direction of indiscreet questions that must be opened within the immense movement of praxis.

NOTES

1. Theology articulates the communal *act* of faith, and in its former definitions, it was the deepening of the experience itself.

2. In history, as in the totality of the human sciences, what Lévi-Strauss called the "testing of models" replaces the former methods of observation; determination of types of analysis wins over determination of the means or places of information. See Jean Viet, *Les Sciences de l'homme en France* (The Hague: Mouton, 1966), pp. 163–75.

3. Here, as in many other instances (consider "manifestation," "apparition"—and even "action"), a pressure of current language leads meaning to turn from the *act* to its *result,* from the active state of *doing* to the passive state of *being seen,* from a gesture to its image in a mirror. A growing rift between research and popularization cuts across both history and theology. Research takes the form of specific *steps* that are differentiated by their own procedures; but, in their popularization, history and theology become *objects* of knowledge or curiosity that are distributed to and imposed upon a public of consumers having less and less to do with production.

4. Many of the so-called theses of theology, it must be admitted, are simply literary analyses of an author and are hardly distinct from any other literary study except by dint of having a religious subject—as if describing the theological ideas contained in a work could be considered a way of "making theology."

5. Thus, in his great study *Chrétiens sans Eglise: La Conscience religieuse et le lien confessionel au XVIIe siècle* (Paris: Gallimard, 1969), the Marxist Leszek Kolakowsi wishes to take doctrinal and religious fact very seriously as such: "From the standpoint of a materialist interpretation of history, the irreducibility of religious phenomena can be recognized, even while we can admit to being able to explain them genetically through others. . . . We consider their specificity [that of "religious ideas"] understandable in the form of specificity in general, in taking account of the richer whole that is the totality of the social needs of a period in all their interrelations" (pp. 49 and 51). On the methodological problems advanced by the work, see Robert Mandrou, "Mysticisme et méthode marxiste," in *Politique aujourd'hui* (February 1970), pp. 51ff., and my *L'Absent de l'histoire* (Paris: Mame, 1973), pp. 109–15.

6. See Jean Orcibal, *Les Origines du jansénisme*, 5 vols. (Paris: Vrin, 1947–1962); Lucien Goldmann, *Le Dieu caché* (Paris: Gallimard, 1956), available in English as *The Hidden God* (London: Routledge and Kegan Paul, 1977); and my "De Saint-Cyran au jansénisme," *Christus* (1963), 10:399–417.

7. On this subject see Edgar Magnus Carlson, *The Reinterpretations of Luther* (Philadelphia: Westminster Press, 1948); J. V. M. Pollet, "Interprétation de Luther dans l'Allemagne contemporaine," *Revue des sciences religieuses* (1953), pp. 147–61; H. J. Grimm, "Luther Research Since 1920," *Journal of Modern History* (June 1960) vol. 32; R. H. Bainton, "Interpretations of the Reformation," *American Historical Review* (October 1960), vol. 36; Jean Delumeau, *Naissance et affirmation de la Réforme* (Paris: PUF, 1965), especially pp. 281–300; or the notes by R. Stauffer and T. Süss in the *Bulletin de la Société de l'histoire du protestantisme français* (1967), 113:313–46 and 405ff.

8. See "Henri Bremond, historien d'une absence," in my *Absent de l'histoire*, pp. 73–108.

9. Unfortunately Van Gennep (who died in 1956) had not yet been the subject of the collective study Pierre Marot called for in his "Hommage à Arnold Van Gennep," in *Arts et traditions populaires* (1957), 5:113ff. Since that time the lacuna has been filled by Nicole Belmont, in *Arnold Van Gennep* (Paris: Payot, 1974).

10. On the work of Gabriel Le Bras, see the studies of Henri Desroches in the *Revue d'histoire et de philosophie religieuse* (1954), 2:128–58, and François Isambert, in the *Cahiers internationaux de sociologie* (1956), 16:149–69.

11. Le Bras' first article on "La Pratique religieuse en France" took as its object "the popular life of Catholicism"; for its model, "the folklorist"; and as its point of departure, "the planning of investigation proposed by M. Saintyves." It was published in the *Revue de folklore français* (1933), 4:193–206.

12. In his *Introduction à l'histoire de la pratique religieuse en France* (Paris: PUF, 1945), Gabriel Le Bras posits the problem of the relation between a *single* practice and *plural* beliefs (1:116–20), but for him this plural designates "faith." Reacting against the overabundance of studies dedicated to doctrines (see his article of 1933), he short-circuits the ideologies in order to note the enigma of the relation between the practice (i.e., the sociological, the "visible" as he puts it) and the beliefs (for him this is not a sociological concept, but the invisible, the "flame" or "the grace of inner illumination"). Little by little he nuances this division, a product of the theological distinction between nature and the supernatural, at the same time that he has less and less confidence in the practice (the term disappears from the title given to the new edition of his *Introduction* in 1956). To this second evolution Isambert dedicated the article noted above, "Développement et dépassement de l'étude de la pratique religieuse chez G. Le Bras."

13. Thus from obscurity René Taveneaux, in *Le Jansénisme en Lorraine, 1640–1789* (Paris: Vrin, 1960), derives what he calls "the networks of the transmission of thought." In reality, what he brings to light are rifts, polarizations (first Parisian and then Dutch), unexpected combinations (e.g., the reemployment of the monastic bastions of Saint-Vanne in this ensemble), etc., which characterize a

complex social unity. "Thought" allows him to establish a very delicate sociology of a clerical group.

14. It is hardly surprising that this current is born of a widening gap in the history of sciences. See, for example, Edwin Arthur Burtt, *The Metaphysics of Modern Physical Science* (New York: Harcourt Brace, 1925); H. A. Smith, *A History of Modern Culture* (New York, 1930–1934); A. Wolf, *History of Science, Technology, and Philosophy in the Sixteenth and Seventeenth Centuries* (London: Allen, 1935); and A. R. Hall, *The Scientific Revolution, 1500–1800* (London: Longmans, 1954).

15. In *Geistesgeschichte* the notion of *Zeitgeist* has acquired a meaning which almost inverts its origins. Central among the German revolutionaries at the crossroads of the eighteenth and nineteenth centuries (Henning, Rebmann, Niethammer, Arndt, especially in his *Spirit of the Time* in 1806, or Hardenberg, etc.), it designates an irresistible force whose advance throws all institutional obstacles topsy-turvy. It is in this sense that Hegel takes it up, and that in 1829 it is criticized by Schlegel as indeterminate and subversive, in *Philosophie der Geschichte* (1829), 2:18. See Jacques d'Hondt, *Hegel, philosophe de l'histoire vivante* (Paris: PUF, 1966), pp. 211–16. Since that time the *Zeitgeist* has to the contrary defined an established order or the static coherence of a mentality. It is the significant trace of a "liberal" and "ideological" thought which then confronts Marxism.

16. See for example V. P. Zoubov, "L'Histoire de la science et la biographie des savants," *Kwart. Hist. Nauki* (1962), 6:29–42.

17. Arthur O. Lovejoy, *The Great Chain of Being: A Study of the History of an Idea* (Cambridge: Harvard University Press, 1936).

18. On the French "history of mentalities," see especially Georges Duby, *L'Histoire et ses méthodes* (Paris: Gallimard-Pléiade, 1961), pp. 937–66. But reference must be made to historical works more than to theoretical presentations: those of Georges Duby or Jacques Le Goff to be sure, but also Franco Venturi's remarkably lucid study "L'Illuminismo nel settecento europeo," in *Rapports* of the 11th International Congress of Historical Sciences (Stockholm), Uppsala, Almquist (1960), 4:106–35. In historiography of the "modern" period, in the same way that the seventeenth century is at once the object and the archeology of an analysis of practices, the eighteenth century is both object and archeology for a history of ideas. In the eighteenth century, for example with the "Students of Man," the relation between the man of the "Enlightenment" and the popular man, between the elite-subject and the population-object of science, is formed. See Sergio Moravia, *La Scienza dell'uomo nel settecento* (Bari: Laterza, 1970).

19. Gaston Bachelard, *Le Rationalisme appliqué* (Paris: PUF, 1949), pp. 104–5.

20. See Michel Foucault, *L'Archéologie du savoir* (Paris: Gallimard, 1969), pp. 29–101; in English, *The Archeology of Knowledge* (New York: Pantheon, 1972), pp. 21–76.

21. This problem of parallelism is evident all the while that, at least in the case of Georges Duby, the historian is interested in literature as the "transposition" or the "reflection" of the group which is the real object of his study. It would

be necessary to measure the effects proper to this "transposition." Literary expression is not the transparency of social life, but its complement and often its inversion (to the degree where it expresses what is perceived as "lacking").

22. In *Quaderni del carcere* (Turin: Einaudi, 1975), vol. 3, Antonio Gramsci notes, "As these diverse categories of traditional intellectuals experience, with an *esprit de corps,* the feeling of their uninterrupted historical continuity and of their qualification, they consider themselves autonomous and independent of the dominant social group. This self-positioning is not without broad consequences in the political and ideological field: all idealist philosophy can be easily attached to this position taken by the social complex of intellectuals" (p. 1515).

23. The evolution of historiography concerning the notion of "historical fact" can be measured by comparing Henri-Irénée Marrou's synthesis ("Qu'est-ce qu'un fait historique?" in Duby, *L'Histoire et ses méthodes,* pp. 1494–1500) and the problems advanced by François Furet in Jacques Le Goff and Pierre Nora, eds., *Faire de l'histoire* (Paris: Gallimard, 1974), 1:42–61.

24. Raymond Aron, *Introduction à la philosophie de l'histoire: Essai sur les limites de l'objectivité historique* (Paris: Vrin, 1938). The same theses are repeated in *Les Dimensions de la conscience historique* (Paris: Plon, 1961).

25. See the magisterial work of A. Renaudet, *Préréforme et humanisme à Paris pendant les premières guerres d'Italie, 1494–1517* (Geneva: Droz, 1916), and its many descendants.

26. A university tradition which responds to the widespread rejection of Jansenism by academic teaching spreads all the way up through the middle of the nineteenth century, and is maintained even in Antoine Adam's vigorous synthesis *Du mysticisme à la révolte: Les Jansénistes du XVIIe siècle* (Paris: Fayard, 1968).

27. One index of this among many is the place accorded to Newton's theological writings—see *Theological Manuscripts,* Herbert McLachlan, ed. (Liverpool: Liverpool University Press, 1950)—within the interpretation of his work. Alexandre Koyré especially has modified this perspective; see his *De monde clos à l'univers infini* (Paris: PUF, 1961), in English, *From the Closed World to the Infinite Universe* (New York: Harper, 1958). Today it is even emphasized that Western science has developed as a function of theological debates and that it has for example an intrinsic bond with the dogma of the Incarnation; see Alexandre Kojève, "L'Origine chrétienne de la science moderne," in *Mélanges Alexandre Koyré* (Paris: Hermann, 1964), 2:295–306.

28. See Henri Bernard-Maître, "Les 'Théologastres' de l'Université de Paris au temps d'Erasme et de Rabelais," *Bibliothèque d'Humanisme et Renaissance* (1965), 27:248–64; and Jean-Pierre Massaut and Josse Clichtove, *L'Humanisme et la réforme du clergé* (Paris: Belles Letters, 1968).

29. See Louis Bouyer, *Autour d'Erasme: Etudes sur le christianisme des humanistes catholiques* (Paris: Editions du Cerf, 1955), in English, *Erasmus and His Times* (Westminster, Md.: Newman Press, 1954); and Henri de Lubac, *Exégèse médiévale* (Paris: Aubier, 1964), vol. 4.

30. See Etienne Gilson, *Etudes sur le rôle de la pensée médiévale dans la formation du système cartésien* (Paris: Vrin, 1951).

31. See René Rémond, *La Droite en France de 1815 à nos jours* (Paris: Aubier, 1954). The Anglo-American perspective is supplied by Richard Griffiths in his *Reactionary Revolution* (London: Constable, 1966) and by Eugen Weber, *L'Action française* (Paris: Stock, 1962), among others.

32. See Emile Poulat, *Intégrisme et catholicisme intégral* (Paris: Casterman, 1969), and the subsequent debate with Paul Droulers in *Archives de Sociologie des Religions* (1969), 28:131–52.

33. Lucien Febvre, *Au coeur religieux du XVIe siècle* (Paris: Sevpen, 1957), p. 146.

34. See Pierre Goubert, *Beauvais et le Beauvaisis de 1600 à 1730* (Paris: Sevpen, 1960).

35. See Pierre Goubert, *L'Ancien Régime* (Paris: Colin, 1969), vol. 1; available in English as *The Ancien Régime* (London: Weidenfeld and Nicholson, 1973).

36. See Michel Foucault, *Les Mots et les choses* (Paris: Gallimard, 1966), chapters 3–6; available in English as *The Order of Things* (New York: Vintage, 1970).

37. See L. Cognet, *La Spiritualité moderne* (Paris: Aubier, 1966), and M. Venard's book review in *Revue d'Histoire de l'Eglise de France* (1968), 54:101–3.

38. See the remarks by D. Julia, P. Levillain, D. Nordman, and A. Vauchez, "Réflexions sur l'historiographie française contemporaine," *Recherches et débats* (1964), 47:79–94.

39. On the ethnological or folkloric interest through which religion becomes an object of study, and which explains at once the nature of a new "curiosity" and the renewal of studies on ideologies (from now on held to be unbelievable, but symbolic of a meaning to be deciphered), see "Les Révolutions du *croyable*," in my *Culture au pluriel* (Paris: Union Générale d'Editions, "10/18," 1974), pp. 11–34.

40. Here the problem is one of knowing what event or what sociopolitical transformation *makes possible* for twentieth-century historiography an analysis analogous to that which R. Mousnier recently devoted to historians of the eighteenth century. But most probably the terms of the question ought to be inverted: a new scientific point of view is clearly one of the indices by which an "event" is expressed and located.

41. See in particular the new series of *Annales E. S. C.* (since 1969), or *The Journal of Interdisciplinary History* (Boston: MIT Press, 1970).

42. Karl Marx, *Das Kapital* (Berlin, 1947), 1:7 (first preface); in English, *Capital* (New York: International Publishers, 1979).

43. Foucault has strongly underscored this point, in particular in *The Archeology of Knowledge*, pp. 8–9.

44. See Emmanuel Le Roy Ladurie, *Les Paysans de Languedoc* (Paris: Sevpen, 1966), 1:7–11, available in English as *The Peasants of Languedoc* (Urbana: University of Illinois Press, 1974); and especially Pierre Vilar, *La Catalogne dans l'Espagne moderne* (Paris: Sevpen, 1962), 1:11–38.

45. See Marc Soriano, *Les Contes de Perrault: Culture savante et traditions populaires* (Paris: Gallimard, 1969).

46. Alphonse Dupront, in *Revue de Synthèse*, nos. 37–39, p. 329. See also some particularly important studies, namely: "Lourdes: Perspectives d'une sociologie du sacré," *La Table ronde* (May 1958), 125:74–96; "Problèmes et méthodes d'une histoire de la psychologie collective," *Annales E. S. C.* (1961), 16:3–11; and "Formes de la culture des masses: De la doléance politique au pèlerinage panique (XVIIIe–XXe siècles)," in *Niveaux de culture et groupes sociaux* (The Hague: Mouton, 1968), pp. 149–67.

47. Vilar, *La Catalogne* preface, 1:36–37. The confrontation between cultural expression and economic structures is especially rich (because of the very object to be studied) in "Le Temps du Quichotte," *Europe* (January 1956), pp. 3–16; in "Les Primitifs espagnols de la pensée économique," *Mélanges Marcel Bataillon* (Bordeaux: Féret, 1962), pp. 261–84; or, from a more methodological standpoint, in "Marxisme et histoire, dans le développement des sciences humaines," *Studi storici* (1960), 1(5):1008–43.

48. See Michel Foucault, *Madness and Civilization* (New York: Pantheon, 1965), tr. of *Folie et déraison: Histoire de la folie à l'âge classique* (Paris: Plon, 1961; 2d. ed., Gallimard, 1972).

49. On this topic see Jacques Derrida's pointed remarks in "Cogito et histoire de la folie," in *L'Ecriture et la différence* (Paris: Seuil, 1967), pp. 51–97; available in English as "Cogito and the History of Madness," in *Writing and Difference* (Chicago: University of Chicago Press, 1978), pp. 1–63.

50. See Foucault, "The Discursive Regularities," in *The Archeology of Knowledge*, pp. 21–76.

51. *Ibid.*, pp. 5 and 8.

52. Roland Barthes, "Le Discours de l'histoire," *Social Science Information* (1967), 6(4):65–75; to be compared on the same question, with "L'effet de réel," *Communications* (1968), 11:84–90, and "L'Ecriture de l'événement," *Communications* (1968), 12:108–13. [These essays are reprinted in *Le Bruissement de la Langue* (Paris: Seuil, 1984).

53. Barthes, "Le Discours de l'histoire," p. 65.

54. *Ibid.*, pp. 73–74.

55. *Ibid.*, p. 75. In the "referential illusion" of the real in "realism," Barthes discerns a new verisimilitude ("L'Effet de réel," p. 88). This "real" is the connotation of *what can be thought*.

56. A. J. Greimas, *Du sens: Essais sémiotiques* (Paris: Seuil, 1970), p. 111. See the entire chapter entitled "Histoire et structure," pp. 103–16.

57. A problem that is not without analogy to what the first philosophies of language had dealt with at the end of the Middle Ages. See J. Claude Piguet, "La Querelle des universaux et le problème contemporain du langage," *Revue de Théologie et de Philosophie* (1969), 19:392–411.

58. In "L'Histoire et l'unité des sciences de l'homme," *Annales E. S. C.* (1968), 23(2):233–40, Charles Morazé using this approach envisions the central role of history: it is because the relation between human sciences is transferred and is played out in history that the latter is "syncretic" and seems fragmented today by its adhesion to more and more divergent disciplines.

59. After having said "the preceding regime," as of November 1789 one speaks

of the "ancien régime." See Albert Soboul, *La Civilisation et la Révolution française* (Paris: Arthaud, 1970), 1:37, and Goubert's thoughts in *The Ancien Régime*, vol. 1, ch. 10.

60. Barthes, "Le Discours de l'histoire," p. 71.

61. This is said leaving aside the examination—sketched elsewhere—of the problems opened by the intervention of psychoanalysis in the field of history. See chapter 8, "What Freud Makes of History."

2

The Historiographical Operation

W HAT do historians really fabricate when they "make history"? What are they "working on"? What do they produce? Interrupting their erudite perambulations around the rooms of the National Archives, for a moment they detach themselves from the monumental studies that will place them among their peers, and walking out into the street, they ask, "What in God's name is this business? What about the bizarre relation I am keeping with current society and, through the intermediary of my technical activities, with death?

To be sure, however general or extensive it may be, no thought or reading is capable of effacing the *specificity* of the place, the origin of my speech, or the area in which I am researching. This mark is indelible. Within the discourse in which I am putting global questions on stage, an "idiotism" comes forth: my way of speaking, my patois, represents my relation to a given place.

But the gesture which attaches ideas to places is precisely the historians'

Part of this study, originally entitled "The Historical Operation," was published in Jacques Le Goff and Pierre Nora, eds., *Faire de l'histoire* (Paris: Gallimard, 1974), 1:3–41. It is presented here in reviewed and corrected form.

gesture. For them, comprehension is tantamount to analyzing the raw data—which every method first establishes according to its own criteria of relevance—in terms of productions whose locality can be determined.[1] When for its practitioners history becomes the very object of their reflection,[2] can they ever invert the process of comprehension which relates a product to a place? Historians would then be rogues; they would give way to an ideological alibi if, in order to establish the correct status of their work, they were to have recourse to a philosophical *elsewhere*, to a *truth* formed and received outside of the channels through which, in history, every system of thought is referred to "places"—social, economic, cultural, and so on. Such a dichotomy between what they practice and what they preach might, besides, serve the reigning ideology by isolating it from effective praxis. The dichotomy would also relegate the historians' experiments to a theoretical sonambulism. Even more, in history as in other fields, one day or another a practice without theory will necessarily drift into the dogmatism of "eternal values" or into an apology for a "timelessness." Suspicion could never be extended over every theoretical analysis.

In this sector, Serge Moscovici, Michel Foucault, Paul Veyne, and many others point to an epistemological awakening.[3] A new urgency is becoming manifest in France. But only a theory which articulates a practice can be accepted, that is, a theory which on the one hand opens the practices to the space of a society, while on the other it organizes the procedures belonging to a given discipline. On a necessarily limited scale, envisaging history as an operation would be equivalent to understanding it as the relation between a *place* (a recruitment, a milieu, a profession or business, etc.), analytical *procedures* (a discipline), and the construction of a *text* (a literature). That would be to admit that it is part of the "reality" with which it deals, and that this reality can be grasped "as a human activity," or "as a practice."[4] From this perspective I would like to show that the historical operation refers to the combination of a social *place*, "scientific" *practices*,[5] and *writing*. Such an analysis of the preconditions that its discourse does not take up will allow us to specify the silent laws which organize the space produced as text. Historical writing is constructed as a function of an institution whose organization it apparently throws into upheaval: it effectively obeys its own rules, which demand to be examined for themselves.

A SOCIAL PLACE

ALL historiographical research is articulated over a socioeconomic, political, and cultural place of production. It implies an area of elaboration that peculiar determinations circumscribe: a liberal profession, a position as an observer or a professor, a group of learned people, and so forth. It is therefore ruled by constraints, bound to privileges, and rooted in a particular situation. It is in terms of this place that its methods are established, its topography of interests can be specified, its dossiers and its interrogation of documents are organized.

The Unspoken

FORTY years ago a first critique of "scientism" revealed the relation of "objective" history to a place, that of the subject. In analyzing what Raymond Aron has termed a "dissolution of the object," this critique took from history the privilege in which the discipline had taken so much pride when it claimed to reconstitute the "truth" of events. Moreover, "objective" history upheld with this idea of truth a model derived from a former philosophy, or from a theology dating from an even earlier time. It limited itself to translating truth in terms of historical "facts"—and the happy days of this positivism are over.

Since then an era of suspicion has reigned. It has been shown that all historical interpretation depends upon a system of reference; that this system remains as an implicitly particular "philosophy"; that, seeping into the work of analysis, it organizes the work surreptitiously by referring to an author's "subjectivity." In popularizing the themes of German historicism, Raymond Aron taught an entire generation the art of enumerating the "philosophical decisions" through which the organizations of raw data were ordered, as well as the code of their decipherment and the order of their exposition.[6] This "critique" represented a theoretical effort. It marked an important step in relation to a French situation where positivistic research prevailed and where there reigned skepticism with regard to German "typologies." It exhumed unadmitted dimensions as well as the philosophical presuppositions of nineteenth-century historiography. It already referred to a circulation of concepts, that is, to the movements which throughout the century had transported philosophical categories into the underground of history, just as in the cases of exegesis or sociology.

Today, the lesson is at our fingertips. "Historical facts" have already been established through the introduction of a meaning into "objectivity." In the language of analysis, "facts" speak of "choices" which are precedents, and which are therefore not the result of observation—and which are not even verifiable but, thanks to critical examination, are only "falsifiable."[7] "Historical relativity" thus forms a grid from which, over the background of a totality of history, multiple individual philosophies can be differentiated, especially those of philosophers dressed in historians' garb.

The return to personal "decisions" takes place on the basis of two assumptions. On the one hand, in isolating a philosophical element from the historiographical text, an *autonomy had been presupposed for ideology*: such was the condition of its extraction. An order of ideas was set apart from historical practice. On the other hand (but the two operations go together), while underscoring divergences among "philosophers" discovered in historians' clothing, by referring to the unfathomed dimensions of their rich intuitions, these thinkers were considered as *a group that could be isolated from society* by virtue of their direct relations to reflection. Recourse to personal options short-circuited the role practiced upon ideas by social localizations.[8] The plurality of these philosophical subjectivities had from that point the discreet effect of retaining a singular position for intellectuals. As questions of meaning had been discussed *among them*, the clarification of their differences of thought came to bestow upon the entire group a privileged relation to ideas. None of the interference of production, of technique, of social constraint, of professional or political position could bother the harmony of this relation: a silence was the postulate of this epistemology.

Raymond Aron granted a reserved status to both the rule of ideas and the kingdom of intellectuals. "Relativity" was at stake only within the closed perimeters of this field. Far from calling the area into question, relativity indeed defended it. Based on the distinction between the scientist and the political figure, one of the weakest links in Weber's theory,[9] such theses demolished a pretension of knowledge, but they also reinforced the "exempted" power belonging to the knowledgeable. A place was marked "off limits" just when the fragility of what was being produced therein was revealed. The favor taken away from works that could be controlled reverted to a group which could not be controlled.

Even nowadays, the most remarkable works on history seem to be dissociated with great difficulty from the very strong position that Raymond Aron had taken by substituting the silent privilege accorded to a *place* for that—in all of its triumph and controversy—of a *product*. While Michel Foucault denies all reference to the subjectivity or the "thought" of an author, he still takes for granted, at least in his first books, the autonomy of the theoretical *place* where, in its "narrative," laws are developed according to which scientific discourses form and combine in global systems.[10] In this respect *The Archaeology of Knowledge* (1969) marks a rupture by introducing at once both social conflicts and the techniques of a discipline into the examination of an epistemological structure, notably that of history (which is not by chance). Likewise when Paul Veyne succeeds in destroying within history what Raymond Aron's passage had still retained as a "causal science"—when in his work interpretive systems crumble into a dust of personal perceptions and personal decisions, leaving nothing subsisting in the way of coherence other than the rules of a literary genre and, as a point of reference, the historian's pleasure[11]—it still appears that the presupposition lives on intact. From the theses of 1938 onward that presupposition implicitly withdrew all epistemological relevance from the study of the social function exercised by history, by the group of historians (and more generally by intellectuals), by this group's practices and laws, by its intervention in the play of public forces, and so on.

The Historical Institution

THIS place left blank or hidden through an analysis which overvalued the relation of individual subjects to their object might be called an *institution of knowledge*. It marks the origin of modern sciences, as shown in the seventeenth century with the assemblies of erudites (for example at Saint-Germain-des-Prés); with the networks of correspondences and of travels that were formed by a milieu of the "curious";[12] or even more clearly in the eighteenth century, with the learned circles and the Academies with which Leibniz was so preoccupied.[13] The birth of "disciplines" is linked to the creation of such groups.

From this relation between a social institution and the definition of a knowledge, the figure coextends from the time of Bacon or Descartes onward, with what has been termed a "depoliticization" of intellectuals. By that we mean not an exile outside of society,[14] but rather the foundation of professional "bodies," those of "engineers," of pensioned needy intellectuals, and so on, at a time when universities fall into sclerosis as they become secluded. Political, erudite, and ecclesiastical institutions become distinctly specialized. We have therefore not an absence, but a particular place in a redistribution of social space. In the fashion of a withdrawal relative to public and religious affairs (which are themselves also organized in particular bodies), a "scientific" place is established. A rupture provides the basis for a social unity which will then become "science." It is a sign of an ongoing global reclassification. Outside of this break is outlined a place which is connected with others within a new whole, while inside is sketched the foundation of a knowledge that cannot be dissociated from a social institution.

Since that time this originary model has become ubiquitous. It is seen also in the form of subgroups or of schools. Whence the persistence of the gesture which circumscribes a "doctrine" by dint of an "institutional basis."[15] The social institution ("A Society for the Study of . . .") provides the ground for a scientific language (the review or the "bulletin", the inheritor and equivalent of yesterday's correspondence). From the "Students of Man" of the Enlightenment up to the creation of the sixth section of the Ecole Pratique des Hautes Etudes, thanks to the school of *Annales* (1947), all through the faculties of the nineteenth century, each "discipline" maintains its ambivalence of being at once the law of a group and the law of a field of scientific research.

The institution does more than give a doctrine a social position. It makes it possible and surreptitiously determines it. But it is far from being the case that one could be the cause of the other! The terms could never be easily inverted (the infrastructure becoming the "cause" of ideas) in assuming unchanged between them the type of relation that liberal thinking established at the moment when it allowed doctrines to lead history by the hand. It is necessary rather to challenge the isolation of these terms, and hence the possibility of turning a correlation back into a relation of cause and effect.

The same movement organizes society and the "ideas" that circulate within it. It is parceled into orders of manifestation (economic, social, scientific, and so forth) which make up overlapping but differential functions, in which none can be either the reality or the cause of another. Thus, socioeconomic and symbolic systems combine without being identified or ranked in hierarchies. In this way a social change can be compared to a biological change in the human body: like the biological change, the social change forms a language which is proportioned to other types of language, such as the verbal. The "medical" isolation of the body results from an interpretive bracketing which does not take into account passages from somatization to symbolization. Inversely, an ideological discourse is proportioned to a social order, just as every individual utterance is produced in relation to silent organizations of the body. That discourse as such can obey its own laws does not impede it from being linked to what it does not say—to the body, which speaks in its own fashion.[16]

In history every "doctrine" which represses its relation to society must be regarded as abstract. It denies the very matter with respect to which it is elaborated. Thus it undergoes effects of distortion owing to the elimination of what in fact situates it, but without its either being expressed or brought to consciousness: a power, which has its own logic; a place, which grounds and "maintains" a discipline in its development in successive works, and so forth. "Scientific" discourse which *does not speak* of its relation to the social "body" could never establish a practice. It would no longer be scientific. Here we face a question central to the historian's labors. This relation with the social body is specifically the object of history and could not be taken up without also calling into question the status of historiographical discourse.

In his "General Report" of 1965 on French historiography, Jean Glénisson evoked some of the discreet connections existing between a *knowledge* and a *place*: the supervision of research by some professors who rose to the highest positions in the academic world and who "ruled over others' university careers";[17] the constraint exercised by the social taboo of the monumental doctoral thesis;[18] the link between the weak influence of Marxist theory and the social recruitment of "scholars provided with tenured chairs and presidencies";[19] the effects of a strongly centralized and stratified institution on the scientific evolution of history, which has experienced a remarkable "tranquillity" for three-quarters of a century.[20] We must also underscore the interests too exclusively national of a historiography consumed by internal debates (historians fight either for or against Seignobos or Febvre), or circumscribed by the linguistic chauvinism of French culture which favors expeditions to the nearest regions of Latin reference (the Mediterranean world, Spain, Italy, Latin America), and which is limited in addition in its financial means, etc.

Among many others, these traits refer the "state of a science" to a social situation which is its unspoken condition. It is therefore impossible to analyze historical discourse independently of the institution in respect to which its silence is organized; or to dream of a renewal in the discipline that would be assured by the mere modification of its concepts without an intervening transformation of acquired situations. From this standpoint, as Jürgen Habermas' research has shown, a "repoliticization" of the human sciences is needed: progress may never be measured or attained without a "critical theory" of the current status of these sciences in society.[21]

Moreover, the question at which Habermas' critical sociology is aiming has already been traced in historical discourse. Without waiting for the theoretician's denunciation, the text in itself avows its relation with the institution. For example, the author's "we" refers to a convention (or, as semiotics would cast the formula, it refers to an "enunciative verisimilitude"). In the text, the "we" stages a social contract "among ourselves," in which a plural subject "utters" the discourse. A "we" takes hold of language for itself by virtue of being placed in the speaking subject's position.[22] In this way historical discourse takes priority over every particular historiographical work,[23] and so does the relation of this discourse to a social institution. The mediation of this "we" eliminates the alternative, which would attribute history either to an individual (the author, his personal philosophy, etc.) *or* to a global subject (the time, society, etc.). It replaces these subjective pretensions or edifying generalities with the positivity of a *place* over which discourse is articulated, but without the latter being reduced to the former.

The authorial "we" corresponds to that of true readers. The public is not the veritable recipient of the history book, even if it may be its financial and moral support. As the student but lately spoke to his class but had his teacher behind him, a work is valued less by its buyers than by the author's peers or colleagues, who rank it according to scientific criteria different from those of the public, but which are decisive for authors as soon as they wish to write a work of historiography. There are *laws* of the milieu. They circumscribe possibilities whose contents vary, but whose constraints do not. They organize a "police" around the work. If it is not "received" by the group, the book falls into the category of a "popularization" which, considered more or less benevolently, could never qualify a study as being "historiographical." It has to be "accredited" in order to accede to historiographical enunciation. What Foucault calls "the status of individuals who are the only ones to have the formal or traditional, juridically defined or spontaneously accepted right to profess a discourse of this sort"[24] depends upon an advanced degree (the *agrégation*) which categorizes the writer's "I" within the "we" of a collective body of work, or which enables a speaking subject to utter historiographical discourse. This discourse—and the group which produces it—*makes* the historian, at the same time that the atomist ideology of a "liberal" profession maintains the fiction of the authorial subject and leads everyone to believe that individual research constructs history.

In a more general fashion, a "historical" text (that is to say, a new interpretation, the application of specific methods, the elaboration of other kinds of relevance, a displacement in the definition and use of documents, a characteristic mode of organization, etc.) expresses an operation which is situated within a totality of practices. This aspect is the initial one. It is basic in scientific research. A particular study will be defined by the relation that it upholds with others that are contemporaneous with it, with a "state of the question," with the problematic issues exploited by the group and the strategic points that they constitute, and with the outposts and divergences thus determined or given pertinence in relation to a work in progress. Every individual result is inserted into a network whose elements narrowly depend upon one another, and whose dynamic combination forms history at a certain time.

Finally, what is a "valued work" in history? It is a work recognized as such by peers, a work that can be situated within an operative set, a work that represents some progress in respect to the current status of historical "objects" and methods, and one that, bound to the milieu in which it has been elaborated, in turn makes new research possible. The historical book or article is together a result and a symptom of the group which functions as a laboratory. Akin to a car produced by a factory, the historical study is bound to the complex of a specific and collective fabrication more than it is the effect merely of a personal philosophy or the resurgence of a past "reality." It is the *product* of a *place*.

Historians in Society

ACCORDING to a rather traditional concept among the French intelligentsia since the elitism of the eighteenth century, it is generally agreed that no element relative to practice will enter theory. "Methods" will thus be discussed, but without risking the impudence of evoking their importance as initiation into a group (to be introduced into a group, an individual must learn or practice "good" methods), nor is their relation to a social force ever expressed (the methods are the means thanks to which the power of an academic or clerical body is defended, differentiated, and made manifest). These methods define the parameters of institutional behavior and the laws of a milieu. They are nonetheless scientific. To suppose that an antinomy exists between a social analysis of science and its interpretation in terms of the history of ideas is the duplicity of those who believe that science is "autonomous." Because of this dichotomy, they also consider the analysis of social determinations as irrelevant, and the constraints it unveils as foreign or accessory.

These constraints are not accidental. They are part of research. Far from representing the shameful and unwarrantable interference of a foreigner in the Saint of saints of intellectual life, they form the texture of scientific process. Labor is based more and more on *teams*, leaders, and financial means, and therefore, too, through the mediation of credits, on favors that social or political proximities bring to this or that study. It is also organized by a *profession* which has its own hierarchies, its centralizing norms, its own type of psychosocial recruitment.[25] Despite attempts to break these barriers, the intellectual labor is established within the circle of *writing*: in the history that is being written, by priority the labor ranks the very ones who have written in such a way that the historical work reinforces a sociocultural tautology between its authors (a learned group), its objects (books, manuscripts, etc.), and its (educated) public. This work is attached to a *teaching activity*, hence to the fluctuations of a clientele; to pressures that it exerts while expanding; to the defensive reactions, the acts of authority or of withdrawal, that students' evolution and movements provoke among teachers; to the introduction of mass culture within a diversified university that is no longer an intimate area reserved for exchanges between research and teaching. The professor is pushed toward popularization aimed at "the greater public" (students or no), while the specialist is exiled from circles of consumption. Historical production finds itself shared between the *literary* work which is "authoritative" and the *scientific* esotericism which "produces research."

A social situation changes at once the mode of work and the type of discourse. Can we say that this is "good" or "bad"? First and foremost, it is a fact. It can be discerned everywhere, even where it is unspoken. Hidden connections can be recognized among sectors first assumed to be foreign, when they begin to move or become immobilized together. Is it by chance that we move from "social history" to "economic history" between the two wars,[26] around the time of the Great Depression of

1929; or that cultural history wins out at the moment when the social, economic, and political importance of "culture" is felt everywhere through mass media and leisure time? Is it by chance that the "historical atomism" of Langlois and Seignobos, explicitly associated with a sociology based on the figure Tarde called the "initiator" and with a "science of psychic facts" (breaking down the mind into rubrics of "motifs," "impulsions," and "representations"),[27] was combined with the liberalism of the reigning bourgeoisie at the end of the nineteenth century? Is it by chance that the dead spots of erudition—those which are neither an object nor a place for research—happen to be, from Lozère to Zambia, underdeveloped regions, but of such kind that economic enrichment creates today historiographical topography and ordering without having either its origin avowed or its relevance assured?

From collecting documents to writing books, historical practice is entirely relative to the structure of society. In the France of a recent past, the existence of firmly constructed social units defined the diverse levels of research: there were archives circumscribed within the events of the group and still close to family papers; a category of patrons or of authorities who signed with their proper names to "protect" a patrimony, clients, and ideals; a recruitment of erudite scholars devoted to a cause and adopting, vis-à-vis their motherland great or small, the motto of the *Monumenta Germaniae*: *Sanctus amor patriae dat animum*; works "dedicated" to subjects of local interest that furnished a language common to limited but faithful readers, and so on.

Studies on broader subjects do not escape this law, but the social unit on which they depend is no longer of the same sort: it is no longer a locality, but the scholarly, then the university intelligentsia, which distinguishes itself at once from the "petty history" and from provincialism and the common people, before its power enlarges with the centralizing extension of the university and it imposes the norms and codes of lay, liberal, and patriotic evangelism developed in the nineteenth century by the "conquering bourgeois."

And also, when Lucien Febvre between the two world wars stated that he wished to remove from sixteenth-century history the "frock" of former quarrels and take it out of the categories produced by the wars between Catholics and Protestants,[28] from the outset he was attesting to the disappearance of those ideological and social struggles which in the nineteenth century bore the flags of religious "parties" in the service of homologous campaigns. In fact, the religious quarrels continued to be waged for a long time, although not on religious grounds: between republicans and traditionalists, or between the *école publique* and the *école libre*. But these struggles lost their sociopolitical importance after the First World War, when the forces that had been opposed were dispersed into different categories, when "gatherings" or common "fronts" were formed, and when the economy began to organize the language of French life. Only then did it become possible to treat Rabelais as a Christian—that is, as a witness to a *past* time—to withdraw from divisions no longer inscribed within the daily life of a society, and therefore to stop favoring the cause of the Reformation or the Christian Democrats in the political or religious historiography of the academy. This brings neither better nor more objective conceptions, but does indicate a different situation. A social change provides historical distance in relation to what is becoming an entirely past time.

In this way Lucien Febvre follows in the footsteps of his forebears. As presuppositions of their understanding, they adopted the social structure and assumptions of their group, even if it entailed making them undergo a critical deviation. Doesn't the founder of the *Annales* do as much when he promotes a hisitorical quest and *Reconquista* of "Man," the "sovereign" figure at the center of the universe of his bourgeois milieu;[29] when he calls "global history" the panorama which is offered to the scrutiny of the regents of a university; when, with "mentality," "collective psychology," and all the equipment of *Zusammenhang*, he founds one more "idealist" structure,[30] which functions as the antidote to Marxist analysis and hides under a "cultural" homogeneity the class conflicts in which he, too, is implicated?[31] However genial and new it may be, his history is no less socially *marked* than those which he rejects, and if he is able to go beyond them, it is only because they correspond to *past* situations, and because another ready-made "frock" is cast over him by the place he fills in the conflicts of his present time.

With or without the fire that burns through Lucien Febvre's books, the same issues are ubiquitously at stake today—even if we leave aside the role of the social and political rifts which extend to publications or nominations, where tacit interdictions are in play. It is doubtless no longer a question of a war between the parties or great bodies of yesterday (the army, the university, the church, etc.): the hemorrhage of their forces has brought with it a folklorizing of their programs, and the true battles are no longer settled there.[32] "Neutrality" refers to the metamorphosis of convictions into ideologies, in a technocratic and anonymously productivist society that can no longer either designate its choices or keep track of its powers (in order to avow or to denounce them). Thus, the colonized university, a body deprived of autonomy in measure with its expansion, is now left open to orders and pressures coming from without. Within it, the scientistic expansionism or the "humanistic" crusades of earlier times are replaced by retreats. In matters of options, silence replaces affirmation. Discourse takes on the color of the walls; it is "neutral." It even becomes the means of defending *places* instead of being the statement of "causes" which might express a desire. Discourse can no longer speak of the elements which specify it, a labyrinth of positions to be respected and of patronizing practitioners to be solicited. Here, the *unexpressed* is at once the unavowed dimension of texts that have become pretexts, the exteriority of what is done in relation to what is said, and the disappearance of a place where a force is connected to a certain language. Besides, would this unexpressed not betray the reference of conservative historiography to an "unconscious" both endowed with a magic stability and transformed into a fetish by the need one has, "all the same," to affirm a power that everyone "surely knows" has already vanished?[32]

What Permits and What Prohibits: The Place

BEFORE knowing what history says of a society, we have to analyze how history functions within it. The historiographical institution is inscribed within a complex that permits only one kind of production for it and prohibits others. Such is the double function of the place. It makes possible certain researches through the fact of common conjunctures and problematics. But it makes others impossible; it excludes from discourse what is its basis at a given moment; it plays the role of a censor with respect to current—social, economic, political—postulates of analysis. This combination of permission and interdiction is doubtless the blind spot of historical research, and also the reason why it is incompatible with *n'importe quoi*, just anything. It is equally within this combination that work destined to modify it plays its role.

In any event, research is circumscribed by the place that a connection of the possible and impossible defines. If it were envisaged solely as a "saying," *legend* would be reintroduced into history, that is, a non-place, or an imaginary place, would be substituted for the connection of discourse to social places. To the contrary, history is defined entirely by a relation of language to the (social) body, and therefore by its relation to the limits that the body assigns either in respect to the particular place whence one speaks, or in respect to the other object (past, dead) that is spoken about.

History is entirely shaped by the system within which it is developed. Today as yesterday, it is determined by the fact of a localized fabrication at such and such a point within this system. Therefore, taking account of the place where it is produced only allows historiographical knowledge to escape from the unawareness of a class that would fail to recognize itself as a class in relations of production, and that would likewise fail to recognize the society in which it is inserted. Connecting history to a place is the condition of possibility for any social analysis. It is known for a fact that, in Marxism as in Freudianism, there can be no analysis which does not depend wholly upon the situation created by a social or analytical relation.

To take seriously the site of historiography is still not tantamount to expounding history. Nothing of what is produced in it is yet said about it. But taking the place seriously is the condition that allows something to be stated that is neither legendary (or "edifying") nor atopical (lacking relevance). Denial of the specificity of the place being the very principle of ideology, all theory is excluded. Even more, by moving discourse into a non-place, ideology forbids history from speaking of society and of death—in other words, from being history.

A PRACTICE

"MAKING history" is a practice. From this point of view we can now move to a more programmatic perspective, envisage paths that are opened, and cease to pursue the epistemological situation that thus far a sociology of historiography has been revealing.

Insofar as the university is foreign to practice and to technicalities,[34] everything that places history in rapport with techniques is classified as "auxiliary science." Formerly, this meant epigraphy, papyrology, paleography, diplomatics, codicology, etc.; today, musicology, "folklorism," computer science, etc. History would only begin with the "noble speech" of interpretation. It would finally be an art of discourse delicately erasing all traces of labor. In fact, there is a decisive option here: the importance that is accorded to technicalities turns history either in the direction of literature or the direction of science.

If it is true that the organization of history is relative to a place and a time, this is first of all because of its techniques of production. Generally speaking, every society thinks of itself "historically," with the instruments that pertain to it. But the term "instrument" is equivocal. At stake are not only means. Serge Moscovici has most convincingly shown[35]—although from another perspective—that history is mediated by technique. In this fashion is relativized the privilege invested in social history throughout the nineteenth century, and often enough today. A society's relation with itself, the "becoming other" of the group according to a *human* dialectic, is combined with what is crucial to current scientific activity, the becoming of *nature*, which is "at once a given and a work."[36]

Research follows along this changing border between the given and the created, and finally between nature and culture. In "life," biology discovers a language spoken before speakers ever appear. Psychoanalysis discerns the articulation of a desire in discourse that is organized in ways other than those expressed through consciousness. In a different field, environmental science modifies the moving combinations of nature and industry, but it can no longer isolate the indefinite extension of *social* constructions from the natural structures that it changes.

This immense work site promotes, as Moscovici has said, a "renewal [of nature], instigated through our intervention."[37] It "reunites humanity to matter differently."[38] In this way "the social order is marked as a form of the natural order, and not as an entity opposed to it."[39] All of this will modify profoundly a history that assumed its "central sector" to be what Labrousse calls "social history, that is, the history of social groups and their relations."[40] Already history has been directed first toward economy, then toward "mentalities," thus oscillating between the two terms of the relation that research is increasingly honoring: nature and culture. The signs are multiplying. An orientation that was already outlined during the period between the wars, the interest in geography and in a "history of men in their close relations with the earth,"[41] is emphasized with studies on the construction and the combinations of urban spaces,[42] on the migrations of plants and their socioeconomic effects,[43] on the history of techniques,[44] on mutations of sexuality, on sickness, medicine, and the history of the body, and so forth.[45]

But the fields open to history can never be solely new objects furnished to an unchanged institution. History as such becomes involved in this relation of discourse with the techniques engendering it. We must envisage how it deals with "natural" elements in order to change them into a cultural *environment,* and how it makes transformations effected within the relation of a society and its nature accede to literary symbolization. From wastes, papers, vegetables, indeed from glaciers and "eternal snows,"[46] historians *make something different:* they make history. They fashion an artifice of nature. They participate in the work that changes nature into environment, and thus modify the nature of man. Their techniques situate them specifically in this articulation. Placed as we are at the level of this practice, no longer do we face the dichotomy which opposes the *social* to the *natural,* but the connection between a socialization of nature and a "naturalization" (or a materialization) of social relations.

The Nature-Culture Connection

NO doubt it is an overstatement to say that "time" provides the "raw data of historical analysis" or its "specific object." According to their methods, historians deal with the physical objects (papers, stones, images, sounds, and so on) that are distinguished within the continuum of perception through the organization of a society and the systems of relevance which belong to a "science." They work on materials in order to transform them into history. Here they undertake a practice of manipulation which, like others, is subject to rules. A comparable manipulation would be the manufacturing of goods made of already refined matter. First transforming the raw material (a primary source) into a standard product (secondary source), the work of the historian carries it from one region of culture ("curiosities," archives, collections, etc.) to another (history). Historical work participates in the movement through which a society transforms its relation to nature by changing the "natural" into the utilitarian (for example, a forest that is exploited), or into the esthetic (for example, a mountain turned into a landscape), or by making a social institution shift from one status to another (for example, a church that is converted into a museum).

But historians are not satisfied with *translating* one cultural language into another, that is, social productions into historical objects. They can change elements into culture that they have extracted from natural areas. From their documentation (in which they include pebbles, sounds, etc.) to their books (where plants, microbes, and glaciers acquire the status of symbolic objects), they proceed to a displacement of the separation between nature and culture. They modify space in the manner of the urban designer who integrates fields into the town's network of transportation, of the architect who regulates the lake with dams, of Pierre Henry, who changes a squeaking door into a musical motif, or of the poet who completely transforms the relations between a "noise" and a "message." Historians metamorphose the environment through a series of transformations which change the boundaries and the internal topography of culture. They "civilize" nature—which has always meant that they "colonize" and change it.

To be sure, we can observe nowadays that an increasing mass of historical books are becoming novelistic or mythic. Such books no longer produce these transformations in the fields of culture, while in contrast "literature" intends to work upon languge and make a "text" stage what Raymond Roussel describes as a *"movement of reorganization,* a mortuary circulation which engenders as it destroys."[47] In other words, in this form history ceases to be "scientific," while literature becomes more and more so. When historians suppose that a past already given is unveiled in their text, they align themselves all the more with the consumer's behavior. They passively receive objects distributed by producers.

What is "scientific" in history and in other disciplines is the operation that changes the "milieu"—or what makes an organization (whether social, literary, etc.) the condition and place of a *transformation.* In a society, at one of its strategic points, it displaces the connection tying culture to nature. In history, the operation establishes a "government of nature" in a way that concerns the relation of the present to the past—insofar as the latter is not so much a "given" as a product.

From this feature common to all scientific research we can specify precisely those points where technique is marked. Here I do not wish to hark back to historical methods. By means of several probings, I intend only to raise the type of theoretical problem that an examination of its "apparatus" and technical procedures can open in history.

The Establishment of Sources or the Redistribution of Space

IN history everything begins with the gesture of *setting aside,* of putting together, of transforming certain classified objects into "documents." This new cultural distribution is the first task. In reality it consists in *producing* such documents by dint of copying, transcribing, or photographing these objects, simultaneously changing their locus and their status. This gesture consists in "isolating" a body—as in physics—and "denaturing" things in order to turn them into parts which will fill the lacunae inside an a priori totality. It forms the "collection" of documents. In the words of Jean Baudrillard, it places things in a "marginal system."[48] It exiles them from practice in order to confer upon them the status of "abstract" objects of knowledge. Far from accepting "data," this gesture forms them. The material is created through concerted actions which delimit it by carving it out from the sphere of use, actions which seek also to know it beyond the limits of use, and which aim at giving it a coherent new use. It becomes the vestige of actions which modify a received order and a social vision.[49] The establishment of signs offered for specific treatments, this rupture is therefore neither uniquely nor from the first the effect of a "gaze." A technical operation is necessary.

The origins of our National Archives already imply, in effect, the combination of a *group* (the "erudite"), *places* ("libraries"), and *practices* (of copying, printing, communication, classification, etc.). In fine point, they are a token of a technical system which was inaugurated in the West with "collections" assembled in Italy, then in France, from the fifteenth century onward. They were financed by great patrons who wanted to appropriate history for themselves (the Medici family, the dukes of Milan, Charles of Orleans, Louis XII, and so on). In these areas the creation of a new *task* ("collecting") is combined with the satisfaction of new *needs* (justification of recent and familial groups thanks to the establishment of their own traditions, titles, and "property rights") and with the production of new *objects* (documents that are set aside, conserved, and copied) whose meaning is hereafter defined by the relation of every item to the whole set (the collection). The science that is born (the "erudition" of the seventeenth century) inherits with these "establishments of sources" —technical institutions—its basis and rules.

First linked with juridical activity among men of letters, lawyers, bureaucrats, and recorder-keepers, the enterprise expands and conquers as soon as it passes into the hands of specialists.[50] It is productive and reproductive. It observes the laws of multiplication. From 1470 on, it is allied with printing: the "collection" becomes a "library."[51] "Collecting" for a long time actually means manufacturing objects: copying or printing, binding, classifying—and with the products he multiplies, the collector becomes an agent in the concatenation of a *history to be made* (or remade) according to new intellectual and social relevances. Hence the collection, as it topples the instruments of work, redistributes things, redefines elements of knowledge, and inaugurates a place for a new beginning through the building of what Pierre Chaunu calls a "gigantic machine" that will make an entirely different history possible.

Erudite scholars want to develop into a whole the innumerable "rarities" that the endless trajectories of their curiosity bring back to them; they want to invent languages that will assure their understanding of them. If one can judge from the evolution of their work, from the end of the sixteenth century up to Leibniz through Peiresc and Kircher, these scholars are oriented toward the methodical *invention* of new systems of signs thanks to analytical procedures, especially analysis and synthesis.[52] They are preoccupied by the dream of a totalizing taxonomy and by the will to create universal instruments proportioned to their passion for comprehensiveness. Through the intermediary of the *cipher*, which plays a central role in this "art of decipherment," homologies between erudition and mathematics are crucially important. To be sure, to the cipher, a code destined to construct an "order," is opposed the symbol. Linked to a received text which refers to a hidden meaning within the figure (allegory, blazon, emblem, etc.), symbol implies the necessity for an *authorized commentary* by whomever is "wise" or profound enough to detect this meaning.[53] But on the other side, even if the thresholds and detours are numerous, the systems made possible by the cipher—from the series of "curiosities" to the artifical or universal languages (we might say from Peiresc to Leibniz)—are however inscribed along the line of development that establishes the *construction of a language* and, therefore, the production of techniques and objects proper to it.

Today the establishment of sources requires also a founding gesture, signified, as in former times, by the combination of a place, an "apparatus," and techniques. A first sign of this displacement: there is no task which does not have to use common sources *otherwise* and, for example, change the function of archives formerly defined by a religious or "familial" use.[54] Accordingly, in the name of new relevance, the work shapes tools, recipes, songs, popular imagery, the layout of farmlands, urban topography, and so forth, into documents. The issue is not only one of bringing these "immense dormant sectors of documentation" to life,[55] of giving a voice to silence, or of lending currency to a possibility. It means changing something which had its own definite status and role into *something else* which functions differently. And, too, the label "research" cannot be applied to a study that purely and simply adopts former classifications, which sticks to the limits posed for example by series H in the National Archives, and which therefore does not define its own field of study. A work is "scientific" when it produces a *redistribution* of space and when it consists, first of all, in *ascribing* a place for itself through the "establishment of sources"—that is to say, through an institutionalizing action and through transformational techniques.

Nowadays the institutional procedures raise more fundamental problems than are indicated by these initial signs. For every historical practice establishes its place only thanks to the apparatus which is at once the condition, means, and result of a displacement.[56] Similar to paleotechnical factories, national or municipal archives formed a segment of the apparatus that formerly determined operations adopted to a system of research. Any change in the use of archives cannot be foreseen without their overall form being changed. The same technical institution prohibits formulation of new answers to different questions. In fact, the situation is the inverse: from now on, other kinds of "apparatus" allow the study of new questions and answers. Certainly, an ideology of "real" or "true" historical "facts" still hovers in the air of our time; it even proliferates in a literature *on* history. Yet this is tantamount to folklorizing former practices: such frozen words outlive battles long ended; they only show the gap between received "ideas" and practices which will change them sooner or later.

The transformation of "archivistic" activity is the point of departure and the condition for a new history. It is destined to play the same role that the erudite "machine" had played in the seventeenth and eighteenth centuries. I will choose only one example, the use of the computer. François Furet has shown several of the effects produced by the "constitution of new archives recorded on perforated tapes": meaning is made only as a function of seriality, and not in relation to a "reality." The objects of investigation can only be those which can be constructed formally before programming takes place, and so on.[57] Yet this is nothing more than a particular element and, in part, a symptom of a larger scientific institution. Contemporary analysis upsets procedures linked to the "symbolic analysis" which had prevailed since the time of romanticism and which sought to recognize a given and hidden meaning. Analysis regains the confidence in *abstraction* which characterized the classical period—but an abstraction which today is a formal set of relations, or "structure."[58] Its practice consists in constructing "models" that are posited deliberately, as André Régnier says, "replacing the study of concrete phenomena by that of an object shaped through its definition," judging the scientific value of this object according to the "field of questions" to which it allows response and the answers that it furnishes, and, finally, "establishing the limits of the model's range of meaning."[59]

This last point is crucial for history. For if it is true that, in a broad fashion, contemporary scientific analysis aims at *reconstructing* objects from "simulacra" or "scenarios," that is, at providing itself through the relational models and languages (or metalanguages) it produces with the means for multiplying or transforming given systems (whether physical, literary, or biological), history tends to manifest the "limits of the range of meaning" of these models or languages; in this form of a limit relative to models, it meets again what formerly appeared as a past relative to an epistemology of origins or ends. In this way, it seems, history is faithful to its fundamental purpose, which doubtless always remains to be defined—but we must already note that this purpose links history simultaneously to the real and to death.

The specification of its role is not determined by the apparatus itself (for example, the computer) which places history into a network of constraints and possibilities born of the present scientific institution. Elucidation of what is proper to history is marginalized in respect to the apparatus: it flows back into the preparatory time of programming that the use of the apparatus necessitates, and it is rejected at the other end, in the time of exploitation yielded by the obtained results. It is developed in relation to the prohibitions that the machine establishes, through the objects of research that have to be constructed, and in relation to what this machine permits, through a way of dealing with the standard products of the computer. But these two operations are necessarily based on the technical institution which inserts *every* piece of research into a generalized system.

Libraries of the past also exercised the function of "placing" erudition within a system of research. But it was a regional system. Thus the epistemological moments (of conceptualization, documentation, of treatment or interpretation) that are currently distinguished inside a generalized system could be mixed in the regional system of former erudition. The *establishment* of sources (through the mediation of its current apparatus) therefore involves not only a new delimitation of the relation between reason and the real, or between culture and nature; it is the principle of an epistemological redistribution of the moments of scientific research.

In the seventeenth century, the library of Colbert's design—or its homologues—was the common ground on which the very rules of erudition developed. A science grew around this apparatus, which is still the place where researchers circulate, to which they make reference, and whose ruling they accept. "Going to the archives" is the statement of a tacit law of history. Now another institution is replacing this central locus. It also imposes its law on practice, but a different one. So we ought first of all to account for the technical institution which, like a monument, organizes the locus where from now on all scientific research circulates, before we analyze in depth the operational trajectories that history maps over this new space.

Bringing Forth Differences: From the Model to Its Deviation

THE use of current techniques of information retrieval brings historians to the point of separating what until now was combined in their work: the construction of objects of research and hence also of units of comprehension; the accumulation of "data" (secondary sources, or refined material) and their arrangement in places where they can be categorized and shifted;[60] the exploitation made possible by the diverse operations to which this material is susceptible.

In this way historical research is staged, strictly speaking, in the relation between the extreme poles of the entire operation: on the one hand, in the construction of models, and on the other, in the attachment of a "degree of meaning" to the results obtained after all of the combinations of processed information have been completed. The most visible form of this relation ultimately consists in granting relevance to *differences* proportioned to the formal units built beforehand; in discovering heterogeneity that can be of technical use. In relation to material produced through the advent of serial constructs and their combinations, former "interpretation" becomes the manifestation of a *deviation relative to these models*.

This schema is probably still quite abstract. Many current studies make the movement and meaning more comprehensible. As an example, historical analysis does not have as an essential result a quantitative relation between the size and the degree of literacy among men drafted into the armed forces from 1819 to 1826, nor even proof of a survival of the ancien régime in postrevolutionary France, but only the unforeseen coincidences, the incoherences, or the unknowns that this inquiry brings forth.[61] What is important is not the combination of series obtained thanks to a preliminary isolation of significant points according to preconceived models, but, on the one hand, the relation among these models and the limits that their systematic use brings to light, and on the other, the capacity to transform these limits into problems with which available techniques can deal. These two aspects are moreover coordinated, for if the difference is made obvious by virtue of the rigorous extension of constructed models, it is *significant* thanks to the relation that it keeps with them in the form of a deviation—and through this it leads to a return to these models with the aim of correcting them. It might be said that the formalization of research has as its goal precisely the production of "errors"—insufficiencies, lacunae—that may be put to scientific use.

This way of proceeding appears to overturn history as it has been practiced in the past. It customarily began with limited evidence (manuscripts, rarities, etc.), and it took as its task the sponging of all diversity off of them, unifying everything into coherent comprehension.[62] But the value of this inductive totalization depended then on the quantity of accumulated information. It vacillated when its documentary basis was compromised by the results harvested from new investigations. Research—and its prototype, the thesis—tended to prolong the time of information-gathering indefinitely, in view of deferring the nonetheless inevitable moment when unknown elements would come and demolish its basis. The often monstrous quantitative development of the search for documents had the result of introducing into the interminable process of research the very law that made it obsolete as soon as it was completed. A threshold has been passed, and beyond it this situation is inverted. From quantitative development according to a stable model, history is turning to endless changes of models.

Today, the study is initially developed over units that it has itself defined, insofar as research becomes—and must become—capable of choosing a priori its objects, levels, and taxonomies of analysis. The coherence is initial. With the computer, the quantity of information that can be studied in relation to these norms has become endless. Research has totally changed. Based on formal entities that are deliberately put forward, it is drawn toward the deviations that are revealed through logical combinations of series. It plays on the limits of models. To use a former vocabulary that no longer corresponds to its new trajectory, we might say that research no longer begins with "rarities" (remainders from past time) in order to advance to a synthesis (present understanding), but that it begins from a formalization (a present system) in order to give occasion to "remainders" (signs of limits and, through this logic, of a "past" which is the product of historical work).

This movement has doubtless been accelerated through the use of the computer. It preceded it—just as a technical organization preceded the computer, which is but one more of its symptoms. A strange phenomenon in contemporary historiography must be observed. The historian is no longer a person who shapes an empire. He or she no longer envisages the paradise of a global history. The historian comes to circulate *around* acquired rationalizations. He or she works in the margins. In this respect the historian becomes a prowler. In a society gifted at generalization, endowed with powerful centralizing strategies, the historian moves in the direction of the frontiers of great regions already exploited. He or she "deviates" by going back to sorcery,[63] madness,[64] festival,[65] popular literature,[66] the forgotten world of the peasant,[67] Occitania,[68] etc., all these zones of silence.

These new objects of research attest to a movement which has been clearly visible for several years in the strategies of history. Thus Fernand Braudel has shown how studies on "cultural areas" benefit when being situated in places of transit, where "borderline," "borrowed," or "rejected" phenomena can be perceived.[69] The scientific interest of these works consists of the relation that they keep with supposed or posited totalities—"a coherence in space," "a permanence in time"—and to the corrective that they allow to be brought to them. No doubt we must envisage in this perspective many types of current research. Even biography plays a role of a distance and a margin proportioned to global constructions. Research ascribes objects for itself that take the shape of its practice: they furnish it with the means of *bringing forth differences* relative to continuities or to elements from which analysis proceeds.

Research on the Borderlines

THIS strategy of historical practice prepares it for a theorization that conforms better to the possibilities offered by the sciences of information. It could be that more and more this strategy specifies not only the methods but also the function of history within the totality of sciences today. Its methods no longer consist in providing knowledge with "authentic" objects; its social role is no longer—except in specular literature, which is to say popularizations—one of supplying society with global representations of its genesis. History no longer occupies as it did in the nine-teenth century this central locus organized by an epistemology that, los-ing reality as an ontological substance, sought to rediscover it in the form of historical force, *Zeitgeist* and the future hidden inside the social body. It no longer has the totalizing function which consisted in taking the place of philosophy in its role of stating sense and meaning.

History now intervenes in the mode of a critical experimentation with sociological, economic, psychological, or cultural models. It is said, to quote Pierre Vilar, that it uses "borrowed tools." This is true. But to be precise, it *tests* these tools by transferring them to different areas, in the same way that a touring car is "tested" by being driven on racetracks, at speeds and in conditions which exceed the norms. History becomes a place of "control." In it a "function of falsification" is put to work.[70] In it the limits of what might be significant can be made obvious relative to models which, in turn, are "essayed" by history in areas foreign to that of their elaboration.

This functioning can be shown, by virtue of example, in two of its essential moments: one aims at the relation with the real in the mode of the historical fact; the other, at the use of received "models" and hence the relation of history to a contemporary form of reason. The former deals with the internal organization of historical procedures, while the latter takes up the connection of these procedures with different scientific fields.

Facts have found their champion in Paul Veyne, a marvelous butcher of abstract heads. As is always the case, he raises the flag of a movement that has preceded him—not just because every true historian is a poet of meticulous detail who plays, as does the esthetician, on the thousand har-monic levels that a rare piece awakens within a broad network of knowl-edge, but also because, nowadays, many formalisms can furnish new rel-evance for the *exceptional detail*. Put otherwise, such a return to facts cannot be recruited into a campaign against the structuralist "monster," nor can it be pressed into the service of a regression toward former ideologies and practices. To the contrary, it is inscribed in the line of structural analysis, but as a development. For the "fact" hereafter in question is not the one which offered to an observer's knowledge the emergence of a reality. Combined with a constructed model, it assumes the form of a *difference*. The historian is therefore not faced with the choice of "your money or your life"—the "law" or the "fact" (two concepts that are, moreover, effaced from contemporary epistemology).[71] Historians find in their models a means to make deviations visible. If, for some time, they hoped for a "totalization" and believed that they could reconcile diverse systems of interpretation in a fashion accounting for all of their information,[72] by priority historians are now concerned with the complex manifestations of these differences. In this way the area in which they are settling can still, by analogy, bear the venerable name of the "fact": the fact, such is the difference.

And, too, the relation with the real becomes a relation among the terms of an operation. Fernand Braudel has already given an entirely functional meaning to the analysis of borderline phenomena. The objects that he proposed for research were determined in relation to an operation to be undertaken (not to a reality to be rejoined), and in respect to existing models.[73] A result of this enterprise, the "fact" is the designation of a relation. The "event" can also in this way recover its definition of being a caesura. To be sure, it no longer cuts through the thickness of a reality whose ground we would see across a transparency of language, or which would rise to the surface of our knowledge in the form of fragments. The event pertains entirely to combinatory relations of rationally isolated series within which it serves to *mark* in turn crossing points, conditions of possibility, and the limits of validity.[74]

This already implies a "historical" way of using models that are taken from other sciences, and of situating a function of history in respect to these sciences. One of Pierre Vilar's studies helps to make the principle explicit. Apropos of the work of J. Marczewski and J.-C. Toutain, Vilar has shown the errors that would be encountered with the systematic "application" of our contemporary economic concepts and models to the ancien régime. But the problem is much more vast. For Marczewski, the economist is characterized by the "construction of a system of references," and the historian is the individual "who uses economic theory." To say this is to pose a problematic which makes one science into the instrument of another, and which can be inverted infinitely: finally, who indeed is "using" whom? Pierre Vilar shifts a similar conception. In his opinion, history has assigned itself the task of analyzing the "conditions" in which these models are valid and, for example, specifying the "exact limits of possibility" of a "retrospective econometrics." History manifests a *heterogeneity* relative to the *homogenous* wholes established by each discipline. It also might put into dynamic relation the limits proper to every system or "level" of analysis (economic, social, and so forth).[75] In consequence, history becomes an "auxiliary," in the words of Pierre Chaunu;[76] not that it is "in the service" of economy, but the relation that it maintains with diverse sciences allows it to hold, in respect to each of them, a necessary critical function. This relation also suggests the purpose of connecting the limits thus made obvious.

In other sectors the same complementarity is also found. In urban studies, Choay remarks that history might be able "to have us comprehend, through *difference,* the specificity of the space that we have reason to require of contemporary developers"; to permit "a radical critique of the operative concepts of urbanism"; and, inversely, in respect to the models of a new spatial organization, to give an account of social *resistances* through analysis of "deep structures with slow evolution."[77] A tactic of deviation would specify the intervention of history. From its standpoint, the epistemology of sciences begins with a present theory (in biology, for example) and meets history in the fashion of *what was not* clarified, or thought possible, or even formerly articulated.[78] The past surges up first as "what lacks." Intelligence of history is linked to the capacity of organizing differences or absences that are pertinent, that can be ranked, because they are relative to current scientific formalizations.

One of Georges Canguilhem's remarks about the history of science can be generalized to give breadth to this "auxiliary" position.[79] In effect, history seems to have a fluctuating *object* whose determination comes less from an autonomous decision than from its interest and importance for other sciences. Scientific interest exterior to history defines the objects that the discipline ascribes for itself and the areas to which it is successively drawn, according to the fields (sociological, economic, demographic, cultural, psychoanalytical, etc.) which have in turn become the most decisive ones, and in conformity to the problematics which organize them. But historians accept responsibility for this interest as a task belonging to the greater entity of Research. Thus they create laboratories of epistemological experimentation.[80] Certainly they can give an objective form to these investigations only by combining the models with other sectors of their documentation about a society. Whence their paradox: they put *scientific* formalizations into play in order to test them, using the nonscientific objects with which they practice such testing. History thus continues to maintain no less than ever the function that it has exercised over the centuries in regard to many different "reasons," which concerns each of the established sciences: namely, its function as a form of criticism.

Criticism and History

WORK on the limits could be located elsewhere, and not exclusively where there is recourse to historical "facts" or a treatment of theoretical "models." If they are accepted, however, already these few indications direct us toward a definition of research as a whole. The strategy of historical practice implies a status of history. So it is hardly surprising to note that the nature of a science is the presupposition which must be exhumed from its effective procedures, and that this is the means to make these procedures more precise. Without this, every discipline would be associated with an essence that presumably exists within its successive technical reincarnations, that outlives each of them (somewhere) and that keeps a merely accidental relation with practice.

A brief study of historical practice seems to allow three connected aspects to be specified: the mutation of "meaning" or of the "real" in the production of *significant deviations;* the position of a particular event as a *limit of what can be thought;* and the composition of a place which establishes within present time the *ambivalent figuration of the past and future.*

The first aspect presupposes a sudden change in historical knowledge in the last century. One hundred years ago, history represented a society as a collection and recollection of its entire development. It is true that history was fragmented into a plurality of histories (biological, economic, linguistic, and so on).[81] But among these scattered positivities, as among the differentiated cycles that characterized each one of them, historical knowledge restored the *same* through their common ground of an *evolution.* It sewed all of these discontinuities together by running through them as if they were the successive or coexisting figures of a same meaning—that is, of an orientation—and by evincing in a more or less teleological writing the interior unity of a direction or a development.[82]

Currently, history is judged rather according to its capacity to measure *deviations* exactly—not only of a quantitative nature (statistics of population, salary, or publication) but also qualitative (structural) differences—in relation to current formal constructs. In other words, the conclusion of history is what used to take the form of the *incipit* in former historical narratives: "In times past, life was not the way it is today."

Cultivated methodically, this distance ("life was not. . .") has become the result of research, instead of being its postulate and question. Thus, through hypothesis, "meaning" is eliminated from scientific fields all the while that they are being established. Historical knowledge does not reveal a meaning, but rather the exceptions that the application of economic, demographic, or sociological models uncovers from various areas of documentation. Research consists in producing significant negative factors. It specializes in forging pertinent differences which increased rigor in programming and its systematic exploitation allow it to "bring out."

In proximity to this first aspect, the second involves the element which has rightfully established the historical discipline: the *particular* (what G. R. Elton correctly distinguishes from the "individual"). If it is true that the particular designates at once both historical scrutiny and research, this is not insofar as it is an object actually thought, but rather because it is, to the contrary, the limit of what can be thought. Only universal issues are thought. The historian settles on the frontier where the law of an intelligibility meets its limit in the form of what it must endlessly overcome through its own movement, and what it endlessly meets again in new and different shapes. If historical "comprehension" is not enclosed within the tautology of legend or has not taken flight into ideology, its primary characteristic is not making series of selected data understandable (although that may be its "basis"), but rather *never denying* the relation that these "regularities" keep with "particularities" which escape them. Biographical detail, an aberrant toponymy, a local drop in salary, and so forth: all these forms of exception, symbolized in history by the importance of the proper name, renew the tension between systems of explanation and the always unexplained "that." To designate the "that" as a "fact" is only a way of naming what cannot be understood; it is a *Meinen* and not a *Verstehen*. But it is also tantamount to maintaining as necessary what is still unthought.[83]

Certainly this experience must be attached to the pragmatism that lives in all historians, and that drives them to turn theory into ridicule so quickly. But it would be illusory to believe that the mere mention of "that's a fact" or "it happened" is equivalent to an understanding. Chronicle or erudition limited to collecting particular information only ignores the law which organizes it. Like that of hagiography or news items,[84] such discourse only illustrates in a thousand variants the general antinomies that belong to a rhetoric of the exceptional. It falls into the platitude of repetition. In reality, particularities have as their jurisdiction a play over the base of an explicit formalization; they function by investing it with interrogation; they signify by referring back to acts, to persons, and to everything that remains outside of both knowledge and discourse.

The place that history creates by combining the model with its deviations—or by playing on the borderlines of regularity—represents a third aspect of its definition. More important than reference to the past is the introduction of the past by way of an assumed distance. A gap is folded into the scientific coherence of a present time, and how could this be, effectively, unless through something that can be objectified, the past, whose function is to indicate alterity? Even if ethnology has partially relieved history in this task of establishing a staging of the other in present time—the reason why these two disciplines have been in intimate rapport—the past is first of all the means of *representing a difference*. The historical operation consists in classifying the given according to a present law that is distinguished from its "other" (the past), in assuming a distance in respect to an acquired situation, and thus in marking through a discourse the effective change that precipitated this distancing.

This operation has a double-edged effect. On the one hand, it historicizes current time. Properly speaking, it stages the present time of a lived situation. It necessitates clarification of the relation of dominant forms of reasoning to a proper *place* which, in opposition to a "past," becomes the present. A reciprocal relation between the law and its limit simultaneously engenders the differentiation of a present from a past time.

But on the other hand, the figure of the past keeps its primary value of representing *what is lacking*. With a material which in order to be objective is necessarily *there*, but which connotes a past insofar as it refers first of all to an absence, this figure also introduces the rift of a future. It is well known that a group can express what it faces—what is still lacking—only through a redistribution of its past. Thus history is always ambivalent: the locus that it carves for the past is equally a fashion of *making a place for a future*. As it vacillates between exoticism and criticism through a staging of the other, it oscillates between conservatism and utopianism through its function of signifying a lack. In these extreme forms it becomes, in the first case, either legendary or polemical; in the second, it becomes reactionary or revolutionary. But these excesses could never allow us to forget what is written in its most rigorous practice, that of *symbolizing limits* and thus of enabling us to *go beyond those limits*. The old slogan about "the lessons of history" acquires new meaning in this perspective, if, as we leave an ideology of inheritors aside, we can identify the "moral of history" with this interstice created within the events of the day through the representation of differences.

A WRITING

REPRESENTATION—literary staging—is "historical" only if it can be articulated within a social place of scientific operation, and only if linked both institutionally and technically to a practice of deviation in respect to contemporary theoretical or cultural models. There is no historical narrative where the relation to a social body and an institution of knowledge is not made explicit. Nonetheless there has to be a form of "representation." A space of figuration must be composed. Even if we cast aside everything that deals, properly speaking, with a structural analysis of historical discourse,[85] we still must envision the operation that turns the practice of investigation into writing.

Scriptural Inversion

WRITING, or the construction of an *écriture* (in the broad meaning of the organization of signifiers), is an uncanny sort of passage.[86] It leads from practice to text. A transformation assures the passage from the unlimited field of research to what Marrou calls the "servitude" of writing[87]—"servitude" because, in effect, the foundation of a textual space carries with it a series of distortions in respect to analytical procedures. With discourse a law contrary to the rules of practice is seemingly imposed.

The first constraint of discourse consists in prescribing for beginnings what is in reality a point of arrival, and even what would be a vanishing point in research. While the latter begins in the currency of a certain social place and a certain conceptual or institutional apparatus, the exposition follows a chronological order. It takes the oldest point as its beginning. In becoming a text, history conforms to a second constraint. The priority that practice gives to a tactic of deviation (in respect to the base furnished by models) appears to be contradicted by the closure of the book or article. While research is interminable, the text must have an ending, and this structure of finality bends back upon the introduction, which is already organized by the need to finish. Thus the whole is presented as a stable architecture of elements, rules, and historical concepts which form a system among themselves, and whose coherence is owing to a unity designated by the author's proper name. Finally, in order to maintain itself by means of some few examples, scriptural representation becomes "full"; it fills or obliterates the lacunae that are to the contrary the very principle of research, for research is always sharpened through lack. Put otherwise, the text makes *present*, it represents through an ensemble of figures, stories, and proper names, what practice seizes as its limit, as exception or as difference, as past. The "servitude" that discourse imposes on research is measured with these few features—the inversion of the order, the closure of the text, and the substitution of a presence of meaning where lacunae were at work.

Could writing therefore be the inverted image of practice? It would have the merit of mirror writing,[88] as in all cryptographies, in children's games, or in counterfeiters' imitations of coins, fictions forging deceit and secrets, tracing the sign of a silence through the inversion of a normative practice and its social coding. This is the case for the "mirrors of history." To be sure, they hide their relation to practices that are no longer historical but now political and commercial; but in using a past in order to deny the present that they repeat, they set apart something foreign to current social relations, they *produce secrets* within language; their games designate a withdrawal that can be told in legends inverting the normal channels of research and superseding them. Mirror writing is serious because of what it does—it states something other through the inversion of the code of practice; it is illusory only insofar as, not realizing what it is doing, one takes its secret to be what it puts into language, and not what it subtracts from it.

In fact, historical writing—or historiography—has been controlled by the practices from which it results; even more, it is itself a social practice which establishes a well-determined place for readers by redistributing the space of symbolic references and by thus impressing a "lesson" upon them; it is didactic and magisterial. Yet at the same time, it functions as an inverted image; it gives way to lack and yet hides it; it creates these narratives of the past which are the equivalent of cemeteries within cities; it exorcises and confesses a presence of death amidst the living. Playing on both sides, at once contractual and legendary, both performative writing (discussed in the final two sections of this chapter) and mirror writing, historiography has the ambivalent status of "producing history" (as Jean-Pierre Faye has shown),[89] and also of "telling stories"—that is, it imposes the constraints of a power, and it provides loopholes. It edifies as it amuses, so to speak. By specifying a few aspects of historiographical construction, we can better clarify the relations of difference and continuity that writing keeps with the discipline of research,[91] and also its social function as a practice.

In effect, by being dissociated from the daily work, the gaps in logic, the conflicts, and the combinations of microdecisions that characterize concrete research, discourse is located outside of the experience that gives it credibility; it is separated from *passing time*, oblivious to the flow of everyday labor, in order to furnish models within the fictional cadre of *past time*. What is arbitrary in this construction has been shown. This is a general problem. Thus, Claude Bernard's *Cahier rouge* (1850–1860) represents a chronicle that is already distinct from the actual experimentation in his laboratory, and his theory, the *Introduction à l'étude de la médecine expérimentale* (1865), is in its turn a simplification, out of touch and reductive in respect to the *Cahier*.[91] Among a thousand other examples, this one shows the passage from practice to chronicle and from chronicle to a didactics. Only a distortion allows the introduction of "experiment" into another practice equally social but symbolic, scriptural, which substitutes the authority of a knowledge for the labor of a given research. What do historians *fabricate* when they become writers? Their very discourse ought to betray what they are doing.

Chronology, or the Masked Law

THE results of research are clarified according to a chronological order. To be sure, the composition of series, the isolation of global "conjunctures," just like narrative or cinematic techniques, have made this order more flexible, permitting the innovation of synchronic tables and renewing the traditional means of putting different moments into play with one another. Nonetheless, every historiography puts forward a *time of things* as the counterpoint and condition of a *discursive time* (discourse "advances" at different speeds, slowing down or rushing ahead). By means of this referential time, it can condense or stretch its own time,[92] produce effects of meaning, redistribute and codify the uniformity of flowing time. This difference already takes the form of a splitting in two. It allows for play and furnishes an area of knowledge with the possibility of being produced in a "discursive" time (or a "diegetic" time, as Gérard Genette says) placed at a distance from "real" time. The service that allusion to this referential time renders to historiography can be envisaged under three diverse aspects.

The first (which can also be located in other forms) is one of *making oppositions compatible*. A simple example: we can say that "the weather is good" or "the weather is bad." These two propositions cannot be maintained at the same time, but only one or the other. In contrast, if we introduce temporal difference so as to transform the propositions into "yesterday, the weather was good," and "today, the weather is bad," it is now legitimate to maintain them together. Contraries are therefore compatible within the same text under the condition that it is *narrative*. Temporalization creates the possibility of making coherent an order and its "heteroclite," its irregularity. In respect to the flat space of a system, narrativization creates a "depth" which allows the contrary or the remainder of the system to be placed *near* it. Historical perspective therefore authorizes the operation which, from the same place and within the same text, substitutes conjunction for disjunction, holds contrary statements together, and, more broadly, overcomes the difference between an order and what it leaves aside. Thus it is the instrument par excellence of all discourse that aims to "understand" antinomical positions (it suffices that one of the terms of conflict be classified as past), to "reduce" the aberrant element (it becomes a "particular" case which is marked as a positive detail within a narrative), or to maintain as "lacking" (pertaining to another period) what does not fit into a present system and therefore acquires an uncanny appearance.

But this temporalization, skittering away as it does from rigorously imposed limits, creating a stage on which incompatible elements can be put into play together, indeed has to be paid for with its counterpart. Narrative can keep only the appearance of syllogism; where it explicates, it is enthymematic,[93] it "pretends" to be reasoning. To be sure, in maintaining the relation of a rationality with what takes place outside of it, on its borderlines, narrative preserves the possibility of a science or a philosophy (it is heuristic); but, as such, it occupies their place and hides their absence. We can therefore wonder what authorizes historiography to be synthesized from contraries, if this is not a rational stricture. In fact, if we adopt Benveniste's distinctions between "discourse" and "narrative,"[94] it is a narrative that functions as a discourse organized by the locus of "interlocutors" and based on what the "author" ascribes for himself in respect to his readers. It is the locus whence the text is being produced that authorizes it, and before any other sign, the recourse to chronology avows it.

Chronology indicates a second aspect of the service that time renders to history. It is the condition that allows a classification by periods. But, in the geometric sense, it applies the inverted image of time upon the text, an image that in research proceeds from the present to the past. Chronology follows this path in reverse. Historical exposition supposes the choice of a new "vector space" which transforms the direction of the path marked by the temporal vector and inverts its orientation. This reversal alone appears to make the connection of practice and writing possible. If it indicates an ambivalence of time,[95] it posits first of all the problem of a *re-commencement: where* does writing begin? Where is it established so that historiography can exist?

At first sight writing leads time toward the moment of the individual receiver. It thus constructs the locus of readers in 1988. From the depths of the ages, it comes to them. Whether or not it participates in a thematic of progress, whether it drains long durations or relates a succession of *epistemès,* no matter what its content may be, historiography attempts to rejoin a present which is the end of a more or less protracted course along a chronological trajectory (the history of a century, of a period, or of a series of cycles). The present, the postulate of discourse, becomes the *profit* of the scriptural operation: the place of the production of the text is transformed into a place produced by the text.

The narrative, however, has it duplicity. The chronology of the historical work is only a limited segment (for example, we describe the evolution of Languedoc from the fifteenth to the eighteenth century), set apart first on a longer axis that exceeds it on one end and the other. (figure 2.1). On one side, chronology aims at the present moment across a distance—the right half of the line left blank, defined only in its origin (from the eighteenth century up to contemporary times). On the other, it presupposes a finite series whose terms are always uncertain; it ultimately postulates recourse to the empty and necessary concept of a zero-point, an origin (of time), indispensable for any orientation.[96] The narrative therefore masks this initial and unassignable reference, the absolute condition for any possibility of its historicization, on the entire surface of its organization. By allowing the present to be "situated" in time and, finally, to be symbolized, narrative posits it within a necessary relation to a "beginning" which is *nothing,* or which serves merely as a limit. The anchoring of the narrative conveys everywhere a tacit relation to something which cannot have a place in history—an originary non-place—without which, however, there would be no historiography. Writing disperses through its chronological staging the reference of the entire narrative to something unspoken that is its postulate.

This non-place marks the interstice between practice and writing. The qualitative gap between one and the other is doubtless manifested through the fact that writing de-natures and inverts the time of practice. But only a silent passage to the borderline effectively poses their difference. A zero-point in time connects one to the other. It is the threshold which leads from the fabrication of the object to the construction of the sign.

This initial nothing traces out the disguised return of an uncanny past. It could be said that it is myth transformed into a chronological postulate—at once erased from the narrative but everywhere presupposed in it, impossible to eliminate. A necessary relation to the other, to this mythic "zero," is still inscribed in the narrative content with all the transformations of genealogy, with all the modulations of dynastic or familial histories concerning politics, economy, or mentalities. In order for the narrative to "come down" to present time, it must be authorized by this higher "nothing" whose formula the *Odyssey* has already provided: "No one knows by himself who his father really is."[97] Expulsed from knowledge, a ghost insinuates itself into historiography and determines its organization: it is what we do not know, what is not endowed with a proper name. In the form of a past which has no locus that can be designated—but which cannot be eliminated—it is *the law of the other*.[98]

"Law always takes advantage of what is written," Maurice Blanchot has said.[99] If it results from a current and localized operation, insofar as it is writing historiography reiterates another beginning, one that is impossible to date or to represent, a beginning presupposed by the deployment of chronology, a deployment which at first sight appears to be very simple.[100] Historiography doubles the gratifying time—the time which comes toward you, the readers, and which valorizes your position—with the shadow of a forbidden time. The absence through which all literature begins inverts—and allows—the manner by which narrative is filled with meaning, and by which discourse establishes a position for the reader. The two are combined, and we can see that historiography acquires its

FIGURE 2.1

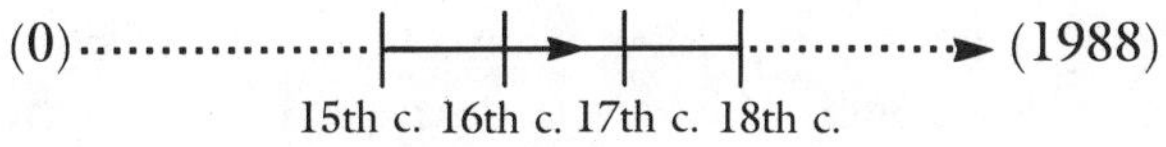

$(0)\cdots\cdots\cdots\vdash\!\!-\!\!\rightarrow\!\!-\!\!\vdash\!\!\cdots\cdots\blacktriangleright (1988)$

15th c. 16th c. 17th c. 18th c.

force by transforming genealogy into a message and by being situated "higher" than the reader, simply because it is nearer to that which authorizes. The text holds together the contradictions of this unstable time. It discreetly restores its ambivalence. It secretly betrays the contrary of "meaning" by which the present time claims to understand the past. Indeed, unlike what it does when it assumes itself as its object, this writing does not acknowledge that it is the "labor of negation." Yet it does witness to it. The construction of meaning is built upon its contrary. Here too, as Blanchot remarks, the language of the writer "does not present by rendering present what he is showing, but in showing it behind everything, as both the meaning and the absence of that everything."[101]

When it becomes historical, narrative nevertheless resists the seduction of beginning; it does not yield to the Eros of the origin. Unlike myth, it does not assume as its goal the staging of a necessary and lost authority in the guise of an event that never took place.[102] It does not state what it presupposes, for its objective is one of making room for a *labor*. The law is conveyed only through a particular study, whose organization assures the relation among the terms (the origin, the present time) left out of view.

Split Constructions

AMONG the problems related to narrative envisioned as a discursive form,[103] there are a number that have to do specifically with the construction of historiography. They concern a *will* for which temporalization provides a frame, allowing a sum of contradictions to be held together without the need for resolving them. This "globalizing" purpose is at work everywhere in the historiographical work. It ultimately refers to a political will to manage conflicts and to regulate them from a single point of view. This purpose literally produces texts which, in various ways, have the double quality of combining a *semanticization* (the edification of a system of meaning) with a *selection* (a sorting having its basis in the place where a present is separated from a past), and of directing an *intelligibility* toward a *normativity*. The mixed function of historiography can be specified by several features that deal first of all with its status in a typology of discourses, and second, with the organization of its contents.

In developing a general typology of discourse, a first approximation concerns the mode through which every discourse organizes the relation between its "content" and its "expansion." In narrative both refer to an order of succession; in exposition, referential time (a series of moments cast as A, B, C, D, E, etc.) can be subject to omissions and inversions capable of producing effects of meaning (for example, literary or cinematic narrative will offer an order of E, E, A, B, etc.). In logical discourse, content is defined by the status of truth (and/or of verifiability) that can be assigned to statements, and it implies syllogistic (or "legal") relations between statements which determine the mode of the exposition (induction and deduction). Now historical discourse claims to provide a true content (which pertains to verifiability) but in the form of a narration (figure 2.2).

Combining heteroclite systems, this mixed discourse (made of two others and situated between them) can be fashioned according to two contrary movements: a *narrativization* makes content move in the direction of its expansion, from nonchronological models to a chronologization, from a doctrine to a manifestation of a narrative type; inversely, a *semanticization* of raw data makes descriptive elements move toward a syntagmatic linkage of utterances and an establishment of programmed historical sequences. But these generative procedures of the text cannot entirely conceal the *metaphorical* slippage where, following Aristotle's definition, the "passage from one genre to another" is effected. As a sign of this mixed discourse, metaphor is omnipresent. It brings to historical explanation an enthymematic character. It carries causality off in the direction of successivity (*post hoc, ergo propter hoc*). It takes relations of coexistence

FIGURE 2.2

	content	expansion
narration	temporal series (A, B, C, D . . .)	temporal sequence (E, C, A, D . . .)
historical discourse	"truth"	temporal sequence
logical discourse	truth of propositions	syllogism (induction, deduction)

as coherence, and so forth. The likelihood of statements is constantly substituted for their verifiability. Whence the authority which historical discourse needs in order to uphold itself: what it loses in rigor must be compensated for by an increase in reliability.

Another form of splitting can be linked to this need for reliability. We admit as historiographical discourse that can "include" its other—chronicle, archive, document—in other words, discourse that is organized in a *laminated* text in which one continuous half is based on another disseminated half. The former is thus allowed to state what the latter is unknowingly signifying. Through "quotations," references, notes, and the whole mechanism of permanent references to a prime language (what Michelet called the "chronicle"),[104] historiographical discourse is constructed as a *knowledge of the other*. It is constructed according to a problematic of procedure and trial, or of *citation*, that can at the same time "subpoena" a referential language that acts therein as reality, and judge it in the name of knowledge. Moreover, the convocation of raw data obeys the jurisdiction which is pronounced upon it in the historiographical staging. This stratification of discourse does not assume the form of a "dialogue" or a "collage." Into the singular it combines knowledge citing the plural of the documents that are quoted. In this play, the basic tenet and limit of the decomposition of raw data (through analysis or division) is the *uniqueness* of a textual recomposition. The role of quoted language is thus one of accrediting discourse. With its referential function, it introduces into the text an effect of reality; and through its crumbling, it discreetly refers to a locus of authority. From this angle, the split structure of discourse functions like a machinery that extracts from the citation a verisimilitude of narrative and a validation of knowledge. It produces a sense of reliability.

By these divided texts a particular epistemological and literary functioning is also implied. On the one hand, to use Karl Popper's categories, the question here is one of "interpretation" rather than "explication." Insofar as historical discourse acquires from its internal relation with "chronicle" its status of being the knowledge of this chronicle, it is built upon a certain number of epistemological presuppositions: the need for a referential semanticization which comes to it from culture; the possibility of transcribing the already coded languages which it interprets; the possibility of fashioning a metalanguage through the very language of the documents it uses. In these diverse forms, quotation introduces a necessary outer text within the text. And reciprocally, quotation is the means of attaching the text to its semantic outer surface, of letting it appear to play a role in culture, and of thus giving it the stamp of referential credibility. In this respect, quotation is only a particular instance of the rule that necessitates, for all production of "realistic illusion," the multiplication of proper names, descriptions, and deictics.[105] Thus, to take just one example, proper names already play the role of quotation in this discourse. From all outer appearances, they are reliable. While the novel must slowly fill with predicates the proper names (such as "Julien Sorel"), that it poses at its beginning, historiography receives proper names already filled (for example, "Robespierre") and is satisfied with working on a referential language.[106] Yet this external condition of a knowledge of the other, or of a heterology,[107] has as its corollary the possibility of discourse itself being the equivalent of a semiotics, a metalanguage of natural languages, and therefore a text which presupposes and manifests the transcriptibility of different codifications. In fact, this metalanguage is developed in the very lexicon of the documents it decodes; it is not formally distinguished (in exception to what is the case in every science) from the language it interprets. Therefore it cannot control the distance that it claims to maintain from the level of analysis, nor establish in its own field and univocally the concepts that organize it. It is narrated *in* the language of its other. It plays with it. The status of metalanguage is thus the postulate of a "will to understand." At stake is an a priori rather than a product. Interpretation has the characteristic of reproducing inside of its split discourse the relation between a place of knowledge and its exteriority.

As it quotes, this discourse transforms every quoted element into a source of reliability and the lexicon of a knowledge. But in this way it places the reader in the position of what is quoted; it introduces the reader into the relation between a knowledge and a non-knowledge. In other words, this discourse produces an enunciative contract between the sender and the receiver. It functions as a didactic discourse, and does so all the more as it dissimulates the place whence it speaks (it erases the "I" of the author), as it presents in the form of a referential language (it is the "real" that is addressing you), as it narrates more than it reasons (one does not debate a story), and as it takes hold of its readers right where they are (it speaks their language, though otherwise and better than they do). This discourse has no openings: it is semantically saturated (there are no gaps in intelligibility), "pressed" (thanks to a "maximum shortening of the passage and of the distance between two functional focal points of narration"),[108] and tightly organized (a network of cata-phoras and anaphoras assures endless reference of the text to itself as an oriented totality). The structure inherent to the discourse produces both chicanery and a certain type of reader: that is, a receiver cited, identified, and taught by the very fact of being placed in the situation of the chron-icle that stands before a knowledge. In organizing textual space, the struc-ture establishes a contract and also orders social space. In this respect, the discourse does what it says. It is performative. The ruse of histo-riography consists in creating what Barthes describes as "a fake perfor-mative discourse in which the apparent declarative element is in fact no more than the signifier of the speech-act taken to be an act of author-ity."[109]

A third aspect of splitting concerns neither the degree of mixture nor the stratification of discourse but, rather, the problematic of its manifes-tation, or the relation between the *event* and the *fact*. On a very debated subject I shall make but one point relative to the construction of writing. From this perspective, the event is that which must *delimit*, if there is to be intelligibility; the historical fact is that which must *fill*, if there is to be meaningful statement. The former conditions the organization of dis-course, while the latter provides the signifiers intended to form a series of significant elements in the mode of narrative. In sum, the former de-fines, and the latter spells out.

In effect, what is an event if not what must be presupposed, in order for an organization of documents to be possible? The event is the means thanks to which disorder is turned into order. The event does not explain, but permits an intelligibility. It is the postulate and the point of departure—but also the blind spot—of comprehension. "Something must have taken place" right *there*, by means of which one can construct a series of facts, or transport them from one regularity to another. Far from being the base or the substantial landmark on which information would be founded, the event is the hypothetical support for an ordering along a chronological axis; that is, the condition of a classification. Sometimes it is no more than a simple localization of disorder: in that instance, an event names what cannot be understood.

In providing the uncanny with a place *useful* for a discourse of intel-ligibility, by exorcising what is not understood in order to make of it a means of comprehension, historiography nevertheless does not avoid the surreptitious return of what it effaces from manifestation. We can doubt-less recognize this return in the process of erosion that never stops undermining concepts built by this discourse. To be sure, it works there as a secret movement within the text, nonetheless constant, like a slow hemorrhage of knowledge. We apprehend it, for example, in relation to the order shown by an organization of historical units. The scriptural staging is assured by a certain number of semantic choices. François Châtelet gives the name of "concept" to these units, but these are concepts "which we can call, through analogy with the epistemology of natural sciences, *historical categories*."[110] They are of many diverse types: thus the "period," the "century," etc., but also the "mentality," the "social class," the "economic conjuncture," or the "family," the "city," the "region," the "people," the "nation,", the "civilization," or even the "war," the "heresy," the "festival," the "plague," the "book," etc., not to speak of notions such as "antiquity," the "ancien régime," the "Enlightenment," etc. These units often convey stereotypical combinations. A predictable montage offers the familiar patterns: the life—the work—the doctrine; or its collective equivalent: economic life—social life—intellectual life. "Levels" are piled up. Concepts are packaged. Every code has its logic.

The question here is hardly one of going back over the social constraints (see "A Social Place," above) or the theoretical and practical programming necessities (see "A Practice") that intervene in the determination of these units; rather, it is one of grasping their scriptural function. Occasionally it is said that the organization of these concepts is almost automatically triggered by the very title of the text, and that it is in sum only a frame, more or less artificial (finally, it matters little!), where treasures of information are amassed. According to this conception, the units make up the checkerboard of a display in which every square must be filled. In the last resort, these concepts are indifferent to the riches they bear: in the storehouse of history, only content counts, never presentation (provided that it is clear and classical). But this is to make (or to believe) historiographical composition inert, as if it simply arrested research in order to replace it with the moment of addition and to proceed to the summation of acquired capital. Writing would consist in "coming to an end." In reality, it is nothing of the sort from the moment historical discourse exists. The writing imposes rules which obviously are not those of practice; different and complementary, they are the rules of a text which organizes places in view of a production.

Historical writing indeed assembles a coherent set of great units into a structure analogous to the architecture of places and characters in a tragedy. But the system of this drama is the space where the *movement* of documentation, that is, of smaller units, sows disorder within this order, escapes from established divisions, and brings about a slow erosion of organizing concepts. In approximate terms, we might say that the text is the place where a labor of "content" is exacted upon the "form." To take the more precise words of Raymond Roussel, it "*produces* as it destroys." Through the moving and complex mass that it throws into historiographical delimitation and which stirs things up there, information appears to involve a *wearing out* of the classificatory divisions that cement the foundation of the textual system. And indeed, discourse no longer "stands up" if the structural organization falls apart, but it is historical insofar as a labor jostles and corrodes the conceptual apparatus that is nonetheless necessary for the formation of the space which welcomes this movement.

Following this procedure, which allows the arranging of the unknown within a blank square prepared for it ahead of time and named "event," a "reason" of history becomes thinkable. A full and saturating semanticization is then possible: the "facts" enunciate this semanticization by accrediting it with a referential language; the event obfuscates its gaps with a proper name that is added to the continuous narrative and masks its ruptures. In other words, the serial architecture plays upon what contradicts it, namely events, as if upon a limit that it *also* names in order to turn itself into a didactic discourse which suffers neither interruption nor lapsus from erudite authority. These two elements are necessary to one another: a strange reciprocity admits each of them only in relation to the other. But the text *at once* admits the fulfillment of meaning and its condition; it conjoins and levels them within the expansion of discourse. In this way it is global, but only at the expense of camouflaging this difference, and thanks to the system that establishes beforehand, by virtue of an acquired place, an authority capable of "understanding" the relation between an organization of meaning (of "facts") and its limit (the "event").

A construction and erosion of units: all historical writing combines these two operations. An economic or demographic architecture must be posited so that the stirrings that soften it, move it, and ultimately refer to another grouping (whether social or cultural) can appear. A geographic unit (regional or national) must be delimited so that all which cannot be enclosed becomes manifest. The organization of conceptual "bodies" through a delimitation is at once the cause and the means of a slow hemorrhage. The structure of a composition does not retain what it represents, but it must "hold" enough so that, with this escape, the past, the real, or the death of which the text speaks can be truly staged —"produced." Thus is symbolized the relation of discourse with what it designates through losing it; that is, its relation with the past which it is not—but which could never be conceived without writing, which articulates "compositions of place" over an erosion of these places.

The combination of *breakages* (macro-units) and *erosions* (displacements of concepts) is, to be sure, only an abstract schema. Besides, it does not deal with the structure of discourse itself, but only describes one movement of writing, one intended to produce meaning authorized by knowledge. Yet it can be recognized in the most important texts of contemporary French historiography.

In order to explain the apparition of a national consciousness in Catalonia—a problem that a socioeconomic study of this region "brings forth"—Pierre Vilar argues for the connection between mercantilism (to which the formation of a dominant class is linked) and nationalism (an instrument used by this class with the goal of establishing a political dominion). An economic "place" is the base for a very rich analysis. But certain outer elements penetrate it: thus, the observation that nationalism grows with the unhappy consciousness of a threatened nation.[111] This intervention of a heterogenous element does not inaugurate another conceptual delimitation and certainly not a "global" history. It shifts the initial drama of the text. This is one example among hundreds showing the process of erosion which works on a strongly erected composition, and precisely because it is not an inert framework.

Erosion is also the movement that shifts the unit of "the Beauvais region" so firmly traced in Pierre Goubert's "regional study," and which then lets it run toward Beauce, or toward Picardy.[112] In the text, the labor which moves the place and mixes what had been excluded back into it sketches within the text a disappearance (never total) of concepts, as if the study led its representation (always, however, upheld as long as there is a text) to the borderline of the absence that it outlines.

The Place of the Dead and the Place of the Reader

A THIRD paradox of history: writing places a population of the dead on stage—characters, mentalities, or prizes. In different fashions and with different contents, it remains linked to its archeology of the beginning of the seventeenth century ("one of the zero-points in the history of France," notes Philippe Ariès),[113] as the "gallery of history," as can still be seen in the Beauregard château:[114] a line of portraits, effigies, or emblems painted on the wall before being described by the text organizes the relation between a space (the museum) and a route (the guided visit). Historiography has this same structure, of painting linked together through a trajectory. It represents the dead along a narrative itinerary.

Many signs in history attest to this "gallery" structure; for example, the multiplication of proper names (personages, localities, coins, etc.), and their duplication in the "Index of Proper Names." Thus what proliferates in historical discourse are elements "below which nothing more can be done except display,"[115] and through which *saying* reaches its limit, as near as possible to *showing*. With these proper names the signifying system is grossly expanded on its extreme deictic border, as if the very absence it studied made it turn in the direction where "showing" tended to stand for "signifying." But there are many other indications: the role of maps, of figures, or of graphics; the importance of panoramic views and recapitulative "conclusions," of countrysides which the book stakes out, etc. These are foreign elements in the treatise of sociology or of physics.

Must we again recognize in these qualities a literary inversion of procedures belonging to research? Practice in effect discovers the past through a relevant deviation from current models. In reality, the specific function of writing is not contrary to that of practice, but different and complementary to it. Writing can be specified under two rubrics. On the one hand, writing plays the role of a burial rite, in the ethnological and quasi-religious meaning of the term; it exorcises death by inserting it into discourse. On the other hand, it possesses a symbolizing function; it allows a society to situate itself by giving itself a past through language, and it thus opens to the present a space of its own. "To mark" a past is to make a place for the dead, but also to redistribute the space of possibility, to determine negatively what *must be done,* and consequently to use the narrativity that buries the dead as a way of establishing a place for the living. The ordering of what is absent is the inverse of a normativity which aims at the living reader and which establishes a didactic relation between the sender and the receiver.

The past occupies the place of the subject-king in the text. A scriptural conversion is effected. Where research had brought about a critique of current models, writing constructs a *tombeau* for the dead.[116] The locus ascribed to the past thus plays, here and there, upon two different types of operation, one technical and the other scriptural. Only across this difference of functioning can an analogy be discovered between the two positions of the past—within the technique of research and within the representation of the text.

Writing speaks of the past only in order to inter it. Writing is a tomb in the double sense of the word in that, in the very same text, it both honors and eliminates. Here the function of language is to introduce through *saying* what can no longer be *done*. Language exorcises death and arranges it in the narrative that pedagogically replaces it with something that the reader must believe and do. This process is repeated in other unscientific ways, from the funeral eulogy in the streets to burial ceremonies. But unlike other artistic or social "tombs," here taking the dead or the past back to a symbolic place is connected to the labor aimed at creating in the present a place (past or future) to be filled, a "something that must be done." Writing gathers together the products of this labor. In this way it liberates the present without having to name it. Thus it can be said that writing makes the dead so that the living can exist elsewhere. More exactly, it receives the dead that a social change has produced, so that the space opened by this past can be marked, and so that it will still be possible to connect what appears with what disappears. Naming the absent of the household and inserting them into the language of the scriptural gallery is equivalent to liberating the apartment for the living, through an act of communication which combines the absence of the living in language with the absence of the dead in the household. A society furnishes itself with a present time by virtue of historical writing. The literary founding of this space thus rejoins the labors that historical practice had brought about.

As a substitute for the absent being, an enclosure of the evil genius of death, the historical text plays a performative role. Language allows a practice to be situated in respect to its *other,* the past. In fact, in itself it is a practice. Historiography uses death in order to articulate a law (of the present). It does not describe the silent practices that construct it, but it effects a new distribution of already semanticized practices. It is an operation of an order other than that of research. Through its narrativity, historiography furnishes death with a representation that, in placing the lack within language, outside of existence, has the value of an exorcism against anguish. But, through its performativity, historiography fills the lacuna that it represents; it uses this locus to impose upon the receiver a will, a wisdom, and a lesson. In sum, narrativity, the metaphor of performative discourse, finds its support precisely in what it hides: the dead of which it speaks become the vocabulary of a task to be undertaken. Such is the ambivalence of historiography: it is the condition of a process and the denial of an absence; by turns it acts as the discourse of a law (historical saying opens a present to be made) and as an alibi, a realistic illusion (the realistic effect creates the fiction of another history). It oscillates between "producing history" and "telling stories," but without being reducible to either one or the other. No doubt we can recognize the same splitting in another form which completes the simultaneously critical and constructive historical operation: writing follows a path between blasphemy and curiosity; between what it eliminates in establishing it as past, and what it organizes from the present; between the privation or dispossession that it postulates, and the social normativity that it imposes on the unknowing reader. Through all these aspects combined in the literary drama, writing symbolizes the desire that constitutes the relation with the other. It is the mark of this law.

It is not surprising that something other than destiny or the possibility of an "objective science" is in question here. Insofar as our relation with language is always a relation with death, historical discourse is the favored representation, in Jacques Lacan's words, of a "science of the subject," and of the subject "taken in a constituent division"[117]—but with a staging of the relations that a social body keeps with its language.

NOTES

1. If, as Paul Veyne has shown in *Comment on écrit l'histoire* (Paris: Seuil, 1971), pp. 258–73—available in English as *Writing History: Essay on Epistemology* (Middletown, Conn.: Wesleyan University Press, 1984)—historical research is characterized by the determination of relevant places, that is, by a topical arrangement, it does not so much refuse to inscribe units of meaning (or "facts") determined as such into relations of productions, as it aims at showing the relations between *products* and *places* of production.

2. At once and for all of the following I would like to specify that I am using the word "history" in the sense of "historiography." In other words, by "history" I mean a practice (a discipline), its results (a discourse), and the relation between them. See chapter 1, "Making History."

3. See Serge Moscovici, *Essai sur l'histoire humaine de la nature* (Paris: Flammarion, 1968); Michel Foucault, *L'Archéologie du savoir* (Paris: Gallimard, 1969),

available in English as *The Archaeology of Knowledge* (New York: Pantheon, 1972); and Veyne, *Comment on écrit l'histoire*.

4. See Karl Marx, the first of his *Theses on Feuerbach*, in Karl Marx and Friedrich Engels, *Basic Writings on Politics and Philosophy*, L. S. Feuer, ed. (New York: Doubleday, 1959).

5. However suspect it may be within the ensemble of the "human sciences," the term "scientific" (where it is replaced by the term "analytical"), is no less so in the field of the so-called exact sciences, at least insofar as it would refer to "laws." With this term we can nonetheless define the possibility of conceiving an ensemble of *rules* allowing control of operations adapted to the production of specific objects or ends.

6. See Raymond Aron, *Introduction à la philosophie de l'histoire: Essai sur les limites de l'objectivité historique* (Paris: Vrin, 1938); and his *La Philosophie critique de l'histoire* (Paris: Vrin, 1938; reissued in 1969). On the theses of Raymond Aron, see Pierre Vilar's critique "Marxisme et histoire dans le développement des sciences humaines," *Studi storici* (1960), 1(5):1008–43, especially pp. 1011–19.

7. On the "principle of falsification," see Karl Popper, *Logik der Forschung* (Vienna, 1934); or the quite expanded and reviewed English translation, *The Logic of Scientific Discovery* (London: Hutchinson, 1959), the basic work concerning "critical rationalism."

8. See Antonio Gramsci, *Gli intelletuali e l'organizzazione della cultura* (Turin: Einaudi, 1949), pp. 6–38.

9. Returning to the Weberian thesis according to which "scientific elaboration begins with a choice whose only justification is subjective" in his *Les Etapes de la pensée sociologique* (Paris: Gallimard, 1967), p. 510, Raymond Aron once again underlines the crisscrossing of "subjective choice" and the rational system of "causal" explanation in Weber's work (pp. 500–22). In that way he obliterates the influence on intellectuals of their place in society, and once again holds Weber in the position of the anti-Marx.

10. See in particular Michel Foucault's *Les Mots et les choses* (Paris: Gallimard, 1966), available in English as *The Order of Things* (New York: Vintage, 1970), whose purpose has since been specified and situated (notably in Foucault's remarkable introduction to *The Archaeology of Knowledge*, pp. 3–17). See also my "Le Noir soleil du langage: Michel Foucault," in *L'Absent de l'histoire* (Paris: Mame, 1973), pp. 115–32.

11. See my "Une épistémologie de transition: Paul Veyne," *Annales E.S.C.* (1972), 27:1317–27.

12. See Philippe Ariès, *Le Temps de l'histoire* (Monaco: Editions du Rocher, 1954), p. 224 [reissued in 1986 by Editions Gallimard, Paris——Tr.]; and Pierre Chaunu, *La Civilisation de l'Europe classique* (Paris: Arthaud, 1966), pp. 404–9, on "the establishment of a small world of research throughout Europe." Many others have noted this situation. But only detail can show to what point this social "establishment" marks an epistemological break. For example, there is a strong tie between a delimitation of correspondents (or of travels) and the development of an erudite language among them; on these correspondences, see Baudouin de

Gaiffier, *Religion, érudition, et critique à la fin du XVIIe siècle* (Paris: PUF, 1968), pp. 2–9. There is also a tie between the Wednesday "assemblies" at the Bibliothèque Colbertine from 1675 to 1751 and the elaboration of historical *research;* on these meetings, see Léopold Delisle, *Le Cabinet des manuscrits de la Bibliothèque Nationale* (Paris: 1868), 1:476–77.

13. Daniel Roche illustrates the close connection between encyclopedism (a "complex of ideas") and these institutions, which are the Parisian or provincial academies; see "Encyclopédistes et académiciens," in *Livre et société dans la France du XVIIIe siècle* (The Hague: Mouton, 1970), 2:73–92. Similarly, Sergio Moravia links the birth of ethnology to the constitution of the group of the "Students of Man," in *La Scienza dell'uomo nel settecento* (Bari, Italy: Laterza, 1970), pp. 151–72. Examples could be multiplied.

14. Despite Gaston Bachelard, who in *Le Rationalisme appliqué* (Paris: PUF, 1966) says, "The scientific citadel is built along the borders of social society" (p. 23); see also his *La Formation de l'esprit scientifique* (Paris: Vrin, 1972), pp. 32–34. Alexandre Koyré takes up the same thesis, but in order to sustain "a life of its own, an immanent history" of science which "can only be understood in relation to its own problems, to its own history"; see "Perspectives sur l'histoire des sciences," in *Etudes d'histoire de la pensée scientifique* (Paris: Gallimard, 1973), p. 399. It seems that here there is, following Max Weber, a confusion between differentiation and isolation, as if the establishment of a "proper" place were not linked to a general redistribution and, therefore, to reciprocal redefinitions; and a conception of the "history of ideas" which withdraws all relevance from *social* partitions, while epistemological divisions are at once social and intellectual.

15. See Jean Glénisson, "L'Historiographie française contemporaine," in *Vingt-cinq ans de recherche historique en France* (Paris: CNRS, 1965), p. xxiv, n. 3, with respect to the *Annales.*

16. Psychoanalysis would even say that speech hides and that the body speaks.

17. Glénisson, "L'Historiographie," p. xxvi.

18. *Ibid.,* p. xxiv. On these two points, see Terry N. and Priscilla P. Clark, "Le Patron et son cercle: Clef de l'Université française," *Revue française de sociologie* (1971), 12:19–39, a perspicacious study that only "outside observers" were capable of writing. The authors define the "system" through four essential elements: centralization of control, the monopolistic character of the system, the restricted number of important positions, and the multiplication of the patron's functions.

19. Glénisson, "L'Historiographie," pp. xxii–xxiii.

20. *Ibid.,* p. xl.

21. In sociological theories (we could add: historical theories) of a purely technical and "gnoseological" type, Jürgen Habermas criticizes in particular the presupposition of neutrality in respect to values postulated at the epistemological beginnings of research; see his "Analytische Wissenschaftstheorie und Dialektik," in *Zeugnisse: Theodor W. Adorno zum sechzigsten Geburtstag* (Frankfurt: Suhrkamp, 1963), pp. 500–1. See also the basic works, *Zur Logik der Sozialwissenschaft* (Tübingen: Mohr, 1967) and *Technik und Wissenschaft als Ideologie* (Frankfurt: Suhrkamp, 1968).

22. On the role and meaning of "I" or of "we," the locus marked in language for the speaker who "appropriates" it for himself as speaking subject, see Emile Benveniste, *Problèmes de linguistique générale* (Paris: Gallimard, 1966), pp. 258–66. Available in English as *Problems in General Linguistics* (Miami: University of Miami Press, 1971).

23. By "discourse" I mean the historical genre itself or, rather, in Foucault's perspective, "a discursive practice"—"the group of rules that characterize a discursive practice" (*The Archaeology of Knowledge*, pp. 55 and 127).

24. Foucault, *The Archaeology of Knowledge*, p. 54, apropos of medical discourse.

25. Unfortunately, there does not exist concerning the recruitment of historians the equivalent of Monique de Saint Martin's *Les Fonctions sociales de l'enseignement scientifique* (The Hague: Mouton, 1971).

26. Here the essential date is that of George Lefebvre's thesis *Paysans du nord de la France pendant la Révolution*, 1924. But a whole plethora of historians mark this turning point: Hauser, Sée, Simiand, etc.

27. *Introduction aux études historiques* (1898) is still the great work of a historiography, even if today the book is no longer what it had been for an entire epoch: the statue of the Commander. Lo and behold, it can still be read with great interest. Its clarity is admirable, especially in ch. 8 of book 2 and chs. 1–4 of book 3, all thanks to Seignobos, who explains the authors' scientific references.

28. Lucien Febvre, *Au coeur religieux du XVIe siècle* (Paris: Sevpen, 1957), p. 146.

29. "Everything that belongs to man depends on man, serves man, expresses man, signifies the presence, activity, the tastes and fashions of man's being," Febvre declares in *Combats pour l'histoire* (Paris: Colin, 1953), p. 428. Since that time the figure created by this conquering optimism has lost much of its credibility.

30. Already in 1920 Henri Berr pointed to the "idealist" character of history in Febvre's work, in the *Revue de synthèse historique* (1920), 30:15.

31. On the fluctuating and rich "theory of *Zusammenhang*" in Febvre's work, see Hans-Dieter Mann, *Lucien Febvre: La Pensée vivante d'un historien* (Paris: Colin, 1971), pp. 93–119. Febvre refers to "class" in order to explain the sixteenth century—see for example *Pour une histoire à part et entière* (Paris: Service d'Edition et de vente des publications de l'Education nationale, 1963), pp. 350–60, on the bourgeoisie—even if he does so with a good deal of reticence (see pp. 185–99). But he does not introduce the problem of his own social localization when he analyzes his own historical practice and concepts. His anti-Marxism surfaces, for example, in his review of Daniel Guérin's work (in *Combats pour l'histoire*, pp. 109–13), in which the convergence of Michelet and Marx is, in Febvre's view, "incestuous."

32. See "Les Révolutions du croyable" in my *Culture au pluriel* (Paris: Union Générale des Éditions, 1974), pp. 11–34.

33. See Octave Mannoni, "Je sais bien, mais quand même," in *Clefs pour l'imaginaire, ou l'Autre Scène* (Paris: Seuil, 1969), pp. 9–33.

34. See Frédéric Bon and Michel-Antoine Burnier, *Les Nouveaux Intellectuels*

(Paris: Seuil, 1971), p. 180, and my "Les Universités devant la culture de masse," in *La Culture au pluriel*, pp. 111–37.

35. Serge Moscovici, *Essai sur l'histoire humaine de la nature* (Paris: Flammarion, 1968).

36. *Ibid.*, p. 20.

37. *Ibid.*

38. *Ibid.*, pp. 7 and 21.

39. *Ibid.*, p. 590.

40. Ernest Labrousse, introduction, in *L'Histoire sociale* (Paris: PUF, 1967), p. 2.

41. The expression is Fernand Braudel's, in his *Leçon inaugurale au Collège de France* (Paris: Annuaire du Collège de France, 1950). In *La Catalogne dans l'Espagne moderne* (Paris: Sevpen, 1962), 1:12, Pierre Vilar reminds us that between the two world wars, "the great questions, whose dominance of our century we could divine more or less clearly, were scarcely put before us, unless through the lessons of our geography teachers."

42. See in particular Françoise Choay, "L'Histoire et la méthode en urbanisme," *Annales E.S.C.* (1970), a special issue on "History and Urbanization," 25:1143–54; and Stephan Thernstrom, "Reflections on the New Urban History," *Daedalus* (Spring 1971), pp. 359–76. *L'Enquête sur le bâtiment* (The Hague: Mouton, 1971), edited by Pierre Chaunu, is also a fine example of the new interest brought to spatial organizations.

43. See for example the chapter on "vegetal civilization" in Emmanuel Le Roy Ladurie, *Les Paysans de Languedoc* (Paris: Sevpen, 1966), pp. 53–76. This very original study on the "biological fundaments" of rural life shows that vegetables are "objects of history" by "the very fact of their plasticity, of the unending changes that man has brought to them." The paperback edition (Paris: Flammarion, 1969) unfortunately does not include this chapter. [Nor does the English edition—see ch. 1, n. 44—which was translated from the paperback.——TR.]

44. See the great *Histoire générale des techniques,* Maurice Daumas, ed., 4 vols. (Paris: PUF, 1963–1968), or the works of Bertrand Gille, such as *Les Ingénieurs de la Renaissance* (Paris: Herman, 1964).

45. See for example the special issue of *Annales E.S.C.* (November–December 1969), vol. 24, entitled "Biological History and Society"; Michel Foucault, *Naissance de la clinique* (Paris: PUF, 1963), available in English as *The Birth of the Clinic* (New York: Vintage, 1973); and Jean-Pierre Peter, "Le Corps du delit," *Nouvelle Revue de Psychanalyse* (1971), no. 3, pp. 71–108.

46. See Emmanuel Le Roy Ladurie, *Histoire du climat depuis l'an mil* (Paris: Flammarion, 1967).

47. Raymond Roussel, *Impressions d'Afrique* (Paris: Gallimard, 1963), p. 209. [My translation, but available in English as *Impressions of Africa* (Berkeley and Los Angeles: University of California Press, 1967).——TR.] See also Julia Kristeva, "La Productivité dite texte," in *Sèmeiôtikè: Recherches pour une sémanalyse* (Paris: Seuil, 1969), pp. 208–45; in English, "The Bounded Text," in *Desire in Language: A Semiotic Approach to Literature and Art* (New York: Columbia University Press, 1980), pp. 36–63.

48. Jean Baudrillard, "La Collection," in *Le Système des objets* (Paris: Gallimard, 1968), pp. 120–50.

49. Seen from this angle, historical "documents" can be assimilated into "iconic signs" whose organization Umberto Eco analyzes in noting how they "reproduce some conditions of common perception on the basis of normal perceptive codes"; See "Sémiologie des messages visuels," *Communications* (1970), no. 15, pp. 11–51. From this perspective we can add that scientific work is found where there are changes in the "codes of recognition" and in the "systems of expectation."

50. See Ariès, *Le Temps de l'histoire,* pp. 214–18.

51. See Gilbert Ouy, "Les Bibliothèques," in *L'Histoire et ses méthodes: Encyclopédie de la Pléiade* (Paris: Gallimard, Encyclopédie de la Pléiade, 1961), p. 1066, on the agreement passed between Guillaume Fichet and three German printers aimed toward founding the typographical workshop of the Sorbonne and relaying copies of manuscripts that Fichet himself partially assured for its library.

52. Since, for the erudite scholar, his "library" was what he *constituted* (and not what he *received,* as will later be the case for the "curators" of the great libraries created before them), we can detect a continuity on the grounds of writing, between the production of the collection of texts and the production of ciphers destined to decode them.

53. See Madeleine V.-David, *Le Débat sur les écritures et l'hiéroglyphe aux XVIIe et XVIIIe siècles* (Paris: Sevpen, 1965), pp. 19–30.

54. Thus, in his *Guide des archives diocésaines françaises* (Lyon: Centre d'Histoire du Catholicisme, 1971), Jacques Gadille underscores "the value of these archives for historical research" by noting that they allow for the constitution of new "series" valuable for both an economic history and a history of mentalities (pp. 7–14).

55. François Furet, "L'Histoire quantitative et la construction du fait historique," in Jacques Le Goff and Pierre Nora, eds., *Faire de l'histoire* (Paris: Gallimard, 1974), 1:49.

56. By "historical practice" we must understand not methods particular to a given historian but, as in the exact sciences, the *complex of procedures* that characterizes a period or a sector of research.

57. Furet, "L'Histoire quantitative," pp. 47–48.

58. On this subject, see Michel Serres' pointed reflections in *Hermès ou la communication* (Paris: Editions de Minuit, 1968), 1:26–35; in English, *Hermes: Literature, Science, Philosophy,* Josué Harari and David Bell, eds. (Baltimore: Johns Hopkins University Press, 1982), pp. 16–28.

59. André Régnier, "Mathématiser les sciences de l'Homme?" in P. Richard and R. Jaulin, *Anthropologie et calcul* (Paris: Union Générale des Editions, 1971), pp. 13–37.

60. Insofar as it is linked to the use of the computer, information science, between "input" and "output," organizes arrangements of symbols in reserved sites within a memory and transfers them to agreed-upon addresses according to instructions that can be programmed. It orders placements and displacements in a space of information which is not without analogy to the libraries of the past.

61. See Emmanuel Le Roy Ladurie and P. Dumont, "Quantitative and Car-

tographical Exploitation of French Military Archives, 1819–1826," *Daedalus* (Spring 1971), pp. 397–441; and also Le Roy Ladurie, *Le Territoire de l'historien* (Paris: Gallimard, 1973), pp. 38–87.

62. In reality, the "synthesis" was not terminal; it was elaborated in the course of the manipulation of documents. Already too, it deviated finally in relation to the preconceived ideas that the practice of texts had been unveiling and shifting in the course of operations themselves set up by an institutional discipline.

63. See Robert Mandrou, *Magistrats et sorciers en France au XVIIᵉ siècle* (Paris: Plon, 1968), and the abundant historical literature on the topic.

64. This is especially so since Michel Foucault's *Histoire de la folie à l'âge classique* (Paris: Plon, 1961; new edition, Gallimard, 1972); available in English as *Madness and Civilization* (New York: Pantheon, 1965).

65. See in particular Mona Ozouf, "De Thermidor à Brumaire: Les Discours de la Révolution sur elle-même," *Au siècle des Lumières* (Paris: Sevpen, 1970), pp. 157–87, and "Le Cortège et la ville: Les Itinéraires parisiens des fêtes révolutionnaires," *Annales E.S.C.* (1971), 26:889–916.

66. See Paul Delarue, *Le Conte populaire français* (Paris: Erasme, 1957); Robert Mandrou, *De la culture populaire en France aux XVIIᵉ et XVIIIᵉ siècles* (Paris: Stock, 1964); Geneviève Bollème, *Les Almanachs populaires aux XVIIᵉ et XVIIIᵉ siècles* (The Hague: Mouton, 1969); Marie-Louise Tenèze, "Introduction à l'étude de la littérature orale: Le Conte," *Annales E.S.C.* (1969), 24:1104–20; not to mention the more "literary" works by Marc Soriano, *Les Contes de Perrault* (Paris: Gallimard, 1968), or Mikhaïl Bakhtine, *L'Oeuvre de François Rabelais et la culture populaire au Moyen Age et sous la Renaissance* (Paris: Gallimard, 1970), available in English as *Rabelais and His World* (Cambridge: MIT Press, 1968).

67. On peasants, above all see the entire work of Emmanuel Le Roy Ladurie cited above; on the poor, see the works of Jacques Le Goff and, in the last two decades, the research on the poor and poverty in the Middle Ages directed by Michel Mollat. [See especially his *Les Pauvres au Moyen Age* (Paris: Hachette, 1978).——Tʀ.]

68. See Robert Lafont, *Renaissance du Sud* (Paris: Gallimard, 1970), and also André Larzac, "Décoloniser l'histoire occitane," *Les Temps modernes* (November 1971), 676–96.

69. "L'Histoire des civilisations: Le Passé explique le présent," one of Fernand Braudel's most important methodological works, is reprinted in *Ecrits sur l'histoire* (Paris: Flammarion, 1969), pp. 255–314 (see especially pp. 292–96).

70. See note 7 above.

71. Adopting a rather shopworn conception of the exact sciences ("Physics is a body of laws," he writes), Paul Veyne opposes it to a history that would be a "body of facts" (*Writing History: Essays on Epistemology,* pp. 21–22).

72. Since Henri Berr in his conception of history combined the comparative method, the primacy of the "social," and the "permanent taste for general ideas," this "totalization" has represented a return to the spirit of *synthesis* and a reaction against the erudite, exhausting crumbling of "atomist history," rather than a pretension of establishing a universal historical discourse. After Mauss, Durkheim, Vidal de La Blache, the idea of organization tends to prevail over that of "fact"

or of "event." See Mann, *Lucien Febvre,* pp. 73–92. In "Théorie et pratique de l'histoire," in *Revue historique* (1965), 89:139–70, Henri-Irénée Marrou takes up the idea of a "general history" which resists the specialization of methods and the diversification of chronologies according to levels. He wishes for a "total history which would be forced to grasp the tangled skein of these particular histories in all its complexity" (p. 169).

73. In Braudel's work the object of study acquires the meaning of being a "touchstone," a tactical operation relative to a situation of research, and proportioned to a "definition" (of civilization), itself posited not as the truest but as *the easiest to handle* in order to *pursue* our work in the best ways." *Ecrits sur l'histoire,* pp. 288–94 (my emphasis).

74. It appears to me that apropos of Paul Bois' *Les Paysans de l'Ouest* (The Hague: Mouton, 1960; paperback edition, Paris: Flammarion, 1971), Le Roy Ladurie argues for a closely related issue in what he calls "eventual-structural" history; see his "Evénement et longue durée dans l'histoire sociale: L'Exemple chouan," in *Le Territoire de l'historien,* pp. 169–86. In my opinion, the event seems to be at once the *question posited by the relation* between two more rigorously isolated series (the economic infrastructure of La Sarthe and the mental structure that divides the country into two political groups) and the *means to respond by articulating them* (in order for the relation among them to change, something has to happen). In the form of the "moment" of the years 1790–1799, the event serves to designate a difference in their relation. For Bois, the more systematic delimitation of both series has the double effect of on the one hand, "bringing forth" (as a question) a difference of relation, and on the other, establishing in this intersection the locus of *what,* in the discourse, assumes the historical figure of the event.

75. See Pierre Vilar, "Pour une meilleure compréhension entre économistes et historiens," *Revue historique* (1965), 233:293–312.

76. Pierre Chaunu, "Histoire quantitative et histoire sérielle," *Cahiers Vilfredo Pareto* (Geneva: Droz, 1964), 3:165–75, or *Histoire science sociale* (Paris: SEDES, 1974), p. 61.

77. Choay, "L'Histoire et la méthode en urbanisme," pp. 1151–53 (my emphasis). As Christopher Alexander, in *De la synthèse de la forme* (Paris: Dunod, 1971), pp. 6–9, suggests from his standpoint, it is precisely thanks to logical explanation, to the current *construction* of "structures of totalities," and therefore to a "loss" of their intuitive "innocence," that specialists in urban problems discover a relevance in historical differences—either in order to distinguish themselves from past conceptions, to make their own conceptions more relative, or even to bind them to complex situations which resist the rigor of a theoretical model.

78. Thus Foucault: "Up to the end of the eighteenth century, in fact, life does not exist: only living beings" (*The Order of Things,* p. 160); or, see François Jacob on the "inexistence of the idea of life" up to the beginning of the nineteenth century, in *La Logique du vivant* (Paris: Gallimard, 1970), p. 103; available in English as *The Logic of Life: A History of Heredity* (New York: Pantheon, 1974). These are but two examples among thousands.

79. Georges Canguilhem, *Etudes d'histoire et de philosophie des sciences* (Paris: Vrin, 1968), p. 18. See also Michel Fichant's remarks in *Sur l'histoire des sciences* (Paris: Maspéro, 1969), p. 55.

80. "A field of epistemological inquiry," Gordon Leff calls it, in *History and Social Theory* (Tuscaloosa: University of Alabama Press, 1969), p. 1. A typical and probably excessively methodological example is John McLeish's original study, *Evangelical Religion and Popular Education* (London: Methuen, 1969), which "essays" successively diverse theories (Marx, Malinowski, Freud, Parsons). From the historical problem (the school campaigns of Griffith Jones and Hannah More in the eighteenth century), he produces a case study method (p. 165), the means for verifying the validity and the limits proper to each of these theories.

81. See Foucault's closely related reflections on "History" in *The Order of Things,* (pp. 367–73), dealing with the link between the division of History into particular positive histories (of nature, of riches, or of language) and their common grounds of possibility—historicity or the finite nature of man.

82. For a long time, American historians and theoreticians have shown their reticence concerning the "dangerous" use of the notions of "meaning" or "significance" in history. See Patrick Gardiner, *Theories of History* (New York: Free Press, 1959; reprinted 1967), pp. 7–8; and Arthur C. Danto, *Analytical Philosophy of History* (Cambridge: Cambridge University Press, 1965), pp. 7–9.

83. See my *Absent de l'histoire* (Paris: Mame, 1973), especially "Altérations," pp. 171ff.

84. See Roland Barthes, "Structure du fait-divers," in *Essais critiques* (Paris: Seuil, 1964), available in English in *Critical Essays* (Evanston, Ill.: Northwestern University Press, 1972); see also chapter 7 below, "Hagio-graphical Edification."

85. On this subject, see also Roland Barthes, "Le Discours de l'histoire," *Social Science Information* (1967), 6(4):65–75, reprinted in *Le Bruissement de la langue* (Paris: Seuil, 1984), pp. 153–66; Erhardt Güttgemans, "*Texte* et *histoire,* catégories fondamentales d'une Poétique générative," *Linguistica Biblica* (Bonn) (1972), no. 11; and note 103 below.

86. In *The Practice of History* (New York: Crowell, 1970), pp. 88–141, G. R. Elton dedicates the central part of his analysis to *écriture*—Writing.

87. Henri-Irénée Marrou, *De la connaissance historique* (Paris: Seuil, 1954), p. 279.

88. See J. M. Lévy, "L'Ecriture en miroir des petits écoliers," *Journal de psychologie normale et pathologique* (1935), 32:443–54, and especially J. de Ajuriaguerra, R. Diatkine, and H. de Gobineau, "L'Ecriture en miroir," *La Semaine des hôpitaux de Paris* (1956), no. 2, pp. 80–86.

89. See Jean-Pierre Faye, *Langages totalitaires,* et *Théorie du récit* (Paris: Hermann, 1972).

90. See Roberto Minguelez, "Le Récit historique: Légalité et signification," *Semiotica* (1971), 3(1):20–36; and the same author's *Sujet et histoire* (Ottawa: Editions de l'Université, 1973).

91. See M. D. Grmek, *Raisonnement expérimental et recherches toxicologiques chez Claude Bernard* (Geneva: Droz, 1973). This highly detailed study—whose

interest goes far beyond the individual case of Claude Bernard—allows us to grasp immediately the distances that generate movement from *experiment* (here as it is controlled) to *chronicle,* and from chronicle to *didactic* discourse—theory or "history."

92. From this standpoint, historiography would do well to draw on the technical means refined by cinema. See as an interesting example Gilbert Rouget's "Une expérience de cinéma synchrone au ralenti," *L'Homme* (1971), 11(2):113–17, on the *Zeitregler,* or "distender of time" (or "stretcher"), which allows sonorous time to be expanded or contracted without deformation, and hence to slow down or accelerate the image. See also Pierre Schaeffer, *Traité des objets musicaux* (Paris: Seuil, 1966), pp. 425–26, on these accelerations and decelerations that are part of a traditional process in history.

93. Barthes has noted this in "Le Discours de l'histoire," pp. 71–72. See also, especially, C. G. Hempel, "The Function of General Laws in History," *Journal of Philosophy* (1942), vol. 39, on the explanatory sketches that historiography furnishes. This is still the basic reference on the subject.

94. See Benveniste, *Problèmes de linguistique générale.* In discourse, he says, the "instance is in the *hic* and *nunc* of interlocutors . . . in their act of speech" (we say: the chief of police left *yesterday*); in narrative, the instance is made from the "terms . . . which refer to 'real' objects . . . to 'historical' times and places" (pp. 253–54). [My translation.——TR.]

95. See, for example, André Viel's remarks in "Du chronique au chronologique," *Histoire de notre image* (Mont-Blanc, 1965), pp. 109–41, on "nonoriented time and ambivalence."

96. From this point of view there is, within the Greek *epistēmē,* a link between the absence of zero in mathematics and the absence of a history which thinks of the past as a difference. On the "concept" of zero, see Frege's remarks in *Les Fondements de l'arithmétique* (Paris: Seuil, 1969), paragraphs 8 and especially 64.

97. *The Odyssey,* Rhapsody 1. [In Leconte de Lisle's translation used above, the text reads, "Nul ne sait par lui-même qui est son père."——TR.]

98. On this topic, see Jean Laplanche and Jean-Baptiste Pontalis, "Fantasme originaire, fantasme des origines, origine du fantasme," *Les Temps modernes* (1964), 19:1832–68. This study on the "staging of desire" in sequences of images also enlightens the problems broached by historical discourse. "The subject can be in a desubjectified form, that is to say, in the very syntax of the sequence in question," the authors write; "Desire is voiced in the phrase of the phantasm which is the elected place of the most primitive defensive operations, such as the return against oneself, the reversal into contraries, projection, denial" (p. 1868). Akin to a staged drama, the historical narrative also presents these aspects of phantasm.

99. Maurice Blanchot, *L'Entretien infini* (Paris: Gallimard, 1969), p. 625. See also Henri Meschonnic, "Maurice Blanchot ou l'écriture hors langage," *Les Cahiers du chemin* (January 15, 1974), no. 20, pp. 79–116.

100. Philip Rieff has especially emphasized recommencement and repetition, which characterize the Freudian "model of time"; see "The Authority of the Past," in *Freud: The Mind of the Moralist* (New York: Viking, 1959), and his "The

Meaning of History and Religion in Freud's Thought," in Bruce Mazlisch, ed., *Psychoanalysis and History* (Englewood Cliffs, N.J.: Prentice-Hall, 1963), pp. 23–44.

101. See Maurice Blanchot, "Le Règne animal de l'esprit," *Critique* (1947), no. 18, pp. 387–405, and "La Littérature et le droit à la mort," *Critique* (1948), no. 20, pp. 30–47. [I have translated the remark quoted in the text, but the articles cited here are available in English in Blanchot, *The Gaze of Orpheus and Other Literary Essays* (Barrytown, N.Y.: Station Hill Press, 1981).——Tr.]

102. On this conception of myth, see Claude Rabant, "Le Mythe à l'avenir (re)commence," *Esprit* (April 1971), pp. 631–43.

103. On this point, see Harald Weinrich, "Narrative Strukturen in der Geschichtschreibung," in R. Koselleck and W. D. Stempel, eds., *Geschichte. Ereignis und Erzählung* (Munich: W. Fink, 1973), pp. 519–23.

104. This discourse—a montage of other discourses—is produced by virtue of quite varied mechanisms: indirect style (historiography states that someone else stated that . . .), quotation marks, illustrations, etc. It can be said that the represented "past" is the effect of the manner in which the discourse conducts its relations with the "chronicle." From this standpoint, the "chronicle" may be more or less ground to pieces. There are many ways of dealing with it, from the "outline" which reduces it to a series of "facts," to the extraction of data usable for a serial history.

105. See for example J.-L. Bachelier's remarks on the "Sur-Nom," *Communications* (1972), no. 19; and Philippe Hamon, "Un discours contraint," *Poétique* (1973), 16:426–27. Inversely, the "I," the essential mark of fantastic discourse, must be avoided; it would erase all nomination. See Tzvetan Todorov, *Introduction à la litterature fantastique;* in English, *The Fantastic: A Structural Approach to a Literary Genre* (Ithaca, N.Y.: Cornell University Press, 1975). Thus the "lack of name creates a serious deflation of the realistic illusion," notes Roland Barthes in *S/Z* (New York: Hill and Wang, 1974), p. 95; see p. 102 in the French edition (Paris: Seuil, 1970).

106. The proper name allows a double effect. On the one hand, it signifies: "'Robespierre,' you know what that is." It is *believable.* On the other, it is the object of a didactic difference: "'Robespierre,' that is something other than what you know, so I am going to have you learn about it." It is the evidence of a bonus of knowledge that is accredited with *a competence.*

107. See my *Absent de l'histoire,* pp. 173ff.

108. Hamon, "Un discours contraint," pp. 440–41.

109. Barthes, "Le Discours de l'histoire," p. 74.

110. François Châtelet, *La Naissance de l'histoire* (Paris: Minuit, 1962), p. 115. On this topic, see also Chaïm Perelman in *Les Catégories en histoire* (Brussels: Editions de l'Institut de Sociologie, 1969), pp. 11–16.

111. Vilar, *La Catalogne dans l'Espagne moderne,* vol. 1, pp. 29–38.

112. See Pierre Goubert, *Beauvais et le Beauvaisis de 1600 à 1730* (Paris: Sevpen, 1960), especially pp. 123–38 and 413–19.

113. Ariès, *Le Temps de l'histoire,* p. 255.

114. See *ibid.*, pp. 195–214, on these "galleries of history" or collections of historical portraits.

115. Claude Lévi-Strauss, apropos of proper names, in *The Savage Mind* (Chicago: University of Chicago Press, 1968), p. 215; see p. 285 in the French, *La Pensée sauvage* (Paris: Plon, 1962).

116. The "tombeau" is a literary and musical commemorative genre dating to the seventeenth century. The historiographical narrative also belongs to this genre.

117. Jacques Lacan, *Ecrits* (Paris: Seuil, 1966), p. 857. "There are no human sciences because there exists only the subject, but not the man, of science" (p. 859).

II

Productions of Time:
A Religious Archeology

INTRODUCTION
Questions of Method

A COLLAPSE of religious practice takes place everywhere in France during and after the Revolution. This sudden change naturally calls for an explanation: something must have taken place earlier so that this rupture could occur. "The fact that this change occurred very quickly under the effect of the shock of the Revolution," write Etienne Gautier and Louis Henry, "gives us reason to believe that minds were ready to accept it."[1] What does one do when one is a historian, if not challenge chance, posit reasons—in other words, understand? Yet understanding does not mean flight into ideology, nor providing an alias for what remains hidden. It means having to discover through the very stuff of historical information what allows it to be conceived.

What Makes Something Thinkable

THIS research has several effects. It permits a series of indications to be advanced which had not been studied until then and which, from that point, become "recognized" because one roughly knows the functions to which they correspond. But the research can also question the concepts, the historical "units" or "levels" of analysis, that had been adopted up to that point. Thus, it happens that the idea of "Christianization" in the seventeenth century can be revised;[2] so can the isolation of an "ancien régime" as a totality distinct from what follows it,[3] or the scope of the results that a "quantitative" analysis of practice can furnish (on the ambivalence of quantitative data concerning religious practices, see chapter 3 below). These divisions (of different types) are necessary for historiography and are constantly eroded at their limits by the very questions that they allow to be raised. The inner orders of analysis are taken in reverse from their very deployments, their extremities, and their consequences. They are fragile at their outer perimeters. Work upon their "borders" will bring about a modification or a replacement. That is the area where we see passages taking place from one model to another.

Thus we happen upon a break, no longer of interest solely for the evolution of a society (for example, the collapse of religious practices), but also for the evolution of the instruments of its analysis (for example, the questioning of a quantitative description)—no longer of interest solely for the passage from one period to another, but also for the shift of models according to which such a historical rupture has been marked. A close connection exists between these two sorts of transformation. Historiography constantly moves with the history that it studies and the historical place from which it is written (see chapter 1). Here, research on *what must have taken place* in the seventeenth and eighteenth centuries in order to produce what undeniably happened at the end of the eighteenth century will normally call for reflection on *what must take place* today and what must be changed in our historiographical procedures in order for these procedures to cast light upon this or that series of elements which have not yet entered into the field of analytical procedures used until now.

A special case of this connection can be seen with a well-known historical problem: the growing divergence in the seventeenth century and even more in the eighteenth between, on the one hand, the rapid autonomy of the "philosophes" in respect to religious criteria, and, on the other, the calm persistence, indeed the objective extension, of religious practices in the mass of the nation during the same period. We can wonder what kind of relation the ideologies of the Enlightenment kept with this latency of contemporary social behaviors. This distortion clearly has a social and economic grounding in the enrichment of a "high bourgeoisie" more and more isolated from the rural "masses." But within our interpretation, it is equally necessary to question the consequences of the distinct methods we use in these two sectors: an ideological and literary method in respect to the systems of thought; but a sociological method in respect to the practices. Perhaps our difficulty in perceiving a relation between the "radical" ideologies and the sociocultural "resistances" stems from the heterogeneity posed a priori, before any analysis, by two methods that were born in reaction to one another; the quantification of positive "facts" was promoted by Gabriel Le Bras in opposition to doctrinal French history (whether of a literary or theological type), or theoretical German typologies.[4]

Because of the very innovations that it made possible, this sociological analysis makes its own limits visible. In a word, we might say that it makes the *specificity* of ideological or religious organizations *unthinkable*. It transforms them into "representations" or into "reflections" of social structures. Put otherwise, it eliminates them as real factors of history: they become additions and secondary effects, precious only insofar as, through their transparency, they shed light on what instigated them.

Formalities in Historiography

THIS is how G. E. Swanson, for example, proceeds in the quite novel study in which he tries to show the dependency of sixteenth-century religious formations and doctrines upon structures of political power.[5] Just like theologies, the regional partitions in religious matters are, in his view, ultimately the projection—or "reflection"—of forms of government that he had previously codified and classified. Swanson's thesis on the political origin of doctrines of the Reformation has the clarity of a position that directly engages a fundamental problem. It allows us to take sight of several principles that also inhabit many of our historical works, although erudition generally obliterates them. I shall describe below only a few of them.

History furnishes "facts" destined to fill formal frameworks determined by an economic, sociological, demographic, or psychoanalytical theory. This conception tends to direct history toward "examples" which must illustrate a doctrine which has been defined elsewhere.

The inverse affirmation can lead to the same result. In their devotion to "facts," erudite scholars gather elements necessary for their research, but these are framed and mobilized with an order of knowledge of which they are unaware and which functions unbeknownst to them. The vindication of facts repeats the forms of their identification. Its implicit corollary is one of the preservation of norms and ideologies which determine the division, classification, and organization depending on the *same* postulates. The vindication of facts therefore indeed "illustrates" a doctrine, but a doctrine which is invisible and of which no more is given than the "examples"—the "facts."

Taxonomy, in Swanson's study, originates in a socioethnology of political forms.[6] From it he draws the criteria of his historical work on the social roots of religious doctrines—a normal position, since the interpretive codes of the past never come to us from this past. But he also presupposes that a sociological grid of this kind is directly connected with the reality of every society, and that the grid introduces the very referent into the analysis. He endows that grid with the ability to correspond with social "truth," in such a way that all other taxonomies must be reduced to the one in question through a series of tranformations. This is tantamount to forgetting that no code as such is any more faithfully reflective of the "real" than another, except by way of its operative power, that is, insofar as it is the instrument of an operation that society imposes upon itself. Even supposing that in contemporary societies change is effected and is thought of according to sociological modes, such has not always been the case. A historical perspective must take into consideration the successive substitutions of these codes of reference and, for example, the fact that in the thirteenth century the theological code played the role that today is attributed to sociological or economic codes. The differences among the frames of reference in terms of which a society organizes its actions and thoughts cannot be held as insignificant. Reducing one to the other would mean that the very labor of history is denied.

Finally, it appears to Swanson and many others that a *single model* (here, a political model) can *in fact* explain a society in its totality. In principle, a single system of clarification ought to integrate and account for its complexity. In this light, the objective of a scientific analysis would be one of bringing to the uniqueness of a theoretical model the fleeting multiplicity of social organizations. This conviction has at least two self-reinforcing origins: on the one hand there is an ethnological postulate according to which "primitive" societies are reducible to *one* system; on the other there is a hierarchical postulate—founded on the operation which transposes the relation between the civilized and the savage into a relation inherent within modern societies—according to which some of the forces or values circulating in a society receive the privilege of representing the "predominant factor," the "progress," or the "essential" and are used in categorizing all of the others. The central place awarded to one category of signs establishes the possibility of classifying others as "delays" or "resistances," and furnishes the base—or the partial base—for a "coherence," for a "mentality," or for a system to which everything is referred.

It is clear that this place accorded to signs refers to the social place of historians.[7] In any event, reference to a "coherence" that might embrace the totality of data from a period or of a country collides with the resistance of this raw material. From this point on, what these data call forth is no longer a change of the interpretive model, but rather the idea that it may be possible to think of them *in the singular*. Hence the impression that a single society advances a *plurality of heterogenous but combined developments*. For example, according to Jacques Berque, the society is characterized by a specific relation between a "base" or a "ground" (a referential *x*, on the basis of which the multiplicity is to be situated) and the play among a plurality of "predicates" knowable only through analysis (the political "dimension," or predicate; the artistic or literary dimension, the industrial predicate, etc.).[8] The model of a "pluridimensional" evolution must then be elaborated; it must allow one to conceive of these "dimensions" as connected and balanced, yet obeying "inherent logical patterns" and various rhythms of growth.[9]

Mentioned here by way of example, this schema is directed to the problem that all historiography faces. In effect, it combines two apparently contradictory elements: *the singularity of a proper name,* the uniqueness of the referent, which is at once inevitable (the history of France, of the Maghreb, of the seventeenth century, etc.) and elusive (the proper name designates the analytical postulate, but not its content); and *the plurality of systems* of development, which are in themselves relative to a plurality in the levels, methods, and materials of analysis. Between the singular and the plural, Jacques Berque argues for a relation analogous to what an invisible "subject" keeps with visible "predicates."

Without even specifying the difficulties offered by this grounding of "dimensions" or "predicates" in a quasi-mystical *x* from which they receive a real but unknown support,[10] we can note that this ultimate trace of an ontologism of language, so frequent in history, has the consequence of our presupposing that this partition into "dimensions" has a universal and constant validity. But such a distinction is unstable. For example, the dissociation of the "political" from the "sacral" or the "esthetic" is a historical production. It results from the advent of a modern type of civilization that has not always existed. Furthermore, the systems of development that have been qualified here as "dimensions" do not correspond

to homologous areas: political, religious, or intellectual units do not co-
incide; they do not have the same extension in time and space, so that
to suppose that they have a same "base" (France, the seventeenth century,
etc.) is an operation which simply consists in taking a *code* (whether political, religious, chronological, etc.) as the basis for the analysis of one
area's relations with others. Historians are strongly obliged to use this
kind of procedure; there exists no universal point of view. But this referent is also a result of their operation. It is therefore not closer to the
real, even if it may be the condition for an analysis which draws a real
knowledge (albeit relative to an interpretive model) from raw data.

As current studies in the social sciences have shown,[11] it appears that
we have to conceive of the possibility of distinct and combined systems,
without having to introduce into their analysis the support of an originary and unitary reality. This implies that we should be able to think of
a plurality of systems specified through heterogenous types and surfaces
of functioning; that the very nature of these systems varies (the religious
system, for example, has not always been either stable or distinct from
what became a political system); that compatibilities, relations, and reciprocal compensations among different systems specify the units marked
off by history; that finally the process by which these units are broken
down or changed in order to give way to others can be analyzed as the
path these combinations follow toward thresholds of compatibility or tolerance among the elements that they are combining.

The identification of these systems is clearly relative to conditions and
models of investigation. But this is equivalent to saying that scientific
analyses intervene, classify, and operate without ever being able either to
integrate or overcome through discourse the history, the *reality* with which
they are dealing; such analyses are part of that reality, and they depend
on it as if on a ground whose displacements are directing their movements.

It has proved interesting to examine from the standpoint of this global
scheme the movement produced on the level of religious practices in the
course of the seventeenth and eighteenth centuries. To do so puts in
question simultaneously the social changes and the transformations in the
axiomatic of the operation:

- We can observe how first a political system, then an economic system, *organized themselves as manifestly distinct* from a "religious" system even while, as R. R. Palmer has shown, Christianity still influ-

enced the general course of philosophy.[12] Another social combination of distinct systems, and simultaneously another mode of the thinkable, were slowly inserted into the still massively religious element —not to imply necessarily Christian element—of the French population.

• *A new formality of practices* allows us to apprehend these structural transformations and their functioning at the very level of religious behavior, without necessarily having to pass through the ideologies which an intellectual elite was elaborating.

• From this given, by way of the possibility of isolating these two series, perhaps we now have the means of analyzing how, on the one hand, *practices and ideologies are connected* in a particular case and how, on the other, the *passage* from one type of social connection to another can take place.

NOTES

1. Etienne Gautier and Louis Henry, *La Population de Crulai, paroisse normande* (Paris: Presses Univeritaires de France, 1958), p. 119. The conclusion of this study, a model of its genre, is justly quoted and emphasized as "capital" in Jean Delumeau, *Le Catholicisme entre Luther et Voltaire* (Paris, 1971), p. 322.

2. "In order to be de-Christianized, it's certainly necessary that they [populations] at one time had been Christianized! It is the measure of this *Christianization* which will reveal the measure of *de-Christianization*," writes Delumeau (*Le Catholicisme*, p. 326). Inversely, if we return from the collapse of religious practice to its causes (the superficial character of Christian practices), we can better gauge the degree of "Christianization," and perhaps even dispense with this notion.

3. The break between "modern" and "contemporary" history has become progressively relativized, we know, through the analysis of economic, demographic, cultural, and other *continuities,* or by the creation of *discontinuities* which do not correspond to the break at the end of the eighteenth century.

4. On the topic of Gabriel Le Bras, see Henri Desroche's studies in the *Revue d'Histoire et de Philosophie religieuses* (1954), 2:128–58, and those of François Isambert in *Cahiers internationaux de sociologie* (1956), 16:149–69.

5. Guy E. Swanson, *Religion and Regime: A Sociological Account of the Reformation* (Ann Arbor: University of Michigan Press, 1967). In his work, Swanson (a professor of sociology at the University of California, Berkeley) provoked a very interesting debate on methodology (the participants were Natalie Z. Davis, T. V. Brodek, H. G. Koenigsberger, and G. E. Swanson) entitled "Reevaluating the Reformation: A Symposium," published in the *Journal of Interdisciplinary History* (1971), 3:379–446. The problems raised by Swanson are not without analogy to those that Lucien Goldmann had formerly touched upon in his *Le Dieu*

caché (Paris: Gallimard, 1956); available in English as *The Hidden God* (London: Routledge and Kegan Paul, 1977).

6. Swanson distinguishes no less than forty-one forms of government, each engendering a religious type proportioned to it.

7. For example, the place occupied by historians themselves, insofar as they are intellectuals in a society, does determine in a large measure the privilege they allocate to a particular category of signs that are *at once* the indications of "progress" and the principle of the synthetic comprehension of a period. There is a relation between the social place of the "scholars" and the epistemological role of criteria of their choice. See chapter 1.

8. Jacques Berque, in "Logiques plurales du progrès," *Diogènes* (1972), no. 79, pp. 6–7 and 10, uses in turn "predicate" and "dimension."

9. *Ibid.,* p. 19.

10. Berque speaks of a "statutory ambiguity" in respect to this "basis of indistinction prior to all differentiation" (*ibid.,* p. 6). He would like to make an economy of it without believing in its possibility. Here indeed is a limit—and also a remainder—of scientific realism. Beyond it, an epistemology begins which refuses to take *reality* into the webbings of *language*, even in the name of an unknowable subject displaying recognizable attributes.

11. Thus, in urban studies, a plurality of systems are sought for consideration, overlapping and self-balancing but not reducible to the theoretical (integrative) model of the tree. See Christopher Alexander, *De la synthèse de la forme* (Paris: Dunod, 1971), and his article "Une ville n'est pas un arbre," in *Architecture aujourd'hui* (1967).

12. Robert R. Palmer, *Catholics and Unbelievers in Eighteenth-Century France* (Princeton: Princeton University Press, 1970).

3

The Inversion
of What Can Be Thought

Religious History in the Seventeenth Century

FIRST envisaged on the basis of what we might call "spiritual life,"
and hence in a relatively narrow field, the religious history of
seventeenth-century France nevertheless offers a certain number
of problems touching on the very methods and definition of this history.[1]

In presenting them here in the form of questions I am classifying these
problems somewhat arbitrarily, within the determinations which typify
our current research, into (a) those problems which first appear to be
bound to the *content* of history, to the ecclesiastical society or the religious phenomena that we study; and (b) those which bear upon its *scientific organization*, that is, upon our way of "understanding" history and
hence the relation that obtains between our present historical point of
view and our religious object of study. From the first standpoint, things
are moving all around us, but they can be analyzed. From the second, it
is we who have to move in respect to the ways things were lived and
thought by their contemporaries or by the historians who preceded us.
We can eliminate neither one nor the other of these two aspects. Their
conjunction defines the historian's work.

This study was first published in *Recherches de science religieuse* (1969), 57:
231–50.

RELIGION IN THE CLASSICAL AGE

THE sources of religious history determine the landscape that we "re-constitute" with the help of the documentation that they have provided for us. Choices are made from the outset about the type of history we will produce, with the sources that we establish for ourselves and what we decide to look for in them. I will reserve this fundamental question for the second part of my chapter in order to devote the first part exclusively to history which is already made; that is, the narrative that has resulted already from abundant harvests of erudition. This "content" is presented according to different types of organization. Seen from this angle, dynamic and structural factors can be distinguished depending on whether they deal primarily with the *internal* functioning of religious society and the Christian experience (for example, the designation of heresy, the relation between the "elite" and the "masses," the status and role of doctrine, and so on), or as they instead allow this society to be defined in respect to an *exteriority* (a past, a hostile or different present, the religious "assimilation" of nonreligious elements, etc.). It will be necessary to go beyond this division. Yet it helps us to take up and to classify several problems.

Stabilities and Internal Tensions
(the Dynamics of Religious Society)

AMONG the tensions inherent to the seventeenth century, the three that follow are presented here in an antinomical and necessarily simplified form. They are obviously bound to a contemporary perception (but up to what point?—a question that must be debated); but this is a sign that they indicate new "places" of research, and that an apparatus must be refined in order to analyze more delicately the problems born of our questions.

Heresy

AS Alphonse Dupront has shown, "a first piece of raw material, as obvious as capital for the modern mind, is the progressive promotion of heresy in confession and of confession in church. . . . Such, in my opinion, is the great modern fact: the notorious heretic has become publicly and officially a minister of the Church, but of another church."[2]

A capital sign, in effect, for hereafter the status of the conformist and the nonconformist, of the orthodox, and, as Bossuet puts it, of the "errant," becomes *problematic,* especially in the sense that the doctrinal criteria are discredited by the very fact of their opposition, and that adhesion to the religious group is progressively imposed as a substitute criterion. From the moment when principles become relative and are inverted, the *membership* of a church (or of a "body"), more than content (which has become debatable because it is partial; or common but hidden, "mystical"), tends to found the certitude of "truths" proper to each. The antinomy (indeed the aggressivity) among groups wins over the disputes concerning "truth"; it involves a skepticism that can be observed everywhere;[3] it also prepares (and already sketches) a *nonreligious* type of certitude—that is, participation in civil *society.* Because of its fragmentation into coexisting and mutually warring churches, the values once invested in the Church appear directed toward political or national unity. A defrocked Church favors the structure over the message, and geographical unity over all forms of "catholicity." Thus the nation is born.[4]

From this standpoint, the multiplication of iconic representations and doctrinal elucidations devoted to the "victory" of faith over heresy probably announces, in each church, the opposite of what they are supposed to prove or demonstrate. For the intransigence carries over to the strict membership of the group. The suspicion that touches upon dogma makes more necessary the rigidity and the self-defense of the group. Whence the new meaning of education as an instrument of cohesion in a campaign to maintain or restore unity. Knowledge becomes, for a religious society, a means of self-definition in its catechisms or in its controversies. Ignorance designates an indecision or a no-man's-land that is hereafter intolerable among the conflicting "bodies." Truth appears less as what the group defends and more as what it uses to defend itself: finally, truth is what it *does,* it is its style of fashioning, of diffusing, and of centralizing what the group *is.* A transformation inverting the reciprocal roles of the society and of the truth takes place. In the end, the former will be what will found and determine the latter. Hence a relativization of "truths" is prepared. More precisely, they function in a new way. Soon, doctrines are going to be held as effects, then as ideological "superstructures" or as instruments of coherence both proper and relative to the societies that have produced them.

This global "heresy" substitutes a social criterion for its religious counterpart. It doubtless corresponds to the historical phenomenon filed until
now within the (religious) category of "de-Christianization." It can be
analyzed through the reemployment within the seventeenth-century milieu of rules that until then had qualified as "heretical" those movements
which were either breaking away from the *unique* religious society, or
were threatening it. These rules (of discernment) begin to function differently through their inscription in a new situation. For example, they
serve to restore the barriers separating institutional "bodies," at a time
when a more and more homogenous "mystic" life (hidden under the visible divisions) seems to emerge among the members of these opposed
groups, "foreign," as it were, to these superficial determinations: the
"spirituals," Protestant or Catholic, Jansenist or Jesuit, are distinguished
much less by the nature of their experience than by the fact of their being
associated with opposite camps. Besides, they often have the common
quality of being suspect (sometimes to themselves as much as to their
religion) because, in the name of an "interiority," they betray the traditional institutions of their society (consider antimysticism as a case in
point). In this way, so to speak, both a social use of religious criteria and
a mystical reinterpretation (which is personal, "hidden," and very similar
among individuals belonging to opposed groups) are lifted from the same
religious structures.[5]

The recovery of the *visible*, which the Council of Trent took as its task
to assure pastorally and doctrinally,[6] seems in reality to lead to two contrary effects. On the one hand, religious institutions become progressively
"politicized," and, without knowing it, they wind up obeying the norms
of the societies or nations that affront one another. On the other hand,
experience sinks into a hidden "underside," or it is marginalized, localized
in a "mystical body" or in "devout circles." Between the two, for a while
maintaining the structure and mental vocabulary of an ecclesiastical hierarchy, "state policy" imposes its law and makes old theological systems
function in a new way:[7] for example, the idea of Christendom resurges
in private societies (thus the Company of the Saint-Sacrament), in the
form of a totalitarian project, a utopia whose mental baggage tends toward the archaic (even if certain of its ideas are reformist) and whose
support is no longer anything more than a secret group. Or else the idea
of a Christian order is opposed, as its antithesis, to political reality; a
spirituality is formulated as the inverse—first "mystical," then "crazy,"

"idiotic"—of the new order of things, which is "lay." Or Christian re-flection even turns the laws and rules that had formerly organized social life toward the sphere of "intention."

Collective Religious Conscience and Doctrinal Representations

IN the same period, a difference revives—once considered intolerable—between the religious *conscience* of Christians and the ideological or in-stitutional *representations* of their faith. Is this a truly new fact? Especially striking in these texts is less the *fact* of difference (which is always very difficult to judge) than the explicit *feeling* of a gap between beliefs and doctrines, or between experience and institutions.

Many signs appear to suggest this hypothesis. Sorcery and skepticism are converging signs (one is popular, the other intellectual) of the im-mense disputes among institutions.[8] The best of the theologians have re-course to the experience of the "illiterate," of the "maiden" of the country or of the common people's urban districts.[9] The return of missionaries to the provinces (the goal of a new *reconquista* through knowledge, as we shall see) turns the French countryside into an area where renewal is to appear, the saintly origins of an apostolic rebirth in "savage" lands[10]— a movement parallel to what then led so many Catholic hermits into the French "deserts."[11] More intimately, among the many great Christians of the seventeenth century there arises doubt in respect to expressions of faith, or difficulty in seeing in the authorities anything other than a means of practicing humility. Reference to what is *experienced* (illuminating or devastating) endlessly opens up the problem of its relation to what is *represented* (official, received, or imposed).

This evolution is accompanied by two apparently contradictory phe-nomena, but I believe them to be coherent and patent in every respect. On the one hand, throughout the entire seventeenth century, religion is progressively brought back to the field of *practice*. Practice is a fact which can be oberved. A proof that faith makes itself, practice is the justifying visibility of a belief that from then on also obeys the imperatives of social utility under the bias of philanthropy and the defense of order. These diverse elements have a variable importance. They seek to defend a Chris-tian originality (a "Jansenist" tendency) or to introduce the Christian ele-ment into the laws of public morality (a "Jesuit" tendency). But they have in common the fact that, attesting equally to defiance in respect to religious representations, they substitute a *social gesture* for interior assimilation of a universal Christian truth recognized in law. At its extreme, this gesture creates truth more than it consists in a "putting into practice" of Christian truths. From now on the decisive areas are mores rather than faith. The religious criterion changes slowly; and what is thus elaborated inside the Church in the seventeenth century is probably exactly what is resurgent today, elevated to the status of a scientific criterion, in "religious sociology."

The other phenomenon is the new function that *knowledge* acquires in the establishment or restoration of an order at the same time served by and justified by the pedagogical crusades of the Church. The great schooling and missionary campaigns of the churches in the seventeenth century are well known: they aim especially at geographical, social, and cultural "regions" that were left fallow until then because they were felt to be assimilated within global structures: the countryside, the child, the woman.[12] These regions are emancipated and thus become dangerous in respect to a new order. I wonder if the explanation that, in the course of the seventeenth century, tends to interpret these resistances as the consequence of ignorance may be nothing more than a sign of the function that this *reconquista* through learning has progressively received. A national unity is thus promoted and framed by the acquisition—first all by way of catechism—of knowledge. The "remainder" will either be relegated to folklore or eliminated.[13]

Perhaps in this respect, in "classical" rural France, an area remaining to be discovered,[14] we must refine the relation between on the one hand the "peasant furies" evoked by Roland Mousnier,[15] the "wild rebellions" and festivals transformed into revolts,[16] the criminality in the country, the remnants of sorcery and so forth, and, on the other, the intellectual character of the catechetical movement and the effort at education of which the Church had been the instigator.[17] Just as the philanthropy of its devotees works to "confine" the poor as it benefits them, just as in one action it defends evangelical poverty and represses felonious poverty,[18] so in the same fashion might the educaional campaign have played these two roles. The church obeys the imperative of public order. Thus a national redefinition divides the country according to cultural criteria imposed by conjuncture; they might have been accepted by the Christian apostolate, but they were no longer determined by it, and perhaps their efficacy remained unknown to it. Once again the hypothesis of a new function of religious structures is suggested.

Religious Ideology and Social Reality

THE question posed by this social function of religion refers to a broader inquiry. This inquiry concerns first the relations that religious representation or ideologies keep with the organization of a society; secondarily, it concerns the criteria that we currently use to evaluate a social "reality," criteria that might allow us to appraise either the delusion of religious expressions (if these are superficial effects) or their effectiveness (if they have a determining role)—in any event, their meaning.

Lucien Goldmann poses the question bluntly in its initial shape when he demonstrates a reaction against royal absolutism among lawyers, but a reaction that accompanies an increasing economic dependence upon the monarchy. The "Jansenist" retreat would express only the inevitable outcome of an opposition stripped of power: it would be a sublimated resignation.[19] In Goldmann's view, understanding Jansenist "ideology" means identifying the "social and economic infrastructure" which accounts for it.[20] Today this problem weighs on every analysis of theologies or spiritualities. But Goldmann's brilliant demonstration does not resolve the issue, to the extent that it remains a tautology—that is, to the extent that, scouring all resistance from the historical raw data, his demonstration makes a selection from among them and extracts only data conforming to a predetermined "Marxist" system of interpretation. The question persists, however, even if it can be cut through by the substitution of a recent ideology (Marxist) for another, older one (of theology).

Before envisaging how a religious historiography can define the relation between a current mode of understanding and the way in which men of former times might have understood themselves, we can notice among the elements that we perceive in the seventeenth century a homology between mental and social structures. There seems to be a connection between the intellectual movements revealed by a history of ideas and the shifts or hierarchizations described by social history. Noting this is a first task. Qualifying this connection (and perhaps having to modify the idea we had of it at the outset, or recognizing in it the result of the "perception" that makes this parallelism appear) is still another task. I shall therefore only indicate initially some of the data that can suggest a parallelism among ideologies and social modifications.

The organization of ecclesiastical sciences changes in the course of the seventeenth century. Through new divisions *among* fields of knowledge and a redefinition *of* knowledge as a whole, a shift takes effect which has its analogues in the society: the place given to religious wisdom within the general culture; the growing localization of social recruitment proper to this genre of men of letters; the sale, if not the format, the specialized illustration, etc., of these diverse works, and the sociocultural networks that their circulation allows to be remarked on the surface of the country or categorized within its depth and breadth (places of sale, prices, quotations or references in other texts or in letters—an entire series of indications draws a stippled image of mental stratifications and groups that are otherwise difficult to recognize). These dispersed factors indeed appear to compose a homogenous phenomenon. To an organization of sciences and literary genres corresponds a social geography.[21]

On the very turf that an analysis of ideologies defines, a thousand signs indicate the bond among particular evolutions and structural shifts. Any division of sciences (here, religious studies) always reveals the construction of knowledge in its global and formal aspect. It is already evident in the bibliographies (too rare at this time),[22] the "libraries" (very numerous), or the directories for clerical studies[23]—all eminently classificatory documents. In comparing and cross-referencing them, we recognize signs—generally late in coming—of shifts in the order which stratifies and distributes forms of knowledge.

This movement classifies the same contents differently, or provides the same general frames with new contents: these are two opposite forms of a single evolution that engages the *nature* of knowledge. Thus, in a specific sector, we see a "mystical theology" break away from theology and become "mysticism," then "piety"—a specialty whose counterpart is "positive theology," also increasingly separated from theology and sent off in the direction of erudition.[24] In reality, it is the criterion of knowledge that is changing here, at the same time that the formerly globalizing and vivifying theology is rent to pieces. Instead of a rational and spiritual interpretation of *tradition,* one seeks observable *facts* (which are psychological, in spirituality; historical, in "positive theology"). On one side, extraordinary phenomena, and on the other, "positive" realities, are hereafter taken to be the foundations of religious science—and an analogous process was simultaneously taking place in the other sciences.

Experiment establishes these sciences and furnishes them with the title in whose name they obtained the right to "verify" received information.[25] The same recourse functions in different modes, to be sure, but in ways that are already directed toward sciences (psychology, history) of which religious life will be more and more the object and less and less the principle. Science imposes its criteria upon everyone; one's belief or unbelief is of no importance here. It places religious facts outside of scientific process; religious facts are either before science as an *object,* or behind it, with the status of an interior *motivation* (the learned man's "pious intention") or of a place in society (the scholar is Christian only in living in the style of a "solitary" or a monk). A geography of ideas outlines a sociocultural geography, and here we doubtless must recognize the symptom of a global movement, in the logic that apportions the language of spirituality between psychologism and casuistry, or which pushes "mysticism" back into the heart of the countryside and into sects, and bears "positive" theology toward "a certain historical rationalism."[26]

A more limited but also sharper analysis can reveal other phenomena of the same order. Between 1630 and 1660, sciences and techniques (astronomy, weaving, etc.) replace natural realities (water, fire, etc.), and "urban references" or "references to Versailles" pick up the slack of rural or medieval images within the raw material of comparisons used by spiritual literature. Spiritual treatises are then organized according to the "states of life," in other words, according to a social model and to professional classifications, and no longer according to determinations belonging to the Church (clerical-lay, regular-secular, parishes, missions, etc.).

Through this configuration we can certainly better understand the *intolerable options* and the *interior divisions* to which believers of the seventeenth century seem so often to be driven. Gallicanism, or support of the administrative autonomy of the French Catholic Church, and quietism faced each other, as if the new "reason" which placed ecclesiastical action within the framework of national politics and positivity had for its contrary and correspondent a spirituality of abandon and passivity, as much more foreign to institutional boundaries (religious ones included) as it was more "interior."[27] Again through this configuration, in the second half of the seventeenth century doctrinal positions reveal and refer back to sociocultural changes. Earlier, in the middle of the century, a neighboring phenomenon is met, for example, not in the shape of an opposition, but of a juxtaposition: in the case of such and such an intendant,[28] an ethic ordered entirely by fidelity to the king is conjoined to—but without interfering with—a mystical docility to the universal Creator. What will be rejected later on is already dissociated here within personal experience.

Many other fields are subject to this study: thus the *sociocultural localization of religious ideologies*. I believe this can be perceived in various shapes:
in more or less secret networks through which the same ideas circulate—
those of the Jansenists,[29] of the "devouts,"[30] or of the "spirituals";[31] libertine or erudite circles whose recruitment is relatively homogenous, and
whose activity is equally occult;[32] and the social and professional specialization of religious congregations which are progressively defined on
the ladder of a social hierarchy and within an increasingly rigid organization of trades. Partitions are therefore reinforced, either among small
private circuits (themselves dissociated from public "reason"), or among
groups hereafter determined more and more by objective tasks, by the
milieus where they are recruited, and by the ideologies that become the
sign of this fragmentation. From this standpoint, René Taveneaux's *Le
Jansénisme en Lorraine, 1640–1789* appears to be a scientific model that
might bring out problems referring to a new organization of religious
life.

Religious Life Within Seventeenth-Century Society

THE internal relations among groups, doctrines, or levels of expression
already implicate the relations that communities of believers keep with
what we might call their "outside," what they designate as alterity ("pa-
ganism," "atheism," "naturalism"), and in terms of which these communities define their own existence. This can be considered from different points of view, which seem to encourage the analysis of global
structurings characterizing the religious experience of the period. Thus,
as examples, we can discern several general categories of language.

The Hidden

HERE we have a fundamental quality of the seventeenth century of both
religious and cultural stamp: *a nonvisibility* of meaning (or even of God).
It is first revealed between the scene and what lies "behind" it,[33] by the
insecurity (forcibly aggressive) that marks all expression; by the disconnection of the "indicible" and the "positive," and so on. It orders "style,"
rhetoric—in other words, an art of speech in which allegory everywhere
plays a decisive role that consists of stating something by uttering *something else:* painting and literature use mythology or religious representa-

tions in order to express an "underside" that only an apprenticeship (from school all the way up to the court) slowly allows to be perceived and suggested. "A word to the wise is enough!" defines this language. And there are many of the wise, informed and "refined" enough to play the game of an entire society. Enigmas, allegories, medallions, and so forth: the most perceptible signs must be brought out, since they refer to a very general structure which is legible too in the shape of libertine "academies" or pious "associations," private groupings establishing a project and language beneath the official surface of the country.

It might seem that an entire society expresses what it is in the process of fabricating through the representations of what it is in the process of losing. The sacred becomes the allegory of a new culture at the time when, inversely, adventures of the body provide spiritual experience with its new language.[34]

Displacements of a Bipolar Structure

ANOTHER "law" (if it can be termed one) appears to rule over the evolution of religious society and become proper to it even while it will cease to characterize civil society: the bipolar structure that always constitutes into an exterior *unity* whatever does not pertain to the Church. This will be for example, the infidel, the atheist, the heretic, or "the world." This "law" governed medieval Christianity; it had its symbolic expression in the Crusades. But the birth of Europe makes a national unity of each state among *several* others. Catholicity itself crumbles into a *plural* organization. Perhaps because of its ideological nature, religious society continues to consider what it opposes or what it is distinguished from as a *unique* totality. The permanence of this structure can be observed across the mobility of ideas and groups in the course of the seventeenth century, even despite the diversity of doctrines or situations which condition its expression. The bipolar relation is thus maintained even while its terms are being transformed.

In this respect it is important to analyze the successive contents of the same binomial. For example, the ideological position of the atheist is successively filled by *alhumbrados* or "spirituals," by Protestants or Catholics, by Jansenists or Jesuits, by theists, and so on. These definitions display at once the movements of a boundary (retractions, or new modalities of Christianity), and the rigidity of the principle by which a society organizes events in order to define itself.[35]

The problem can be shown in multiple and sometimes inverted forms. For instance, American Indians or Chinese "Sages" are granted the role of representing a truth (a "natural" truth, but bound to revelation through a regress of biblical chronology) which may have been corrupted among the colonizers. The positive pole is an elsewhere, opposed to a corrupt and "infidel" Europe. Here we can locate another form of the hidden, since civilizations thus acquire a mystical meaning and constitute the immense allegory of God who is under veil in the West. Thus begins a nostalgia—soon to become philosophical—for a truth which rises, masked, in the East, and which is tarnished in the mirrors where the West had believed it could take hold of it: the next form of the bipolar structure within the mythologies of the nineteenth century.

The Relation with the Past

AN equally telling fact is that relations to tradition change. The "return to origins" always states the contrary of what it believes, at least in the sense that it presupposes a *distancing* in respect to a past (that space which precisely defines history: through it is effected the mutation of lived tradition by which one makes a "past," the "ob-ject" of study), and a will to *recover* what, in one fashion or another, seems lost in a received language. In this way the "return to origins" is always a modernism as well.[36]

However that may be, the "exegetical" methods of the time, their differences from or their analogies with "historical" methods, the progressive homology between the two—but compensated through an often ferocious distinction between the areas studied ("profane" or "sacred"); the slow replacement of the apostolic era with the patristic in the interest of historians; the subtle terrorism that erudition wields over theology or apologetics; the selection effected in history (which is more and more "latinized"): all of these elements would have to be studied (a model of the sort being Alphonse Dupront's work on Huet).[37] They characterize religious society on three fronts, equally historical: namely, on what it consciously *lacks* (a lost tradition); what it *rejects* in order to fashion a "legend" from it or to "forget" it; and what it *states* about itself in reinterpreting its past—in other words, its other (what that society is no longer). Every particular question is the mirror of the greater overall complex of problems set before the Church. Here everything concerning interpretation takes on a social meaning. And exegesis of the past must be endlessly compared with the form that it assumes vis-à-vis the coexisting "other"—the Indian, the Chinaman, other cultures.

As a UNESCO report notes in passing,[38] the "knowledge of the past is 'structural' to the extent that it plays a unifying role in each nation's ways of thinking." We must add: and each period's. The reinterpretation of the past, the type of historical "understanding," and renewed use of former elements have a supplementary dimension in Christian religious life. They are given either the role of reference to originary history, or they show the persistence of the bipolar structure—they are signs of a selection between what is excluded as obsolete, and what is considered as homogenous to the present time, or "fundamental"; that is, between what has *become* unthinkable, and what has *become* thinkable.[39]

HISTORICAL INTERPRETATION

THAT knowledge of the past is an integral part of a present time is a problem that also concerns *us*. It requires an elucidation of the relation between our ways of thinking and those which we want to study. Put otherwise, there is no historiography without an explicit or hidden philosophy of history. I will put forward just a few general thoughts on these two points.

"Social" History and Religious History

"SOCIAL" history makes use of many constraints that victimize as much as they benefit religious history. I shall pause to reflect on the first aspect, as the second is rather patent.

Sociological or ideological "models" tend to become an imperialism and to define a new orthodoxy. They are necessary because they determine a process of research, hence an intelligibility of history. Yet for us they are an element in a relation to which history must offer some form of resistance. If not, all different societies will seem to conform to our ideology or to our experience, and, lacking this "deviation," historiography would no longer exist in any practical sense. In other words, we cannot forget, as Pierre Goubert has quoted Maurice Crubellier as often saying, that social history is still "a project and a way of seeing"—a method, and not a truth.

More fundamentally, historians spontaneously take their task to be the need to determine what a field delineated as "religious" can teach them about a society (we all go about our job in the same way). What they place under the rubric of "society" is not one of the poles of a confrontation with religion but, rather, the axis of reference, the obvious model of all possible intelligibility, the current postulate of all historical comprehension. In this perspective, "comprehending" religious phenomena is tantamount to repeatedly asking something else of them than what they meant to say; to questioning them about what they teach us concerning a social status through personal or collective forms of spiritual life; to taking as a *representation* of the society what, from *their* point of view, *founded* that society. We claim to understand, by referring it to the organization of their society, what religious phenomena stated not only to justify but also to account for this social status. The very questions that they had to explain through a truth (God, Providence, etc.) have become what makes their explanations intelligible to us. Between their time and ours, the signifier and the signified have castled. We postulate a coding which inverts that of the time we are studying.[40]

The religious history of the seventeenth century, for example, thus implicates a difference between two systems of interpretation, one "social" (so to speak) and the other "religious"; that is, between two periods of consciousness, or between two historical types of intelligibility, ours and theirs. Thus, we have to wonder what may be the meaning of an enterprise that consists of "understanding" a time organized as a function of a standard of comprehension other than ours.

Because of this very difference, currently the "religious" aspect of religious history seems to pass from the historical object to the historian subject. With the religious object (for example, priests, sacramental practice, spirituality) having been hereafter handled *as a function* of a society (according to criteria common to everyone today, which are no longer "religious"), believing historians can do no more than surreptitiously slip *subjective* convictions into their scientific study. These motivations intervene in the choice of their objects (relative to a religious interest) or in the *overall thrust* of the study (in relation to present preoccupations; for example, de-Christianization and its origins, the reality of a popular Christianity, etc.). As a kind of before and after, they frame historical investigation without having any intrinsic relation to it. On the one hand, one writes religious history *because* one is a Christian (or a priest, or a member of an order), while one can no longer write it *as* a Christian.

On the other hand, at the other end of the scale, one mobilizes its results *in the service* of one's belief, and this intention (more or less "apologetic") provokes a certain number of distortions in research itself, simply because the intended goal modifies the process leading historians to it.

In other words, the believer's conviction has no internal relation with the postulates that his or her methods imply; it tends to become a pressure which only seeks to "make use" of the results produced. This pressure can also be seen, for example, in the illusion which consists in our believing ourselves Christian solely because we have established a work site on objectively religious grounds, which masks under Christian intentions the logic of a historical comprehension sapped of religious character. By some kind of fiction we succeed in thinking that a history is religious simply because our motivations are religious.

Religious Fact, Religious Determination, Religious Meaning

THE relation among Christian intentions and a type of historical "comprehension" already poses a problem within the present time of research which must be clarified also in its object, in the past. In the form of historiographical labor, just as in the form of what it can teach us about a period (or more exactly, in the form of a relation to be established between our present and the past), the same problem comes forward: what is "religious"? What is grasped as such?

Religious Fact

ONE example will refine the question. An inquiry by historical religious sociology can furnish a certain number of indications about Christian practices. But it leaves open (even if this seems obvious) the question of the interpretation to be assigned to them. Thus, how can we know whether the result would situate historians before or after the religious moment for which they claim to be accounting? A flourishing practice might be only the *survival* of crumbling convictions or, to the contrary, the hasty adoption of a Christian language whose meaning would *not yet be lived*. For example, who will tell us the precise relation in seventeenth-century Brittany between a waning of Christian practices and a spiritual vitality that was perhaps invested into other modes of expression (non-Christian or nonreligious, that is, not conforming to what we define as such)—or even between the sacramentalization of the crowds following popular missions and the "pagan" basis which perhaps it only covers? The image that sociological historiography provides risks being late (in the first case) or premature (in the second), depending on whether the catalogued phenomena that outline it for us represent a remainder of the Christian past or a layer of paint lightly brushed over a flourishing non-Christian religious system. How can we remove this doubt?

The problem here concerns the relation between *lived meaning* and *designated fact*. Historians can neither be satisfied with describing the fact by blindly postulating its meaning, nor can they admit an unfathomable meaning which could be conveyed by any kind of expression (in the latter case, religious experience would be the night in which all cows are black, since, in the last analysis, we would admit a total break between lived meaning and religious expressions). Thus between the signifier and the signified, a relation has to be cleared up. But it cannot be done at the very level of facts.

Religious Determination and Social Determination

HERE is another example. A sixteenth-century scientist, such as Van Helmont, within whose body of work we consider only a "scientific" part delimited after our present conception of science, organized his entire inquiry according to a religious optic that consisted of deciphering Truth written in the cosmos and the microcosm.[41] Inversely, an erudite Benedictine in the eighteenth century will be classed by us in the "religious" area of endeavor, even though he undertakes study defined by scientific goals and criteria imposed by Enlightenment epistemology. In the first instance, the determination of the research is religious, even though it is expressed in a "scientific" area; this is no longer the case in the second, although its social position (within a religious order) or its motivations are religious.

Now from this we can deduce two kinds of open questions that turn on both methodological and theological options:

1) We can wonder whether the object of religious history should be sought not at the level of an objective localization (relative to our own distinctions between what is religious and what is not), nor at the level of motivations (attested in the past), but rather at the level of an *order* or a *mental organization*. For example, we have seen very firmly that in

the second half of the seventeenth century, spiritual treatises are organized according to "states of life," that is, according to a social model. A social configuration—and no longer a religious hierarchization—is the law determining the partitions and defining the "reemployment" of Christian elements inherited from the past. The fact is even more noteworthy in the nineteenth century apropos of science or social questions: a society which is no longer religious imposes *its* rationality, *its* own categories, *its* problems, and *its* type of organization upon religious formulations. This is doubtless what we can observe today in the place that religion occupies within contemporary historiography. From this perspective the only possible religious history would be a history of religious *societies*.

2) We can also wonder whether the same type of "religion" is in question in the Middle Ages as in the seventeenth or the nineteenth century. The concept and the experience of religion do not always refer to the same thing. At stake are systems whose common term, "religion," may be equivocal. In this perspective, social history conspicuously demystifies religious history into the singular (and therefore the univocality of its conceptual apparatus), but it does not suppress the necessity of religious histories. At the very least, the latter would have the function of preventing one type of interpretation from being treated as the only one. These histories would become *critical* in respect to contemporary models of explanation, and they would assure the resistance of *other* pasts: they would defend history itself and, by virtue of the gap between explanatory systems never truly global, they would also defend the possibility of an option concerning the meaning of this history.

In the one instance as in the other, we would first have to differentiate the modes according to which religious "facts" *function* (supposing even that these facts may be identical). That is, we would have to distinguish the orders which determine the new uses of these facts and therefore their successive meanings; all this before—and with the end of—being able to grasp what historical relation exists among these modes, and therefore our means of "understanding" or interpreting them "accurately."

NOTES

1. In matters of bibliography I refer to the two lists that René Taveneaux has compiled in "La vie religieuse en France de l'avènement d'Henri IV à la mort de Louis XIV (1589–1715)," *Historiens et géographes* (October 1966), no. 200, pp. 119–30; and Pierre Chaunu, "Le XVIIe siècle religieux: Réflexions préalables," *Annales E. S. C.* (1967), 22:279–302.

2. See Alphonse Dupront, "Réflexions sur l'hérésie moderne," in *Hérésies et sociétés dans l'Europe pré-industrielle, XI–XVIIIe siècles* (The Hague: Mouton, 1968), p. 291.

3. See especially Henri Busson, *La Pensée religieuse en France de Charron à Pascal* (Paris: Vrin, 1933); René Pintard, *Le Libertinage érudit* (Paris: Boivin, 1943); and above all Richard Popkin, *The History of Scepticism from Erasmus to Descartes,* rev. ed., (Berkeley and Los Angeles: University of California Press, 1979).

4. See Frederico Chabod, *L'Idea di nazione* (Bari, Italy: Laterza, 1961).

5. The fact is patent in Jean Orcibal, *La Rencontre du Carmel thérésien avec les mystiques du Nord* (Paris: PUF, 1959); and in J. B. Neveux, *Vie spirituelle et vie sociale entre Rhin et Danube au XVIIe siècle* (Paris: Klincksieck, 1967), pp. 361–524.

6. See Alphonse Dupront, "Du concile de Trente . . . ," *Revue historique* (October–December 1951) vol. 206, and "Le Concile de Trente," in *Le Concile et les conciles* (Chevetogne, 1960), pp. 195–243.

7. Homologies and ruptures between the ecclesiastical society and the new political society appear clearly in Etienne Thuau's study, *Raison d'Etat et pensée politique à l'époque de Richelieu* (Paris: Armand Colin, 1966). The insinuation of a political criterion into seventeenth-century ecclesiology is mentioned in Jean Orcibal's "L'Idée d'Eglise chez les catholiques du XVIIe siècle," in *Relazioni del X Congresso Internazionale di Scienze Storiche* (1955), 4:111–35.

8. Today historians willingly ascribe the first to a lack of knowledge; but they thus adapt precisely the interpretation that had already been that of the missionaries or judges in the seventeenth century. In that fashion do they not both attest together to the social a priori (new, I believe, in the seventeenth century) which makes *participation in knowledge* (defined by an elite) the prerequisite for being part of a society, and makes this very knowledge the means by which a society places its members in hierarchies or eliminates the "errants" who do not conform to common reason? This is an open question. See my "Une mutation culturelle et religieuse: Les Magistrats devant les sorciers du XVIIe siècle," in *L'Absent de l'histoire* (Paris: Mame, 1973), pp. 13–39; and Marc Soriano, *Les Contes de Perrault* (Paris: Gallimard, 1968), pp. 90–92.

9. Henri Bremond was quite struck by this fact, and he has often made note of it. Since then, other cases have confirmed his intuition. No doubt there would be a more systematic work to be undertaken on the simultaneously anti-intellectual (but equally ideological) and pauperist themes of the "illiterate," the "poor maiden," and so on. It is the revival (in a new direction) of the theme which,

two hundred years before (in the fifteenth and sixteenth centuries), opposed the inspired lay to the theologian priest, in other words, two categories of the Church; on this topic, see my research in "L'Illettré éclairé: L'Histoire de la lettre de Surin sur le jeune homme du coche," *Revue d'ascétique et de Mystique* (1968), 44:369–412. The entire "spiritual" current (whose local manifestations vary a good deal) is constructed from this perspective. In the seventeenth century, it begins with the primacy granted to the "wisdom of the Saints" (which was often opposed to "positive" theology, and especially to "scholasticism"); it ends with the apologia for the "idiot" at the dawn of the Enlightenment. Even saints are recruited in this anti-intellectual campaign; such is Saint Joseph, considered the mystic of silence before becoming in the nineteenth century the patron saint of the virtues of the family. See Jacques Le Brun, *Nouvelle Histoire de l'Eglise* (Paris: Seuil, 1968), 3:428–30.

10. I feel that we can thus read as affected by this double meaning the data that Charles Berthelot du Chesnay puts together in *Les Missions de Saint Jean Eudes* (Paris: Procure des Eudistes, 1967). The "savage" of the homelands or abroad is a theme common to all missionary literature; it is opposed to that of the civilized person. See René Gonnard, *La Légende du bon sauvage* (Paris: Médicis, 1945), pp. 54–70.

11. See Pierre Doyère's studies, especially the article "Erémitisme" in the *Dictionnaire de spiritualité* (1960), vol. 4, cols. 971–82.

12. An analysis analogous to what Philippe Ariès has argued in *L'Enfant et la vie familiale sous l'Ancien Régime* (Paris: Plon, 1960) would have to be undertaken in respect to the woman. We can already find suggestive leads in Robert Mandrou's *Introduction à la France moderne* (Paris: Albin Michel, 1961), pp. 112ff., or in Gustave Reynier's older study, *La Femme au XVIIe siècle* (Paris: Tallandier, 1929).

13. Obviously this is only one aspect (and, in a sense, the inverse) of the immense pedagogical work which was then achieved in France.

14. See J. Jacquart, "L'Histoire rurale," in *Historiens et géographes* (April 1967), no. 204, pp. 715–21, where it is surprising not to see mention of Marc Vénard's *Bourgeois et paysans au XVIIe siècle* (Paris: Sevpen, 1957); and especially Pierre Goubert, *L'Ancien Régime* (Paris: Armand Colin, 1969), pp. 77–144; available in English as *The Ancien Régime* (London: Weidenfeld and Nicholson, 1973).

15. Roland Mousnier, *Fureurs paysannes: Les Paysans dans les révoltes du XVIIe siècle* (Paris: Calmann-Lévy, 1967), pp. 13–156.

16. See Emmanuel Le Roy Ladurie, *Les Paysans de Languedoc* (Paris: Sevpen, 1966), 1:391–414 and 605–29; available in English as *The Peasants of Languedoc* (Urbana: University of Illinois Press, 1974). From this book, astounding in so many respects, it happens also that in Languedoc (a "cold society" according to Lévi-Strauss' categories) the teaching of literacy (pedagogy of *writing* and of "Northern" language) and the Reformation (primacy of the Book and of *Writing*) follow the same paths. Here acculturation is the principle of autonomy.

17. See Jean-Claude Dhôtel, "La Prodigieuse ignorance," in *Les Origines du catéchisme moderne* (Paris: Aubier, 1967), pp. 149–278.

18. See Pierre Deyon, "Peinture et charité chrétienne," in *Annales E. S. C.*

(1967), 22:137–53. From this standpoint, through its own activity, the company of the Saint-Sacrement would work against its utopian projects (a return to a "Christian" politics) or "subversive" projects (opposition to power).

19. Lucien Goldmann, "Jansénisme et noblesse de robe" in *Le Dieu caché* (Paris: Gallimard, 1955), pp. 115–16; in English, *The Hidden God* (London: Routledge and Kegan Paul, 1977), pp. 103–6. For these "officers," whose attributions are transmitted to the king's commissaries (1635–1640), Jansenist ideology represents "the radical impossibility of attaining a worthwhile life in the world" (p. 117).

20. *Ibid.*, p. 156.

21. In this respect we find some very precious methodological indications in Pierre Jeannin's "Attitudes culturelles et stratifications sociales: Réflexions sur le XVIIe siècle européen," in *Niveaux de culture et groupes sociaux* (The Hague: Mouton, 1967), pp. 67–145. The author shows how, without being identified as such, "a cultural and a social dynamic constantly react against each other" (p. 101).

22. For example, the classifications which F. Jacob de Saint-Charles adopts first in his *Bibliographia parisiana* and then in *Gallica* (which is unfortunately ephemeral: 1646–1651) are, in this respect, even more precious than the information that he furnishes on the publications. See L. N. Malclès, "Le Fondateur de la bibliographie nationale en France: Le R. P. Louis Jacob de Saint-Charles (1608–1670)," *Mélanges Frantz Calot* (Paris: D'Argences, 1960), pp. 245–55.

23. We can go back to the beginning of the seventeenth century from the very elaborate directory—a final point, dating from 1713–1717—published by Raymond Darricau, in *La Formation des professeurs de Séminaire au début du XVIIIe siècle d'après un Directoire de M. Jean Bonnet (1664–1735)* (Piacenza, Italy: Collegio Alberoni, 1966).

24. See Robert Guelluy, "L'Evolution des méthodes théologiques à Louvain d'Erasme à Jansénius," *Revue d'Histoire ecclésiastique* (1941), 37:31–144; and my "Mystique au XVIIe siècle: Le Problème du langage mystique," in *Mélanges de Lubac* (Paris: Aubier, 1964), 2:267–91.

25. See Bruno Neveu, "Sébastien Le Nain de Tillemont (1637–1693)," in *Religion, érudition, et critique* (Paris: PUF, 1968), p. 30.

26. Bruno Neveu, "La Vie érudite à Paris à la fin du XVIIe siècle," *Bibliothèque de l'Ecole des Chartes* (1967), 124:510.

27. In this respect we must combine the reading of Aimé George Martimort's *Le Gallicanisme de Bossuet* (Paris: Cerf, 1953) with J. Coudy's *Les Moyens d'action de l'ordre du clergé au conseil du roi, 1561–1715* (Paris: Sirey, 1954), Pierre Blet's *Le Clergé de France et la monarchie; étude sur les Assemblées générales du clergé de 1615 à 1666* (Rome: Université Grégorienne, 1959) on the clergy, and L. Cognet's *Crépuscule des mystiques* (Tournai, Belgium: Desclée, 1958).

28. See my "Politique et mystique: René d'Argenson (1596–1651)," *Revue d'Ascétique et de Mystique* (1963), 39:45–82.

29. See René Taveneaux, *Le Jansénisme en Lorraine, 1640–1789* (Paris: Vrin, 1960).

30. See the literature dedicated to the Company of the Saint-Sacrament since

Allier's *La Cabale des dévots* (Paris, 1902): A. Auguste (1913), J. Aulagne (1906), Begouen (1913), A. Bessières (1931), J. Brucker, *La Compagnie de Jésus* (Paris, 1919), J. Calvet (1903), F. Cavallera (1933–35), E. Stanley Chill (1960), J. Croulbois (1904), P. Emard (1932), A. Féron (1926), M. Formon (1953–54), L. Grillon (1957), G. Guigues (1922), A. Lagier (1916), G. Le Bras (1940–41), B. Pocquet (1904), N. Prunel (1911), A. Rebelliau (1903 and 1908), L. C. Rosett (1954), M. Souriau (1913), F. Uzureau (1906). A whole literature on the topic calls for new historical synthesis.

31. For example, the Aa; see Y. Poutet and J. Roubert's very exhaustive study "Les 'Assemblées secrètes' des XVIIe–XVIIIe siècles en relation avec l'Aa de Lyon," excerpted from *Divus Thomas* (1968).

32. The role of the academies grows not only in Paris—see Jacques Le Brun in the *Revue d'Histoire littéraire* (1961), 61:153–76—but in the provinces as well, although up to now, only regional studies have noted this fact; see for example L. Desgraves on President Salomon's Assembly in Bordeaux, in *Histoire de Bordeaux* (1966), 4:425ff.; and J. Brelot on the Boisot library in Besançon, in Claude Fohlen, *Histoire de Besançon* (1965), 1:122ff.

33. Studies on the baroque, a spectacle of metamorphoses which ceaselessly hide what they show, particularly enlighten literature dedicated to the mystical experience. In order to understand the "spirituality" of the first half of the seventeenth century, we must compare it to an art (an expression) where the shimmering of appearances speaks for the inaccessibility of the "real." From the works of Pierre Charpentrat to Jean Rousset, the bibliography on this topic is immense.

34. The life of the body becomes in effect the allegory (the theater) of spiritual life. It is the current that has been qualified as "psychological." A language written in terms of sicknesses, levitations, visions, odors, etc., in other words in corporal terms, replaces the "spiritual" vocabulary forged by the medieval tradition. This is not a decadence, but another cultural situation of the Christian experience.

35. Another effect or sign of this structure is the new status of the priest. From the time when Christian society is no longer totalizing and cannot be defined by differentiating itself from other totalities (the Turks, etc.), from the time when it becomes a particular unit within the nation, differentiation is directed toward the distinction between the priest and the laity. An artisan for a long time, a man of rural profession depending upon his lord within the organization of Christendom all the way up to the sixteenth century (and often much later), the priest *becomes* the one thanks to whom the Church may be differentiated, as a religious society, from "civil" society. He tends to establish the new frontier of the sacred at the same time that it defines him in practice or in theory.

36. On this topic, see Maria Isaura Pereira de Queiroz's methodological remarks in *Réforme et révolution dans les sociétés traditionnelles* (Paris: Editions Anthropos, 1968), pp. 162–63, 262, 338–42.

37. Alphonse Dupront, *P.-D. Huet et l'exégèse comparatiste au XVIIe siècle* (E. Leroux, 1930). Through apologetic intent and the very constraint of the comparative and erudite method that he uses, the author shows how Huet finally inscribes the Bible within the "prodigious work of divine fabrication which fills all of antiquity" (p. 161). In that way the exegete is the victim of his historiog-

raphy; he drowns revelation in fabulation. What he fights against as a Christian, the genial scholar admits—by the very fact of the logic of his scientific methods.

38. SHC/CS/90/7.

39. Whence the importance of studies dedicated to the conceptions and organization of classical religious historiography. See Alphonse Dupront, "Clairvoyance de Vico," *Les Etudes philosophiques* (1968), 30:271–95; Corrado Vivanti, *Lotta politica e pace religiosa in Francia fra Cinque e Seicento* (Turin: Einaudi, 1963); and Y. M. Bercé's bibliography in *Bibliothèque de l'Ecole des Chartes* (1966), 214:281–95.

40. Thus, as a model of the genre, we have Pierre Vilar's remarkable study "Les Primitifs espagnols de la pensée économique," in *Mélanges Marcel Batillon* (Bordeaux: Féret, 1962), pp. 261–84, which, *for a history of economic theories,* draws on the great moralist theologians of Spain in the sixteenth and seventeenth centuries.

41. J.-B. Van Helmont, *Ortus medicinae* (Amsterdam, 1652; Lyon: Ioannis Baptistae Devenet, 1655). From how many other "scientists" ought we not to admit as much, among whom we discard everything that is "theological" as an insignificant "remainder"? For their reactions against these abstract divisions imposed by contemporary classifications, see H. Fisch, "The Scientist as Priest: A Note on Robert Boyle's Natural Theology," *Isis* (1953), 48:252–65; above all, Alexandre Koyré, in for example *Du monde clos à l'univers infini* (Paris: PUF, 1962), available in English as *From the Closed World to the Infinite Universe* (New York: Harper, 1958); R. Lenoble, *Histoire de l'idée de nature* (Paris: Albin Michel, 1969), pp. 309–37; and Abraham Wolf, *History of Science, Technology, and Philosophy in the Sixteenth and Seventeenth Centuries* (New York: Macmillan, 1935).

4

The Formality of Practices

From Religious Systems
to the Ethics of the Enlightenment
(the Seventeenth and Eighteenth Centuries)

T
HE work to follow was born of a question: how can a sociology
of behavior and a history of doctrines be articulated? The analysis of documents concerning religious practices in the seventeenth and eighteenth centuries must have some relation with the analysis
of ideological or symbolic discourses. The relation has yet to be clearly
specified. It obviously cannot be reducible to an immediate and univocal
causality. In any society, collective symbols and "ideas" are no more the
"cause" than the "reflections" of change.[1] No more shall one hypothesize
that the channels are unknowingly organized by something either implicit
or unconscious. Identified with the "unsaid" dimension of theories or the
"unshown" areas of practices, and hence accredited with an indefinite
virtue of explication, in fact this unknown would fill with historians' own
ideologies the void left open by their knowledge or methods.

The sociocultural slippages at work in the seventeenth and eighteenth
centuries have much to do with frames of reference. They move from a
religious organization to an economic or political *ethic*. The field favors

This study first appeared in *La Società religiosa nell'età moderna* (Naples: Guida,
1973), pp. 447–509.

the analysis of the mutations that touch both upon the structures and upon the "believable" in a society.[2] These changes seem to be manifested on the level of practice by a series of new *functionings* that are not yet accompanied either by properly apportioned theoretical expressions or by spectacular crumblings. Yet the pieces of the totality already begin to "turn" otherwise. The *content* of practices scarcely changes, but what I call their *formality* indeed does. From this bias it appears that we can apprehend the following: processes of transition and *types of mobility "hidden" inside a system* (here, a religious system) which is nonetheless objectively maintained; a possible *connection between the principles invested within practice and the theories elaborated in "philosophical" production;* finally, in a more general fashion, relations among *systems* that, momentarily or for a longer duration of time, are *coexisting, irreducible* to each other, that can neither be located in any one of the levels of a social stratification,[3] nor placed within a Manichaean ranking which classifies some in the direction of "progress" and others in that of "resistances."

From Religion to Ethics: A Displacement in the Frames of Reference

IN the seventeenth and eighteenth centuries a rift between religion and morals was produced—and then declared[4]—which made their distinction effective and their subsequent connection indeed quite problematic. The rift changed the experience and the conceptions that Western societies had had of them. For the system that made *beliefs* the frame of reference for practices, a social *ethic* was substituted, formulating an "order" of social practices and relativizing religious beliefs as an "object" to be put to use. If we formulate the problem in terms that have since become our own, both the relation between morality and religion and the relation that practice maintains with theory were thus simultaneously inverted.

In order to outline this trajectory at the outset in a global fashion and as it expressed itself, one can say that the seventeenth and eighteenth centuries stage the history of a divorce. Not that the relations between "morality" and "religion" were ever easy or harmonious in times past; many studies have shown that they were stormy and always unstable, for example in matters of usury, sexuality, or temporal power,[5] but the referential *principle* of their union was never questioned. All through the Middle Ages and up to the sixteenth century it was accepted that morality and religion have *the same* origin: reference to a single God organizes at once a historical revelation and an order of the cosmos; this reference considers Christian institutions the legible form of a law of the world. Society is built in terms of an integrative belief. On the level of practice, expressed on the visible surface of society (although there may be rural "depths" which seem to have escaped Christianity), just as in the case of public and professional existence, private life moves within a Christian framework;[6] religion envelops modes of behavior.

In the seventeenth and eighteenth centuries this unity is fissured, then falls apart. Churches are divided; we witness the breakup of the institutional alliance between Christian *language,* attesting to the tradition of a revealed truth, and the *practices* apportioned to an order of the world. Social life and scientific investigation are slowly exiled from religious allegiance. Memberships in different churches, now opposing one another, become relativized. They become signs of contingent, local, and partial determinations. It becomes necessary and possible to find a *legality* of a different order. A new system of axioms on thought and action moves initially into a third position, between the adversary churches of Catholic and Protestant denomination. It progressively defines the very ground which is uncovered beneath the fragmentation of beliefs. An autonomous ethics is thus established, one whose frame of reference is either the social order or the conscience. Jean-Jacques Rousseau designates the mutation which comes about when he writes to Voltaire, "Dogma is nothing, morality is everything."[7] Similarly, he writes for the *Encyclopédie,* "morality wins over faith . . . because all morality . . . is of an unchanging nature and will last into all of eternity, when faith will subsist no longer and be changed into conviction."[8]

With *ethics,* social practice becomes the area in relation to which a theory of behaviors can be elaborated. At the same time, the doctrine of past time is changed into a fact of "belief"; it is a "conviction" (that is, an opinion combined with a passion), or a "superstition"; in sum, the *object* of an analysis built over autonomous criteria. In other words, ethics plays the role formerly allocated to theology. A "science of mores" hereafter *judges* religious ideology and its effects, at the very point where a "science of faith" used to classify conduct under a subsection entitled "moral theology," which ranked behavior according to the codes of doctrine. There are many signs of this evolution: the epistemological primacy of ethics in reflections on society; the appraising of religion according to "values" no longer its own (the common good, the demands of conscience, progress, etc.); the withdrawal of religion to "religious practices" or its alignment with categories imposed by a society; the marginalization of worship in respect to civil or moral law, and so forth.

We should adjoin an analysis of practices to this general sketch of a trajectory, at least insofar as they state a meaning. Numerous studies on this topic allow the formulation of several hypotheses that particular investigations may deny, specify, or confirm. They are classified here in stages destined to underscore some connections perceived on a basis of religious practices: from the division of the churches to state policy (in the seventeenth century); a new formality of practices: the politicization of conduct; the logic of the practicing believer: the alternatives of stately duties and prophecy; philosophical ethics: legality and utility in the eighteenth century; and laws belonging to the religious group: reduction to silence and administration of worship.

FROM THE DIVISION OF THE CHURCHES TO STATE POLICY (THE SEVENTEENTH CENTURY)

AT the end of the sixteenth century and at the beginning of the seventeenth, the role of the division of the churches is not only that of revealing what Joseph Lortz calls a "disaggregation of the principles and structures fundamental to the Middle Ages."[9] The division accelerates this disaggregation, and has the net effect of a dissuasion. Its impact is multiplied elsewhere by the discovery of other religions in the New World, in Africa, and in Asia.

A *uniqueness* of frame of reference formerly imposed its own, "theological" system even onto heresy itself, and on the defense of an autonomy of royal rights as well. Thus social manifestations of medieval heresies are theological, precisely because they have no other common ground, and because theology, the medieval equivalent of our sociological or economic codes, was the only way by which a difference *could be marked*. Alterity was hence eliminated, effaced, or integrated, not only for lack of strong political or social bases, but just as much—or more—for lack of a capacity for being shown to differ in respect to the system of reference, for lack of situating its practice within a code other than the highly doctrinal one it had called into question.

Division and Doubt

WITH the pluralization of these systems a new social space is created. *Heresy* becomes alterity which is insinuated into the margins *next to* common law,[10] into a given space that cannot be reduced to an antilaw. This situation is always tolerated with difficulty because it questions the coherence of the group. In the seventeenth century, it is effectively experienced in the mutual aggressiveness between groups—and thus can only be transitory, before another law is set in place. During this period, violent therapeutics are multiplied to combat the hemorrhages of interpretive systems (religious wars, bloody struggles against sorcery, etc.) and many attempts are made to reconstitute a new order.

Totalizing references and dogmatic discourses originating in tradition appear as mere *particulars*. Within the very experience of practicing believers, they are elements *among others* in a picture in which every element speaks of a vanished unity. What used to be totalizing is no more than a feature within a landscape of disorder which requires another principle of coherence. The criteria of each believing community come to be relativized. In addition to these segmented religious formations, entire zones are discovered (such as the New Worlds) which are impossible to frame within traditional terms. Thus the popular masses, uprooted and seemingly wandering across social and symbolic frames, are delivered up to witches' hallucinations created by this absence. Rampant skepticism attests to the same absence, but within educated milieus.[11] Sorcery and skepticism indeed outline the void that a universal Reason or a natural Law will have to fill.

From a religious viewpoint, *doubt,* the great problem of the time, is linked to division everywhere. From Montaigne to Pascal, all meditation is invaded by the doubt to which plurality gives birth: "I see several contrary religions, and consequently all are false," writes Pascal.[12] An apologetic mode proliferates in an atmosphere where violence and "controversies" among religious groups grow with the suspicion that attends their particular imperatives. Even Christian philosophy is mobilized by the task that Malebranche defines: "Through reason to discover, among all the religions, the one that God has established."[13]

Such an apologetics is inscribed upon a backdrop of "perplexity and anguish": Calvin already echoes it when he underscores that the object of this anguish is not the resistance of the "Turks" or the "Pagans" ("We wouldn't be astonished by them," he says), but the multiplication of those who "tear up piece by piece, ripping asunder the union of our faith with the end of perverting the truth of God."[14] Scandal is on the inside. It is born of internal "in-coherence." Is not religion, writes Du Plessis Mornay in 1581, the "means of reuniting and reconciling?" But it is here that the means of unification is divided: "Is there one or are there several?"[15] To use an image dear to this author, the "bridge" has been fragmented into a plurality of religions![16]

In order to recover certitude with unity, it is necessary then either to go back to a *natural* religion more fundamental than historical religions, which are entirely contingent; to try to bring back to *one* of these religions all of its rivals, which shall be held to be "false" thanks to the establishment of "marks" guaranteeing the "true" one;[17] to try to seek in *politics,* in science, and in still other areas, another "way of unifying" which will hereafter fill the role that religion had been playing up until then; indeed, with Descartes, to move during this period of research into the "provisional morality" whose first rule for him was "to obey the laws and the customs of my country, constantly keeping the religion which God gave me the grace of being taught from my earliest childhood."[18]

By virtue of this movement, religion begins to be perceived from the outside. It is classified in the category of customs, or else in that of historical contingencies. In this fashion, it is opposed to "Reason" or to "Nature."[19] In the eighteenth century it will be seen from an already ethnographical bias from the standpoint of the "students of man."[20] The very term designating it now acquires a new meaning. *Religion* no longer signifies a religious order or the Church in the singular: as Georges Gusdorf has remarked, "Hereafter religion can be spoken of in the plural."[21] It is a socioeconomic positivity bound to a body of abstract hypotheses. Bayle or Fontenelle will call it "the system of the Christian religion."[22] A totality is set in place that must be understood, criticized, or situated according to criteria which are not its own. The *quod creditur* (what is believed) is dissociated from the *fides qua creditur* (faith which causes belief) and is transformed into "belief" in the objective sense of the term. The contents of belief are subject to analysis from an increasing distance in respect to the act of believing. Religion tends to become a social *object,* and hence an object for study, in ceasing to be for the *subjects* that which allows them to think or to behave.

Atheism, Sorcery, Mysticism

AN "atheism" develops in the course of the second third of the seventeenth century,[23] with the "erudite Libertines."[24] To be sure, it will soon be effaced by the political order that Louis XIV institutes, but from then, it is merely partially hidden and covered by official power; it will spring out of the shadows at the beginning of the eighteenth century. This "libertine" eruption of a morality without religion at the heart of the seventeenth century must be linked to other contemporary symptoms: the explosion of sorcery in popular areas, diabolical "possessions" in cities,[25] the "mystical invasion" during the same years.[26]

Atheism, sorcery, mysticism: these three simultaneous phenomena all betray the fact that the churches have become incapable of providing the references that integrate social life. Divided among and within themselves, churches are *localized*. They can no longer supply thought or practice with the statement of general laws. Thus, with the phenomena that I assume to be three variants of a new social structuring, two reciprocal movements are produced. On the one hand, doctrinal elements that had been combined until this time are now disconnected. Among libertines, modes of knowledge are dissociated from the unitary "reason" whose principle was faith; in sorcery, collective symbols concerning church membership are detached from the churches in order to form the imaginary lexicon of an antisociety; with "spirituals," personal experience furrows biographical or psychological itineraries foreign to the institutional and theological languages that had organized its development until then. On the other hand, this disconnection follows *social cleavages,* which are increasing (while religious "allegiances" continue to play an important role, they are staged and apportioned according to sociological categories): libertines are urban masters of writing, already endowed with a social rank and the very technical instrument with which the new power of the middle class will be affirmed; sorcery finds its recruits in rural areas less controlled than in the past and seemingly turned into a single mass by the very fact of mobilities that stir up local hierarchies; mystics are often localized among those lawyers subjected to contradiction between their allegiance to a cultural tradition and the decrease of their political or economic power.

Everything happens as if doctrinal elements, thrown out of the orbit of an integrative system, had then been following differentiated *social gravities*. Social ranks become determining factors, but religious language is still used to designate them. Social distribution acquires a capacity to classify. It slowly models a new order, but all the while this evolution is still hidden under cultural symbols and is betrayed only by the reorganizations that it puts into motion. Already true ecclesiology assumes the form of a political system before, later, it becomes a sociology.

Because this fragmentation is constantly effected through more and more *social* divisions, it points to something that is nascent. It is also organized around something that is disappearing, that is, this integrative virtue that the religious frame of reference had represented until this time. It is here that this principle of unity turns out to be lacking. In each respective group its uncertainty is marked, by "libertine" critical doubt, by returns in sorcery of the "pagan" repressed, or by voyages toward the invisible secrets of received language which the absence of God instigates. The *loss of the absolute object* is inscribed within these three movements, although in characters relative to what specifies each of these groups. It is the question to which they will respond differently.

State Policy

BECAUSE they are still only symptoms, these currents will disappear— almost simultaneously—around the years 1650–1660,[27] as political law is imposed which replaces the order whose explosion they manifest. From the middle of the century, royal power is not mistaken when, in the same move, it represses atheists, sorcerers, and mystics, in view of defending not a religious orthodoxy but rather the "state policy": these movements are symptoms of *an order that is being undone*. They can no longer be tolerated by the innovative politics of an order which will take the place of religion in its role of providing the frame of reference for a society.

Inaugurated under Richelieu in the middle of this "turmoil," and within the context of the skepticism which envelops all existing doctrines, state reinforcement "turns former mental structures topsy-turvy" because, fundamentally, it reorganizes *modes of behavior* relieved of criteria and frames of reference.[28] No matter what may be the condition of belief destined for uncertainty, a basis for *practice* is quickly perceived as both lacking and necessary. An axiomatic of action is needed. Modern science will be formed as it seeks a way for ordering procedures.

A problem of passions is at stake; that is, of action thrust forward by the eruptions of an unfathomable will, disconnected from intellectual or social language. So then, for a period of time, a morality holds sway that is based on exceptions, the ambitious, unstable and risky morality of the "noble" man, of the "hero," of the stoic or the mystic, in sum, of the "savage" and "rare" sublime: morality flows back toward the individual act, as is always the case when normative references to a society tend to weaken.

State policy comes to fill the void by ordering laws of behavior. Based on Tacitus and Machiavelli—"the lands of Machiavelli and Tacitus," Balzac used to say—in the area of *practices*, it *in fact* overcomes the contradiction betwen reason and violence. Managed by "the Great" (they themselves are the only ones who "have the right to reason" about affairs),[29] an order is imposed with royal power. It is accompanied by a "classical" humanism, which, skeptical in matters of ideology, cynical with respect to power, "lucid in scrutinizing the defects of nature," owes much more to philosophy than to "religion."[30] "The Queen of all virtues,"[31] force, founds an order. As Hobbes believes, this legitimation finds its beginnings in the illegitimacy of a violence. It constructs the circle of the state on three points which will organize the writing of a society—"affairs" (a practice), "The Great" (a power), an "order" (a rationality)—and whose certitude is represented in the "mortal God," the king.

Thus as Etienne Thuau has said, "the policy of the seventeenth century is born in a large measure through collective action and the practical needs of the state enterprise." In the field of national or scientific activities, this policy develops a desire both to master and possess social nature. State policy already turns the country into a mercantilist and capitalist enterprise.[32] And it recruits beliefs: "To govern is to make subjects believe."[33] Mersenne saw a legitimate "management of minds" in this political rationalization of convictions and mentalities. For Campanella it was a "spiritual war," a crusade, the equivalent of "spiritual combat." Policy conscripts predicators and men of letters into the service of power; it orients "public" instruction into a pedagogical battle; it aggravates the "crimes of opinion." What could be more astonishing than the chores of morality and knowledge being centered again on the prince, a strategic point of direction? What could be more astonishing than having the "education of the prince" become the practice par excellence where the new political order focuses the formation of a referential social language? The education of the prince is the employment in respect to which "it was often heard said" of Pascal himself "that, had he been engaged in it, there was nothing to which he wanted to contribute more, and that he would have willingly sacrificed his life for such an important cause."[34]

A NEW FORMALITY OF PRACTICES:
THE POLITICIZATION OF CONDUCT

THE establishment of a practical policy with the reinforcement of monarchic power is one thing; the readjustment of religious formations whose internal division was "compensated" by state reinforcement, but which were not vanishing so easily, is another. They functioned quite well indeed. But how did these two systems mesh together? Where can we grasp the connections that are established—as soon as we cease to assume that power possesses the capacity of expanding everywhere the policy that it founds, or the capacity of taking away the relevance or the existence of conducts and beliefs which are still being posited as religious? Practices allow us to grasp the process of a new combination: they indeed define the field where modifications are taking place that will soon flow back upon ideologies. Their different *formality* evinces their *renewed deployment* in the name of another function.

The Formality of Practices

THE nation is normalized into a society of orders arranged around the royal throne, which furnishes both its center and, as in a mirror, the possibility of self-representation.[35] There is a *revival* of religious structures, but one based upon *another system*. Christian organizations are put to renewed use, in relation to an order which they no longer have the power of directing. This is a significant point, for to the king is attributed the privilege of "having God at his side" and "around his person."[36] Like God, the churches happen to be right beside the king. If Louis XIV is part of the Counter-Reformation, he inverts its principle through his *manner* of bringing it to a close.[37] To be sure, as his power becomes increasingly visible, in matters of religion he becomes more and more conservative. The goal of his "great plan" seems to be a "restoration" of the splintered Church, but in reality his goal involves "giving peace to the state and rights to authority"[38]—a surreptitious revolution indeed, where ends are transformed into means. Political institutions *use* religious institutions, infusing them with their own criteria, dominating them with their protection, aiming them toward their goals.

So what is new is not so much religious *ideology* (power imposing a return to Catholic orthodoxy) as the *practice* which, from now on, makes religion serve a politics of order. The religious investiture accrediting this order is intended to win over existing organizations and to consolidate political unity. On this level the weakened Christian "system" is transformed into a sacred theater of the system which will take its place. It also assures the shift of Christian conscience toward a new public morality.

The ways state policy slips under the cover of what it replaces become evident with a politicization of conduct—if by "politicization" we mean movement toward a system which articulates behavior in terms of *forces* facing it, of social *contracts* placing these forces in hierarchies, and of common *values* postulated by these contracts. In order to account for the changes that occur within this *practical policy,* to discern the new order which is inscribed within traditional behaviors, it is not sufficient simply to analyze their contents: the same ideas or institutions can be perpetuated at the very time they are changing their meaning within the social sphere. This is the case with religious conceptions or organizations at the end of the seventeenth century; they follow the same trajectory. They are maintained, even while certain additional elements join them which are already symptoms of another totality. Yet, just as a system of thought is doubtless designated through the invention of a few additional notions, but even more through a different organization of the ideas that it receives from other areas—that is, through its own way of "making them work" within the totality of a discourse—so then religious beliefs and institutions begin to "work" differently and thus betray another kind of dynamic, of which a subsequent recapitulation will be able to grasp the principles in order to make it accede to the status of theory.

Even though intact within themselves, modes of moral behavior are inscribed upon other social trajectories. They are obedient to *criteria,* they are classified according to *categories,* they aim at *objectives* which are changing. These questions have much to do with a formality of practices (practices of language, professional or devotional practices, etc.)—analogous to what Pierre Bourdieu calls a "logic in its practical state."[39] This formality is more or less in accord with official or theoretical discourses; it calls them into question, since it also organizes a practice of reading or hearing; in other words, a practice *of* these discourses, not to speak of the practices which they forget or exclude. One of the tasks of history consists of measuring the distance or the relations between the formality of practices and that of their representations; in this way, with the tensions that are at work throughout a society, we can analyze the nature and forms of its mobility.

New Uses

UNDER the ancien régime and especially throughout the seventeenth century, religious behaviors and conceptions offer a favorable area for this type of analysis. Religious structures begin to "turn" quite differently, as if they were taken up en masse into the political element. We must direct our attention to the erosion of these structures, and especially to their new movements, in order to apprehend the transformation that is in progress. All kinds of indications exist within modes of religious behavior that allow us to specify the more or less explicit, more or less new means under which the "formality of a practice" can be shown.

Some are of a directly political type. These are the most obvious cases. Thus the "monarchic service" and the "king's religion" among Protestants[40] have their more grandiose Catholic equivalents in ecclesiastical "docility" in respect to power, in the royalist feeling which relativizes membership in the Roman churrch (qualified as ultramontane) and pushes the Church of France toward a "political Gallicanism" at times close to schism,[41] and finally with the fact that from 1675 on, the Assemblies of the Clergy are, as Jean Orcibal notes, "completely in the hands of the court."[42] An *identical functioning* overwhelms the division among churches and "makes them work" according to the political system that their fundamentally different theologies are all vainly attempting to deny. Opposed religions follow identical paths. Operations follow "obligatory ways" marked by the political space in which churches are moving. This is not cowardice or a lack of lucidity among men. We will see that the position of "refusal" or of "sanctuary" undergoes and also manifests the same law, although on another scale. At stake first are the attractions and displacements within a system that its combination with a stronger element will precipitate.

If we pass over to particular practices, we can observe the same kind of dysfunction. In the Offices of Charity, the measure by which the needy to be helped are chosen is no longer solely membership in the municipality or in the same social milieu (the impoverished aristocrats), as had already been the case in the sixteenth century, but the possibility or the effectiveness of a "conversion" to Catholicism, an instrument of national unity.[43] Donations made by particular groups and lay masses for schools or missions seem to organize a geography of political interests and social alliances.[44] There is a growing seizure by royal tribunals on religious questions, and a new "relevance" of state affairs in ecclesiastical trials.[45] Religious obedience is subjected to a more fundamental loyalism which founds obedience to the king upon a "divine and human right" or a "natural law" and which divides the clergy according to the rift between "rebels" and "clients" of the king.[46] Theological quarrels generate a theater of conflicts among "parties," and they follow their logic far more than they determine it (see, for example, "Jansenists and Jesuits" in this chapter). For more than a century an instrument of religious propaganda, education becomes an immense social campaign launched against evil, of which a thousand contemporary documents show that the three heads— ignorance, delinquency, division—are part of the same monster (see the remarks on this topic in chapter 3).

Other indications attest to the degree to which religious practices conform to social forms. A few examples will suffice. In the discipline ruling secondary schools, sociocultural and economic "virtues" are imposed more and more—politeness, composure, "bearing," and even more, hygiene (bound to a mastery of life), productivity (the student's *condition* aims toward a social usefulness), competition (knowledge is enjoined in a struggle for promotion), "civility" (the established order of social conventions), and so forth, while "Christian virtues," whose elements are established on a stable list, are simply reclassified within a social restructuring of practices.[47] In the same fashion, a reorientation occurs in institutions and religious foundations with the logic introduced there first by concern for efficacy, then rationalization aiming at an "order" and the sense of method. Within the very practice of prayer, this rationalization replaces "inspirations" with "the usefulness of good thoughts," or "affections" of the heart with "reasons" and "methods."[48] New religious congregations are created—and, often, the former ones are specialized (as in the case of the Benedictines)—in conformation with a topography of urgency or assignments established by society (the struggle against ignorance among the masses, help for the victims of disaster or abandoned children, the quarantine of the sick, education for young women, erudition, etc.): determinations according to social functions are more decisive than the former classifications of religious orders following church functions ("contemplative," "active," "predicatory," and so on).

Many other examples could adduce these functions, whose reciprocals involve privatizing and interiorizing the bases of Christian life. "Sanctities" outline "subjective" and "psychological" itineraries which can no longer be drawn on the checkerboard of civil and political organizations. Withdrawal from the body into the "sanctuary" of the heart is an act that mimes a fundamental incompatibility with the social body; before being a doctrine, rupture is a situation. The "spirituals" of the period are lucid when they regress from practices to the "motives" of action, and when they situate the Christian options below language and works, outside of the social text, within the purity of intention, in the purposes of the heart, in the formal element of action.[49] But since it is deprived of social moorings, this option seems to be lost in an unfathomable night—or must be identified with "extraordinary" phenomena that the scientific optic is already changing into psychological or medical *objects*. "Mystical experience" indeed vacillates between these two poles.

From the bias of their formalities, it also appears that Christian modes of behavior are all affected by the transformation which, on the one hand, brought the problem of order into a field of practice and, on the other, provided it with a sociopolitical solution. It is hardly surprising that one of the clearest signs of this slow revolution in religious structures of action is precisely the place held by the figure of the "practicing believer."

THE LOGIC
OF THE PRACTICING BELIEVER:
THE ALTERNATIVES OF STATELY DUTIES
AND PROPHECY

Between the Law of Acting and the Place of Enunciation

Acting is socialized: it follows the criteria apportioned to the social order being established. Such is the overall displacement at work—a displacement that is difficult to pinpoint, since the distinction between politics and religion (and no longer only between the temporal and the spiritual) is precisely what is being produced. It is therefore impossible to count on these two concepts as if they were solid and stable columns on which a historical analysis could be based in order to account for transformations in progress. Yet something strange is happening. Religious behaviors which used to manifest a Christian *meaning* within a social *practice* are broken. The need to express meaning is dissociated from the social logic of doing. Affirmation of a Christian meaning is isolated in a speech and appears to be less and less compatible with the axiomatic of practices.

The will to state a faith is accompanied by a retreat to the "interior" or to the "anywhere out of this world." It is marked by the foundation of a place apart, from which it may be possible to speak. In representations and images, the "heart" plays this role; it depicts a space, a retreat, closed and cut away from the rest of the world. On the map of France the multiplication of sanctuaries, hermitages, secret societies, etc., is the social equivalent to these closed hearts defending against the intrusions of the world. In these marginal areas a "prophetism" of a new type is established.

An inverse phenomenon corresponds to this. The need to "do" (there is no faith without "works") forcibly submits the action that is undertaken to the organization of civil and political tasks, which are the first to be changed by the new order of practices (professional or familial activities appear to be "laicized" at a slower rate). Unconsciously, the act of "doing" allows the very thing to escape that it wanted to produce, that is, formally Christian actions. It ends in what contemporaries are correct in calling "compromises"—yet these compromises have less to do with a doctrine than with the law which is imposed as soon as one chooses to act on society. In this respect, conciliatory "humanism" and even moral "laxity" are first of all the signals of a situation. The order which they betray can only be compensated (according to the modes which also refer to the same situation) by correctives proportioned to the detail of each element of social behavior (in view of inserting into it a specifically Christian deviation), and especially by reinforcing the marks of differentiation that are called "religious."

This break of Christian action separates the *place of meaning* (that is, the possibility of finding a place for enunciating) from the *work of social production* (that is, the effective work on which a society is built).[50] Doubtless some account could be made of the great debates at the end of the century in terms of the tension between the necessity of "re-constituting" a place of enunciation and the logic of production in which a society is mantled. Options diverge. Sometimes they favor *prophetic* urgency, and at others, they confirm the *politicization* of fact in order to correct it. By crossing one another and even inverting their positions, nevertheless they bear witness to the common situation as a function of which various doctrines and choices affront one another.

The "Marks"

UNDER the figure of collective *retreats* effected by prophetism, or with the series of *arrests* (or rectifications) that casuistry places everywhere along the trajectories of action, a single and same necessity is born—that of "marks," a word recurring infinitely in texts of the period. By "mark" we must understand an objective combination of a *practice* and a *sign*, a crossing point between the language of society and the enunciation of a faith—in sum, an effective way of surmounting the rupture between one and the other. The mark can be a miracle, a sanctuary, a priestly or charismatic personage, a devotion, a sacramental gesture, and so forth. In every manner of its appearance it focuses religious expression upon particular actions. Everything is concentrated on practices. A religious group experiences its cohesion through them. In them it finds its mooring and its differentiation in respect to other social units, whether religious or of other fabric. From them it gains the confidence that beliefs themselves provide less and less. Soon, apropos of Christians, Montesquieu will state that they "are no more firm in their unbelief than in their faith; they live in the ebb and flow that endlessly carries them from one to the other."[51] Humorous perhaps, lucid in any event, his remark indicates the difficulty that these Christians have in finding social landmarks for their faith; it helps us understand the decisive, and in certain respects the fetishistic, role that this or that religious practice will play in their lives.

Jansenists and Jesuits

THE choice between Christianities is effected in terms of practices. Opposition between the currents which are designated as "Jansenist" and "Jesuit" is quite revealing of the choices that had to be made. The battlefield is that of practical morality.[52] If the "spirituals" are cast aside— whose reactions all the way from Port-Royal to the Company of Jesus have more and more in common, despite the social barrier between the two "parties"[53]—there is a quite rapid reduction of Christian faith to practices, or at least an identification of faith with practices. But *the same practices are not in question:* this is the difference which orders doctrinal divergence. The Jansenists opt for practices of *worship;* they aim at emphasis on liturgical or sacramental observances, whose very importance requires greater spiritual preparation; they wrestle especially against social institutions which must threaten observances (from the cabaret to the court).

To the contrary, the Jesuits deliberately place themselves within the field of *civil* practices. As partisans of adaptation, as the principal legislators of "civility,"[54] of "honesty," of "stately duties," and soon—into the eighteenth century—even of "honor" or of a "legitimate self-respect" in Christian morality,[55] they try to proportion to these practices a *deviation* that in every instance is relative to a social task. Here we see the infinite work of casuistry, endlessly correcting the situations that it had first confirmed. In the long run, this task becomes increasingly difficult to fulfill. Choices have to be made: a growing incompatibility is uncovered between, on the one hand, an *ethics* founded on the effective law of "civil society" and, on the other, the *places* where Christian life is located, for lack of being able to correct the norms of social life—the practices of devotion (the Sacred Heart), secret associations (the Congregations of Gentlemen, for example), spiritual retreats, and so forth. A new form of sanctuary appears among the Jesuits themselves, when these signs become polarizers precisely because they are isolated from an ethics considered to be "atheistic" in nature.

Thus in the eighteenth century the Jansenists and Jesuits will meet again in the importance they grant to worship. Their contrary options become minute inside this sphere. To a *sacramental* polarization (with which comes a reinforcement of sacerdotal authority or of the severity of measures concerning misconduct in this respect) is opposed from now on a *devotional* polarization (which goes hand in hand with an overvaluation of the "spiritual guide" or of imperatives concerning the execution of actions and the literal fidelity to formulas).[56] It goes without saying that these two tendencies intersect and are often mixed together. They are also frequently encapsulated in a single term: *piety.* The real problem rather consists in relating *piety* and *morality,* which has become separated from the former and which is explicitly expressed in terms of social practices. The countless titles in which the binomial *piety and morality* appears betray the evidence of the rift through the very conjunction "and" that binds the combination.

Stately Duties

NONETHELESS the debates between the Jansenists and the Jesuits remain above all a "theater." The changes and tensions of a society are represented in antinomical figures.[57] Thus, like a tragedy, they impassion the learned world. But this dramatic staging refers to a more obscure force at work. One of the most striking indications of it is to be found in the role that the apology of "stately duties" begins to play in Christian morality. An entire religious literature is devoted to it, popular works generally, midway between works of literature and pamphlets hawked in the streets. In turn it circumscribes the "duties of the prince," as well as those of socialites, masters, soldiers, artisans, peasants, domestics, the "poor," even of spouses, fathers, widows, schoolboys, and so on.[58]

In this literature, the word "state"[59] arrives on the scene bearing a spiritual and theological tradition in which the term designates a habitual "disposition of the soul,"[60] a "degree" or an "order" of grace,[61] one of the stages or "paths" that are distinguished in a mystical or Christian itinerary, divided into three,[62] four,[63] five,[64] or more states. In the early seventeenth century, the analysis of the states of prayer or of the states of perfection acquires an importance that it had never before enjoyed: a scholasticism of the spiritual itinerary is substituted for that of beings or of ideas. It participates in the work of a society in transit, in the search for a new order. As Loyseau says, "state" is the "verbal name of the verb *to be*"; from this point on the word is attributed to *offices* "because their true nature is one of being a permanent quality inherent in the individual."[65] It refers the movements of praxis to stabilities. It posits the intermediary of a disposition between multiple activities and the unique *being* or *essence* of former philosophy.

Now it is symptomatic that the social order hereafter furnishes Christian morality and spirituality with the principle of their new organization, and that the ranking of socioprofessional "states" in a hierarchy slowly begins to play the role that was held until then by a ranking of ecclesial functions or of spiritual degrees.[66] The established order thus becomes the base for a redistribution of the old religious virtues: obedience is befitting to the domestic; justice, to the master, and so on. The social delimitation of a "situation" within a totality indicates the virtues that have to be cultivated. It has a categorical value. This delimitation also replaces with "state" what "being" represented in former metaphysics (*operatio sequitur esse*), that is, a foundation and an order of operations. Social organization thus becomes a sort of code basic to all practices; it is the place (the supremely philosophical place) of their stabilization and of their distribution. This evolution is also parallel to what, on a political level, reshapes churches to correspond with nations (with Anglicanism, Gallicanism, and soon Josephism, etc.) and makes nations at once the "patterns" and the inheritors of churches.

Access to Christian meaning appears to be linked here to the locus an individual occupies and to the function he exercises in society. Something still more decisive for the future is sketched out on a practical level in these apologies of "stately duties" (but unknowingly and without theoretical elaboration): the adjustment of *meaning* (whether Christian or not) to one's *social position*. What henceforth figures in the history of the West is an ethics expressed in terms of social divisions and ecconomic relations. This connection becomes a structure of modern and contemporary societies.

In relation to this determining of moral categories by means of a socioeconomic organization, "the practices of piety" are presented as an extra. With the first violent tremor they fall, without the essential being shaken—unless, for Christians driven to the brink of the alternative, they become everything that is left for them.

As for the ethics that will organize the meaning of existence around work, status, and therefore around social conflicts as well, here we find one of its points of emergence. This moment inaugurates two and a half centuries of identification between the social *duty* and the *meaning* of man, as by turns the "bourgeois," the liberal, the patriot, the socialist or scientist. Perhaps the "meaning of history" goes back to this combination. We have had to wait until the middle of the twentieth century, with its extension of leisure and socioeconomic rationalization, to see this alliance established at the end of the seventeenth century break down—so that social units no longer delimit beliefs, values, and virtues; and meanings, metamorphosed into questions, can move in the direction of one's liberation from work.

From Prophetism to Radicalism: The Practice of Division

IN the seventeeth century there also exists a polemic prophetism of deliberately marginal stripe. A "righteous" faith defends its ability to define the criteria of behavior proper to it. Port-Royal is the most famous case. But the "spiritual" resistances, the "sects," the pious "parties," the withdrawn "companies," the secret "associations," or the "little churches" abound everywhere, with an accompanying multiplication of hermitages or of occult groups such as the Rosicrucians.[67] Within this flowering of *ecclesiolae*[68] a common element wins over and crosses through all clerical differences, making all of these new retreats distinct from heresies or from former sects. Everywhere we witness a *practice of division* winning over a "gnosis." These isolationist formations (squeezed into little islands, or distended into parallel networks) are defined less by knowledge or by a type of initiation than by a practical way of resisting the surrounding milieu. Put another way, the noting of difference is of a moral more than of a theological order. Through these forms of behavior division is brought forth, but not essentially—as was the case in the twelfth or the thirteenth century—by way of conceptions or ideologies.

The act of differentiating oneself from the world leads to a proliferation of lines of application; this is ultimately what the doctrines speak of, more than it is a consequence of theory. The action wins over the content. It becomes the most *sure* sign of belief. It simultaneously posits and "expresses" belief as a mode of behavior. The "spiritual meaning" is hereafter linked to a language composed of practices, whereas in the Middle Ages it had moved within a cosmological universe of ideas and of words that were also things. The enunciation of a word now acquires the institutional form of a visible and social opposition to other kinds of conduct. It changes its nature when, instead of consisting of stating truths, it already falls under the regime of an operation of separation which now has an ethical value.

Furthermore, most of the "spirituals" individually manifest the same motion: just as their doctrine moves toward what Henri Bremond correctly called a "mystical moralism,"[69] the writing which they inaugurate is characterized by a *peculiar* treatment of *common* language. For the most lucid individuals among them there no longer exists any language other than that of the "world." The expression of spiritual experience consists in making that language play against itself; it effects a division within the social text rather than constituting an autonomous linguistic or ideological corpus. Because mystics cannot draw upon statements which would be specific to this experience, they express themselves through a particular style of practicing everyone's language, through a kind of intervention, a *modus loquendi*.[70] Here, as in all movements of this marginal type, the theological statement has the same status as other statements; it is the raw material that ways of acting or speaking—all that is truly relevant— are remodeling.

These minorities and "old believers" often defend themselves through a "return to origins" that is once again the principal symbolic indication of a new practice. In France, in England, even in Russia and elsewhere, they form pockets of irreducible believers. Camisards, Jansenists, "underground churches," Puritans, not to speak of the Raskol of Avvakum, and many others, are of this order. Despite all of their predecessors, it can be said that they invent the tradition of a "Christian radicalism."[71] Here faith is a practice, and its "work" is hereafter indissociable from a political opposition. It even aims at a political foundation, when exile becomes possible.[72] Along similar lines, the investment of religious conscience in a sociopolitical conduct or category is and will become more and more tellingly crucial.[73]

In their beginnings, the Jansenist, Camisard, Puritan, or even Raskol movements are distinguished by the frontier of a sacramental practice, by a form of assembly and prayer, by liturgical gestures, and so on. This social edge brings the value of a sign to the retreat from society, itself accompanied by (or taking the place of) a "spiritual" retreat outside of common language. Yet what provokes this retreat is precisely what changes the nature of its signs: the "world" that is left behind *socializes* these signs of rupture and therefore brings them back to itself. Acts of separation thus lose their religious meaning. They are understood and lived within "sanctuaries" otherwise than as they would be on the outside. They constitute an increasingly unintelligible message for those at whom they are aimed. The retreats of the Camisards, the Jansenists, the faithful members of Raskol are judged as political acts. And furthermore, this common interpretation flows back into these groups. The very individuals who posited religious signs begin to think and practice them as a sociopolitical resistance. To be sure, there are exceptions. Hence the Camisards are able to defend the meaning they ascribe to their actions against this ambient pressure. But this is due less to the fact that they rely on their international religious relations than by reason of a further retreat into the secret of an intimacy (of the family, the village, the monastic cell),[74] and thanks to its established symbol of the martyr, who is the public mark of a social elimination (in prophetic antisociety, the martyrdom of the witness corresponds to what in a traditional church would be the saint's virtue).

The effective and visible organization of society demonstrates that in most cases a transformation of meaning occurs even inside reformist and contentious practices. There appears to be a substitution of living creatures inside the same shell. Thus, between the Jansenism of Port-Royal and that of the eighteenth century, a mutation occurs.[75] Prophetic beginnings make room for a sociopolitical opposition; the same can also be observed earlier (between 1640 and 1644) within Puritanism.[76] The enunciation of meaning becomes a resistance to royal power or to ecclesiastical hierarchy (another form of power). This change has less to do with laxity or an abandonment of "primitive" conducts than with the internal inversion of their working. The surrounding interpretation modifies the religious substance of the same objective signs.

Hence traditional "heresy," a social form modeled on a theological truth, becomes less and less possible. The orthodoxy in terms of which this form was determined will now be more of a civil than religious nature. That is, just like action, heresy becomes socialized. Social heresy is born. Because of this transformation first of all marked in practices, a "prophetic" group will be progressively less able to avoid slipping toward either defense of a *civic* morality, an *occult* existence, or even an organization of *worship* that will soon become "folkloric" and foreign to what is truly at stake in a society.

PHILOSOPHICAL ETHICS: LEGALITY AND UTILITY IN THE EIGHTEENTH CENTURY

POLITICIZATION or folklorization of religious practices: at best these are the alternatives the situation announces, even if the evolution toward them is slowed by the upholding of religious contents carried with them or whose system they overtake or corrode. In this combination of two systems, the protection which royal power still accords to the institutions of the Church also plays an important role, because it simultaneously accelerates politicization and preserves Catholic representations. There is hence a great diversity of positions ranged along the course of the transformation taking place.

Nevertheless, from the seventeenth century onward, the most lucid minds perceive the weight of social use and public order on forms of religious conduct. For many of them an essentially Christian ethics no longer exists. When Pascal analyzes access to faith, the truth of which he speaks is no longer identified with either any particular behavior or any doctrinal statement. Within the present time, it is the vanishing point implied by entirely civic but contradictory realities; it is the intermediate space (the unspoken moment) to which social combinations of violence and order, of legitimacy and illegitimacy, of prejudices and reason, allude. Truth no longer has an assigned place in the world, unless it is the line that miracle traces over the martyrdom of saints: it is precisely a place-"off" and away. The analogies between the thought of Pascal and of Hobbes have been noted.[77] In fact, Pascal has an entirely political and "worldly" philosophy of society which his experience, his visits to Roannez and such, had taught him.[78] From this standpoint he is more modern and more perspicacious than his casuist adversaries. He runs far ahead of them when he inscribes the believer within a dialectic of "uses" and conflicts of power, and so forth. All the same he does not attempt to find a place for faith somewhere within language, but rather he brings it forth from contrary formalities of social practice.

Within the milieu of the Company of the Saint-Sacrament, the ambassador and intendent to the king, René d'Argenson, already avowed the autonomy of the social and political organization. He was a true mystic. He kept as the rules of his public life, however, only the faithful execution of the king's orders and the service of the populations that he administered. For him these rules had a moral value, without any need for justification or reference to religion. Less lucid than Pascal, he situated spiritual experience within the "particular" (in every sense of the term),[79] but this religious privatization belonged to a "mystical" order that was for him the evanescent double of the objective public order.[80] Destined to a play between the invisibility of its "order" and the marginal position of a few particular indications (the "works" of the Company of the Saint-Sacrament, the accomplishments of "pious duties," a few private devotions), the expression of Christian life was separated from civil practices.

One Grounding Principle of Its Folklore

THIS type of combination already outlines an organization which will become a general fact in the eighteenth century. We might also state that Enlightenment reflection exhumes its postulates and draws theoretical consequences from them. Clearly, it is no longer through aggressive forms that morality is politicized among the apologists of "state policy" under Richelieu. Its place nonetheless remains the same: a political policy made of interconnected practices. But it is no longer traced solely by jurists or the king's clients; it is built in the decisive years from 1660 to 1680. The state becomes the powerful center of national administration, the great enterprise of economic, financial, and statistical rationalization. It "almost entirely belongs to the area of the will, of what is deliberate": it is the arch of the new alliance between reason (*logos*) and *action* (the practices which produce history). The eighteenth century is "the century of politics *par excellence*, hence the century of the state."[81] Frederic II is the model of the eighteenth century just as Louis XIV had been that of the seventeenth.

This *reason* is bound to the *power* of organizing *practices*. It considers as distinct from itself, as the field of its conquests, the immense space of irrational "beliefs" and the inert extension of that Nature which is now offered up to those who will know its previously silent laws. Expressions not endowed with this operative capacity no longer merit the name of discourse, because they are broken off from "business." A *passive* sector of language flows in the direction of areas where opinions, ideologies, and superstitions will finally be reunited, ultimately forming a pocket isolated from politics and science (despite the frictions, two areas indissolubly united by the marriage of rationality and efficiency). From every outward sign, religious expressions are the most important element of this inert sector (while later this place will be filled by folklore and popular literature). Enlightened society of the eighteenth century tries to make them profitable, that is, to introduce them into its "order." It thus establishes as an object for politics or knowledge these expressions that it constitutes as *other* in respect to the rational organization of power or, in what amounts to the same thing, in respect to power acquired by virtue of the rationalization of practices. A rift is thus cut between reason and its "remainder"—or between the discourses of *action* and the more or less exploitable mass of *sayings* lacking "force," or what Machiavelli had already called, in discussing religious discourses, speech with *virtù*.[82]

All is intensified by another rift which is by no means identical: that which separates the popular masses from a noble and bourgeois elite. "The Great" are no longer only those who have the privilege of "reasoning" about business: in France, although they are more limited by nobility than in neighboring countries,[83] merchants, bankers, clerical workers, notables, and the like take part in this calculating and ambitious reason which makes of figures and writing the weapon of its conquests. The power to manage and to produce is the standpoint from which theoreticians speak. Pierre Chaunu has said, "The central affirmation of the Enlightenment is that of legality and intelligibility."[84] Yet who utters this affirmation? Where does it come from? From a bourgeoisie that authorizes for itself the power of being "civilization" by separating itself from a superstitious and still-savage population. From cities established as centers and points of departure for crusades to the "deserts" of the rural world; at this moment there occurs an urban swarm toward the country, and toward the East.[85] "Culture" is elaborated right where the power of *producing* history is built, and it is opposed to the social regions that it establishes within the inertia of a kind of "Nature"—originary, passive, and unfathomable.

Following this movement, religion, although it is still massively received, becomes divided. Precisely where it takes part in the practices of power, it confirms a reason that it no longer defines and which slowly inverts religion's own principles. From another point of view, religion is directed toward *nonoperative* languages and *popular* masses. Surely the Church itself had already prepared for this localization when for more than a century it worked in favor of a return to the people (popular missions, primary education, devotional literature, etc.), at the time when it was losing the ascending elite. The consequences were to be manifold. They cannot be reduced to social problems. In particular, because it was constructed in a direct relation with its other, the "savage," culture established a double language: that of an "enlightened" reason, avowable, productive, organizing an *axiomatic of social utility;* and that of beliefs, disavowed but always there, denied in the present but assuming the figure of an obscure origin, an "obscurantist" past of the systems which took their place.

This set of "fables" is an immense conglomeration of signs which returns to the people the support of the nation. It is an "unknown language" which bears within itself the secret which reason betrays. It is not only a space to be occupied so that "culture" may be planted in it; it also expresses—but in terms that cannot be received—the truth at which "philosophical" categories of "the common good," of "public utility," of universality, and so on aimed. It is the apologue of reality. This language to be decoded is the *follklore of an essential*. Thus, from the middle of the eighteenth century onward, a durable combination—quasi-structural for at least a century—is formed between a "popular" foundation to be deciphered, and a scientific rationality whose effective content is posed as exterior to itself. Reason has its own treasure hidden within the people and inscribed within history. Reason transforms it, while receiving it from what preceded reason. A popular flood rises, from which everything comes. Finally, in calling itself the most advanced part of this flood, enlightened science also admits that it is nothing more than its metaphor.

An anthropological literature attempts to designate, if not to exhume, this secret hidden within the obscure intimacy of common language. This literature forces the relation between *reason* and *fabulation* to vacillate. It goes along with a "distancing"[86] in respect to learned language, as if, in its success, the literature had been losing the presence of what it was designating, as if it had been instituting its own secret while constituting the indigenous object. The novel and the philosophical treatise demonstrate the play of masks by which an elite situates meaning *in the background*, in an illegibility, in a lost origin which is fable and music.

The Ambivalence of "Utility"

THE evolution which makes popular religion the object of an enlightened anthropology is presented first as a selection aiming to extract from beliefs and religious practices whatever is admissible in the name of a social reason. This operation had been taking place for a long time. One of its essential forms consisted of "isolating" an axiomatic from religion, just as physics proposed as its goal the isolation of "real" bodies from within received material.

As of 1624, Lord Herbert of Cherbury took as his principle that *virtue* is the essence of worship.[87] In 1678, Joseph Glanvil opposed to the historical dispersion of beliefs the necessity of extracting from them a few simple rules of common practice: "Religion consists not in knowing many things, but in practicing the few plain things that we know."[88] Before us is a work of translation whose goal is to transform religious language into social discourse. At stake is the establishment of a legality based on effective practices. The *critical* analysis of religion henceforth acquires the meaning of an *ethical* task. To explain religion and to discern the laws that make so many disparate religious formations comprehensible is a task of making explicit what can and must direct the choices of a society being constructed.

Montesquieu outlines the method of this hermeneutics (quite traditional for more than a century) when he writes: "All religions contain principles useful for a society."[89] This law has a scientific meaning and moral implication; it indicates how the elite wished to dispose of religions—to transform them into social *utility*. The birth of a normality invested within the multiplicity of observed facts allows rules of action to be clarified with respect to this society, which replaces the Church in its role of providing the space of meaning, the body of the absolute, and also a clergy of reason.

With increasing urbanization and commerce, a "merchant morality" is established, linked to the development of capitalism. Numerous moral treatises celebrate it.[90] They cannot be separated from the process that conveys this discourse: it was in the renewed rise of the bourgeoisie after the arrest that, during the second half of the seventeenth century, had marked what Pierre Chaunu has called the "reinforcement of aristocratic structures of a society based on order."[91] Even the imaginary dimension of spiritual literature speaks of bourgeois practices. The symbols or the comparisons that it uses are drawn no longer especially from natural elements (water, fire, etc.) as they had been in the sixteenth century, or from civil and technical life, as in the last third of the seventeenth century. Now they are taken from commerce.

The rule of the *utile* is imposed everywhere. Soon Hegel will characterize the truth of the *Aufklärung* in terms of utility (*Nützlichkeit*). As he writes in 1807, "Just as everything is of use to man, so then man is equally useful to man, and his destiny is equally that of making himself a member of the flock which is useful and of universal service to the community. . . . He uses others and is so used."[92] Insofar as beliefs and religious practices are concerned, we can therefore judge them according to the criterion adopted by Morelly; that is, according to what they "produce" among the populations:[93] either nefarious or beneficial, their social *effect* allows a distinction to be made between "superstitions" and "useful principles." This hermeneutics is furthermore able to explain the apparition of religious facts through general laws (climate, temperament, types of society). But it is still an operation, always marked by the principle from which its force is drawn. Reason, which organizes a society's practice upon itself, always takes for granted that its "essence" and its truth are buried within "vulgar" strata and hence are foreign to it. Whatever might be its successes, the method is relative to a foundation which remains extrinsic. It is *for others*—it assumes a civilizing and pedagogical form— just as this popular other is *for itself,* destined to join the enlightened bourgeoisie. Each of the two terms can find its truth only in its other.

The legality of the Enlightenment, a peculiar system within eighteenth-century France, implies an internal contradiction which makes it at once *precede* the masses that it dominates (but which remain foreign to it), and *wait for* the essence hidden within the people to be revealed in a "transparent" society—as Rousseau's great contemporary myth or the revolutionary experience would have it.[94] Education in particular, a crusade of the eighteenth century, is obsessed with the same insurmountable ambivalence. It colonizes, to be sure, but it is also an eschatological quest: it *awaits the coming* of the confirmation and the effectivity of what it already asserts. The illiterate populous, the child, the savage, and also the sick and the insane—enigmatic gods of a society that believes it has expelled them—hold within the folds of their language the proof of that reason which imposes its law upon them. The educational task will thus ceaselessly perfect its methods and expand the field of its progress in order to surmount the rupture that keeps reason outside of its own truth and forces it to depend on its adversary. Yet this rupture is a constitutive one. It could not be suppressed without obliterating the reason that had been defined through its establishment. In antithetical but homologous modes of domination or seduction, the rationality of the Enlightenment maintains a necessary relation with its other.

From the time when a tautological faith taking signs to be the presence of the truth they designate becomes impossible to conceive, "culture" seems destined to reiterate the law which urges it to multiply practices which are always relative to what it lacks. Henceforth, truth will no longer be given in signs. Reason has in its other, outside of itself, what makes it endlessly *produce:* economies of needs, scientific expansions, scholarly strategies, Jacobin democratizations, and civilizing colonizations are rooted in an elitist culture linked indissolubly with its contrary.

Christian Formalities of Philosophical Practices?

AN ethics cannot be based on its objects, since they signify for reason the exteriority of its truth. It authorizes its own postulates as its foundations. Between the Spinozist *conatus* and the Kantian "categorical imperative" at the two extreme ends of the century, many philosophies build the rationality of practice on a principle of action—on a will or a need to do which organizes the construction of reason. Whatever the form that this dynamic postulate may assume, it must be noted that its elucidation (*Aufklärung*) in every instance implies the double reference to the culture which "is fashioned" (that of the Enlightenment) and to the situation which is a "fact" (and still a religious one). The operation refers to its entrenchment within a will to know or a will to do, but also within a general conjuncture that conditions it. By distinguishing these two elements, we shall have, on the one hand, the experience which engenders a new philosophy of man, and on the other, the object of reinterpretation which transforms religion into a past.

In fact, the two enterprises cannot be separated so easily. An economic, political, or scientific *labor* allows a perspective to be taken with respect to religion, which establishes it in "another" place (which is going to be, for example, that of history or of ethnology). In its turn, such an assumption of distance in respect to religious contents works as if it had made possible a transposition upholding religious formalities, but according to a philosophical "regime." Thus is born a "civil religion," as Rousseau correctly puts it in the *Social Contract* (IV, 8). The exegesis which exiles the literality of religion into a past or into the area of the "vulgar" allows a new functioning of structures that had been characteristic of Christianity up until that time. Hereafter, these structures are disburdened of their ideological contents or practices, and can be reinterpreted—and also remain—within the language of "politics," "conscience," or "progress." The contents become the *object* of religious sciences which soar in this period,[95] while the "subject" of science is still organized along the lines of formalities belonging to the diverse historical types of modern Christian experience.

On this basis it is really inexact to persist in thinking of these formalities in religious terms, since they have precisely ceased to be such. In a certain way we might consider the time of their religious "filling" as a moment in the history of these cultural forms. In every study devoted to it since the eighteenth century, religion has always presented this ambiguity of its object: for example, its past is by turns explained through the very sociology it has nonetheless organized, and offered as the explanation for this sociology which has replaced it. More generally, every society born and issued forth from a religious matrix (are there any other kinds of society?) must affront the relation that it keeps with its archeology. This problem is inscribed within contemporary culture by dint of the fact that religious structures have been peeled away from religious contents in organizing rational forms of behavior. In this respect, the study of religion is tantamount to reflecting on what its contents have become in our societies (that is, "religious phenomena"), in the name of what its formalities have also become in our scientific practice.[96]

In any event, the eighteenth century offers this transport of religious structures into philosophical discourses. This is the reciprocal of the process that, as we have observed, makes religious manifestations work according to political formalities. In other words, it seems that "enlightened" practice is organized along the lines of formalities which *were* of religious nature before being taken up as postulates of a morality. What it produces still obeys the principles of what it replaces. The pattern is the same for the three great stages of ethics which can be designated by the privileged reference: politics, conscience, progress. These moments refer to historical experiences of Christianity and bear the mark of religious forms whose very archeology they establish, whether it be an ecclesiology, a spirituality or pietism, or a messianism of a people elected by God for a universal mission.

First of all, a dominant *political* ethics is born of the enormous effort that allowed the eighteenth century to create nations and pass from Christianity to modern Europe.[97] It accredits the state with the role that until this time the Church had claimed, that of being the social mediation of common salvation—the sacrament of the absolute. This is a Catholic ecclesiology, but it is transferred to the state, which sets hierarchies among social orders, initiates liturgies for its power, distributes graces, and rationalizes individual interests. In theory, universal discourse is still political when it replaces its royal symbol with the austere law of the common good and maximum development. The imperative of state policy orders at once the criticism of Christian prohibitions and new prescriptions. For example, in the thought of Morelly,[98] of Diderot,[99] and of many others, sexual liberty has as its goal and criterion production: not love, but demographic growth which, in the populationist perspective of the economists of the time, produces a nation's strength and wealth.

A *will to make the state* founds the rationalization of practices; here we might compare these new eighteenth-century theologians with those whose missionary will to "establish the church" was invested in reorganizing, normalizing, and spreading Christian behavior. "We need missionaries of reason in Europe," said Leibniz in 1709. But this "mission" of the Enlightenment is deployed on another level. It follows other crusades. Combining the key notions of the century, it connects scientific laws with energies that, in an immanent dynamic, must be placed in the service of a public utility in view of a collective creation.

Recourse to *conscience* originates more within economic liberalism and within a "bourgeois individualism." But it is the locus that reformed churches had circumscribed, that which "speech"—impossible to introduce into discourse—had marked and left void.[100] Following the reference to ecclesiological Christianity comes the experience of "Christians without a church," those who challenge the mediations of the ecclesiastic body or language henceforth localized within a political order.[101] In every case, nearest to this ethic is a spiritual tradition: the Quakers' "light within"; the truth which speaks at the bottom of the "heart" in Wesley, in the Northern revivals, or in the mystical *Aufklärung* of the European East (Swedenborg, Franke, etc.). At the eastern extremity of Western Europe, at the end of the century, Kant becomes the great religious witness to the moral conscience to which scientific knowledge refers. But unlike most spiritualities, this conscience is not a gnosis, that is, another knowledge (in the way that for Mesmer magnetism becomes a common ground for mysticism and science). To take up a category dear to Emmanuel Levinas, "subjectivity" remains here as an irreducible and as a condition of possibility in respect to political or scientific legality.

For Rousseau, "the immediate principle of conscience, independent of reason itself,"[102] is a "moral instinct," also called a "divine instinct" and thought of as a "natural instinct." He makes of religious practice—and not of belief[103]—the path by which "self-love" is accomplished in happiness,[104] if one however "retreats into oneself": there the "natural goodness" of men survives, which sociability alters, for "evil is exterior and it is the passion for the exterior."[105] In all of this how can we fail to recognize the organization of a spirituality? But through recourse to the power that man has "to change himself" and to fabricate his happiness, Rousseau erases original sin (but is that not what can be found in modern mystics?), while it is the sore point of theologies of grace in the seventeenth and eighteenth centuries. The formality of religious practice therefore slides onto another terrain. As Lefranc de Pompignan had stated so rightly to him, Rousseau "rationalizes over virtue in the way of pagan philosophers, who did not believe that it had to be asked of God."[106] But he comes from Christianity. Spirituality is transformed into the morality of an autogenesis—a typical case of a form upheld, but within a regime that emptied it of its original meaning.

The metamorphosis of Christianity into ethics and, more broadly, into culture can be located ultimately under the sign of *progress*. To be sure, the appearance of this problematic issue, essential to all of the latter period of the eighteenth century, emerges from difficulties and experiences that had just preceded it. Thus the impossibility of having *social* reality gain a structural coherence or of identifying language with a logic leads to envisaging reason as a story of progress; that is, to categorizing observed phenomena along the line of a development of reason. Dates become a means of recovering an order, since exceptions can be ranked among resistances and former prejudices. Moreover, the role that the "milieu" plays for individuals is envisioned from the perspective of a production. "Custom" is not only a fact, but also a tool: a society acquires through it the power of endlessly "perfecting" itself, of acting on itself, of changing its nature, of constructing itself. From custom we pass to education: toward the end of the century this "myth" confers upon civilization the form of a conquest binding reason to the ability to transform man through the diffusion of the Enlightenment,[107] and coloring all action that works toward progress with a moral value.

Messianism, evangelism, crusade: these Christian structures can be recognized in the enterprise which associates the Enlightenment with their predication, this civilizing mission with the power of changing nature, and the task of converting the meaning of being and of doing with the truth of history. Hegel will be the theologian of this future of the Spirit. But this new evangelism inverts the principle of a Providence which is made manifest in the conversion of man. It is a mission, but it belongs to an elite that receives its privilege and power from itself, that no longer derives them from the heavens above.

Paradoxically, the Enlightenment must become a risk and a task; it must lose the assurance of a past revelation, and it must depend upon what the labor of culture already shows and what it promises with regard to it—in sum, reason must be bound to the exteriority of its future if a function of Christianity is to be revealed in its purity. Detached from the certitude which controlled it in its founding, the evangelical and missionary mechanism is exacerbated. It becomes for itself its own essence. It is now measured only by the limits that it meets, and not by the truth that it bears. *De-Christianization reveals in its formality the Christian practice,* but hereafter that practice is thrown out of the orbit of the *Logos* which had verified it. In this way, too, De-Christianization is an elucidation—an *Aufklärung*. It "betrays" Christianity in both senses of the term: it abandons it, and it unveils it. A social reinterpretation of Christianity is thus inaugurated, which will flow back over Christian milieus: in them it will develop missionary practices turned toward the "other" as toward the future witnesses of an uncertain inner truth; in them it will later provoke the reproduction of the ethics of progress in the form of a theology of history, and so forth.

Whatever the case may be for future embodiments belonging to the churches, the elitist society that extracts a functioning of Christian practices from religious beliefs, that for a period of time takes its ethics to be the infinite progress of its rationalized practices, will find a hidden god once more in the French Revolution. The "savage" or the "commonfolk" were only a foreshadowing of it. This new god will be *the people*, revealed in the revolutionary event which heralds their power; present as an origin; time and again a control and an object for the intelligentsia in the course of a slow democratization; finally held to be the truth of history—a truth that had always been there, but without words, *in-fans*. Feuerbach describes quite exactly what took place: "In the sphere of religious practice, man replaced the Christian"[108]—but this was a cloven man, always divided in two by the distinction which separates the ministers of history from the population to be evangelized, or a bourgeois clergy from the "masses."

LAWS BELONGING TO THE RELIGIOUS GROUP: REDUCTION TO SILENCE AND ADMINISTRATION OF WORSHIP

INSOFAR as the practical organization of Christianity is "socialized" in being stripped of beliefs, what is left for Christian groups? Some ideological contents—a discourse; and some specific practices—a worship. At least that is what may be observed in the ecclesiastical milieu. But among believers the Christian group is still a clerical group. It is found precisely in the area where the displacement occurs that has just been indicated. In order to defend itself through saving believers, the clergy therefore concentrates on a language and on rites considered as objectively Christian signs left by the exile of the practical structures of Christianity. Were the process to be schematized before being nuanced, it could be said that this fixation will simultaneously engender silence in the matter of effective convictions, and behavior like that of civil servants in issues concerning the "administration" of rites. What is experienced in faith can no longer be said in a language that is hereafter focused on a defensive operation and transformed into the verbal ramparts of a silent citadel. For lack of adjustment to social practices, practices of worship also lose their symbolic strength. Analyses of the eighteenth-century clergy all show this obfuscation of living meaning under the proliferation of administrative measures aimed at protecting or spreading patented discourse and deeds.

The clerics were not the only believers, however, even though the charge of representing the church fell more and more to them for over a century. In addition to this clerical "sanctuary"—a reduction and a miniaturization of the Church on the priestly stage—we have the Christian crowds. Can we be sure that in these masses there is a dichotomy between beliefs and civil or scientific techniques, when this rupture is engendered by the ability to produce, and is characteristic of the social category which has the power of rationalizing practices? The category which, likewise, having become apt in *producing* culture, leaves in the margins of its activity those representations associated with a received world and with given truths? Can we suppose that the French populations are entirely modeled by what an elite would like them to be?

Two Practices of Language

RESEARCHES on "popular literature" or on religious iconography do not allow us to take this alignment for granted. It is true that in fact they bear upon the fabricators of these almanacs, pamphlets, or "popular" images (that is, upon clerics or artists specializing in this genre, and not upon their readers).[109] In addition, such works have much to do with a particularly conservative expression where cultural themes and structures, often upheld despite the ambient evolution, are not really good tests of change.

According to these studies, the devotion for souls in purgatory, for example, continues to be diffused within the iconography of Provençal churches in the eighteenth century. Here we observe, however, that "Purgatory softens": the image illustrates God's judgment less than the deliverance of souls.[110] The idea of happiness thus imposes itself here, as everywhere else in the course of the Enlightenment.[111] But, conforming as it does to many others—see the last pages of this chapter and note 142 concerning popular almanacs and the *Bibliothèque Bleue*—such an indication opens a much broader question, at least to the degree that it shows that the idea of happiness is folded *into* traditional collective symbols which it alters from within, but without occasioning any kind of expression that would be its own. Here we witness a perversion internal to language, but not the creation of a new formality. We are nearer to medieval heresy than to modern ethical or scientific discourse: a change is formulated in the very terms and modality of an established corpus; it does not recast collective symbols; it does not impose a different organization upon them. The turbulence of a group is inscribed within this repertoire, but it does not call the repertoire into question. It merely traces variants relative to a stable structure. We remain on the level of expression. What "happens" springs up and is *expressed in the language* without a *language having to be made* in order to "produce" events (which is the property of scientific discourse since the time of the Enlightenment). The displacements of mentality are marked solely within received representations. Here practices are not the very place where an ordering reason is elaborated, a reason which through its own genesis relegates collective symbols to the role—now *become* "ideological"—of adjacent or historical remnants.

In this case, discourses (verbal, iconic, and gestural) *do not have the same function, and therefore do not have the same meaning* when they are contiguous and even foreign to techniques of social or professional work, as when they organize these techniques and in the hands of a social group become a tool for production. Seen from one perspective, discourse is operative: in science or in the culture of the Enlightenment, theory interconnects practices. We have "writing" in the modern sense of the term, when the *cipher* aims at an *operation*.[112] Seen from another, where practices are not interconnected in a rational field through an order of doing, discourse establishes a symbolic space where existential differences can be traced. Here the *symbol* allows for an *expression*.[113]

Since the uses of language are not always the same, can we deal with every language according to identical procedures, namely ours, which are historical or sociological, and which are inscribed within the line of the cipher? Of what can our interpretive methods take account when they are applied to "expressions" which function in ways other than our "productions"? This is a fundamental question in the history of mentalities or in cultural sociology. In the eighteenth century a work of dissuasion is effected between two cultures. One, which is elitist and learned or "bourgeois," is distinguished from the other, which is "traditional" and which is both the object and the term of the action of the former. The combination leads us to demarcate from this point a culture of practioners and of science versus a *theatrical* and consequently medieval culture.[114] How can one account for the other? To these two functionings of language must correspond two different interpretations, since in reality, the signs are not emitted in the same way in one case as in the other, even if they are saying the same thing. Statements play over heterogenous modes of enunciation. Here there are two overlapping but different systems whose heteronomy no model could either explain or overcome, since the model would refer to a place of enunciation and a practice of language that belongs to only one of these systems.

The interpretation of this difference in terms of an opposition between "the elite" and "the masses" runs the risk of being misleading if it does not make explicit the fact that the rupture which the Enlightenment produces indeed changes the nature of this elite/masses division. To recognize this caesura is tantamount to admitting that, having functioned in different ways, the distinction elite/masses cannot be generalized without ambiguity; it is therefore not a good instrument of analysis. To be sure, generally speaking there have always been elite groups and masses. But in the Middle Ages the intellectual elite represents a superior status within a hierarchy of beings. The cleric has the power of *stating the order* of the universe, which he allows and causes to appear through his knowledge, while thus justifying his place within the same world.[115] The elite group of the eighteenth century, however, is not based on the fact of a difference posited by the ordering of the cosmos, but on a practice of rupture, on a *differentiation* that it *effects*. For the elite this action consists in distinguishing itself from the masses by its ability to "produce"; it transposes the separation through which the Judeo-Christian God established himself as the creator.[116] This bourgeoisie-god *makes* the world (its *reason* is the capacity to "produce"), and, in the same movement, it dissociates itself from the masses or the "common" class which in myth or symbol *receives* the world as a meaning.

"De-Christianization"—it would be better to speak of a deterioration of the religious universe (Christian faith is still compatible with this disappearance)—is, for the enlightened elite, the reciprocal of its self-genesis. But this is specific to this particular elite. The eighteenth century is the moment when two practices of language coexist, compensate for each other, and are mutually altered without our being able to reduce one to the other. And we cannot suppose valid for both of them the analytical methods born precisely of the discourse that rationally organizes practices, that is already, in the form of so many *Critical Examinations*,[117] capable of interpreting popular or religious representations as "productions" (of climate, social mechanics, etc.).[118] Now what happens in each practice from the fact of this new coexistence and the reciprocal reorganizations which are caused by it?

Writing and Orality

THE problem appears, for instance, in the form of a new relation between writing and speech. Popular culture, which comes to be defined by its opposite, is oral; but orality becomes something else from the moment when writing is no longer a symbol, but rather a cipher and the instrument of a "production of history" in the hands of a particular social category. Everyone is aware of the confidence that the eighteenth century and the French Revolution had in the book: writing was to refashion society in the same way that it had indicated the power that the enlightened bourgeoisie was ascribing for itself. But on the very interior of this enlightened culture, orality changes its status to the degree that writing *becomes* the interconnection and communication of works through which a society constructs its progress. Orality is displaced, as if excluded from writing. It is isolated, lost, and found again in a "voice" which is that of nature, of the woman, of childhood, of the people. It is pronunciation apart from the technical logic of consonants-ciphers. It is "speech," foreign but relative to the "artificial" language of written combinations. It is music, the language of the indicible and of passion; song and opera, a space where the organizing power of reason is effaced, but where the "energy of expression" deploys its variations within the framework of fiction and speaks of the indeterminate or of the depths of the self.[119] Hardly by chance, the age of the Enlightenment is at once the reign of normalizing writing and the "empire of music."[120] It appears that in the culture born of Gutenberg, former speech is partitioned between a *writing* fab-

ricating objects and the *song* of a passion without content, of an origin
outside the text, or of an infinity of desire which flees and fascinates all
writers at the turn of the century. A music is established in relation to
the triumphs of reason. It is voice separated from contents hereafter in-
strumentalized; it is localized elsewhere, in areas where it evanesces and
disappears from Enlightenment discourse.

We can hardly be surprised to realize that religion and popular culture
are also manifested as voice. Speech, which since the Reformation had
already been dissociated from rational discourse, is directed toward music
through spiritual experience; writes Hasso Jaeger, "A Paul Gerhardt and
a Johann Sebastian Bach are those marking the zenith of Lutheran mysticism."[121] The results of the anti-intellectualism to which mysticism is
driven by the new intelligentsia are music, the poem, the cantata—with
the slight exception that in the eighteenth century, with the Catholic tradition holding more tenaciously to social discourse, musical, poetic, and
oratorial mysticism flees toward the Protestant East of Europe, or everywhere changes into esotericism and occultism.[122] More broadly, an entire
aspect of religion flows back toward popular hymn, toward religious festival, toward the inner life of the family, forming the counterpoint of the
other aspect which we shall meet—official and superficial, organizing
and administrative, but ultimately alienated through its immense work of
clerical governance. Before underlining the dangers of a localization within
what pertains to worship, we must understand the social constraints inspiring it, and their meaning. The movement that brings religiosity back
to a kind of "history without words" identifies it with a festivity incapable
of being based upon a scientific discourse (the inverse of what took place
in the relation between liturgy and former dogmatics). In the philosophy
of the Enlightenment, religion is placed in this "vulgar" stratum which
retains a voice, but one which is superstitious, deprived of reason, and
foreign to the knowledge already possessed by the enlightened milieus.
In relation to the elite which defines itself by writing and which circumscribes "civilization" within what comprises writing—productions extending from science to language itself, identified with the "good usage"
of "authors"—*a secret pact is formed with orality*. A remnant of the festival,
a concert of voices, a silence of meaning in the plenitude of sound, a
popular background, orality is offered to elitist knowledge, which edu-
cates it just as orality exploits the secrets or the savageries of the New
World.[123]

Is this an indication that a culture loses its speech as it founds writing?

It is always the case that something happens in the sphere of orality. But what can we say of it, now that with historiography we are settled into written science? To be able to speak of it, it is not sufficient that from the end of the eighteenth century history plays the role of maintaining the relation of reason with the larger totality that it cannot contain—of being the bigamous discourse in which knowledge is simultaneously married to the science which *produces* history (see chapter 1), and to the novel, the "extenuation of myth"[124] that allows the "spirit of the time," the *Zeitgeist*, to be *expressed*.

A World Between: The Priests

IF we come back from the zones outside of historiography and return to what emerges in documents of the eighteenth century, we can observe within the interior of Christianity a cleavage analogous to what divides society between learned writing and popular orality. What we apprehend is not really the rupture, since that is not something that can be analyzed from a standpoint outside of the division scientific observation created; we apprehend instead its effects and its aftereffects within the area where a Christian reason develops according to the model that the ethics and the philosophy of Enlightenment imposes upon it. Here a considerable amount of organization is effected, but it is governed by social "utility"—as in the other sectors of the enlightened clergy—and is characterized by the rarefaction of speech or the silence of Christian expression; these clerics appear to lose speech to the very extent that they are producing a Church. No longer can they *speak*, and furthermore, no longer do they really *have anything to say*,[125] essentially because the reason with which they are aligned as a minority within the enlightened bourgeoisie directs their activity toward production, even while they still charge this utilitarianism to the account of received Christian "truths."

At the level of its social function, the eighteenth-century Church is influenced by two processes that reinforce each other. On the one hand, because of its marginalization (still relative) in a society in which Christianity is no longer a totalizing frame of reference, the priest becomes the agent by which the Church is differentiated from other groups. The practice and theory of Christianity are mobilized on this frontier of the sacred. Since the end of the seventeenth century, the Church has been reduced and miniaturized into its clergy (see chapter 3). Even if many

of the laity are believers, it is in terms of the priesthood, as a social visibility of difference, that the problems of the Christian life are formulated.

But on the other hand, the center of this new system of defense or
mission is specifically defined by *clerics* who have little to do with the new
culture. They had been converted into men dedicated to writing through
work that for over a century was devoted to reform and to the formation
of the clergy, the first goal of the post-Tridentine Church. Seminaries,
ecclesiastical conferences, synodal statutes, or pastoral visitations aimed
first at educating clerics and normalizing an administrative personnel. This
great campaign put the priests in an increasingly difficult situation. For
if its explicit end was to defend or diffuse religious beliefs, it provided
as means a technical administration whose logic was contrary to the end
it had been intended for. The *organization of practices was stronger than
the system of representations* whose circulation and upkeep it maintained.
As we have seen, this is evident in the process that substitutes the primacy
of practices for that of beliefs. Furthermore, *Christian discourse became the
object and the means of a production*—that which built a religious social
body. Far from having the true Word articulate practices and provide
them with a frame of reference, it was transformed into a means in an
axiomatic of the "production of society." It became rarefied as speech,
frozen into an established discourse which, to be sure, did not make explicit the operation whose object it was (in this respect it is inert and
foreign to the ethical discourse of the Enlightenment), but which functioned according to the "practical reason" belonging to the entire contemporary intelligentsia (and the clerics were certainly part of it).

Whence the particularly distended position that these priests occupied.
Placed in the world between what the Church and the society were separately becoming, and living this contradiction in a place binding them
to the producers of society (that is, to the educators), but in the name
of representations that they were obliged to uphold but which allowed
no means of reflecting upon what they were really doing, these priests
were more and more dedicated to administrative *tasks* as well as to *silence*
in matters concerning the meaning of their faith. The solution to this
dilemma consisted in concentrating the exercise of organizational powers
upon the objective sector that was supposed to represent the conservation
of Christian fidelity; in other words, upon the conservation of the "religious practices" of established discourse: worship and ideology.

The Clerical Hermeneutic

NONETHELESS, a common trait marks the clerical elite: a retreat to the language of Scripture. It is inspired more and more by a nostalgia for origins. The work that brought the history of Christianity back to its beginnings through exegesis,[126] or which tried to tear morality away from probabilistic casuistry and found a "purer" rigor upon a return to the Gospels,[127] orchestrates the exclamation of one of the most lucid priests of the time, Monseigneur Jean Soanen: "O great days of Christianity, when will you return?"[128] But in fact this work made a selection among ancient texts; to the "superstitions" or to the "sensibility" of men "different," "more simple" and "more ignorant than we,"[129] it referred everything which had fallen under disbelief in the eighteenth century, extracting a content conforming to the Enlightenment. Such a hermeneutic strategy produced an object according to operative rules no longer dependent upon religious convictions (even if their practice was still under the influence of ecclesiastical pressures), rules which determined the results obtained more surely than the "motives" or "intentions" invested in the work. The logic of the techniques employed prevailed over the spirit that they were supposed to defend. Among the Protestants, we witness in addition to this scientific exegesis a resurgence of a "spiritual" interpretation that had been left aside since the days of the Reformation:[130] an edifying, pietistic, popular reading. So the Bible becomes an allegory covering over heterogenous religious practices; it is the symbolic space where individual experiences find what they need for expression.

Pious exegesis was also present in Catholicism, where it was equally marginal in respect to approved science. But there it was more suspect, since it escaped the ecclesial institution. Clerical concerns were expressed through the multiplication of directions and "methods" of reading: the "proper use" of Scripture won over its truth.[131] What prevailed once more was a Catholic *practice* of the Bible organized through the pastors whom Fénelon already called "living Scriptures"—a phrase with which the eighteenth century would designate the scribes and technicians of religious practices. When operating on the terrain of ecclesiastical institutions, Catholic pastors brought about a selection among practices analogous to what learned exegesis performed through texts: popular "superstitions" were chased away, sent back to an inadmissible past in

order to avoid "discredit to religion."[132] The hermeneutics of practices
and that of texts followed the same principles.

In effect, these men were first of all *clerics*. As a group, they distanced
themselves from popular culture by tolerating or ignoring what they could
not impede. Rupture was aggravated from about 1750. Contact between
pastors and populations diminished; the clergy made a retreat to a discourse constructed in the seventeenth century as "reformist" but which
became the formal means of priestly regrouping; there occurred an almost
total disappearance of pastoral visits. Among many others, these facts simultaneously attest to the attraction offered by the Enlightenment intelligentsia (born of a rift in respect to the "vulgar"), and the paralysis that
followed from the impossibility of introducing into religious discourse
(frozen in the spot where the Church had to be defended by its Levites)
the epistemological revolution that provided the force of this intelligentsia. To be sure, a slow mutation changed these priests, but it always
remained secret or marginal. Meslier is an extreme—but not an
exceptional—case when he defers the statement of his true thought until
after his death.[133] The content of discourse and the speech act are posited
outside of one another, each foreign to the other, as are the text and its
author: where there is enunciation, the statement lies; when it speaks the
truth, no longer can there be enunciation. Speech is dissociated into a
voice lacking truth and a *writing* lacking voice—a structure which combines, as it pushes them to their limit, the positions of the vulgar and of
the enlightened.

Such an occult transformation does not appear in official texts or acts,
and it does not burst forth publicly until the time of the Revolution,
when so many priests played a decisive role in the national revelation that
referred so specifically to their particular situation. In the preceding time,
cornered between popular religiosity and the enlightened bourgeoisie, they
could only manage their ideological discourse and organize religious
practices by applying the ethics of the Enlightenment to the masses in
matters of education.

A Governance of Language and Religion

IN the eighteenth century the French word *police* designates both the
culture (one is *policé* if civilized) and the order that it takes for granted.
It cannot be dissociated from education. Within strictly ecclesiastical institutions, culture involves participation in a civil philosophy whose prin-

ciples originate elsewhere. Thus this culture occupies little space in ministerial activity. It is therefore the establishment of an order that carries the day in both discourse and worship.

Insofar as *language* is concerned, investigation that deals with masses of official clerical discourse tells us how the clerics became the functionaries of a *religious ideology*. What had been the dynamics of a reform in the seventeenth century changes in the eighteenth into an extremely precise administrative apparatus fully devoted to managing the principles or, in other words, to defending the language of a given group. This apparatus can be considered when we analyze the impressive series of archives put together by the "Ecclesiastical Conferences" and the assemblies of itinerant vicars, sacerdotal reunions organized by district every month or every two months, and always devoted to three subjects: "The Explication of Scripture," "Ecclesiastical Virtues," and "Practical" or "Moral Theology".

The erudition of the priests had replaced their former ignorance. But it was itself stifled under the repetition of books or responses imposed by authority in the form of "duties," and "corrected" by vicars-general. This discourse was uniform and without internal contradictions; it was ruled by quotation, impermeable to personal experience, and docile to the group's "neuter" elements. It ordered promotion to church offices (the priesthood is a "career just like any other"),[134] and was no longer made up of references to real local life. Whatever had to do with sexuality or violence in the country was repressed in order to be replaced by the abstract "cases" exposed in received books.[135] The same observation can be made about pastoral rulings or priestly literature. The task of organizing a group gave birth to this administrative language, which was no more permeable to the real existence of priests than to that of their congregations. The formation of a productive practice robbed discourse of its power to express reality. The revolutionary explosion was needed before any expression of spiritual experience could erupt (as in Grou, Clorivière, etc.), and both the latent theism shrouded under clerical language and the religious insignificance masked by the continuity of traditional customs could at the same time be unveiled.

In everyday practice, *worship* is the major preoccupation. In this respect records of pastoral visits make especially helpful documents in revealing —from parish to parish—the reactions of the congregations, of the vicars, and of the bishops. Observance and purification of worship were the essential preoccupations of the local directors who were, moreover, mobilized on two fronts: they struggled against exterior rivalries (in the first place, against the innkeeper, the "anti-vicar") and the elimination of "indecencies" on the inside (and first of all former popular traditions that peopled the church with therapeutic saints, familiar and professional images, and noisy festivities). An "iconographical repression" excluded nudity, animals, representations which did not conform to "historical truth"—in a word, everything prompting "derision"; that is, what might not conform to the taste of the intelligentsia which was a model for these clerics.[136] That this cultural criterion had importance in moral judgments is shown by the opinions which the vicars had of their congregations, since the "vulgarity" of manners was more often criticized than "sin."[137]

At stake was a governance of practices. In addition to what authority upheld in religion from its standpoint, it was a limited but necessary instrument of worship. In Delamare's great *Traité de la Police* (1705), after a first book of generalities he devotes an entire second book to religion, "the first and principal object of governance." This was done only in order to take up two subjects: on the one hand, the treatment of non-Catholics, and on the other, the respect for worship (festivals, time of penitence, processions, pilgrimages, etc.).[138] Here we have one indication among many others of a "saintly alliance" (as Holbach would say),[139] but even more of a homology in the order of practices, even when they were conveying different truths. A single logic localizes sin right where an obstacle or a deviation appears in respect to a governance of mores. Nonetheless, the ecclesiastical administration obviously constituted a body of its own, and it "marked" this specificity with prohibitions—limits or extra requirements—aimed at rectifying common normality along its borders.[140] In the same fashion it kept up some "magnificent objects" of thought—"astonishing spectacles" and "inestimable treasures"—that it "let the people behold."[141] Therefore we find particularities in Christian action—essentially in practices of worship—and a theatricalization of representations. But they were inscribed within a civil economy. What this administration itself accomplished, when it organized spectacles or a discipline for the people, indeed obeys the laws of an "enlightened" reason, or the formality of practices as they were defined by the Age of Enlightenment.

What happened to these popular masses which embodied "voice" within elitist culture, that voice which it was losing while fabricating writing? What became of these oral traditions that scientific analysis placed outside of its concerns, and eliminated in order to establish itself? They escaped ecclesiastical authority, even if they accepted religious symbols and rites. No doubt they allegorized (but up to what point?) these signs and gestures, just as individual pietistic experience allegorized Scripture. To us these practical displacements of interpretation on the surface of fixed texts still remain unknown, simply because they were not written. Surely, no matter how fragile it may be, the popular literature of almanacs can furnish us with some indications: it replaced ecclesiastical "lies" with the sureness of household techniques; the fear of Last Judgment after death with therapeutic recipes drawn from an ancestral experience and with methods of "good behavior" or *savoir-vivre*.[142] Is this the vulgarization of the spirit of the Enlightenment by authors who are "educators," or is it a proof of popular practices that find a language for their expression in the margins of the religious tradition? Probably both. Yet in order to specify the second aspect, what in the nineteenth century will be repressed by obligatory education and developed by democratization, we would need to look to the language of gestures and utensils, to those discourses called "tacit" which were only made audible in the course of revolts or revolutions with scythes, pitch-forks, hoes, and the like. We would have to take very seriously the *formality of practices other than writing*.[143] Perhaps this reflection would lead us to recover within language its function of speech.

In any event, a break has henceforth "un-done" the organizing myths of behavior, giving way to, on the one hand, a "rationale of practice"—a type of science—and, on the other, to "representations"—ideologies or beliefs. A new historiography will be born when a rationality of "revolutionary" tasks will have ordered beliefs amidst "ancient" fables. From then on the very comprehension of former periods will meet representations as an effect or a remnant in respect to what, from the past, has *become* homogenous with the present; that is, with an economic or political science of social operations.

NOTES

1. Jacques Berque recently recalled this in his "Logiques plurales du progrès," *Diogènes* (1972), no. 79, pp. 3–26, by analyzing the developments, uneven but compensated, of distinct "dimensions" (morphological, technological, esthetic, sacred) within a society.

2. The notion of "what can be believed" calls into question both the frames

of reference and the bases upon which a society situates its possibilities of thinking. See "Les Révolutions du croyable," in my *Culture au pluriel* (Paris: Union Générale d'Editions, 1980), pp. 11–34.

3. Which is to say that we cannot identify *mental* systems with *social* levels. These are two types of classification that often cross but that cannot be reduced to each other.

4. "In the course of the fifty years from 1700 to 1750, religion and morality finish off the transformation through which they took man to be the center in the place of God," writes Roger Mercier in *La Réhabilitation de la nature humaine, 1700–1750* (Villemomble: Editions de la Balance, 1960), p. 441.

5. See especially John T. Noonan's *The Scholastic Analysis of Usury* (Cambridge: Harvard University Press, 1957) and *Contraception: A History of Its Treatment by the Catholic Theologians and Canonists* (Cambridge: Harvard University Press, 1965).

6. See Lucien Febvre, "Prises de la religion sur la vie," in *Le Problème de l'incroyance au XVIe siècle* (Paris: Albin Michel, 1968), pp. 307–23; available in English as "Religion's Domination of Life," in *The Problem of Unbelief in the Sixteenth Century* (Cambridge: Harvard University Press, 1982), pp. 335–53.

7. A draft of a letter quoted in Pierre-Maurice Masson, *La Religion de Jean-Jacques Rousseau*, 2 vols. (Paris: Hachette, 1916): "We do not have the same faith," Jean-Jacques added; "at least we have the same morality" (2:48). Morality furnishes universal principles, while dogmas and beliefs belong to the domain of particularity.

8. Jean-Jacques Rousseau, in *Encyclopédie, ou Dictionnaire raisonné des sciences, des arts, et des métiers*, new ed. (Geneva, 1778), article on "Foi," 17:1019.

9. Joseph Lortz, *La Réforme de Luther* (Paris: Cerf, 1970), 1:22.

10. See Alphonse Dupront, "Réflexions sur l'hérésie moderne," in Jacques Le Goff, ed., *Hérésies et sociétés* (The Hague: Mouton, 1968), pp. 291-300, apropos of the new phenomenon called "heresy in the public arena."

11. See Richard H. Popkin, *The History of Scepticism from Erasmus to Descartes*, rev. ed. (Berkeley and Los Angeles: University of California Press, 1979), and numerous articles by the same author on this topic.

12. Blaise Pascal, *Pensées* (Paris: Gallimard-Pléiade, 1954), Brunschvicg fragment 693, p. 1191.

13. Nicolas de Malebranche, *Entretiens sur la métaphysique et la religion* (Paris: Vrin, 1964), 2:178.

14. There we are in such perplexity and anguish," added Calvin, "that we don't know what to do. And this is what upsets so many simple people. What are we to do? For we see so many disputes in the Church and so many diverse opinions: better that we inquire about nothing." Calvin went about calming this disquiet. See his commentary on chapter 13 of Deuteronomy in *Corpus Reformatorum*, vol. 55 of *Opera*, (Brunswick, Germany, 1884), col. 229.

15. Philippe Du Plessis Mornay, *De la vérité de la religion chrétienne* (Paris, 1581), ch. 20.

16. See La Mothe Le Vayer, the dialogue on "De la diversité des Religions," in *Cinq dialogues . . .* (Mons, Belgium, 1671).

17. See for example René Voeltzel, *Vraie et Fausse Eglise selon les théologiens protestants français du XVII*ᵉ *siècle* (Paris: PUF, 1956), pp. 99ff., on the search for the "marks of the true Church."

18. René Descartes, *Discours de la méthode*, in *Oeuvres complètes* (Paris: Garnier, 1963), ch. 3, p. 592.

19. In his *Histoire de l'idée de nature* (Paris: Albin Michel, 1969), Robert Lenoble thus sums up the position of many: "We follow *customs*, but Reason and Nature are elsewhere" (p. 283).

20. See Sergio Moravia, *La Scienza dell'uomo nel Settecento* (Bari, Italy: Laterza, 1970), pp. 80–112.

21. Georges Gusdorf, *Dieu, la nature, l'homme au siècle des Lumières* (Paris: Payot, 1972), p. 45.

22. Already in Pascal the word "system" has a pejorative meaning (see the *Pensées*, Brunschvicg fragment 194, note). In the eighteenth century, in the *Encyclopédie*, "system" designates a set of abstract, or in reality hypothetical principles, which too quickly signal "experiments and observations." More generally, writes the author of the article entitled "System," "Cartesianism, which had succeeded Peripateticism, put into vogue the taste for *systems* of thought. Today, thanks to Newton, it appears that we have gotten away from this prejudice"; *Encyclopédie*, 32:305. Jean-François Delamare, in his *La Foi justifiée de tout reproche de contradiction avec la raison* (Paris, 1762), saw in Bayle's use of the word the sign of incredulity: for those who use the term, he wrote, "in religion everything is system" because "everything is problematic in these matters"; in Migne, *Démonstrations évangéliques* (1843), vol. 2, col. 861.

23. We know that in the seventeenth century "atheist" and "atheism" referred first of all to the division of churches. Protestants and Catholics mutually treated each other as atheists: "atheism" is the religion of the other. In the accepted meaning in the eighteenth century, the atheist of the seventeenth century was the "libertine."

24. See René Pintard's fundamental study *Le Libertinage érudit dans la première moitié du XVII*ᵉ *siècle* (Paris: Boivin, 1943).

25. See Robert Mandrou, *Magistrats et sorciers en France au XVII*ᵉ *siècle* (Paris: Plon, 1968); Michel de Certeau, *La Possession de Loudun* (Paris: Julliard, 1970); Alan MacFarlane, *Witchcraft in Tudor and Stuart England* (London: Routledge and Kegan Paul, 1970); Keith Thomas, *Religion and the Decline of Magic* (London: Weidenfeld and Nicholson, 1971); and Julio Caro Baroja, *The World of the Witches* (Chicago: University of Chicago Press, 1964).

26. See most obviously Henri Bremond's *Histoire littéraire du sentiment religieux* (Paris: A. Colin, 1967–1968) and Jean Orcibal's *La Rencontre du Carmel thérésien avec les mystiques du Nord* (Paris: Presses Universitaires de France, 1959); Louis Cognet, *Histoire de la Spiritualité moderne* (Paris: Aubier, 1960); and Michel de Certeau, "Mystique au XVII*ᵉ siècle," in *Mélanges de Lubac* (Paris, 1964) 2:267–91, and *La Fable mystique* (Paris: Gallimard, 1982).

27. Around 1660 we witness a general fallout of the expression or forms of *doctrinal* intransigence. Then they are politicized or, more broadly, they give way before the law of social or political cohesions. At about this time, Jansenism ac-

quires a more learned or more social style, and there appears between the opposed churches the "accommodators of religion." Christopher Hill also establishes 1660 as the date of the fall of English millenarianism, in his *Anti-Christ in Seventeenth-Century England* (New York: Oxford University Press, 1971), p. 164. Here there seems to exist a phenomenon common to all of Western Europe.

28. Etienne Thuau, *La Raison d'Etat et pensée politique à l'époque de Richelieu* (Paris: Armand Colin, 1966), p. 10.

29. This phrase from Jérémie Ferrier, a religious mind, in *Catholique d'Etat* (1625), has a thousand equivalents: only power "reasons" by exercising the reason that it creates.

30. Paul Bénichou, *Morales du Grand Siècle* (Paris: Gallimard, 1948), p. 223.

31. Quoted in Thuau, *La Raison d'Etat*, p. 185.

32. *Ibid.*, p. 416. "The transformation that the policy of the state engenders in political thinking is linked to changes in society and to the development from a rural France to a merchant and bourgeois France. From certain points of view, Richelieu's state, which both conquers and organizes, and which is modern and mercantilist, appears as one of the first forms of the capitalistic enterprise. His rationalism and his politics of excessive intervention, his search for self-interest erected into law, his conception of international life as a permanent competition, and his half-morality which is justified by the care for general interest, are some of the many qualities of nascent capitalistic enterprise."

33. *Ibid.*, pp. 169ff.

34. Blaise Pascal, *Oeuvres complètes* (Paris: Hachette, Les Grands Ecrivains de la France, 1904–1914), p. 369 (at the beginning of "Discours du feu M. Pascal sur la condition des Grands").

35. See the alert reading that Michel Foucault has made of Velasquez's *Las Meninas,* a painting that "the king's reflection" organizes, in *Les Mots et les choses* (Paris: Gallimard, 1966), pp. 19–32; in English, *The Order of Things* (New York: Vintage, 1970), pp. 3–16.

36. Quoted in Thuau, *La Raison d'Etat*, p. 184.

37. In France, 1685 (the date of the revocation of the Edict of Nantes by the Edict of Fontainebleau) marks at once the *objective* success and the *religious* collapse of the efforts of the Counter-Reformation. See Jean Orcibal's strong conclusion to *Louis XIV et les protestants* (Paris: Vrin, 1951), pp. 159–67.

38. The phrase is Louis XIV's, quoted *ibid.,* p. 94, n. 13.

39. Pierre Bourdieu, "Genèse et structure du champ religieux," *Revue française de sociologie* (1971), 12:310ff. From the standpoint of sociolinguistics, in his "Sprachliches und soziales Handeln: Überlegungen zu einer Handlungstheorie des Spraches," *Linguistische Berichte* (1969), 2:64–70, S. J. Schmidt takes an interest in the "formality of social acts" and in the "normative systems of action." This is another way of noting the problem that I am advancing here.

40. See for example Emile Léonard, *Histoire générale du protestantisme* (Paris: PUF, 1961), 2:362ff.

41. The expression is Victor Martin's in *Le Gallicanisme politique et le clergé de France* (Paris: A. Picard, 1929), and it characterizes the content of the first of four articles approved by the Assembly of the Clergy in 1682, in other words,

the king's absolute independence in the temporal sphere. See also Jean Orcibal, "L'Idée d'Eglise chez les catholiques du XVIIe siècle," in *Relazioni del X Congresso Internazionale di Scienze Storiche* (Rome, 1955), 4:111–35. It can be added that ultramontane ecclesiology adheres to the same criteria. Thus, for Bellarmin, *assurance* and *guarantee* of pontifical authority are based on its visible conformity with "political models"; see Pierre Eyt, "L'Ordre du discours et l'ordre de l'Eglise: Hypothèse sur les structures profondes d'un texte des *Controverses* de Bellarmin," in *Mélanges d'histoire religieuse offerts à Mgr E. Griffe*, special issue of *Bulletin de Littérature ecclésiastique* (1972), 73:230–49.

42. Orcibal, *Louis XIV et les protestants*, p. 93.

43. Thus, in one example among a thousand, for the Abbey du Chaila the offices of charity are a *means* of conversion (see Jean-Robert Armogathe, *Missions et conversions dans le diocèse de Mende au XVIIIe siècle*, unpublished thesis of the Ecole Pratique des Hautes Etudes, 1970, pp. 134ff.); conversion in turn a *means* of obtaining unity.

44. For example, some observations on this topic are provided by Charles Berthelot du Chesnay in *Les Missions de Saint Jean Eudes* (Paris: Procure des Eudistes, 1968), and by Marc Venard in "Les Missions des Oratoriens d'Avignon aux XVIIe et XVIIIe siècles," *Revue d'Histoire de l'Eglise de France* (1962), 58:16–38: often (but not always) the time and place are arranged by the donors, as, too, are the objectives (associating instruction with the struggle against "licentiousness and crime"). In the case of missions, as well as of schools, and despite the conditions imposed by interested religious congregations, a systematic study of acts of donation would probably reveal a mental and political geography. On donations and legacies made to schools, see F. Léon de Marie Aroz's valuable remarks in *Les Biens-fonds des Ecoles chrétiennes et gratuites pour les garçons pauvres de la ville de Reims au XVIIIe siècle* (Reims, 1970), 1:xxv–xxvi and 1–57.

45. From the witchcraft trials up to the doctrinal debates (on Jansenism, for example), all religious affairs manifest this process.

46. Even among the traditional "ultramontanes" who are Jesuits, "political submission" becomes a "veritable obligation of conscience": it wins over religious obligation because it is "older and stronger." In 1681 Father de La Chaise wrote to his general superior, F. Oliva, that the royal ordinances "by way of the most ancient, divine and human, natural and positive law, bind in conscience" and prevail over the orders of the general superior which only bind "by virtue of piety and spontaneously contracted vows"; quoted in Georges Guitton, *Le Père de La Chaise* (Paris: Beauchesne, 1959), 1:91. A few years later, a collective Jesuit report declared: "In the concurrence of two opposite commandments given to a member of a French religious order, one by the king and the other by the legitimate superior . . . it is a grievous sin against religion, against fidelity, and against justice to obey the general or the local superior at the prejudice of the king's orders." Quoted in Pierre Blet, "Jésuites gallicans au XVIIe siècle?" *Archivum Historicum Societatis Iesu* (1960), 29:75–76.

47. For instance, in respect to Jesuit schools, see François de Dainville, *La Naissance de l'humanisme moderne* (Paris: Beauchesne, 1940), part 4, ch. 3, pp. 247–75; or André Schimberg's old but very rich documentary work on a subject

that has hardly been taken up again since, entitled *L'Education morale dans les collèges de la Compagnie de Jésus en France* (Paris: Champion, 1913). It is also striking, in reading the manuals of the period (these are often manuals of "civility"), to see the extent to which rules and social uses constitute the backbone of education. Christian virtues seem to conform to them and to confirm them as yet one more reason in respect to an actual situation (the established order) that carries the value of *law*. But this means that on a second level the established order is still perceived as divine, although it ceases to have that function in social practice.

48. On the insinuation of the "spirit of method" into congregations and missions, see Jean Delumeau's remarks in *Le Catholicisme entre Luther et Voltaire* (Paris, 1971) pp. 104–9 and 278–80; available in English as *Catholicism Between Luther and Voltaire* (Philadelphia: Westminster, 1977). In piety, intellectualism triumphs with Nicole's *Traité de l'oraison* (1678), but this apologia for discursive prayer has countless parallels. One indication suffices, the multiplication of the term "method" in titles of works on devotion. Unfortunately there does not exist for the seventeenth century the equivalent of Alessandro Fontana's analysis of the eighteenth century: "L'Ensemble *méthode*," in Francois Furet, ed., *Livre et société dans la France du XVIIIᵉ siècle* (The Hague: Mouton, 1970), 2:151–228. It shows the importance of the fact that, after grammar and medicine, it is *devotion* that in these titles offers the most numerous occurrences of "method."

49. On the "intention" or "motif" which is the "formal" element of action (as distinguished from its "material"), and on the historical meaning of this recourse, see Jean-Joseph Surin, *Guide spirituel* (Paris: Desclée de Brouwer, 1963), and my introduction to that work, pp. 23–27 and 31–36. In this respect, the notion of "instinct" is equally fundamental; see Michel Dupuy's article "Instinct" in the *Dictionnaire de spiritualité* (Paris: Beauchesne, 1932–), vol. 3, cols. 1803–05.

50. In social acting this dichotomy is analogous to that fundamental one that Madame David discerned in seventeenth-century research on language, especially in respect to Egyptology; to the "symbol" (or allegory) which *expresses* a truth is opposed the "cipher" which *produces* a knowledge. See Madeleine V.-David, *Le Débat sur les écritures et l'hiéroglyphe aux XVIIᵉ et XVIIIᵉ siècles* (Paris: Sevpen, 1965), pp. 11–30.

51. Montesquieu, *Lettres persanes,* letter 75. Under Louis XIV, dragonnades, conversions, and forced communions had already brought a "cruel denial" to everyone who had lauded the importance of interior dispositions. For example, at that time Percin de Montgaillard emphasized that "former Catholics . . . were scandalized to see what was being done under the pretext of religion," and forced communions "threw topsy-turvy their wavering faith" (quoted in Orcibal, *Louis XIV et les protestants,* p. 166, n. 27).

52. See *La Morale pratique des Jésuites*, 8 vols. (1669–1695), by Perrault, Pontchâteau, and Vanet, with the collaboration of Arnauld and Nicole. At stake is the "purity of morality," "moral maxims," "modes of behavior," and a "politics" (see the preface to the first volume). An entire literature illustrates this thema-

tization around moral *practices* all the way up to Quesnel's *Réflexions morales*. Even the dogmatic discussions are grouped under this sign, just as they will be in the *Défense de la morale et de la grâce* . . . (Cologne, 1698).

53. Thus the network formed by the Jesuit Surin's letters and the diffusion of his manuscripts does not recoup those that either Jansenist or Jesuit *memberships* (they were counted!) constituted. Completely different from these "party" circles, and judged with defiance by the totality of the Jesuits, this network is on the contrary in large measure identical to the very one in which are circulating reformist texts and ideas from the spirituals attached to the *spirit* of Port-Royal. See my introduction to Jean-Joseph Surin, *Correspondance* (Paris: Desclée de Brouwer, 1966), pp. 27–94.

54. "Civility" is born of a predominance of human relations over the relation with nature or the world. Its model is the court. "The service of courtiers constitutes perfect civility," writes Jean-Joseph Surin in his *Fondements* (Spes: 1930), 1, 8, p. 87. Its antithesis is "savage" society. As Surin notes in his *Guide spirituel*, it already implies practices "with no goal other than civil society" (5, 7, p. 228). Whence the importance of "civil nobility," which is based on "the opinion of men" and "success in business," writes Pierre du Moulin, *La Philosophie mise en français* . . . (Paris, 1644), *Ethique*, book 8, ch. 7, pp. 272–75. Critical and disputatious, even Christian ethics is hereafter obliged to be part of this dialectic of various powers and glances; see Pierre Nicole, *De la civilité chrétienne* (Paris, 1670); and Antoine de Courtin, *Nouveau traité de la civilité qui se pratique en France parmi les honnestes gens* (Amsterdam: Jacques Le Jeune, 1671). In many school handbooks, as for P. La Cerda, civility is "the sum of all the other" virtues (quoted in de Dainville, *La Naissance de l'humanisme moderne*, p. 271).

55. See *Mémoires de Trévoux* (November 1740), p. 2131. In quoting this text in *L'Idée de nature en France dans la première moitié du XVIIIᵉ siècle* (Paris: Sevpen, 1963), Jean Ehrard adds quite justly, "In itself, the idea is in no way a novelty" (p. 382, n. 4). It is a novelty coming from a member of a religious order.

56. We are aware, for example, of the difficulties that Fénelon encountered in 1686 when he was working with four Jesuits in Saintonge—because he "pronounced too easily on the Invocation of Saints and Images," or because he was not uttering the *Ave Maria* in his sermons; see Henk Hillenaar, *Fénelon et les Jésuites* (The Hague: Nijhoff, 1967), pp. 40–43. Fénelon had to modify his uses; he wrote ironically to Bossuet: "We are Catholics who are authentically recognized by the *Ave Marias* with which we fill our lectures"; letter of March 8, 1686, in Bossuet, *Correspondance*, Urbain-Levesque, ed. (Paris: Hachette, 1909–1925), 7:494. This is but one indication of the role that visible "marks" will play in a piety dissociated from morality.

57. See my "De Saint-Cyran au Jansénisme," in *Christus* (1963), 10:399–417, and *Les Jésuites: Jalons d'une histoire* (Paris: Beauchesne, 1974), pp. 53–110.

58. R. Dognon, P. Collet, Cl. Fleury, J. Girard de Villethierry, etc., are the specialists on this literature. Many studies are needed for this topic along the lines of R. Darricau's "La spiritualité du prince," *XVIIᵉ siècle* (1964), no. 62/63. There is a domestic spirituality, a military spirituality, etc. (pp. 3–36). On the more

doctrinal precedents, see Luis de la Puente, *De la perfección del cristiano en todos sus estados,* 4 vols. (Valladolid, Spain, 1612–13 and Pamplona, 1616); and François de Sales, *Introduction à la vie dévote* (Lyon, 1619).

59. See René Carpentier, article entitled "Devoir d'état," in the *Dictionnaire de spiritualité,* vol. 3, cols. 672–702; Fernand Jetté, article on "Etat," *ibid.,* vol. 4, cols. 1372–88. See also Fernand Guillen Preckler's thesis *"Etat" chez le Cardinal de Bérulle* (Rome: Università Gregoriana, 1974).

60. See Jetté, "Etat," col. 1378.

61. A state of pure nature," "a state of innocence," "a state of sin," "a state of grace," "a state of damnation," "a state of passivity," "a state of prostration," "a state of consolation," etc., according to Molina, Suarez, Vasquez, and hundreds of other theologians.

62. For example, *incipientes, proficientes, perfecti,* in Thomas Aquinas' *Summa theologiae,* IIa–IIae, q. 183, a. 4.

63. In Saint Theresa d'Avila, *Libro de la Vida . . . ,* ch. 11.

64. In the work of Saint Bonaventure, for instance, "De quinque statibus humanis," P. L. 177, c. 511.

65. Charles Loyseau, "Du droit des offices," *Oeuvres de Maître Charles Loyseau, avocat en Parlement* (Paris, 1678), book 1, ch. 1, p. 4.

66. To be sure, "state" had already qualified a civic situation: "Status pertinent proprie ad libertatem vel servitutem sive in spiritualibus sive in civilibus," wrote Thomas Aquinas in the *Summa theologiae* (IIa–IIae, q. 183, a. 1 c). But these various sorts of *status* took place inside a more fundamental religious organization of hierarchies.

67. See Leszek Kolakowski, *Chrétiens sans Eglise: La Conscience religieuse et le lien confessionel au XVIIe sièle* (Warsaw, 1965; Paris; Gallimard, 1969); in English, *Religion, If There Is No God* (New York: Oxford University Press, 1982). See also my *L'Absent de l'histoire,* pp. 109–15. On eremitism, a symptomatic movement—since it is the inner side of the general movement of escapism, which has an outer surface with travels to foreign lands, and because it is one of escapism's extreme and individual forms—see Pierre Doyère's works, in particular the article "Erémitisme" in the *Dictionnaire de spiritualité,* vol. 6, cols. 971–82.

68. The term is given to the restricted informal meetings among the faithful, whose model was created by Philippe Jacob Spener (1635–1705) at Frankfurt-am-Main. These *ecclesiolae in ecclesia* are *collegia pietatis.* They also have the common characteristic of crossing over separations among churches (which thus lose their "religious" relevance): they are designated not as "Lutheran" but as "Christian," and they bring together worshipers of every faith. See Emmanuel Hirsch, *Geschichte der neuern evangelischen Theologie in Zusammenhang mit den allgemeinen Bewegungen des europäischen Denkens* (Gütersloh, W. Germ.: Bertelsmann, 1951), 2:92ff.

69. Bremond, *Histoire littéraire du sentiment religieux,* vol. 5. The expression, applied to Surin and the school of P. Lallemant, can be extended to many other currents.

70. See my "Histoire et mystique" in *L'Absent de l'histoire,* pp. 153–67.

71. See for instance William Haller, *Liberty and Reformation in the Puritan*

Revolution (New York: Columbia University Press, 1955); Michael Walzer, *The Revolution of the Saints* (Cambridge: Harvard University Press, 1965); but also Peter F. Anson, *Underground Catholicism in Scotland, 1622–1878* (Montrose: Standard Press, 1970).

72. Since the "sanctuary" that the reformed camps wished to establish in Rio de Janeiro in 1555–57—whose ups and downs are told by Jean de Léry in his *Histoire d'un voyage fait en la terre du Brésil* (La Rochelle, 1578; Gaffarel edition, Paris, 1880)—the idea of an exile founding a religious society never ceased to inspire voyages to America all through the seventeenth century. We know that to avoid persecution the gentlemen of Port-Royal and their friends "considered acquiring lands in America in order to be established there" and that the court was opposed to it; see Saint-Simon, *Mémoires* (Paris: Hachette, 1880–1893), 3:533. See also Jean Mesnard, *Pascal et les Roannez* (Paris: Desclée de Brouwer, 1965), p. 735.

73. See Sydney E. Ahlstrom, *A Religious History of the American People* (New Haven: Yale University Press, 1972), pp. 785–804, as well as the classic study of the movement, Walter Rauschenbusch's *A Theology for the Social Gospel* (New York: Macmillan, 1917).

74. In the case of a village of the Cévennes, such preservation and obfuscation within the secrecy of family treasures are discovered by Henry Manen and Philippe Joutard, *Une foi enracinée: La Pervenche* (La Pervenche, 1972); this is the admirable dossier of religious "papers" that were hidden for three centuries in the closed rooms of Huguenot families of the Pervenche region.

75. See Jean Orcibal, *Saint-Cyran et le jansénisme* (Paris: Seuil, 1961), pp. 143ff., and also the works of J. Appolis, L. Ceyssens, or R. Taveneaux on Jansenism in the eighteenth century. On the evolution which involves a de facto alliance among the Jansenists and the philosophes, see for instance Robert Shackleton, "Jansenism and the Enlightenment," in *Studies on Voltaire and the Eighteenth Century* (1967), 57:1387–97.

76. Charles H. George has strongly underscored the mutation around the years 1640–44 from Puritan pietism to revolutionary Puritanism and radicalism in *The Protestant Mind of the English Reformation, 1570–1640* (Princeton: Princeton University Press, 1961), and in "Puritanism as History and Historiography," *Past and Present* (1968), 41:77–104. Certainly this "mysterious" discontinuity— according to George—is marked within the continuity of a development, as William M. Lamont shows in "Puritanism as History and Historiography: Some Further Thoughts," *Past and Present* (1969), 44:133–46; yet this is an evolution that the functioning of religious groups in a politicized society will determine.

77. See Klaus M. Kodalle, "Pascals Angriff auf eine politisierte Theologie," *Neue Zeitschrift für systematische Theologie und Religionsphilosophie* (1972), 14:68–88.

78. See Mesnard, *Pascal et les Roannez*, on the "business experience" that Pascal acquired around the Duke of Roannez, the governor of Poitou (pp. 311–82).

79. The "particular" is distinguished at once from the "public" and from the "general," that is, from politics and from reason. On the subject of the rift (which

crosses religion itself) between private and political morality, the author of *Catholique d'Etat* had already written, "The Justice of Kingdoms has laws other than that of Justice which is practiced among individuals" (quoted in Thuau, *La Raison d'Etat*, p. 174).

80. See my "Politique et mystique: René d'Argenson (1596–1651)," *Revue d'Ascétique et de Mystique* (1963), 39:45–92.

81. Pierre Chaunu, *La Civilisation de l'Europe des Lumières* (Paris: Arthaud, 1971), p. 217, quoting Serge Moscovici.

82. To a (discursive) will to deal with this mass of language and to rationalize this immense linguistic inertia, we would probably have to link the studies of local dialects, the "savage" or natural languages, and even folklore during the second half of the eighteenth century. Here we have an equivalent of what in the nineteenth century will become the exploitation of inert "resources" of nature. See for example Michel de Certeau, D. Julia, and J. Revel, *Une politique de la langue: La Révolution et les patois (1790–1794)* (Paris: Gallimard, 1975).

83. See Chaunu, *La Civilisation de l'Europe des Lumières*, pp. 194–203.

84. *Ibid.*, p. 289.

85. See Chaunu's handsome map (*ibid.*, p. 64) detailing this urban *conquista* across Europe toward the East.

86. That is, a "distanced" interpretation, in the style of an ethnologist confronting a foreign language. On this topic, see Claude Labrosse's penetrating study "Récit romanesque et enquête anthropologique," in *Roman et lumières au XVIIIᵉ siècle*, Werner Krauss et al., eds. (Paris: Editions Sociales, 1970), pp. 73–87; and Henri Coulet, "La Distanciation dans le roman et le conte philosophique," *ibid.*, pp. 438–47.

87. Edward Lord Herbert of Cherbury, *De Veritate* (1624). This point is presented in the third of five "notitiae communes circa religionem" in his last chapter, dedicated to bringing forth a few common values from religious particularities. He takes up this theme again in his *Religio laici* of 1645.

88. Joseph Glanvil, *An Essay Concerning Preaching* (London, 1678), p. 33.

89. Montesquieu, *Lettres persanes*, letter 86.

90. See Ehrard, *L'Idée de nature en France*, pp. 382ff., and also Joseph Lecler, "Libéralisme économique et libre pensée au XVIIIᵉ siècle," *Etudes* (March 5, 1937), pp. 624–45.

91. Pierre Chaunu, *La Civilisation de l'Europe classique* (Paris: Arthaud, 1966), p. 352.

92. G. W. F. Hegel, "The Struggle of Enlightenment with Superstition," in *The Phenomenology of Mind*, (New York: Harper and Row, 1967), pp. 578–89. See also Guy Besse, "Philosophie, Apologétique, Utilitarisme," *Dix-huitième siècle* (1970), 2:131–46. On the same topic, see Foucault, *The Order of Things*, pp. 176–200.

93. Morelly, in *Code de la Nature* (1755), part 3; the chapter entitled "Défauts particuliers de la morale vulgaire" takes up the effects of the idea of God. In the revised edition, edited by Gilbert Chinard (Paris, R. Clavreuil, 1950), see pp. 239ff.

94. See Jean Starobinski's great study, *Jean-Jacques Rousseau: La Transparence et l'obstacle* (Paris: Gallimard, 1971).

95. See especially Gusdorf, "L'Avènement des sciences religieuses," in *Dieu, la nature, l'homme,* pp. 143–239.

96. Reference must be made here to the numerous works of Alexandre Koyré, Georges Canguilhem, Alexandre Kojève, etc., on what Kojève himself calls "the Christian origin of modern science" in *Mélanges Alexandre Koyré* (Paris: Hermann, 1964), 2:295–306.

97. Alphonse Dupront, "Europe et Chrétienté dans la seconde moitié du XVIIᵉ siècle," mimeographed notes from a course offered at the Sorbonne, 1957.

98. Morelly, *Code de la nature,* part 4, pp. 310–13, on the "Conjugal Laws that will prevent all debauchery."

99. The political utopia offered by Diderot in 1772–73 in his *Supplément au voyage autour du monde de Bougainville* (especially in the "Entretien de l'aumônier et d'Orou") orders sexual relations as a function of a "growth of fortune" and "force for the nation." At issue above all is the question of "producing" handsome children and of "making" as many as possible: a "fecund" rather than a "gallant" Venus is in the service of "public utility."

100. I refer here to the nondiscursivity of the Word of salvation, to the "theology of the Cross" for the Reformation. We are not dealing with Max Weber's thesis on the coalescence of modern capitalism or with Protestant transcendentalism of the seventeenth and eighteenth centuries, a thesis that has, moreover, been the subject of Kurt Samuelsson's strong critique in *Religion and Economic Action* (London: Heinemann, 1961); see also Robert W. Green, ed., *Protestantism and Capitalism: The Weber Thesis and Its Critics* (Boston: Heath, 1959), and P. Besnard, *Protestantisme et capitalisme: La Controverse Postwéberienne* (Paris: A. Colin, 1970).

101. See Leszek Kolakowski, *Religion, If There is No God.* See also note 67 above.

102. Jean-Jacques Rousseau, letter to M. d'Offreville, October 4, 1761, in his *Correspondance générale* (Paris: Colin, 1924–1934), 4:223–24.

103. Rousseau had written to Monsignor de Beaumont, "I think that the basis of religion consists in practice; that not only ought one to be a good, charitable, human, and merciful man, but that whoever is truly such has belief enough to be saved."

104. See Robert Dérathé, "Les Rapports de la morale et de la religion chez Jean-Jacques Rousseau," *Revue philosophique* (1949), 139:143–73.

105. Starobinski, *Jean-Jacques Rousseau: La Transparence et l'obstacle,* p. 33.

106. De Pompignan's remark is quoted by Robert Dérathé in "Jean-Jacques Rousseau et le christianisme," *Revue de Metaphysique et de Morale* (1948), 53:414. See also Ernst Cassirer, "Das Problem, Jean-Jacques Rousseau," in *Archiv für Geschichte der Philosophie* (1932), 41:177–213 and 479–513.

107. See Ehrard's fine chapter "Naissance d'un mythe: L'Education," in *L'Idée de nature en France.*

108. Between religion and the "radically new philosophy" there is, according

to Feuerbach, a *replacement,* or homology, of structures and an inversion of meaning. "Disbelief replaced faith, reason replaced the Bible, and politics replaced religion and the Church; the earth replaced the sky, work replaced prayer, material misery replaced Hell," and so on. He also adds, "Once again we must become *religious,* and *politics* must become our religion." Whence the state, and "it is the belief in man as the God of man which subjectively accounts for the origins of the state. . . . The state is the God of men, therefore it justly claims the divine predicate of 'Majesty.' We have become well aware of what produces the unconscious principle and bond of the state: practical atheism": Ludwig Feuerbach, *Sämtliche Werke* (Stuttgart–Bad Cannstatt, 1960–64), vol. 2, p. 219.

109. See, for example, "La Beauté du mort: Le Concept de culture populaire," in my *La Culture au pluriel,* pp. 55–94.

110. See Gaby and Michel Vovelle, *Vision de la mort et de l'au-delà en Provence* (Paris: A. Colin, 1970), pp. 37–42. See also V.-L. Tapié, J.-P. Le Flem, and A. Pardailhé-Galabrun, *Retables baroques de Bretagne* (Paris: PUF, 1972), which allows us to grasp the movements of religious mentality through those of iconographical representations.

111. See Robert Mauzi, *L'Idée de bonheur dans la littérature et la pensée française du XVIIIe siècle* (Paris: A. Colin, 1960).

112. See note 50 in respect to the distinction between "cipher" and "symbol." [In these pages the French *chiffre,* translated here as "cipher," actually has the double meaning of "figure" and "cipher."——TR.]

113. This analysis of historical problems can be compared with Luce Irigaray's remarks in "Langage de classe, langage inconscient," *Le Centenaire du "Capital"* (The Hague: Mouton, Décades de Cerisy-la-Salle, 1969), pp. 191–202, on two "divergent functions of any statement" bound to the "status of the working instrument."

114. "Theatrical" to the degree, as Jacques Le Goff writes of the Middle Ages, that it is "unaware of a specific place set for the theater." "The whole medieval society stages itself," he adds, in *La Civilisation de l'Occident médiéval* (Paris: Arthaud, 1964), p. 444. It is an *expression* of itself, a representation of its universe. A society had to be *productive of itself* before theater could be localized—or before there is created the binomial of expressive culture and practical culture. See "La culture dans la société," in my *La Culture au pluriel,* pp. 227–236.

115. See Jacques Le Goff's analyses in *Les Intellectuels au Moyen Age* (Paris: Seuil, 1957).

116. See Paul Beauchamp, *Création et séparation* (Paris: Aubier, Bibliothèque des Sciences Religieuses, 1970).

117. Roland Mortier notes correctly that "after 1700, *Critical Examinations* proliferate in collections of manuscripts." He analyzes a few of these texts (Burigny, Meslier, or the *Militaire philosophe*) in "La Remise en cause du christianisme au XVIIIe siècle," *Revue de l'Université de Bruxelles* (1971), pp. 415–43.

118. This is a new type of interpretation, for in the sixteenth century radical criticism—that of Henri Estienne, for example—notes in Christianity the hidden repetition of classical religion, and not the result of natural causes (that is, ultimately, the unconscious representation of laws discerned through knowledge).

119. On the relation of music to what is inexpressible, to the passions, or to nature, see Georges Snyders, *Le Goût musical en France aux XVIIe et XVIIIe siècles* (Paris: Vrin, 1968), pp. 71ff. and (in respect to Diderot and Rousseau) pp. 108–34. Nonetheless, because of its proximity to writing within enlightened culture, music is also a field where coding, transcription, and ciphering are developed. Even dance becomes a writing and obeys the laws of the cipher. See for example Francine Lancelot, "Ecriture de la danse: Le Système Feuillet," *Ethnologie française* (1971), 1:29–58.

120. This is the title of Chaunu's chapter dedicated to the esthetics of the Enlightenment, in his *La Civilisation de l'Europe des Lumières*, pp. 373–426.

121. Hasso Jaeger, "La Mystique protestante et anglicane," in André Ravier, ed., *La Mystique et les mystiques* (Paris: Desclée de Brouwer, 1965), p. 284. Moreover, Bach's counterpoint has a structural connection with medieval science; his music is inspired by the mystical theology of the Middle Ages or by Tauler, whose *Sermons* were located in his library (pp. 279–80).

122. See for example J. B. Neveux, *Vie spirituelle et vie sociale entre Rhin et Baltique au XVIIe siècle, de J. Arndt à P. J. Spener* (Paris: Klincksieck, 1967); and Pierre Deghaye, *La Doctrine ésotérique de Zinzendorf* (Paris: Klincksieck, 1969).

123. See de Certeau, Julia, and Revel, *Une politique de la langue.*

124. Claude Lévi-Strauss, *The Origin of Table Manners* (New York: Harper and Row, 1979), pp. 130–31.

125. See Dominique Julia, "Le Prêtre au XVIIIe siècle: La Théologie et les institutions," *Recherches de science religieuse* (1970), 58:533–34, on the "relation between an official discourse and an experience that cannot be put into words": there is a "clandestine quality," a "subterranean perseverance," a "silence" of feelings or convictions in respect to public activity.

126. See Gusdorf, *Dieu, la nature, l'homme,* pp. 207–31.

127. See Edouard Hamel, "Retours à l'Evangile et théologie morale, en France et en Italie, aux XVIIe et XVIIIe siècles," *Gregorianum* (1971), 52:639–87, especially the analysis of Concina's works (*De locis theologicis seu purioris ethicae christianae fontibus,* 1751), or those of Zaccharia (*De l'usage des Ecritures en théologie morale tirée des sources très pures de l'Ecriture et de la tradition . . . ,* 1770).

128. Jean Soanen, *Sermon sur l'exemple,* in Migne, *Orateurs sacrés* (Paris, 1854), vol. 40, col. 1370.

129. Georg Christoph Lichtenberg, quoted in Gusdorf, *Dieu, la nature, l'homme,* p. 212.

130. See Gusdorf, *Dieu, la nature, l'homme,* p. 204, for reference to Emmanuel Hirsch's great work *Geschichte der neuern evangelischen Theologie,* 2:169ff.

131. This can be observed from the end of the seventeenth century, in Fénelon's celebrated letter to the Bishop of Arras, *Sur la lecture de l'Ecriture sainte en langue vulgaire,* in *Oeuvres complètes* (Paris, 1848), 2:190–201; or in the reflections that his *Mandement,* on the reception of the *Bulle Unigenitus,* devotes to the same subject: "Listening to the pastors who explain Scriptures is tantamount to reading Scriptures"; *Oeuvres* (1851), 5:140–42. In effect, "pastors are living Scriptures." Therefore the Church used the "right" of "allowing the reading of the sacred text only to whom it judged well enough prepared to read that text with profit"

(*Oeuvres* 2:193). This theology is traditional, but in the eighteenth century it functions as the substitution of the *priest*, the objective social standard, for the *text*, the literary objective standard. There as on many points Monseigneur So-anen stands out because of the vigor with which he presents Scriptures as a "language of God" and a relation with truth (see his sermon *Sur les saintes Ecri-tures*, in Migne, *Orateurs sacrés*, vol. 40, cols. 1444–62); but he already knows that this language is no longer comprehensible.

132. This is an expression that recurs very frequently in the ecclesiastical conferences around Bordeaux that I have been able to study (see note 135), especially in the treatment of moral or liturgical "cases."

133. See Jean Meslier (1664–1729), *Oeuvres*, 3 vols., R. Desné, ed. (Paris: Anthropos, 1970–1971). Meslier's *Mémoire* begins thus: "My dear friends, since I would not have been allowed and because it would have been an overly dangerous and difficult consequence to say it to you overtly during my life, what I had thought . . . I resolved to tell it to you at least after my death" (*Oeuvres* 1:1). "With a very devout appearance" (this is the phrase of his archbishop in 1716, 1:xxviii), Meslier protects an atheism willed by testament, just as many publicly anti-Jansenist priests protest by testament of their contrary convictions (as Julien Brancolini has shown, quoted by R. Desné in *Oeuvres*, 1:xxxvii, n. 1).

134. Julia, "Le Prêtre au XVIIIᵉ siècle," p. 525. See also Charles Berthelot du Chesnay, "Le Clergé français au XVIIIᵉ siècle et les registres d'insinuation ec-clésiastique," *Revue d'Histoire Moderne et Contemporaine* (1963), pp. 241ff.

135. In particular this observation springs from an analysis of the ecclesiastical conferences and congregations of vicars of the diocese of Bordeaux in the seventeenth and eighteenth centuries, a dossier that provides a complete series (for the eighteenth century: Bordeaux, Archives Départementales, G. 591–97). Other limited investigations confirm this analysis if we take into account the fact that, reformed earlier, the diocese of Bordeaux manifests this evolution toward formalism more rapidly than others.

136. I refer to the synthetic report presented by Dominique Julia: *La Réforme post-tridentine en France d'après les procès-verbaux de visites pastorales: Ordres et résistances*, in *La Società religiosa nell'età moderna* (Naples: Guida, 1973), pp. 311–97.

137. See Dominique Julia, "Le Clergé paroissial du diocèse de Reims à la fin de l'Ancien Régime. II: Le Vocabulaire des curés: Essai d'analyse," *Etudes ar-dennaises* (October–December 1968), 55:41–66.

138. Delamare, "De la religion," in *Traité de la Police* (Paris, 1705), pp. 267–378.

139. Paul Henri Thirg Holbach, *Essai sur les Préjugés*, quoted by Mortier in his "La remise en cause du christianisme au XVIIIᵉ siècle," p. 421.

140. For example, in taking up an old obligation recalled by the *Supra Gregem* Bull of Pope Pious V (March 8, 1566) and by the Sacred Congregation of 1699, Church law forbids the doctor to visit those who are dying if he has not seen the confessor's testimonial certifying that they have been heard in confession. See Erneste de S. Joseph, *Le Ministère du confesseur en pratique* . . . (Liège: Barchon, 1718), 2:395. While this measure was inserted into an organization of religious

hierarchies of society, it takes on the meaning of a "mark" and of a "stop" added onto the civil logic of a profession.

141. These are Monsignor Jean Soanen's expressions in his sermon *Sur l'excellence du christianisme* (in Migne, *Orateurs sacrés,* vol. 40, cols. 1162–68). To the "spectacles" offered by religion, he adds the "advantages" and the "treasures" that it provides: "There is found within Christian religion, as inside these mountains that produce gold and diamonds, many inestimable treasures" (col. 1166; cf. col. 1172). But these expressions can also be found among many other authors.

142. See Geneviève Bollème, *Les Almanachs populaires aux XVIIe et XVIIIe siècles: Essai d'histoire sociale* (The Hague: Mouton, 1969), and *La Bibliothèque bleue* (Paris: Julliard, 1971). See also Robert Mandrou, *De la culture populaire aux XVIIe et XVIIIe siècles* (Paris: Stock, 1964).

143. We can also perceive this interrogation in the great panorama that Fernand Braudel began to outline in his *Civilisation matérielle et capitalisme (XVe– XVIIIe siècles)* (Paris: A. Colin, 1967), vol. 1, a book which doubtless concerns the areas of popular culture much more closely than many works on "popular literature."

III

Systems of Meaning:
Speech and Writing

5

Ethno-Graphy

Speech, or the Space of the Other: Jean de Léry

The Historian's Writing and Ethnological Orality

FOUR concepts appear to organize a scientific field whose status was established in the eighteenth century and which Ampère entitled "ethnology":[1] *orality* (communication within a primitive, savage, or traditional society), *spatiality* (the synchronic picture of a system that has no history), *alterity* (the difference which a cultural break puts forward), and *unconsciousness* (the status of collective phenomena, referring to a significance foreign to them and given only to knowledge originating elsewhere). Each of the four guarantees and calls for the other three. Thus, in primitive society, a timeless land as it were is displayed before the observer's eye ("Things have always been like this," remarks the native); it is taken for granted that speech circulates without its users knowing what unspoken rules it obeys. It is the task of ethnology to articulate these rules in writing and to organize this space of the other into a picture of orality.

Taken here as a kind of hypothesis, however partial, this ethnological rectangle can be seen as giving rise to transformations in which the basic scheme will always remain apparent, whether the field be psychoanalysis or pedagogy. At the same time, this rectangle has its corollary in modern historiography, whose construction in the same era puts forward four opposed concepts, namely *writing, temporality, identity,* and *consciousness.*

In this resepct, Lévi-Strauss bears witness to a differentiation that had already been in place for four centuries when he adds his own personal variant to the literary genre of the parallel between ethnology and history. "Ethnology," he says, "is especially interested in what is *not written*." What it deals with is "*different* from everything that men usually dream of engraving in stone or committing to paper." For him this distinction between materials, the written or the unwritten, is doubled by another having to do with each field's relation to knowledge. History organizes "its data in relation to *conscious* expressions, while ethnology organizes its data in relation to *unconscious* conditions of social life."[2]

The "difference" implied by orality and by the unconscious delimits an *expanse of space,* an object of scientific activity. In order to be spoken, oral language waits for a writing to circumscribe it and to recognize what it is expressing. Over this extended area of continents and oceans pregiven in the operations of writing are outlined the itineraries of travelers whose traces will pertain to history. As soon as written works are available, scientific investigation is no longer needed to posit an implicit element— an unconscious nature—underlying phenomena in general. History is homogenous to the documents of Western activity. It credits them with a "consciousness" that it can easily recognize. History is developed in the continuity of signs left by scriptural activities: it is satisfied with arranging them, composing a single text from the thousands of written fragments in which already expressed is that labor which constructs time, which creates consciousness through self-reflection.

From this complex configuration I will initially retain only two terms. I shall inquire about the breadth of this speech instituted on behalf of the other and destined to be heard *otherwise* than in the ways it is spoken. This area of difference puts into question a function of speech in our societies, which are based on writing—a problem that is far too vast to take up here, but that makes the connection of history and ethnology perceptible within the sum of human sciences.

A Figure of Modernity

HERE we can only fathom the depths. I wish only to travel through history and ethnology with a few questions in mind. Even proceeding in this way, however, speech and writing cannot be considered stable elements whose alliances and divorces have only to be analyzed. At stake are categories that make up a system within succeeding sets. The respective positions of writing and speech are mutually determined. Their combinations, which change their terms as much as they change their relations, are written into a succession of historical configurations. Recent works reveal the importance of transformations which took place in Western Europe from the sixteenth to the eighteenth century (see chapter 4). The discovery of the New World, the fragmentation of Christendom, and the social rifts that accompanied the birth of a new politics and rationality gave birth to another functioning of writing and speech. Seen in the light of modern society, the distinction between them acquires a social and epistemological relevance that it did not yet possess; it especially becomes the instrument of a two-sided work that pertains, on the one hand, to "primitive" man, and, on the other, to religious tradition. The distinction between speech and writing is useful for classifying the problems that the rising sun of the New World and the twilight of medieval Christianity would reveal to an intelligentsia.

This new use can be seen in texts—in travel literature and ethnographical descriptions. This means of course that we are staying in a narrative field, by adhering so much to what writing says about speech. Even if they are the products of research, observation, and practices, these texts are nonetheless a tale and a milieu as told to its own members. These scientific *legenda* cannot be identified with the system of real practices. But by indicating to a group of learned individuals what they "must read," in assembling the representations that this group ascribes for itself, these legends symbolize the alterations that were instigated in the encounter that one culture made with another. The new experiences of a society do not unveil their "truth" through a transparency of these texts; these experiences are transformed there according to the laws of a scientific setting which belongs to the period. In this respect the reading of texts has much to do with an interpretation of dreams; texts form discourses about the other, about which we can wonder what is actually told *there*, in those literary regions that are always drawn from what is really occurring.

Finally, in extracting from a series of travel writings a few segments that mark the path of an archeology of ethnology;[3] in paying heed to an episode recounted by Jean de Léry (1578) as if it were the equivalent of a primal scene in the construction of ethnological discourse; in letting words, references, and reflections freely associate with the reader that I am, I must wonder what this analysis will hide or reveal in me. Concerning ethnological discourse, I would like to explain what it articulates in exiling orality outside of the areas which pertain to Western work, in transforming speech into an exotic object. But even so, I do not escape the culture that produced this discourse. I only reduplicate its effect. What ex-voto is my writing dedicating to that absent speech? For what dream, or what lure, is my writing a metaphor? There can be no answer. Self-analysis has been disenfranchised, and I would not know how to replace with a text what only a voice that is other could reveal about the place in which I am writing.

The principal issue is elsewhere. The question to be asked of ethnological research—what does this writing presuppose *about* orality?—is to be asked also of what it makes me bring forth, which reaches back and returns from much further than I. My analysis comes and goes between these two variants of a single structural relation, between the texts that it studies and the text that it produces. Through this double location it upholds the problem without resolving it—that is to say, without being able to move outside of "circum-scription." At least in this way appears one of the rules of the system which was established as being Occidental and modern: the scriptural operation which produces, preserves, and cultivates imperishable "truths" is connected to a rumor of words that vanish no sooner than they are uttered, and which are therefore lost forever. An irreparable loss is the trace of these spoken words in the texts whose object they have become. Hence through *writing* is formed our relation with the other.

Jean de Léry's Writing Lesson (1578)

ALTHOUGH his text is based on a long medieval tradition of utopias and expectations in which was already mapped the locus that the "noble savage" would soon inhabit,[4] Jean de Léry provides us with a "modern" point of departure. In fact, he assures us of a transition.

Published in 1578, his *Histoire d'un voyage faict en la terre du Brésil*—"that masterpiece of anthropological literature," remarks Claude Lévi-Strauss[5]—is the story of a journey into the Bay of Rio in the years 1556–1558. This voyage is part of a number of successive "retreats." A partisan of the Reformation, Léry flees France in favor of Geneva; he leaves Geneva, and with a few companions he sails off for Brazil in order to take part in the foundation of a Calvinist sanctuary. From the island in the Bay of Rio, where the admiral Nicolas Durant de Villegagnon received the Protestant mission after a treaty with Calvin, he withdraws again, disgusted by the admiral's theological fluctuations. He wanders for three months among the Tupinambous along the coast, from the end of October 1557 until the beginning of January 1558, before following the same road in the opposite direction, from Brazil to Geneva, and from Geneva to France, where he settles down as a pastor. His is a reverse pilgrimage: far from rejoining the referential body of an orthodoxy (the sacred city, the tomb, the basilica), his itinerary goes from the center to the borders, in searching for a space where he can find a ground. Upon that ground he envisions building the language of a new—a reformed —conviction. At the end of his journey, after all the comings and goings, the Savage is invented.[6]

In 1556 Jean de Léry is twenty-four years old. Published twenty years later, his *Histoire* casts the movement of departure that had gone from over here (in France), to over there (among the Tupis), into circular form. It transforms the voyage into a cycle. From over there it brings back a literary object, the Savage, that allows him to turn back to his point of departure. The story effects his return to himself through the mediation of the other. Yet something still remains over there, which the words of the text cannot convey; namely, the speech of the Tupis. It is that part of the other that cannot be retrieved—it is an evanescent act that writing cannot convey.

Thus, in the jeweled setting of the tale, native speech takes on the figure of a missing precious stone. It is the moment of ravishment, a stolen instant, a purloined memory beyond the text: "Such a joy it was [writes Léry about his impressions during a Tupi assembly] hearing the beautifully measured rhythms of such a multitude—and especially the cadence and refrain of the ballad, all of them together raising their voices to each couplet, saying: *heu, heuaüre, heüra, heüraüre, heüra, heüra, oueh*—that I remained completely ravished. But moreover, every time the memory comes back to me, my heart throbs, and it seems as if their music still rings in my ears."[7] An absence of meaning opens a rift in time. Here the chant measures *heu, heuaüre* or, further, *Hé, hua, hua,* just as a voice utters *re re,* or *tralala.* Nothing can be either transmitted, conveyed, or preserved. But immediately afterward, Léry appeals to his interpreter for a translation of several things that he was unable to comprehend. With this passing to meaning occurs the task that transforms the ballad into a product that can be put to good use. From these voices the deft translator extracts the story of an initial deluge "which is," Léry notes, "what most resembles Scripture among them":[8] a return is accomplished, to the West and to writing, to which the gift of this confirmation is taken from the distant Tupi shores, a return to the Christian and French text through the exegete's and the voyager's combined efforts. Productive time is sewn back into the fabric, history is generated anew, after the break precipitated by the throbbing heart that was going back over there, toward that instant when, "totally ravished," fascinated by the other's voice, the observer forgot himself.

The connection between speech and writing is staged on one other occasion in the *Histoire*. This connection discreetly focuses the entire narrative, but Léry clarifies his position in a key episode, in the central chapter in which he deals with religion,[9] that is, with the relation that the Christianity of Scripture holds with the oral traditions of the indigenous world. At the dawn of modern times, this episode inaugurates the series of analogous scenes that so many travelogues will project over the next four centuries. Even if, once again, it inverts the meaning and moral, the "Writing Lesson" Lévi-Strauss recounts in *Tristes Tropiques* (1955) reiterates the schema that organizes ethnological literature and gives birth, from afar, to a staging of the actors in play.[10] In the form assumed here, the scene already puts all kinds of sacred and profane writings together in order to appropriate them to the West, the subject of history, and to allocate to them the function of being an expansionist *labor* of knowledge.

> As for writing, whether sacred or profane, not only are the Indians unaware of what it is, but moreover, they are deprived of characters with which they might otherwise be able to signify things: when I was in their country in the beginning and learning their language, I used to write a few sentences. Then, in reading to them afterward, in their eyes it all seemed like some kind of sorcery. One would say to the other: Is it not a marvel that he could not utter a word in our language yesterday, but by virtue of this paper that he keeps and that makes him speak the way he does, we can understand him today?
>
> Which is the same opinion held among the natives of the Spanish Island who were the first there.[11] For he who wrote its *History* thus states:[12] The Indians, knowing that the Spanish conquerors, without either seeing or speaking to one another, except by sending letters from place to place, could be understood in this fashion, believed either that the European had the gift of prophecy or that the missives spoke. In such a way, he said, the savages, fearing being

discovered and surprised in guilt, were held to their duties so well through these means that they no longer dared either to lie or steal from the Spaniards.

For this reason I say that whoever wishes to amplify this matter here has a handsome topic, both to praise and exalt the art of writing and, too, to show how much the nations that inhabit these three parts of the world—Europe, Asia, and Africa—can praise God beyond the savages of this fourth part called America: for unlike those who are unable to communicate anything except through verbal means,[13] to the contrary we have this advantage, that without budging an inch, by means of writing and the letters we send, we can declare our secrets to whomever we please, even if they are removed to the other end of the world. Thus beyond the sciences that we learn through books, of which the natives are seemingly entirely deprived, this invention of writing at our fingertips, which they are also totally lacking, must be even more advanced to the rank of the unique gifts that men of our lands have received from God.[14]

Scriptural Reproduction

BETWEEN "them" and "us" there exists the difference of possessing "either sacred or profane" writing, which immediately raises the question of a relation of *power*. Between the Nambikwara and Lévi-Strauss, from the beginning, the possession of writing will have the same implications.[15] Sorcery, say the Tupinambous, is the power of the strongest. But they are deprived of it. The Westerners have the advantage. They accredit it as being one of the unique gifts that men from their country received from God. Their cultural power is countersigned by the absolute itself; it is not only a fact, but also a right, the effect of an election, a divine heritage.

Still more characteristic is the nature of the rift. It does not result essentially from a selection between (primitive) error and (Christian) truth. Here the decisive element is the possession or privation of an *instrument* that can at the same time "keep things in all their purity" (as Léry will remark further on)[16] and stretch all the way "to the other end of the world." In combining the power to keep the past (while the primitive "fable" forgets and loses its origin)[17] with that of indefinitely conquering distance (while the primitive "voice" is limited to the vanishing circle of its auditors), writing *produces history*. On the one hand, it accumulates, it keeps an inventory of the secrets from the West, it loses nothing, it preserves them in an intact state. Writing is an archive. On the other hand, it declares, it goes to the end of the world, toward those destined to receive it according to the objectives that it desires—and "without budging an inch," without having the center of its action being moved, without any change in it through its progress. With writing the Westerner has a sword in his hand which will extend its gesture but never modify its subject.[18] In this respect, it repeats and diffuses its prototypes.

The power that writing's expansionism leaves intact is colonial in principle. It is extended without being changed. It is tautological, immunized against both any alterity that might transform it and whatever dares to resist it. It can be taken as the play of a double *reproduction* which, as history and as orthodoxy, preserves the past and which, as mission, conquers space by multiplying the same signs. Léry's is the period when critical research on the return to origins—exhuming written "sources"—is built over the innovation of the new empire that, with printing, is permitted by an indefinite reproduction of the same products.

To writing, which invades space and capitalizes on time, is opposed speech, which neither travels very far nor preserves much of anything. In its first aspect speech never leaves the place of its production. In other words, *the signifier cannot be detached from the individual or collective body.* It cannot be exported. Here speech is the body which signifies. Statements are separated neither from the social act of enunciation, nor from a presence that is given, dispensed, and lost in the act of naming. Writing is found only where the signifier can be isolated from presence, while the Tupinambous see a bizarre form of speech, the action of a force, in characters drawn on paper; in their eyes, writing is a form of sorcery; for the Indians of the Spanish Island, missives speak.

In order that writing can function from afar, it has to maintain its relation to the place of production, even from a distance. For Léry, who still bears witness to reformed biblical theology, writing implies a faithful transmission of the origin, a being-there of the Beginning which lasts, intact, throughout avatars of generations and mortal societies. Writing is itself a body of truth, hence it can be isolated from the Church or community. This true object brings from the past to the present the statements that an originary and founding enunciation has produced "without budging." Léry's is a world which is no longer natural but which has become literary, in which the power of a distant (absent) author is reiterated. The religious cosmos—a creature signifying the creator—already appears to be replaced by the text, but in a miniaturization that fashions for man's profit a faithful and mobile instrument in an endless space. Speech is now located in an entirely different position. It does not preserve. That is its second feature. In respect to a Tupi oral tradition concerning the deluge that would have drowned "everyone in the world, except for their grandfathers who took refuge in the highest trees of their country," Léry notes that "being deprived of all kinds of writing, they retain things in their purity only with difficulty; like poets, they added this fable about their grandfathers who took refuge in the treetops."[19] Thanks to his scriptural standard, Léry knows how to determine what orality adds to things, and he knows exactly how things had been. He becomes a historian. Speech, to the contrary, has much to do with custom, which "turns truth into falsehood." And more fundamentally, the Tupi's account is a fable (from *fari*, to speak). So *fable is a drifting away*—adjunction, deviation, diversion, heresy, and poetry of the present, in relation to the "purity" of primitive law.

Through all this Jean de Léry appears to be a good Calvinist. He prefers the letter to a church body; the text to the voice of a presence; origins related by writing to the elocutionary experience of a fugitive communication. But he is already displacing the theology that inspires him. He is laicizing it. To be sure, in his view nature is still a sign to which he responds, while traveling under blooming trees, by singing the 104th Psalm: such a form of "speech" turns his heart to the whispers of the forest and the voices of the Tupis.[20] It is in syncopation with his ravishment at the sound of the communal ballad. The religious elements of the *Histoire* go in the direction of the almost ecstatic and prophetic speech of the primitives, but these elements are dissociated from the *labor* connoted by writing. A structure already appears to be in place. From festive, poetic, ephemeral speech are delineated the tasks of conserving, of verifying, and of conquering. A will to power is invested in its form. It discreetly transforms the Christian categories which provide it with a language. Ecclesial election is turned into a Western privilege; originary revelation into a scientific concern for upholding the truth of things; evangelization into an enterprise of expansion and return to one's self. Writing designates an *operation organized about a center:* departures and dispatches still depend on the impersonal will which is developed there and to which they return. The multiplicity of procedures in which "declarations" of this will are written elaborates the space of an organization around the *same,* which extends without undergoing any modification.

These are scriptural organizations, commercial, scientific, and colonial. The "paths of writing" combine a plurality of itineraries with the singularity of the place of production.[21]

A Hermeneutics of the Other

SIGNIFIED through a concept of writing, the work of redirecting the plurality of ways toward the single productive center is precisely what Jean de Léry's story attains. As his preface already indicates, the tale is fabricated from "memoirs . . . written in Brazilian ink and in America itself," a raw material doubly drawn from the tropics, since the very characters that bring the primitive object into the textual web are made from a red ink extracted from the *pau-brasil,* a wood that is one of the principal imports to sixteenth-century Europe.[22]

Yet only through the effect of its organization does the *Histoire* "yield profit." To be sure, the literary *operation* that brings back to the producer the results of signs that were sent far away has a condition of possibility in a *structural* difference between an area "over here" and another "over there." The narrative plays on the relation between the structure which establishes the separation and the operation which overcomes it, creating effects of meaning in this fashion. The break is what is taken for granted everywhere by the text, itself a labor of suturing.

The Break. At the manifest level, in the distribution of masses, the separation (between "over here" and "over there") first appears as an oceanic division: it is the Atlantic, a rift between the Old and the New World. In telling of tempests, sea monsters, acts of piracy, "marvels," or the ups and downs of transoceanic navigation, the chapters at the beginning and at the end (chapters 1–5 and 21–22) develop this structural rupture along the historical line of a chronicle of a crossing: each episode modulates uncanniness according to a particular element of the cosmological range (air, water, fish, bird, man, etc.), adding its proper effect to the series, in which difference is simultaneously the generative principle and the object to be made credible. The chapters that present Tupi society (7–19), bordered by the preceding, exhibit the same principle but now systematically, according to a scheme of dissimilarity that must affect every genre and every degree of being in order to situate the "over there" within the cosmos: "This American land where, as I shall be deducing, everything that is seen, whether in the customs of its inhabitants, the shapes of its animals, or in general in what the earth produces, is *dissimilar* in respect to what we have in Europe, Asia, and Africa, might well in our eyes be called a *new* world."[23]

In this landscape the figure of dissimilarity is either a deviation from what can be seen "over here" or, more often, the combination of Western forms that seem to have been cut off, and whose fragments seem to be associated in unexpected ways. Thus, among the four-footed animals (of which there exists "not one . . . that in any or every aspect in any fashion can resemble our own"), the *tapiroussou* is "half-cow and half-donkey," "being both of the one and of the other."[24] The primitives incorporate the splitting that divides the universe. Their picture of the world follows a traditional cosmological order whose scaffolding is exposed, but it is a picture covered with countless broken mirrors in which the same fracture is reflected (half this, half that).

The Work of Returning. This structural difference, particularized in the accidents that happen along the way or in the portraits in the gallery of primitives, only forms the area where an operation of return is effected, in a mode drawn according to the literary zones that it crosses. The narrative as a whole belabors the division that is located everywhere in order to show that the *other returns to the same.* In this fashion it inserts itself within the general problem of *crusade* that still rules over the discovery of the world in the sixteenth century: "conquest and conversion."[25] But this narrative displaces that problem through an effect of distortion that is introduced structurally by the breakage of space into two worlds.

It is about this operation of return that we have a first indication of the general dynamics of the *Histoire.* Seen in terms of a geometrical schema, the text is organized around the horizontal bar (figure 5.1) which separates over here (the same) and over there (the other).

The effects that the narrative produces can be represented as a movement of this line ninety degrees that creates, perpendicular to the axis of here-and-there, an axis of other-and-same (figure 5.2). From this we can deduce that "over there" no longer coincides with alterity. A part of the world which appeared to be entirely other is brought back to the same by a displacement that throws uncanniness out of skew in order to turn it into an exteriority behind which an interiority, the unique definition of man, can be recognized.

This operation will be repeated hundreds of times throughout ethnological works. In Léry's case we see it evinced in the staging of the primitive world, through a division between *Nature,* whose uncanniness is exteriority, and *civil* society, in which a truth of man is always legible.

The break between over here and over there is transformed into a rift between nature and culture. Finally, nature is what is other, while man stays the same. By the way, we can observe that this metamorphosis, a product of the displacement generated by the text, makes of nature the area where *esthetic* or *religious* experience and admiration are expressed and where Léry's prayer is spoken, while the social space is the place where an *ethics* is developed through a constant parallel between festivity and work. In this already modern combination, social production, what reproduces sameness and marks an identity, posits nature, esthetics, and religiosity outside of itself.

We can follow in some detail the arc traced by the story as it turns about its vertical axis (figure 5.3). In a first movement, it goes toward alterity: first the travel in the direction of the land over there (chapters 1–5), and then the overview of marvels and natural wonders (chapters 7–13). This movement has its final punctuation with the ecstatic song glorifying God (the end of chapter 13). The poem, Psalm 104, marks a vanishing point opening onto alterity, what is out of this world and unspeakable. At this point, with the analysis of Tupi society (chapters 14–19), a second movement begins: it goes from the most uncanny (war, chapter 14; anthropophagia, chapter 15) in order to progressively unveil a social model (laws and police, chapter 18; therapeutics, health, the cult of the dead, chapter 19). Then passing through the oceanic break, the

FIGURE 5.1

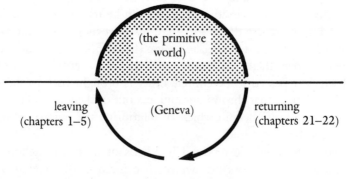

OVER THERE

(the primitive world)

leaving
(chapters 1–5)

(Geneva)

returning
(chapters 21–22)

OVER HERE

narrative can bring this civilized primitive as far back as Geneva by way of return (chapters 21–22).

The initial dangerous and skeptical bipolarity (truth is over here while error is over there) is replaced by a circular schema built over a triangle with three guide points: first of all, *Geneva,* the point of departure and return, of the two terms of the initial relation that the story leaves intact and even reinforces by placing it out of the field, as beginning and ending but not the object of the story; then this strange *nature* and this exemplary *humanity* (however sinful it may be) into which the alterity of the New World is divided, thus reclassified into an exotic universe and an ethical utopia, according to the order that Léry's writing introduces.

This work is indeed a *hermeneutics of the other.* Onto the shores of the New World it transports the Christian exegetical apparatus which, born of a necessary relation with Jewish alterity, has been applied in turn to the biblical tradition, to Greco-Latin antiquity, and to many more foreign totalities. On one more occasion it draws effects of meaning from its relation with the other. Ethnology will become a form of exegesis that has not ceased providing the modern West with what it needs in order to articulate its identity through a relation with the past or the future, with foreigners or with nature.

FIGURE 5.2

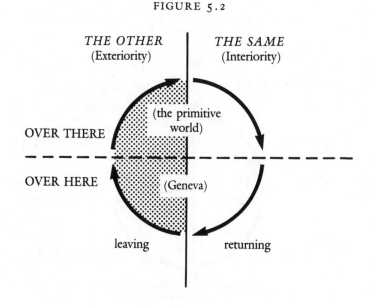

The functioning of this new hermeneutics of the other is already sketched in Léry's text in the shape of two problematic issues that transform its theological usage. These are the linguistic operation of translation, and the position of a subject in relation to an expanse of objects. In both cases the (oceanic) break that characterizes the difference is not suppressed; on the contrary, the text presupposes and thwarts this break in order to be grounded as a discourse of knowledge.

The bar between the Old and the New World is the line on which an *activity of translation* can be seen replacing a theological language. This discreet transformation is indicated by two chapters of which both— since one is devoted to departure and the other to return—constitute a navigational lock, a transit, between the travelogue and the picture of the Tupi world (figure 5.3). The first, chapter 6, tells of theological debates at Fort Coligny in the Rio Bay and of the "inconstancy and variation" of Villegagnon "in matters of religion," the cause for the disembarkation of the Huguenot mission among the Tupis on the coast, "who were incomparably more humane with us."[26] The other, chapter 20, which Léry designates as the "colloquy of the savage's language,"[27] is a dictionary— or rather a French-Tupi Berlitz guide.

According to the first account, the Island of Coligny mediates between the Old and the New World and is a place where divisiveness and the

FIGURE 5.3

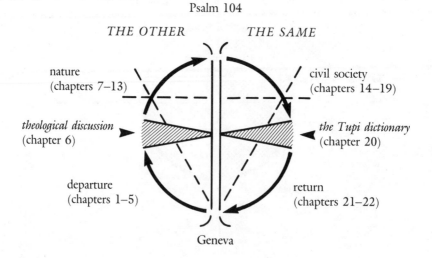

Psalm 104

THE OTHER   *THE SAME*

nature
(chapters 7–13)   civil society
                                           (chapters 14–19)

theological discussion   *the Tupi dictionary*
(chapter 6)   (chapter 20)

departure   return
(chapters 1–5)   (chapters 21–22)

Geneva

confusion of languages reign supreme. It is a Babel in the twilight of the universe. Yet confusion is no longer avowed here. It is hidden in a language of hypocrisy (that of Villegagnon), where what is said is not what is thought, much less what is done. At the end of the globe, at the threshold of the unknown Tupi world, deception proliferates beneath the veil of a literal reproduction of Calvinist theology: such are the public prayers of the "zealot" Villegagnon, whose "inner side and heart it was discomfiting to get to know."[28] Is this not tantamount to saying that at this point language no longer holds an anchor in reality, and that at the farthest borders of the West it floats detached from its truth and from any firm grounding, caught up into the indefinite turnings of a lure?

Chapter 20 comes at the end of the description of the Tupi lands. After the linguistic confusion surrounding the Island of Coligny, this vast picture of the primitive world is an epiphany of things, the *discourse of an effectivity*. Clearly the contents were first given as antinomic, but they were divided and elaborated in such a way as to become, in their human sector, a world which does justice to the truth of Geneva. Thus, a reality is already there, and it saturates Léry's statements. What separates the Western world from that world is no longer an array of things, but their appearance—essentially, a foreign language. From stated difference there only remains a *language to be translated*. Whence the chapter which provides the code for linguistic transformation. It allows unity to be restored by folding upon one another all the heterogenous peelings that cover an identity of substance.

The dictionary becomes a theological instrument. Just as religious language is perverted by a usage which is "discomfiting to get to know" and which refers to unfathomable intentions or "heart,"[29] now, situated on the very line that the rift of the universe demarcated, translation *lets* primitive reality pass into Western discourse. All that is needed is to have one language "converted" into another. As Calvin already suggsted,[30] the operation of translation frees one from reducing language to a first tongue from which all others would be derived; it replaces the being-there of a beginning with a transformation which unravels on the surface of languages, which makes a single meaning pass from tongue to tongue, and which will soon provide linguistics, the science of these transformations, with a decisive role in all recapitulative strategies.

In the place where the *Histoire* locates it, foreign language already acquires the double function of being the way by which a substance (the effectivity of primitive life) happens to uphold the discourse of a European knowledge, and of being a fable, a speech which is unaware of what it expresses before decipherment can provide it with meaning and practical usage. The being which authenticates the discourse is no longer directly received from God; it is made to come from the foreign place itself, where it is the gold mine hidden under an exotic exteriority, the truth to be discerned beneath primitive babble.

For Léry this economy of translation entails, moreover, a general problematic. For example, it orders the analysis of living beings and therein becomes specific. In effect, plants and animals are classified according to the modulations of a constant distinction between what is seen (appearance) and what is eaten (edible substance). Exteriority captivates the eye, it astonishes or horrifies, but this theater is often a lie and a fiction in respect to edibility, which measures the utility, or the essence, of fruits and animals. The double diagnostic of taste corrects seductions or repulsions of the eye: is it healthy or not to eat, raw or cooked? The same holds for exotic fable, the enchanting but often deceptive voice: the interpreter discriminates in terms of utility when, first creating a distance between what it says and what it does not say, he translates what it does not say in forms of truth that are good to hear back in France. An intellectual edibility is the essence that has to be distinguished from ravishments of the ear.

From the baroque spectacle of flora and fauna to their edibility; from primitive festivals to their utopian and moral exemplariness; and finally from exotic language to its intelligibility, the same dynamic unfolds. It is that of *utility*—or, rather, that of *production,* at least insofar as this voyage which increases the initial investment is, analogically, a productive labor, "a labor that produces capital."[31] From the moment of departure from Geneva a language sets out to find a world; at stake is a mission. Deprived of effectivity—without grounding—at the furthermost borders of the West (on the Island of Coligny, chapter 6), it finally appears as a language of pure conviction or subjectivity, a language that is incapable of defending its objective statements against deceptive use, leaving its speakers no recourse but to flee. This language is opposed, on the other side of things, to the world of total alterity, or of primitive nature. Here effectivity is at first uncanniness. But within the breadth of this alterity, analysis introduces a rift between exteriority (esthetics, etc.) and interiority (meaning that can be assimilated). It causes a slow reversion, beginning with the greatest exteriority (the general spectacle of nature, then the forests, etc.), and progresses toward the regions of greater interiority (sickness and death). It thus prepares primitive effectivity to become, by means of translation (chapter 20), *the world that is spoken by an initial language.* The point of departure was an over here (a "we") relativized by an elsewhere (a "they"), and a language deprived of "substance." This point of departure becomes a place for *truth,* since here the *discourse which comprehends the world* is in use. Such is the production for which the primitive is useful: it makes language move from the affirmation of a conviction into a position of knowledge. Yet if, from its point of departure, the language to be restored were theological, what is reinstated upon return is (in principle) either scientific or philosophical.

This position of knowledge is upheld by using the line between *over here and over there* in a way that also results from the transformation that is being performed. This line is used to distinguish between the ethnological subject and object. In Léry's text it is drawn through the difference between two literary forms, that which narrates tales of travel (chapters 1–6 and 21–22), and that which describes a natural and human landscape (chapters 7–19). The *story* of the actions that cross the world draws a frame about the *picture* of the Tupi world: two perpendicular planes (figure 5.4).

On the first is written the chronicle of facts and deeds by the group or by Léry. These events are narrated in terms of *tense:* a *history* is composed with a chronology—very detailed—of actions undertaken or lived

FIGURE 5.4

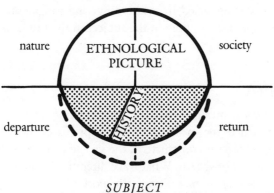

OBJECT
(Sights and Sounds)

nature   ETHNOLOGICAL PICTURE   society

departure   return

SUBJECT
(Facts and Deeds)

by a *subject*. On the second plane *objects* are set out in a space ruled not
by localizations or geographical routes—these indications are very rare
and always vague—but by a taxonomy of living beings,[32] a systematic
inventory of philosophical questions, etc.; in sum, the catalogue raisonné
of a knowledge. The historical parts of the text value time "as an accomplice of our will"[33] and the articulation of *Western acting*. In relation
to this subject who acts, *the other is extension,* where understanding delimits objects.

For Léry, the book is a "History"[34] in which "seen things" are still
attached to the observer's activities. He combines two discourses that will
soon be separated from one another. One discourse is attached to science;
as opposed to "natural history" (left to the philosopher) and to "divine
history" (left to the theologian), it assumes its task, according to Jean
Bodin, to be one of "explaining the actions of contemporary man living
in society" and analyzing "the productions of the human will" insofar as
it is *semper sui dissimilis.*[35] In the sixteenth century, at least for theologians,
history takes for granted the autonomy of a political and juridical *subject*
of actions (the prince, the nation, the "civil order") on the one hand, and
on the other, of *fields* where dissimilitudes between various expressions
of man's will (law, language, institutions, etc.) can be measured.[36] In Léry's
case the subject is momentarily an "exiled prince," a man lost between
sky and earth, between a God who is disappearing and an earth that is
yet to be discovered; the subject's itinerancy connects a language left vacant to the work needed to provide another effectivity for this language.
Later there will be "ethnology," when the picture of the primitive world
will have acquired a homogeneity independent of the displacements of
actual journeys; in other words, when the space of "objective" representation will be distinguished from the observing judgment, and when it
will have become futile to present the subject in the text of a constructive
operation.

Eroticized Speech

IF, in this *Histoire,* meaning moves in the direction of what writing produces (it constructs the meaning of the Tupi "experiment"—just as an
experiment in physics is constructed), the savage is reciprocally associated
with the seduction of speech. What travel literature really fabricates is the
primitive as *a body of pleasure.* Facing the work of the West, that is, Western man's actions that manufacture time and reason, there exists in Léry's

work a place for leisure and bliss, the Tupi world, indeed a feast for the eyes and ears. Such eroticizing of the other's body—of the primitive nudity and the primitive voice—goes hand in hand with the formation of an ethics of production. At the same time that it creates a profit, the voyage creates a lost paradise relative to a body-object, to an erotic body. This figure of the other has no doubt played a role in the modern Western *epistemè*, more crucial than that of the critical ideas circulated through Europe by travel literature.

As we have observed, the profit "brought back" through writing appears to delimit a "remainder" which, although it is unwritten, will also define the primitive. The trace of this remainder is pleasure: Léry's "ravishments," the Tupi festivals—sylvan psalms for the one, dances and country ballads for the others. *Excess* is the quality they share. But they are ephemeral and irrecoupable, unexploitable moments that will neither be regained nor redeemed. Something of Léry himself does not return from over there. These moments rend holes in the fabric of the traveler's time, just as the Tupis' festive organization was beyond all economy of history. Spending and loss designate *a present*; they form a series of "snippets," nearly a lapsus in Western discourse. These rips seem to come in the night to undo the utilitarian construct of the tale. It is the "un-heard" that purloins the text or, more precisely, is stolen from the thief; it is exactly what is *heard* but not understood, hence ravished from the body of productive work: speech without writing, the song of pure enunciation, the act of speaking without knowing—a pleasure in saying or in hearing.

At issue here are not the extraordinary deeds or experiences of which hagiographic or mystical discourses make use, each in their own way, to establish the status of a language of "truth."[37] In the *Histoire,* marvels— the visible marks of alterity—are used not to posit other truths or another discourse, but, on the contrary, to found a language upon its operative capacity for bringing this foreign exteriority back to "sameness." The "remainder" or "leftover" is more likely a fallout, an aftereffect of this operation, a waste that it produces through succeeding in doing what it does, but which comes as a by-product. This waste product of constructive thinking—its fallout and its repressed—will finally become the other.

That the figure of the other, eliminated from objective knowledge, returns in another form along the margins of this knowledge is what the eroticized voice makes manifest. But this displacement has to be situated in the totality which prepares for it, for it is relative to the general representation of the tale, which turns the primitive society into a festive body and an object of pleasure. A series of stable oppositions globally upholds the distinction between the primitive and the civilized man throughout the entire text. Thus:

PRIMITIVE	vs.	CIVILIZED
nudity	vs.	clothing
(festival) ornament	vs.	finery (stylishness)
hobby, leisure, festival	vs.	work (occupation)
unanimity, proximity, cohesion	vs.	division, distance
pleasure	vs.	ethics

Tupis are feathered (from birds to man, the primitive world modulates the combinations of plumed ornaments and pristine nudity). "Frolicking, drinking, and *liquoring* [*caouiner*] is almost their everyday occupation."[38] For Léry, who is an artisan, what are they really doing—or what are they producing? They spend their time celebrating, in pure expression that neither preserves anything nor accrues profit, in a present, eternal time *off*, a pure excess. In the Tupi mirror, the image of the worker appears thus inverted. But the operation which leaves nothing more to difference than an exteriority effectively transforms it into a festive theater. It produces *an estheticization of the primitive.*

A character from a spectacle, the primitive man represents an economy other than work. He reintroduces the other economy into the general picture. By way of hypothesis we can state that in an esthetic and erotic fashion, he is the return of what the economy of production had to repress in order to be founded as such. In the text he is situated in effect at the juncture of a prohibition and a pleasure. For example, the primitive festival is what surprises Léry (he is "ravished"), but equally it is what he surprises, penetrating the Tupi world by effraction. Here we witness a double transgression, in respect both to his law and to theirs. In the village where they are gathered, he feels "some fears" in hearing them sing in the distance: "All the same, after all these indistinct noises and howls turned to silence, the men paused for a moment (the women and children remained very coy all this time), and from then on we heard them singing and making their voices sound on such a marvelous note that, once I regained my confidence in hearing these softer and more gracious sounds, it hardly need be asked if I wanted to see them more intimately."[39]

After a moment of suspense, because of danger, he moves forward in spite of his translator (the interpreter who "had never dared to be seen among the natives during such a festival"): "Thus approaching the place where I heard this singing, as the natives' houses are either very long or are built in a round fashion and (as we might say of the pergolas in our gardens over here) are covered with grasses all the way from the ground to the roof: in order better to see *at my pleasure,* with my hands I fashioned *a little aperture* through the covering."[40] He finally penetrates this area of pleasure protected by a wall, as are the gardens of his native land.

> There, pointing my finger at two Frenchmen who were looking at me—themselves having been emboldened by my example and having approached with neither obstacle nor difficulty—all three of us went into the house. Hence seeing that the primitives were not at all startled (as the interpreter had expected), but rather, on the contrary, held their rank and order in an admirable fashion, and continued to sing their songs, we withdrew quite gently to a corner where we contemplated them *at our delight.*[41]

The tale tells of the pleasure afforded by seeing through the "little aperture," as if it were a keyhole, before the men taking refuge in a corner where they can be fully delighted in the joy of this "sabbath" and these "Bacchanals."[42] Moreover, Léry says the pleasure of hearing the frightening and seductive noises from close proximity makes the temerity of approaching them quite irresistible. Such scenes of ethnological eroticism will repeat themselves in every travelogue. They have their homologue in the inaugural scene of *Sodom and Gomorrha* in Proust's *Remembrance of Things Past.* There, too, is a "New World" and its discovery ("the first appearance of men-women"): it is first *heard* from a little shop "separated from Jupien's merely by an extremely thin wall." The hero hurries there without hesitation:

> The things of this kind that I attended always had in their staging the most imprudent and unreal character, as if the only reward of such revelations were an act fraught with risks, although partially clandestine. . . .
>
> I didn't dare move. The Guermantes' groom, no doubt taking advantage of their absence, had moved into the shop where I was standing on a ladder that had been kept in the shed. And if I had climbed up it I would have been able to open the dormer window

and hear the scene as if I were in Jupien's shop itself. But I was afraid of making a racket, and besides it was useless. I didn't even have to regret not having come into the shop for several minutes. For according to what I heard the first times in Jupien's, what were only inarticulate sounds, I can gather that only a few words were expressed. It is true that these sounds were so violent that, had they not been taken up one octave higher in a parallel lament, I might have believed that one body was cutting the throat of another just beside me and that then the murderer and his revived victim were taking a bath to wash themselves clean of all signs of the crime. I concluded later that there is only one thing as noisy as suffering, and that is pleasure.[43]

The "noises" that resound from the primitive men's festival, like the "inarticulate sounds" that indicate that of "men-women," have no intelligible content. These are "vocations" loosened from the orbits of meaning. An oblivion of precaution, losses of understanding, ravishments— that kind of language draws its power no longer from what it says, but from what it does or from what it is. Thus it cannot be either true or false. It is beyond or before this distinction. The "over there" comes back in this form. Like a cry, the act of enunciation inverts the statement and the whole organization of form, object, or referent. It is senseless. It partakes of orgasm.

Responding to this calling, the gesture of coming nearer reduces but never eliminates distance. It creates a situation of "inter-dict." The voice moves, in effect, in a space between the body and language, but only in a moment of passage from one to the other and as if *in* their weakest difference. Here there is neither the contact of body against body in the violence of love (or festivity), nor the contact of word against word (or text against text) in the semantic order proper to a linguistic linearity. The body, which is a thickening and an obfuscation of phonemes, is not yet the death of language. The articulation of signifiers is stirred up and effaced; there remains nonetheless the vocal modulation, almost lost but not absorbed in the tremors of the body; a strange interval where the voice emits a speech lacking "truths," and where proximity is a presence without possession. The moment evades the legalities and the disciplines of meaning as it evades the violence of bodies. It is the cerebral and illegal pleasure of being right there, where language, as it swoons, announces the coming of a coveted, feared violence which is held at a distance by the space through which one hears. This erotic "excess" plays upon the preservation of the very system that makes the body the observer's other. It takes for granted the legality that it transgresses. That "desire may be the underside of the law" is what the audible voice utters over and over again.[44]

Seen and/or Heard: The Eye and the Ear

THE suppression of the native's effective uncanniness corresponds to the replacement of his exterior reality by a voice. This is a familiar displacement. The other returns in the form of "noises and howls," or "softer and more gracious sounds." These ghostly voices are blended into the spectacle to which the observing and scriptural operation has reduced the Tupi. The space in which the other is circumscribed composes an opera. But if the figures and voices, all remnants transformed from medieval festival, are associated coextensively with pleasure and together form a theater of the esthetic behind which the founding wills (preserved by writing) of operations and judgments on things themselves are upheld, the picture is made double by an opposition between the heard and the seen.[45] In the fashion of those images in books that appear to move when looked at through a pair of spectacles whose lenses are tinted differently, one green, the other red, the native shifts within a single frame according to the way he is perceived, with the eye or with the ear.

We must add a third term to the two others in order to complete the series corresponding to the different ways in which the native can be perceived: *the mouth, the eye, the ear.* The Indian's "edibility" pertains to the *oral* instance, a matter of defining his "substance" and, from the standpoint of the Westerner, confronting his anthropophagia—an obsessive topic whose study has always been central and which establishes the status of future ethnology. Inscribed in the text, as we have seen, this relation of power is moreover what makes the text possible. Here the tale has at its command the object that has been prepared for it through this preliminary action. From now on the compositions of the eye and traversals of voice go along different tracks. For the audiovisual is split into two parts.

The eye is in the service of a "discovery of the world." It is the front line of an encyclopedic curiosity that during the sixteenth century "frenetically heaps up" materials in order to posit the "foundations of modern

science." The rare, the bizarre, the unique—objects already collected
through medieval interest—are apprehended in the fervor of an englobing ambition: "that nothing will remain foreign to man and that everything will be at his service."[46] There exists a "dizzying curiosity" that the
development of all "curious" or occult sciences will be orchestrating. The
frenzy of knowing and the pleasure of looking reach into the darkest
regions and unfold the interiority of bodies as surfaces laid out before
our eyes.

This conquering and orgiastic curiosity, so taken with unveiling hidden
things, has its symbol in travel literature: the dressed, armed, knighted
discoverer face-to-face with the nude Indian woman. A New World arises
from the other side of the ocean with the appearance of the Tupi females,
naked as Venus born in the midst of the sea in Botticelli's painting. To
Léry's stupor, these Indian women wish "to remain nude forever": "With
their two hands they douse water over their heads . . . wash themselves
and plunge their whole bodies in every fountain and glassy river like reeds
of sugar cane, and on one such day, even more than twelve times."[47]

Apparitions of this kind on the banks of glassy rivers have their nocturnal doubles on the Island of Coligny where the French make the Indian women, "prisoners of war," work like slaves: "As soon as night had
fallen, from their bodies they secretly stripped the shirts and other tatters
that had been given to them. For their pleasure, before going to bed they
went about to stroll in the nude all about our island."[48]

The nakedness of these night women wild with pleasure is a very ambivalent vision. Their savagery fascinates and threatens, erupting from an
unknown world where the women are, according to Léry, the only persons who work tirelessly and actively, and who, voracious souls that they
are, are yet the first to practice anthropophagia. Thus the action of the
woman who had been awarded, as a "husband" to look after, a prisoner
doomed to be eaten:

> As soon as the prisoner would have been beaten to death, if he had
> a wife (as I have noted are awarded to a few of them), she placed
> herself beside his body as if she were mourning him a little. I note
> "a little," for truly following what is said to be the way of the
> crocodile—that is, once having killed a man, the animal weeps be-
> side the body before devouring him—immediately after having ex-
> pressed such sorrow and shed a few false tears over her dead hus-
> band, if possible she will be the first to partake of him. That being

done, the other women, and most of the old ones (among whom many covet eating human flesh more than the young women, and constantly solicit all who have prisoners in order to have them dispatched in that way), appear with hot water that they have taken from the fire, rub and scald the dead body in such a way that once they have removed the first layer of skin, they blanch the body just as, over here, cooks prepare a suckling pig that will be roasted on a spit.[49]

"Como era gostoso o meu Frances": "How delicious was my Frenchman," exclaims the Tupi woman in Nelson Pereira dos Santos' film who had taken a French prisoner as her husband immediately before devouring him.[50]

This native reenacts the Western phantasm of witches dancing and crying in the night, wild with pleasure and glutting themselves on children. The "sabbath" that Léry evokes is in continuity with what the Carnival of antiquity has since become, now progressively excluded from cities with the development of bourgeois towns, exiled into the countryside, the forests, and the night.[52] This festive, prohibited, threatening world appears again exiled to the other side of the universe, at the outer limit of the conquerors' enterprise. And like the exorcist, his colleague from over here, the explorer-missionary assigns himself the task of expelling witches from the foreign land. But he does not succeed so well in localizing them on the stage of ethnological exorcism. The other returns: with the image of nudity, "an exorbitant presence";[53] with the phantasm of the *vagina dentata*, which looms in the representation of feminine voracity; or with the dancing eruption of forbidden pleasures. More basically, the native world, like the diabolical cosmos, becomes Woman. It is declined in the feminine gender.

But another image reminiscent of witches is superimposed over this one. In relation to "us," the Tupi are "stronger, sturdier and fuller, fitter, and immune to disease: and there is hardly ever a cripple, a one-eyed, deformed, or baleful soul among them. Furthermore, how many of them live to the age of one hundred or one hundred and twenty years . . . there are few in their old age who have either grey or white hair."

Akin to gods, "they all truly drink from the Fountain of Youth." "The little concern and worry they have for things of this world" harmonizes with a paradise in which "the woods, grasses, and fields are ever greening."[54] In the midst of this endless spring, one of the "doubly strange

and truly marvelous things that I observed among these Brazilian women,"
notes Léry, was their nudity. It is not only innocent, "without any sign
of shame or disgrace,"[55] but primal, prior to human history. In many
images from the Renaissance, nudity has the value of a divine attribute.
It is in effect the sign of theophanies, unveilings of divine Love that a
series of paintings contrasts with the festivals depicting earthly Love, which
is clothed and decorated.[56] Under this sign the apparition of the native
is that of a goddess, "nude, nude beneath her black locks," as Marguerite
Duras writes. But in being born of the sea, the Indian women are no
longer awaited in the nomenclature of the Greco-Latin pantheon; they
surge forth outside of the Mediterranean—the semanticized—space, as
goddesses without proper names, springing forth from an ocean "unknown to the ancients."

These women in whom the diabolical and the divine alternate, who
oscillate between the over-there and the over-here of the human sphere
("This animal takes so much delight in this nudity," writes Léry),[57] are
nevertheless an *object* placed in the space in which the looking itself becomes conspicuous. An image, and no longer an origin—even if the apparition keeps the uncanniness of what it is replacing. As in painting of
the Renaissance, the unclothed Venus replaces the Mother of men,[58] the
mystery of Mary or Eve, and as in Venus the naked truth is what the *eye
is allowed to see,* in the same way the Indian women indicate the secret
that a knowledge transgresses and disenchants. Like the Indian woman's
naked body, the body of the world becomes a surface offered to the in-
quisitions of curiosity. During Léry's time the same will hold true for
the bodies of the city and of the diseased, which are transformed into
legible spaces. Through the "little apertures" of successive "experiments"
the traditional veil that covers the opacity of things is torn and lets the
"world be recognized in ocular ways."[59]

Of the transgression that accompanies the birth of a science, Léry provides a summary with two elements: "a good foot, a good eye."[60] On
another occasion he writes, "See and visit."[61] Light is thrown on his remarks by Freud's comment on the relation that writing (which travels)
and knowledge (which turns subjects into objects) maintain with "treading upon the body of mother earth."[62] From this labor, the women naked, seen, and known designate the finished product metonymically. They
indicate a new, scriptural relation with the world; they are the effect of
a knowledge which "tramples" and travels over the earth visually in order
to fabricate its representation. For Heidegger, "The fundamental event

of the modern age is the conquest of the world as a picture."[63] But the apparition of women in the *Histoire* still retains the traces of risk and incertitude that in the sixteenth century go hand in hand with the inversion of the mother-earth into the earth-object. Through the women the tale therefore tells both of the beginning and of the temerity of a scientific *point of view.*

Whereas the object beheld can be written—made homogenous with the linearities of stated meaning and constructed space—the *voice* can create an *aparté,* opening a breach in the text and restoring a contact of body to body. "Voice off." What comes from the mouth or goes into the ear can produce ravishment. Noises win over messages, and singing over speech. A break of direction and time follows the coming of a "song rally" among both the Indians and the "great forest": "Hearing the chant of an infinity of birds nightingaling through the woods where the sun was shining; seeing myself, I say, as a soul invited to praise God among all these things; moreover with a cheerful heart, I took to singing Psalm 104 out loud: Hark, hark my soul, I must tell you, etc."[64]

There is an analogical structure—resembling many others—in the vocation the "gracious" sounds brought to him through the Tupi festival, and the calling that came from the "birds nightingaling," inviting him to sing. The Indian shaman's vocation often comes of hearing a bird in the forest and gaining the will and the ability to sing.[65] Almost immediately affected with a meaning (whether religious or not), the voice creates the rift of a lapse of memory and an ecstasy. Unlike in shamanism, Léry's calling has no social function; to the contrary, it crosses language, it makes of the senseless soul the void through which an irresistible poem comes to life. "I must tell you": it is still a received formula, but it marks already the locus where the rupture of an excess will expand in the urgency of a "saying," of an act of speech which will be neither docile to a spoken truth nor subject to a statement. The formula no longer goes in the direction of a will conserved in its purity through the writing whose powers Jean de Léry had praised. In a sensorial and symbolic sheath of the winds, of whispers, and of noises foreign to normal sounds is hidden a *birth through the ear.*[66] It designates a violation (or a "ravishment") which cuts across social reason; it is acquiescence to *the other's voice,* "his master's voice" and the voice of the father, the voice of conscience; the voice where there is indication—originally represented in myth as the incestuous demand for sacrifice—of the "obscene and ferocious figure of the superego."[67]

This figure designates the insurmountable alterity from which the subject's desire is modeled. I evoke it here only to emphasize a crucial point. What is heard is not what is expected. What appears "doesn't resemble anything." Hence it cannot be truthful. "Meaning is truthful"; and inversely, "Truthfulness is nothing more than meaning"; finally, "Truthfulness has but one constant characteristic: it *means*, it has the sense of a *meaning*."[68] In this fashion what was heard *cannot be put into words*, unless indirectly, through a metaphorical disruption, breaking the linearity of discourse. It insinuates a rift, a jump, a confusion of genres. It is a *metabasis eis allo genos*, a "passage to another genre" as Aristotle puts it.

Generally speaking, voice itself would have a metaphorical—a delinearizing and altering—function to the degree that it cuts across the metonymical schema of sight. If, as "derision of the signifier," metaphor "is placed at the exact point where meaning is produced in non-meaning,"[69] it would be in effect the movement by which one signifier is replaced by its other:[70] "one word for another," but also the very ruse that subverts the word. Through these metaphorical eruptions of fable and these lapses of meaning, voice, exiled to the distant shores of discourse, would flow back, and with it would come the murmurs and "noises" from which scriptural reproduction is distinguished. Thus an exteriority, with neither beginning nor truth, would return to visit discourse.

In respect to a single text, would it be too much to recognize already in the gap between what is seen and heard the distinction between two functionings of the savage world in relation to the language that deals with it? Either as an *object* of a discourse that constructs schemes and pictures, or as a *distortion*, a rapture, but also a calling of this discourse? These two functions are combined, for the vocal exteriority is also the stimulus and the precondition of its scriptural opposite. It is necessary —insofar as necessity, as Jacques Lacan says, is precisely "what never ceases to be written."[72] The savage becomes a senseless speech ravishing Western discourse, but one which, because of that very fact, generates a productive science of meaning and objects that endlessly writes. *The locus of the other* that this speech represents is hence doubly fabulous: first by virtue of a metaphorical rupture (*fari*, the act of speech not having a subject that can be named), and then by virtue of an object that can be understood (a fiction that can be translated into the terms of knowledge). A saying *arrests* what is said—it is the erasure of writing—and forces it to extend its production; it generates writing.

At the very least, Léry's story sketches the science of this fable, which essentially will become ethnology—or the manner of its intervention in history.

NOTES

1. G. de Rohan-Csermak, "La première apparition du terme ethnologie," in *Ethnologia europea: Revue internationale d'ethnologie européenne* (1967), 1(4):170–84.

2. Claude Lévi-Strauss, *Structural Anthropology* (New York: Doubleday, 1967), pp. 18 and 25; in the French, *Anthropologie structurale* (Paris: Plon, 1958), see "Histoire et ethnologie," pp. 25 and 33.

3. On the series of Franco-Brazilian voyages from the sixteenth to the eighteenth century alone—the object of a work in progress—the bibliography is already immense. I refer only to a few general works which have guided my research: Geoffrey Atkinson, *Les Nouveaux Horizons de la renaissance française* (Paris: Droz, 1935); H. Baudet, *Paradise on Earth: Some Thoughts on European Images of Non-European Man* (New Haven: Yale University Press, 1965); Sergio Buarque de Hollanda, *Visâo do Paraiso* (São Paulo: Editora do Universidade de São Paulo, 1959); Michele Duchet, *Anthropologie et histoire au siècle des Lumières* (Paris: Maspéro, 1971); Sergio Landucci, *I Filosofi e i selvaggi, 1580–1790* (Bari, Italy: Laterza, 1972); Gerard Leclerc, *Anthropologie et colonialisme* (Paris: Fayard, 1972); Frank Edward Manuel, *The Eighteenth Century Confronts the Gods* (Cambridge: Harvard University Press, 1959); Sergio Moravia, *La Scienza dell'uomo nel Settecento* (Bari, Italy: Laterza, 1970); Joaquim V. Serrâo, *O Rio de Janeiro no seculo XVI*, 2 vols. (Lisbon: Comissão Nacional das Comemoragües do le Centenário do Rio de Janeiro, 1965); and naturally, Anatole Louis Garraux, *Bibliographie brésilienne* (French and Latin works relative to Brazil, 1500–1898), 2d. ed. (Rio de Janeiro: J. Olympio, 1962); and Georges Raeders, *Bibliographie franco-brésilienne (1551–1957)* (Rio de Janeiro: Ministerio da Educaçao e Cultura, Instituto Nacional do Livro, 1960).

4. "The Middle Ages also prepare everything that will be necessary for the reception of a 'noble savage': a millenarianism that awaits a return to the Age of Gold; the conviction that, if it exists, historical progress takes place in waves of renaissances, or revivals of an innocent primitivism," notes Jacques Le Goff, "L'Historien et l'homme quotidien," in *L'Historien entre l'ethnologue et le futurologue* (The Hague: Mouton, 1973), p. 240. On the continuity between the idea of the Golden Age and that of the noble savage, see René Gonnard, *La Légende du bon sauvage: Contribution à l'étude des origines du socialisme* (Paris: Librairie Médicis, 1946); and Harry Levin, *The Myth of the Golden Age in the Renaissance* (Bloomington: Indiana University Press, 1969), ch. 3.

5. Claude Lévi-Strauss, *Tristes Tropiques* (New York: Atheneum, 1975), p. 85; p. 89 in the French edition (Paris: Plon, 1955).

6. The Léry dossier is important.

I will be quoting from Paul Gaffarel's edition of the *Histoire d'un Voyage*—the only exact and complete one—except for some details, checked based on the Geneva edition of 1580 (Paris, B. N.: 8° Oy 136 B), in two volumes (Paris: A. Lemerre, 1880). I will refer to this text hereafter with G. followed by the volume and page numbers.

After its first six editions in the late sixteenth and early seventeenth century (La Rochelle, 1578; Geneva, 1580, 1585, 1594, 1599, and 1611), all subsequent editions of *L'Histoire* except for the Gaffarel were abridged. It was republished by Charly Clerc in 1927, by M.-R. Mayeux in 1957, and by A.-M. Chartier in 1972 (with an excellent introduction). Since then there has appeared the superb anastatic reproduction of the 1580 edition, edited by Jean-Claude Morisot (Geneva: Dorz, 1975). I must also mention the Brazilian translation and useful notes by Serge Millet in the "Biblioteca historica brasileira," *Viagem à Terra do Brasil* (São Paulo; Editora da Universidade de São Paolo, 1980), including Plinio Ayrosa's curious reconstitution of chapter 20 on Tupi language (pp. 219–50) that A. Lemos Barbosa, one of the outstanding specialists on ancient Tupi—see his *Curso de Tupi antigo* (Rio de Janeior, 1956)—had nonetheless criticized vehemently; see Barbosa's *Estudos de Tupi: O "Dialogo de Léry" na restauração de Plinio Ayrosa* (Rio de Janeiro, 1944).

In the second half of the sixteenth century an entire literature either surrounds or exploits the knight Durant de Villegagnon's expedition to Rio (1555–1560), especially treatises: the Franciscan André Thévet's *Cosmographie universelle* (Paris: Chez P. L'Huillier, 1575), whose "impostures" Léry aims to refute; *Les Trois Mondes* by Henri Laucelot du Voisin de La Popelinière (Paris: P. L'Huillier, 1582), whose third part (America) deals at great length with the voyage, etc. But these scientific works are published on the heels of documents and pamphlets. Some, of polemic and journalistic stripe, are of the order of *L'Epoussette des armoiries de Pillegaignon* . . . or *L'Etrille de Nicolas Durand* . . . . Others provide a foundation for dossiers on debated questions. Two historical moments are of importance:

1) 1557–1558, after the departure of the "mission" from Geneva, when Villegagnon has dominion over the Island of Coligny in the Bay of Rio. These are political apologia:

> · *Copie de quelques Letres sur la Navigation du Chevallier de Villegaignon es Terres de l'Amerique* . . . *contenant sommairement les fortunes encourues en ce voyage, avec les meurs et façons de vivre des Sauvages du pais: Envoyées par un des gens dudict Seigneur,* Nicolas Barré, ed. (Paris: Martin le Jeune, 1557), in-8°; reissued in 1558, in-8°, 19ff.
>
> · *Discours de Nicolas Barré sur la navigation du chevalier de Villegaignon en Amerique* (Paris: Martin le Jeune, 1558), reissued in Paul Gaffarel, *Histoire du Brésil français au XVIᵉ siècle* (Paris: Maisonneuve, 1877), pp. 373–82.

2) 1561, therefore after the Portuguese victory and the departure of the French (1560). A theological and political debate ensues between Paris and Geneva on the failed occasion for a Protestant sanctuary. Villegagnon is accused of having

betrayed either the reformed religion or the king—or both. The pastor Pierre Richier, a theologian and a member of the "mission" in which Léry played a part, was the most uncompromising for the former governor.

- [Loïs du Rozu], *Histoire des choses mémorables advenues en la terre du Brésil, partie de l'Amérique Australe, sous le gouvernement de M. de Villegagnon depuis l'an 1555 jusqu'à l'an 1558* (Geneva, 1561), in-8°, 48ff.; republished in *Nouvelles Annales des Voyages,* 5th series, (1854), vol. 40.
- *Les Propositions contentieuses entre le Chevallier de Villegagnon sur la Résolution des Sacrements de Maistre Jehan Calvin* (Paris, 1561), in the volume cited above.
- *Response aux Lettres de Nicolas Durant, dict le Chevallier de Villegaignon adressées à la Reyne mere du Roy: Ensemble la confutation d'une hérésie mise en avant par le dit Villegaignon contre la souveraine puissance et authorité des rois* (n.p., n.d.; circa 1561), in-8°, 46ff.
- *Petri Richerii libri duo apologetici ad refutandas noenias, et coarguendos blasphemos errores detegendaque mendacia Nicolai Durandi qui se Villegagnonem cognominat,* "Excusum Hierapoli, per Thrasybulum, Phoenicum" (Geneva, 1561), in-4°. In the same year Richier's text was published in French as *La Refutation des folles rêveries, execrables blasphèmes et mensonges de Nicolas Durand . . .* (Geneva, 1561).
- *Response aux libelles d'injures publiés contre le chevalier de Villegagnon* (Paris: André Wechel, 1561), in-4° (inspired or written by Villegagnon).

It must also be noted that in the subsequent edition of Jean Crespin's famous *Actes des Martyrs* (Geneva, 1564), two reports that have been inserted on the devout Calvinists persecuted by Villegagnon during the mission of 1556–57 at Rio are by Jean de Léry (pp. 857–68 and 880–98).

There are several studies concerning the historical and literary implications of the *Histoire d'un Voyage faict en la terre du Bresil:* Paul Gaffarel, *Jean de Léry: La Langue tupi,* an offprint from the *Revue de linguistique* (Paris: Maisonneuve, 1877); Léry's *Histoire du Brésil français au XVIe siècle* (Paris: Maisonneuve, 1878); *Les Français au delà des mers: Les Découvreurs français du XVIe siècle* (Paris: Challamel, 1888); Arthur Heulhard, *Villegagnon, Roi d'Amérique* (Paris: E. Leroux, 1897) (the panegyric of a colonizer); Gilbert Chinard, *L'Exotisme américain dans la littérature française au XVIe siècle* (Paris: Hachette, 1911), and *Les Réfugiés huguenots en Amérique* (Paris: Belles Lettres, 1925); C. Clerc, "Le Voyage de Léry et la découverte du 'bon sauvage,'" *Revue de l'Institut de Sociologie* (Brussels) (1927), 7:305ff.; Pedro Calmon, *Historia do Brasil, 1500–1800* (São Paulo–Rio: 1939; 2d ed., 1950); Olivier Reverdin, *Quatorze calvinistes chez les Topinambous* (Geneva-Paris: Droz-Minard, 1957); E. Vaucheret, "J. Nicot et l'entreprise de Villegagnon," in *La Découverte de l'Amérique* (Paris: Vrin, 1968), pp. 89ff.; Florestan Fernandes, *Organização social dos Tupinamba,* 2d ed. (São Paulo: Difusão Européia do Livro, 1963).

To a Léry dossier I should also add everything that relates to the importance of the *Histoire* in the history of thought in the sixteenth century (Montaigne, G.

Atkinson, etc.), as well as everything on the materials it furnishes about the Tupi language. In the text of the *Histoire,* this language becomes a linguistic curiosity both hiding and revealing an identity of man; see Vicomte de Porto-Seguro, *L'Origine touranienne des Américains Tupis-Caribes et des Anciens Egyptiens* (Vienna: Faesy and Frick, 1876); P. C. Tatevin, *La Langue tapïhïya dite Tupi ou Neêngatu* (Vienna: A. Hölder, 1910); and Frederico G. Edelweiss, *Estudos Tupis e Tupi-Guaranis* (Rio de Janeiro: Liv. brasil. Edit., 1969).

7. G. 2:71–72.

8. G. 2:72.

9. "Ce qu'on peut appeler religion entre les Sauvages Amériquains. . ." [What Can Be Called Religion Among the American Native Indian Savage . . .], G. 2:59–84.

10. Lévi-Strauss, "Leçon d'ecriture," in *Tristes Tropiques,* pp. 337–49; pp. 294–304 in the English edition. See Jacques Derrida, "La Violence de la lettre: De Lévi-Strauss à Rousseau"; in English, "The Violence of the Letter: From Lévi-Strauss to Rousseau," in *Of Grammatology* (Baltimore: Johns Hopkins University Press, 1976), pp. 101–40; and Roland Barthes, "La Leçon d'écriture," *Tel Quel* (1968), no. 34, pp. 28–33; in English, "Lesson in Writing," in *Image/Music/Text* (New York: Hill and Wang, 1977), pp. 170–78.

11. "L'Isle espagnole": Hispaniola, which is to say Haiti.

12. F. Lopez de Gomara, *Historia de las Indias, con la conquista del Mexico y de la nueva España,* book I, ch. 34, p. 41. Martin Fumée's French translation was published in Paris in 1568; it was published in five subsequent editions from 1577 to 1606. Léry refers to it quite often, as will Montaigne. See Marcel Bataillon, "Gomara et l'historiographe du Pérou," *Annuaire du Collège de France* (1967).

13. This was an error, but of importance here is the coalescence between "primitive" and "oral" or "verbal."

14. G. 2:60–61.

15. Lévi-Strauss, *Tristes Tropiques,* p. 297.

16. G. 2:73.

17. *Ibid.*

18. Following the former tradition that an "old" Tupi recounts to Léry, "a *Mair,* that is, a Frenchman, or a foreigner," hitherto came as the carrier of a religious "language" that the Tupis "did not want to believe"; then "there came another who, in a gesture of malediction, offered them a sword, with which we have been killing each other ever since" (G. 2:77). In this "tale" the Western foreigner is a double figure, representing both the language of a truth and the sword that arms him and punishes resistance.

19. G. 2:72–73.

20. G. 2:27 and G. 2:80. In both cases it is a question of Psalm 104.

21. In "Chemins de l'écriture" in his *Les Paysans du Languedoc* (Paris: Sevpen, 1966), pp. 331–56, Emmanuel Le Roy Ladurie has depicted the narrow geographical and cultural ties between "the linguistic revolution marked by the first diffusion of French (1450–1590)" into the Languedoc, and the "intellectual revolution" which the Reformation introduces. Sign of the extension of French (and

of writing) and Calvinism (a return to Scripture) along the same paths is seen in "the creation of a new kind of man": "at stake is the formal restriction of pleasure and the tacit tolerance of usury; at stake is asceticism through proclamation and capitalism by preterition" (p. 356). Between one form of writing and another there are combinations and mutual reinforcements. But ultimately the introduction of a new law of writing changes Scripture, which had served as a form of mediation. [My translation. *Les Paysans du Languedoc* is available in English, however; see ch. 1, n. 44.——TR.]

22. On Brazil-wood, which is especially used for dyes, see Frédéric Mauro, *Le Portugal et l'Atlantique au XVIIe siècle* (Paris: Sevpen, 1960), pp. 115–45.

23. G. 1:34–35; my emphasis.

24. G. 1:157.

25. Alphonse Dupront, "Espace et humanisme," *Bibliothèque d'Humanisme et Renaissance*, (1946), 8:19.

26. G. 1:112.

27. G. 1:12. See above, note 6, for the bibliography touching on "Léry's Dialogue." This text, whose author probably is not Léry, is part of the *Histoire* from the first edition. It is one of the oldest documents concerning the Tupi language.

28. G. 1:91–96.

29. The effort of numerous French "spirituals" in the seventeenth century will consist specifically in going back from objective religious language that has since become ambivalent and deceptive to "intentions," to "motifs," to one's "heart," and to the "mystical" conditions of a good "style of speech." See chapter 4, "The Formality of Practices."

30. See *Commentaires de M. Jean Calvin sur les cinq livres de Moyse* (Geneva, 1564), on Genesis (pp. 20–21), and Claude-Gilbert Dubois, *Mythe et langage au seizième siècle* (Bordeaux: Ducros, 1970), pp. 54–56.

31. Here we can refer to Marx's analyses in *Introduction to a Critique of Political Economy* and in his *Principles of a Critique of Political Economy*, in *The German Ideology* (New York: International Publishers, 1978). See "Writings and Histories" above, notes 28 and 29.

32. On the taxonomies of living creatures in the sixteenth century, see Paul Delaunay, *La Zoologie au XVIe siècle* (Paris: Hermann, 1962), pp. 191–200; and François Jacob, *La Logique du vivant* (Paris: Gallimard, 1970), pp. 37–41; in English, *The Logic of Life* (New York: Pantheon, 1974), ch. 1. Jean de Léry follows the classics, and when he writes of birds, for example, he refers to Pierre Belon's famous *Histoire de la nature des Oyseaux* (Paris, 1555). Cf. G. 1:176.

33. Louis Dumont, *La Civilisation indienne et nous* (Paris: Armand Colin, 1964), p. 33. The chapter entitled "The Problem of History" (pp. 31–54) strongly underscores the particular character of "evidence" proper to the West: "We should go so far as believing that only change has meaning and that permanence has none, while most societies were of the contrary conviction" (p. 32).

34. Destined to "perpetuate the memory of a voyage" (G. 1:1) and based on "reports" brought back from Brazil, the "story" is held among the "notable things that I observed during my travels" (G. 1:12). Léry therefore places himself among the "cosmographs and other historians of our time" who have written of Brazil

(G. 1:40). The story has a double edge: it recounts an *action* and it challenges a truth that would be neither "observed" nor "experimental" in nature.

35. Jean Bodin, *Methodus ad facilem historiarum cognitionem* (1566), cap. primum, in *Oeuvres philosophiques,* Mesnard, ed. (Paris: PUF, 1951), pp. 114–15.

36. See George Huppert's remarks in *L'Idée de l'histoire parfaite* (Paris: Flammarion, 1973), pp. 93–109 (on Bodin) and 157–76 (on "the meaning of history").

37. On hagiographical discourse, see below, chapter 7. On "mystical" discourse, see my *Absent de l'histoire* (Paris: Mame, 1973), pp. 153–66, and *La Fable mystique* (Paris: Gallimard, 1982).

38. G. 1:130. *Caouiner* means to celebrate by drinking *caouin,* a potion made from corn called *Avati.* In chapter 9 of his *Histoire,* Léry elaborates at length on the fabrication of *caouin* and on *caouinages* at the time of festivities when our "American rogues and rascals" celebrate with such fabulous *beuveries,* or drinking bouts.

39. G. 2:69.

40. G. 2:69–70; my emphasis.

41. G. 2:70.

42. G. 2:71 and 73.

43. *Sodome et Gomorrhe,* part one, in Marcel Proust, *A la recherche du temps perdu* (Paris: Gallimard-Pléiade, 1954), 2:608–9. [My translation.——Tr.]

44. Jacques Lacan, "Kant avec Sade," in *Ecrits* (Paris: Seuil, 1966), p. 787. [My translation.——Tr.]

45. See Guy Rosolato's remarks on hallucinations in *Essais sur le symbolique* (Paris: Gallimard, 1969), pp. 313ff.

46. Alphonse Dupront, "Espace et humanisme," *Bibliothèque d'Humanisme et Renaissance* (1946), 8:26–33, on "curiosity."

47. G. 1:136.

48. G. 1:137.

49. G. 2:47–48. "The older women," Léry notes, "take marvelous appetite in eating human flesh"(G. 2:48); they "love it" (G. 2:50).

50. *Como era gostoso o meu Frances: Uma historia do Brasil* is Nelson Pereira dos Santos' Brazilian film of 1973 on Tupi anthropophagia in the sixteenth century according to the tales of Thévet and Léry. But he also alludes to the Brazilian literary or "anthropophagist" current of the 1920s (Brazil "assimilates" foreign imports), and, by way of fable, he criticizes that "love" which a totalitarian regime has given to its subjects since 1964.

51. G. 2:71.

52. The rise of commercial business in cities has increasingly repressed the free and festive time of carnival; see for example Joël Lefebvre, *Les Fols et la folie* (Paris: Klincksieck, 1968). The bibliography on the witches' Sabbath and sorcery is immense. See Julio Caro Baroja, *Les Sorcières et leur monde* (Paris: Gallimard, 1972), pp. 97–115, or my *L'Absent de l'histoire,* pp. 13–40. Unfortunately travel literature has not yet been studied systematically as a great complement and displacement of demonology. Yet the same structures are common to both.

53. Emmanuel Levinas, *Totalité et infini* (The Hague: Nijhoff, 1971), p. 234, on "exhibitionistic nudity of an exorbitant presence," "lacking signification."

54. G. 1:123.

55. G. 1:136 and 123.

56. On the representations which inspired Renaissance artists in terms of the Platonic opposition (dear to Ficino) between the *Amor divinus* (nude) and the *Amor humanus* (clothed), see Erwin Panofsky, *Renaissance and Renascences in Western Art* (London: Paladin, 1970), pp. 188–200; the Botticelli or Mantegna Venus, Ripa's *Felicità Eterna*, Scipione Francesci's *Bellà disornata*, etc., are theophanies.

57. G. 1:136.

58. Venus "replaces the Virgin," writes Pierre Francastel in respect to Botticelli, in *La Figure et le lieu: L'Ordre visuel du Quattrocento* (Paris: Gallimard, 1967), p. 280. The question is not only that of substituting the profane woman for the sacred woman; it is that of substituting an object to be seen (and to be known) for the mother.

59. Marc Lescarbot, *L'Histoire de la Nouvelle France* (Paris, 1609), p. 542.

60. G. 1:138. [The French proverb is *bon pied, bon oeil.*——TR.]

61. "For the entire year I lived in this country, I was so *curious* about *contemplating* the big and small that, being of the opinion that I always *see them before my eyes*, I would forever have the *idea and image* in my mind." But "to partake in the pleasures, you must *see and visit* them in their country" (G. 1:138; my emphasis). [The French locution is *voir et visiter.*——TR.]

62. Sigmund Freud, "Inhibitions, Symptoms, and Anxiety" in *The Standard Edition of the Complete Psychological Works of Sigmund Freud*, 24 vols., J. Strachey, tr. and ed. (London: The Hogarth Press, 1953–1974), 20:90.

63. Martin Heidegger, "The Age of the World Picture," in *The Question Concerning Technology and Other Essays* (New York: Harper and Row, 1977), p. 134.

64. G. 2:80.

65. See for instance Alfred Métraux, *Religions et magies indiennes d'Amérique du Sud* (Paris: Gallimard, 1967), pp. 82ff. ("The shamans of the Guianas and Amazonia") and pp. 105ff. ("Shamanism among the Indians of the Gran Chaco"), on the shaman's vocation.

66. See Ernest Jones, "The Madonna's Conception Through the Ear," in *Essays in Applied Psycho-analysis*, 2 vols. (London: Hogarth Press, 1951), pp. 266–375.

67. Jacques Lacan, *Ecrits* (Paris: Seuil, 1966), pp. 360, 619, 684. Moreover, it is always in connection with the superego that voice appears in Lacanian analysis.

68. Julia Kristeva, *Sèméiotikè: Recherches pour une sémanalyse* (Paris: Seuil, 1969), pp. 211–12. [My translation; but see ch. 2, n. 47, for English edition.——TR.]

69. Lacan, *Ecrits*, pp. 557 and 508.

70. Metaphor effectively allows us to "designate realities that do not have their own terms," therefore, "to break the barriers of language, and to state what is unspeakable," notes Michel le Guern in *Sémantique de la métaphore et de la métonymie* (Paris: Larousse, 1973), p. 72.

71. Jacques Lacan, *Le Séminaire*, book 20, *Encore* (Paris: Seuil, 1975), p. 99.

6

Discourse Disturbed

The Sorcerer's Speech

THE possessed woman raises a double-edged question. On the one hand, it involves the possibility of acceding to the speech of the other, which is effectively the problem facing historians: what can we apprehend from the discourse of an absent being? How can we interpret documents bound to an insurmountable death, that is to say, to another period of time, and to an "ineffable" experience always approached from an outside evaluation? On the other hand, there is the study of the alteration of language through "possession," the aim of this chapter.

My reflections are a sequel to my research for *La Possession de Loudun*, a model case quite renowned in the series of possessions that increasingly replaced the great epidemics of sorcery in the years 1610–1630.[1] Now Freud also took great interest in sorcery. He read the *Malleus maleficarum* "with ardor." He customarily went so far as saying, in his correspondence with Wilhelm Fliess and others,[2] that between the inquisitor (the exorcist) and the possessed woman (or the sorcerer) there existed something analogous to the relation between the analyst and the client.

But in the "diabolic" and its development for an entire century (roughly between 1550 and 1660), it is necessary to distinguish two successive forms that it suffices simply to recall here. The first form is sorcery, a rural phenomenon; the repression of often pitiless, urban judges is opposed to the massive eruption of sorcerers in the countryside. A dual structure is evident: on one side of the coin, the judges; on the other, the witches. On one side, the city, while on the other, the countryside. A second form appears in possessions which spring up toward the end of the sixteenth century. It is established among microgroups, for example in convents of nuns. Little circles are circumscribed in islets or, if we take up a representation that organizes religion of the seventeenth century, in "sanctuaries," or in "little pockets" in the country. These possessions concern milieus that are either homogenous or identical to those of the judges. While in sorcery a social disparity exists between the judge and the sorcerer, in the case of possession a social homogeneity exists between the judge or the exorcist and the possessed individual. From the binary structure defining the relation of judge and sorcerer a ternary structure is developed, one whose third term—the possessed woman, the victim—is emphasized in this history.

Finally, as a last difference, through possession the struggle against the redoubtable "plague" of witches becomes a trial that oscillates between a debate over a society's frames of reference and a dramatization of the social, religious, philosophical, and political wars of the period. Possession is the scene of a play, while sorcery is a conflict. Possession is a theater where fundamental questions are played out—always in the style of a staging; while sorcery is a struggle—an internecine warfare between two different social categories.

Thus in the case of Loudun, mentioned here because it is a model of its kind, about twenty Ursuline nuns form a group of possessed souls. Not by chance is the possessed body essentially female; behind the scenes a relation between masculine discourse and its feminine alteration is acted out. Yet for six years (1632–1638) these mad nuns furnished a spectacular setting for discussions which attracted thousands of visitors and nourished an overabundant literature by authors who were time and again theologians, doctors, and scholars interested for reasons that must be examined.

The stocks of manuscripts and buried works, now conserved in national or municipal archives, allowed me to analyze initially how a diabolical "place"—a diabolical scene—was organized through the play of social, political, religious, or epistemological tensions, and how this composition of place, this production of theatrical space, enabled a reclassification of social representation to function as shifts in frames of reference. In this respect, possession is a phenomenon parallel to the creation of theater in the sixteenth and seventeenth centuries. From medieval carnival we move to seventeenth-century theater, at a time when a society's image of itself is localized, objectified, and miniaturized by ceasing to be popular liturgy. On the reduced stage of possession a modification of epistemological, political, and religious structures of the period is acted out. Finally, I attempted to analyze how, over a few years' time, displacements that were imposed on this dramatic field acquired the value of a symptom in respect to struggles that were concurrently changing the entire body of society. Loudun is successively a metonymy and a metaphor allowing us to apprehend how a "state policy," a new rationality, replaces a religious reason.

Entitled *La Possession de Loudun*, this first study sought to understand the diabolical spectacle as a social phenomenon; it examined the rules followed by the play of characters in the religious, medical, or political sphere, while in addition it studied the relations that processes of acculturation were maintaining with a logic of the imaginary.

A Discourse of the Other?

AT the present time I should like to attempt an analysis of a question that I had left in the margins and that I would now place initially under the sign of a possessed woman's own transgression: does there exist a "discourse of the other" in cases of possession? In other words, my first attempt at interpretation did not leave sufficient space for a question that nonetheless was lurking on the horizon—that is, the very discourse of possessed women, insofar as this discourse is said to be *spoken by another*. "Someone else is speaking within me": thus speaks the possessed woman. This question could be taken up only after historical study of the sociocultural theater in which it arises. We have yet to analyze closely, through the relation of the actors of Loudun, the combination of two asymmetrical positions—that of the possessed women and that of their judges, exorcists, doctors, and the like.

On the one hand, for the possessed women the place from which they speak is indeterminate, always giving itself as a "somewhere else" that speaks in them. Something other is speaking which cannot be determined. On the other hand, the exorcists or the doctors respond through a labor of naming or designating that is the characteristic answer to possession in any traditional society. Whether in Africa or South America, therapy in cases of possession essentially consists of naming, of ascribing a term to what manifests itself as speech, but as an uncertain speech inseparable from fits, gestures, and cries. A disturbance arises, and therapy, or social treatment, consists of providing a name—a term already listed in a society's catalogues—for this uncertain speech. The task of doctors or exorcists is one of nomination, which aims at categorizing the interlocutors, confining them in a place circumscribed by these doctors' or exorcists' knowledge.

On the one hand, we can never know who is speaking or what is being spoken; on the other, we find a knowledge that tends to reclassify the alterity that it meets. From this standpoint, even if there is divergence among exorcists and doctors over the taxonomies by which they effect their reclassifying—that is, if medical and religious knowledge are not akin—in either instance a form of knowledge is assumed to be capable of *naming*. Both exorcists and doctors are opposed to the delinquent, heretical, or sick exception, to the abnormal represented by the possessed woman. They are opposed to her escape into fancy, because through it she exiles herself from social language, she betrays the very linguistic topography with which social order can be organized.

Exorcists or doctors therefore attempt to resolve or compensate for the possessed woman's flights beyond the fields of an established discourse. Doctors and exorcists are not in agreement about the norm: for the latter, it includes the visible intervention of a supernatural cosmos, while for the former it excludes this intervention. But they fundamentally agree enough to eliminate an exterritoriality of language. What they are fighting through acts of naming is a text-*off*,[3] a writing of alterity, where the possessed woman is located when she presents herself as the statement of something that is fundamentally other.

This way of considering the problem of possession is obviously not innocent. It is based on several hypotheses. In particular, I assume here a distinction between what the possessed or demoniac woman is stating and what is stated by demonological treatises or exorcists who witness demonology. The distinction is analogous to that which exists between the discourse of the person known to be "crazy" and the discourse of psychiatry—as well as, in certain respects, that of psychoanalysis. There must always be a gap between what the possessed woman utters and what the demonological or medical discourse makes of it. It would be no more possible to identify the knowledge of possession with the possessed woman's speech than to identify psychiatric or psychoanalytic knowledge with what the "madman" or "madwoman" (if vague references can be used) is expressing.

Inversely—and this is another postulate—I would not suppose that the possessed woman's discourse surely exists somewhere, like a hidden treasure to be exhumed from under the interpretations piled over it; nor that what she utters as "other" is established as a discourse, analogous but opposed to the discourse of a psychiatric or religious knowledge. In the same way that a relation with the psychiatrist, and therefore the constitution of psychiatry as well, represents for the individual who is termed "mentally ill" the precondition of his discourse in the locus of a hospital that was assigned to him by the doctor, so, too, the treatise of demonology (or the exorcist's interrogations) assigns in advance to the possessed woman the condition and the place of her speech. From psychiatric discourse the "mentally ill" or the "madwoman" gains the possibility of uttering statements; in the same fashion, the "possessed woman" can speak only thanks to the demonological interrogation or knowledge—although her locus is not that of the discourse of knowledge being held about her. The possessed woman's speech is established relative to the discourse that awaits her in *that* place, on the demonological stage, just as the language of the crazed woman in the hospital is only what has been prepared for her on the psychiatric stage.

This means first of all that we cannot attribute to the possessed woman a discourse different from what she effectively is speaking, as if there existed on a lower level another discourse, intact, to be unearthed. And second, it means that we cannot identify *what* she says with the locus (both linguistic and social) where she must be situated in order to be capable of uttering a discourse.

Transgression and Interdiction

TRANSGRESSING signifies crossing. The problem posed here is one of a distortion between the *stability* of demonological discourse (or medical discourse) as a discourse of knowledge, and the function of a *limit* played by the possessed woman's statements. This distortion obliges us to maintain temporarily a distinction between them that does not imply a homology. By virtue of the fact that the possessed woman's speech represents a limit, we cannot conclude that such a limit has the same discursive structure as that of demonological or medical knowledge. Thus an asymmetrical relation is at work: the possessed woman's speech is neither posited as analogous to the discourse of knowledge, nor as hidden by it, as if it were another discourse lying under the surface of what is legible and visible. What is introduced into language here is a question that can neither be erased by assimilation into the given text nor objectified by granting it the status of a discursive positivity buried under a repressive discourse. At issue is a relation of discourse (of demonology, medicine, history, etc.) to a transgression that is not a discourse. Such a relation can be discerned in the very texts that we possess.

The situation is interesting because it is not exceptional. It is reproduced in a series of cases where disturbance becomes, *inside* discourse, the mobile, evanescent, and resurgent figure of the transgression *of* discourse. My question here concerns the nature of this speech which is *interdicted by* discourse and *recurs within* discourse, or, in other words, which is "inter-jected" by the upheavals of the same discourse. It is found again in the mystical process, for I believe more and more in a structural homology between problems raised by sorcery, possession, and mysticism. To be sure, the question remains of why things are black or white, why they are linked to God or to the devil; but fundamentally, the type of manifestation is always identical, insofar as it is reducible to the relation that an altering passage keeps with a semantic order, or to the relation that an enunciation keeps with a system of statements. This relation can appear in mystical or in diabolical ways, or in terms of madness. It can be seen also in ethnological discourse, when the issue is how the Indian is going to speak the language of Occidental knowledge. Or else, it can be asked how the "madman" or "madwoman" is going to speak within the discourse of psychiatric or psychoanalytical knowledge. In various ways, the same interrogation insinuates itself as a text-*off,* about which one must ask how it combines with the known body of writing. What constitutes this text-*off* that is nonetheless marked within the text?

Parallel to diabolical possession in the seventeenth century, mystical language—its homology and its inverse—is defined throughout the period by the introduction of an unspoken dimension into a received text. A *je ne sais pas quoi* is speaking, but this *je ne sais pas quoi* of the *other* is introduced and spoken in a doctrinal system by altering the discourse of theological knowledge, not by constructing another discourse. In the same fashion, the possessed woman's *je ne sais pas quoi* is inserted into the extraordinarily organized discourse of demonology, a network of chicaneries built from the standpoint of a position of knowledge.

According to the status that had been given to "mystical" literary works, or according to the theory that they ascribe for themselves, the issue is how to speak about a so-called ineffable experience which therefore *cannot be spoken about*. Such experience of possession (divine possession, in the case of mysticism) has no language of its own, but it is marked (as a "wound," the mystics say) in theological discourse; it inscribes itself through the labor it effects inside the discourse received from a religious tradition. A (mystical) transgression of the law of (religious) language is written into this very language by a style of practice—by a *modus loquendi*. And, too, the seventeenth-century theoreticians characterize this practice not as a discourse, but by what they call "mystical phrases" or "ways of speaking." In that way they designate an operation performed upon language. In established discourse a practice of elocution and a treatment of language trace an alterity that cannot yet be identified with another discourse. As in the case of the possessed woman, we have a relation between an established discourse and the alteration that the travail of stating "something other" introduces.[4]

Speaking more broadly, similar problems appear in the relation maintained by the ethnographical tale with the "other society" that it recounts and claims to make heard. With respect to the possessed woman, the primitive, and the patient, demonological discourse, ethnographical discourse, and medical discourse effectively assume identical positions: "I know what you are saying better than you"; in other words, "My knowledge can position itself in the place whence you speak." Now when the possessed woman speaks the language which is imposed upon her and which has put itself in her place, the alienating but necessary discourse that she utters will bear the trace—the "wound"—of the alterity that knowledge claims to conceal. First of all I would like to underline the generality of the question opened by the return of the other in the discourse that prohibits it. This "returning" can assume an attenuated and almost surreptitious form. The alteration of discourse through the speech that it is replacing can ultimately take the form of the discreet ambivalence of "repressive" procedures. Such is, for example, the case of citation: in ethnographical texts and travel literature, the savages—like the possessed woman—are *cited*, in both juridical and literary fashion, through the discourse which positions itself in their place, saying about these unknowing people what they do not even know about themselves. Like demonological or medical knowledge, ethnographical knowledge is accredited by citation. From this perspective we must question the role of

citation of the other in historiographical discourse itself. I mean "citation" in a literary sense, but the word can also be understood in the guise
of citation before a tribunal. It is a literary technique of trial and judgment which sets discourse in a position of knowledge from which it can
give voice to the other. Something different returns in this discourse,
however, along with the citation of the other; it remains ambivalent; it
upholds the danger of an uncanniness which alters the translator's or
commentator's knowledge. For discourse, citation is the menace and suspense of a lapsus. Alterity dominated—or possessed—through discourse
maintains the power of being a fantastic ghost, or indeed a possessor in
a latent state. To cite the other is a strategy of law which nevertheless
refers to another place. Clearly the citation is not a hole in the ethnographical text through which another landscape or another discourse might
be revealed; what is cited is fragmented, used over again and patched
together in a text. Therein it is altered. Yet in this position where it keeps
nothing of its own, it remains capable, as in a dream, of bringing forth
something uncanny: the surreptitious and altering power of the repressed.

In the same way, medical discourse has its own code spelled out by
madmen. In order to speak, the madman must answer the questions asked
of him. Therefore, in a psychiatric hospital it is observed that in the course
of a month or two following the internment of a patient, a leveling of
his discourse or an effacement of his idiosyncrasies takes place. The patient can only speak in the code that the hospital provides for him. He
is alienated in the answers to questions, to bodies of knowledge that alone
allow his enunciation. Organized into a therapeutic process, however,
medical discourse bears the mark of another place of enunciation, retaining that ambivalent, ill-formed enunciation, inscribed into itself in these
very citations that are the trophies of its own victories. From these "other"
traces which oscillate between integration and transgression, is it possible
to get back to the repressed speech of madness, not in its primitive state
(which has since become inaccessible), but by examining the succession
of silences organized each time by normalizing "reasons" that are still
marked by what they have eliminated, in order to be established as such?

Here I will only offer a few hypotheses with respect to indications that
have a strange function in narratives of possession, upholding an instability which excludes the possibility of textual closure. In different ways
that may however be interrelated, these indications mark an elsewhere of
discourse *within* discourse. Inside the narrative they play the role of piv-

otal pieces; they inscribe a surreptitious "possession" into the network of theological or medical taxonomies: they shake and push the text toward its text-*off*, but in a fashion that is inherent to the text of knowledge; through this ambiguous functioning, within the text they trace the line of a dangerous division. Perhaps these "forbidden games" make up an autonomous system that, from a semiotic or psychoanalytical point of view, inspires in the text a "diabolical" uncanniness, the current equivalent to the question that had formerly been asked by the possessed woman from depths forever inaccessible to us. As such, something of the interrogation she formerly opened never ceases to be diabolical.

Altered Documents: The Possessed Woman's Texts

WE cannot deal with this problem independently of the nature of the raw material. But what reaches us is a set of altered or fragmentary documents. A few signs are worth reviewing.

Quite often the available sources (archives, manuscripts, etc.) offer, as the possessed woman's "discourse," what is always spoken by someone other than the possessed. In most cases these documents are notaries' minutes, medical reports, theologians' opinions or consultations, witnesses' depositions, or judges' verdicts. From the demoniac woman there only appears the image that the author of such texts has of her, in the mirror where he repeats his knowledge and where he takes her own position through inverting and contradicting it.

That the possessed woman's speech is nothing more than the words of her "other," or that she can only have the discourse of her judge, her doctor, the exorcist, or witnesses is hardly by chance, as I will emphasize below. But from the outset this situation excludes the possibility of tearing the possessed woman's true voice away from its alteration. On the surface of these texts her speech is doubly lost. It is lost by virtue of being "redone" and reformed—that is, it receives its form—by the knowledge that is alone stated. And, too, her speech is lost because even before this speech can be reformed through the discourses in which it figures by dint of citations, a battery of interrogations has determined all response ahead of time; they have fragmented the possessed woman's speech according to classifications that are in no way her own, but rather those of the inquirer's knowledge. In this respect documents constitute a point of no return.

Fabricated out of these questions and answers, hundreds of interrogations have been faithfully transcribed by scriveners. These texts assemble questions from the exorcist, the judge, the doctor, and answers from the possessed woman. Question—answer—question—answer: such is the literary form of the document closest to the interrogation. It has the appearance of dialogical texts (plays, novels, etc.), but can it really be assimilated into texts that have taken the shape of exchanges among characters? In other words, can there be a literary continuity between Beckett's or Diderot's dialogues on the one hand and, on the other, the corpus in which the exorcists' questions are followed by the answers of diverse "demons" possessing the women being interrogated?

Even if the possessed women's answers are still relative to the interrogations and are determined by these questions, even if the entire scene follows the rules of a drama, a complete assimilation of these two types of dialogue appears to me to be difficult. The reason is not that in one case we would have the singularity of one author (for example, in *Rameau's Nephew*) and in the other case, a plurality. A text is at stake in every respect in both cases, and the difference between one or several authors is not pertinent. But to eliminate the hypothesis of a difference between these two literary forms of questions-and-answers is tantamount to refusing a priori the very specificity of "diabolical" texts: the play between the stable place to which the exorcists try to direct the women under question, and the evanescent plurality of places that allow the possessed women to claim that they are elsewhere. The diabolical theater is characterized by the always uncertain relation between the locus assigned to every actor by a very few in the group (the exorcist or the doctor composes the scene by designating a role for everyone, just as the psychiatrist establishes or tends to establish the role for his patient) and the mobility of certain actors (the possessed women), slipping from place to place.

On this stage that the interrogation establishes, we have actors who tend to assign roles and other actors who modify these roles. The possessed woman jumps from one locus to another, creating a stir exactly where the doctor or exorcist is awaiting her. Earmarked for a locus that the therapeutic staging assigns her, the patient or possessed woman moves incessantly. The suspense of the interrogation arises from the question: how and up to what point will the demonological staging tolerate the mobility of actors changing the locus where a social knowledge awaits them? Reducing the play of possession to a checkerboard of squares drawn by demonological or medical discourse, or assimilating it to a theater built on a solid architecture of "characters" (or "proper" names), would be equivalent to forgetting the uncanniness that circulates in this strongly structured network of theatrical relations. But then again the possessed woman's question is constantly lost in the theatrical architecture; it avoids consideration solely of the composition of places and characters.

Upheaval is already part of the document as it falls into our hands, and we cannot determine the nature of the possession that is recounted within a questions-and-answers text.

In a certain number of cases the documents come from the possessed women themselves, such as the declarations, letters, and autobiography of Jeanne des Anges, the prioress of the Ursulines, the most famous of the possessed women of Loudun. Here, then, the sick woman speaks for herself. Yet if we exclude her answers in the course of the interrogation during the exorcisms (the procedure just considered), Jeanne des Anges' texts inscribe themselves within the continuity of a language *on* possession, not from possession. These texts do not originate in the time when, "unconsciously," Jeanne des Anges is the voice of whatever demon is possessing her. These are discourses written later, when she objectifies herself by saying, "I used to be, I used to do." The point seems quite important. Jeanne des Anges can *speak* but she cannot *write* as a possessed woman. Possession is only a voice. As soon as Jeanne passes to writing, she tells what she used to do, she refers to a past time, she describes an object that is distant from her, about which she can utter afterward the discourse of knowledge. She writes from a place other than whence she had been speaking as a possessed woman. Now, speaking of her possession in terms of a former time, she either edits reports, letters, or depositions during the times of calm between demoniac crises, or fifteen years later, toward 1640, she uses the past tense to tell of a period of possession from which she says she has been "delivered" or "freed."

For Jeanne des Anges, writing means keeping a distance, using a language that she can master. To write is to possess. On the contrary, to be possessed is a situation compatible solely with orality: a person cannot be possessed while writing. Between the voice of the possessed and the writing of the possessed there exists a rupture already symptomatic of what we can expect from written documents.

There finally comes the question that I must ask either as historian or interpreter. In analyzing the possessed woman's speech, it is my ambition to hear it better than the doctor or exorcist of former times and to understand much better than the learned figures of the past what her language—or learned language—betrays as *other*. What therefore is the locus that authorizes me, today, to suppose that I can speak the other better than all of them? Lodged like them in knowledge that attempts to understand, with respect to the possessed I am reiterating the position —now with a few variants which must be evaluated—that formerly belonged to the demonologist or the doctor. From this locus, is it possible that I am played upon—possessed—by the desire that produces the possessed woman's transgression? This is one of the questions that we shall have to examine in Freud's *Moses and Monotheism* in chapter 9. In any case, through my work I find myself adding to the disturbances that have already reduced documents concerning possession to the state in which they are handed down to us.

Today an analysis that might show how a text (the one I am writing) relates to demoniac speech in the seventeenth century would perhaps be a way of reiterating the question without risk of falling into folklore or scientism. This would be tantamount to *thinking* the strange remark that Freud picked up from Goethe, "So muss denn doch die Hexe dran"— we must therefore resort to the sorceress—and expecting that she will elucidate (or disturb?) our discourse.

"Je est un autre": The Perversion of Language

THIS sorceress or possessed woman to whom I am resorting will be conjured up first of all through Rimbaud's proverb, "Je est un autre,"[6] or "*I* is another." His motto, although not quite appropriate, nonetheless indicates the spot where the rift that the possessed women opens can be located in language.

We can find a common trait by isolating the texts reporting the speech uttered by the possessed, the discourses in "I" (*Ichberichte*). They all affirm, "Je est un autre." This trait marks their continuity with what the psychiatric tradition has been calling "hysteria" for three hundred years: the hysteric does not know, and therefore cannot name, *who* she is. The sorceress, who alone interests us for the moment, creates in the play of language a trouble connoted by the disconnection of the speaking subject ("je") from a definite proper name; "Je est un autre." The exorcist or doctor engages in determining who this "other" is by placing him in a topography of proper names and by normalizing once again the connection of the speech act with a social system of statements. Thus exorcism is essentially an enterprise of denomination intended to reclassify a protean uncanniness within an established language. It aims at restoring the postulate of all language, that is, a stable relation between the interlocutor, "I," and a social signifier, the proper name. At stake here is the connection of an enunciation with a statement; in other words, the contract that the clause "I am Michel," or I = a (proper) name, expresses between the subject and language.

The proper name assigns to the subject a locus in language and therefore "secures" an order of sociolinguistic practice. And since the possessed woman deviates by offering an uncanniness of the subject ("je est autre," or "I is other"), we must appropriate this aberration by giving it another proper name taken from a (demonological) list that a society has prearranged for cases of this type. From then on the contract—the very principle of knowledge, of the "order of things," and thus also of a therapeutics—is restored.

The madwoman is constantly creating deviance with respect to the postulate $I = x$ (x designating a determinate name). Surely, in the unconsciousness which is a precondition of her being possessed, she enters successively into the loci that a nomenclature of demons provides. Urged by the exorcists to fix her name firmly (it is precisely the avowal of a proper name that they want to extort from her) and to pigeonhole herself within their demonological repertory, she finally declares, "I am Asmodeus": $I = Asmodeus$.

But soon afterward she will respond, "I am Aman"; then, "I am Isacaron," etc. In this fashion, with Jeanne des Anges we have a series of heterogenous identifications:

$$I = \text{Asmodeus}$$
$$I = \text{Isacaron}$$
$$I = \text{Leviathan}$$
$$I = \text{Aman}$$
$$I = \text{Balam}$$
$$I = \text{Behemoth}$$

The plurality of identifications drawn from the same onomastic table ultimately denies the possibility of any localization, but without rejecting the (demonological) social code, since basically nothing else has been provided for this case. The code remains, but the possessed woman passes through it. She slips from locus to locus, challenging the stability of all proper names through her trajectory; no determinate value can be linguistically attached to "I" in any stable way.

The endless rotation of "I" within a limited list of fixed proper names (there is also, we shall see, an element of improvisation in these names) generates demonological discourse, but it impedes the discourse from working in a proper way, requiring it to repeat the denominative operation indefinitely. In the discourse of possession this procedure of perversion is the equivalent of what Rimbaud expressed as a form of commentary about his poetry: "It is false to say: I think. We ought to say, I am thought." Who are the *they* who are thinking him? That is precisely the question put forward by the sorceress: "I am spoken." Rimbaud continues, "I is an other. Too bad for the wood that happens to be a violin."[7] What Rimbaud's poetry *writes*, the possessed woman's onomastic displacement *speaks:* she is thus "wood that happens to be a violin." But played by whom or by what? While Rimbaud traces the trajectory of this hazardous indetermination in the play of *common* nouns, the possessed can only play (with) her *proper* nouns at this very point where language is connected to the enunciation of the subject. Her perverting procedure is nonetheless analogous to Nietzsche's *es denkt* (the *id*, or *ça*, which has no proper noun, is *thinking* within me),[8] or Rilke's paradox: where there is a poem it is not mine, but that of Orpheus who comes and sings it.[9] To take up another of Nietzsche's aphorisms, the possessed woman suggests a "sacrifice" of what is her own and an alteration—possession by an another—of the locus that language reserves for the "I." A renunciation plays itself out in the very linguistic place of the "I." Possessed women's texts do not provide the skeleton key for their language, for it remains indecipherable even to themselves. This is probably the reason why their position as "possessed women" is sustained only by a fluttering from one name to another within the frame imposed upon them. On a checkerboard of proper nouns they slip endlessly from square to square, but they do not create an additional square that would be their own. In regard to received denominations, no additional elements are created which might provide them with a space of their own (figure 6.1).

This deviation, analogous to what distorts or effaces names in chapter 3 of Freud's *The Psychopathology of Everyday Life,* is the way by which there is traced inside a text (and already inside the list of proper nouns) not a plurality of speakers, but rather the speaker's vanishing and a dispossession of language. By designating different proper nouns one after the other, the possessed woman escapes the linguistic contract and steals away from language its power to be the law of speech for the subject.

If it is true that in language the "I" is, as Emile Benveniste writes, the "unique but mobile sign" (like "you," but unlike "he" or "she") that is "bound to the *exercise* of language and declares the locutor as such," it is hardly surprising that the point of emergence and highest intensity of this mobility occurs at the intersection between "I" and the proper name. "The shifters *I* and *you* exist only insofar as they are actualized in the instance of discourse where, each through their own instances, they mark the speaker's process of appropriation," he remarks.[10] It is over this "empty" sign, which becomes "full" as soon as the interlocutor assumes it, that the sorceress's diabolical displacements initially extend. The combats and ruses concerning the possession of language (possession ⇄ dispossession), and therefore the identity of the speaking subject, are focused in this linguistic place of appropriation.

The Construction and Deconstruction of a Place

A SEMANTIC axis of diabolical texts is indicated by the question which the exorcist formulates as "Who is there?" and which the doctor phrases as "What is it?" Both the exorcist and the doctor respond with proper names—either taken from demonological series (Lucifer, Asmodeus, etc.) or medical listings (melancholy, imagination, hypochondria, hysteria, etc.). These names also designate "essences" which are determined by the knowledge of the former or the latter. From this point of view, a difference between them nonetheless exists. The exorcist *must* make the demoniac woman confess the proper name. If the central task of the exorcist

FIGURE 6.1

Disturbance or Linguistic Deviation

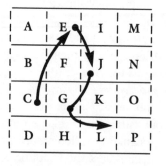

A checkerboard of proper nouns: A, B, C, D, etc.,
and the trajectory of a subject among these proper nouns.

is denomination, such denomination has to be sealed through the possessed woman's avowal; in order for the contract to be restored, she must answer, "Yes, I am Asmodeus." Later, in psychiatry from Pinel's time onward, something analogous takes place: the patients' veritable cure consists in not only naming the sickness, but in having the patients recognize the truth of what their doctors say about them. Then, from denomination to confession, knowledge goes full circle.

The same occurs in the treatment of possession. But the exorcist must also obtain this confession from the demoniac at the moment she is possessed and in a state of "unconsciousness": the confession is awaited from the other who speaks within her. The seventeenth-century doctor does not need this avowal, or at least he obtains it from his observation; in other words, from the corporal surface whose visible symptoms (sweating, pulse, fecal dejecta, deglutitions) take the place of confession. The patient's sweat speaks instead of the possessed woman's words. Yet if the exorcist constrains the voice of the possessed to avow the name of the possessing devil, while the doctor requires the body of the patient to express the illness, to speak, in both cases a nonknowledge on the part of the demoniac or the patient is the postulate of identification posed by a knowledge. The voice of the unconscious possessed woman and the body of the mute patient are there only in order to assent to the knowledge that alone is speaking.

Two parallel movements are therefore traced in the texts. The demonological trajectory begins with the question "Who is there?" Through the mediation of an unconscious voice, it ends up with the name of a devil extracted from a list of beings defined by demonology. The medical movement begins with the question "What is it?" Through interpretation of an array of corporal phenomena, it terminates with the name of an illness taken from a dictionary established by medical science. These two lines are drawn according to the same scheme, which consists in passing from nonidentification to identification.

This diagram outlines the production of a proper noun. But the proper noun is produced only when accompanied by a constellation of adjectives or predicates. Around the name they will create a complex space in which each of the predicates becomes the metonymy of the proper noun and traps the possessed in deviations that only cause her to pass from one equivalent to another of the same identity. "Subversion" is transformed into its theatrical obverse. Thus, around the name "Leviathan" a palette of qualifiers develops slowly, pervading the possessed woman's remarks (mockery), mimicry (laughter, graciousness, etc.), or modes of conduct (cajoling, etc.). This plural repertory widens the circle of the same, the name; it encloses the possessed woman more definitely by awarding her the possibility of movements that no longer question the place of identity, but which produce spectacular effects—surprises, inventions—drawn from relations (of metonymy, of metaphor) between a plurality of attributes (more or less coherent among themselves) and the same proper noun. Once the code is firmly established, "the laughing face," as the written minutes state, replaces Leviathan and begins to circulate on a well-defined semantic surface. The name "Leviathan" becomes a space of play. The name is in the center; around it radiate constellations of postures, mimicry, or verbal equivalents. A theater of allusions and charades is organized among the possessed, the exorcists, and the audience. The possessed woman plays with the audience while the exorcist plays with her. She thus refuses to reveal her name, but she assumes a cajoling expression, as if saying to the audience, "Can you guess who it is?" And they answer, "Of course, it's Leviathan." From this perspective, the staging transforms games of identity into games of rhetoric; it replaces the subject's vanishing with unforeseen metamorphoses or relations of her attributes. This baroque theater marks the success of an order.

Yet, even if slowed down by surface effects, the initial procedure is carried out. It destines the operation of identification to an infinite series of beginnings. The circle is vicious. The process of establishing places is incessantly returned to its point of departure; the possessed continue to move to other areas, and the task of establishing them in firm onomastic spaces must begin from zero over and over again. Finally, since enclosure within the religious onomastic checkerboard does not work, it will be replaced by another grid, that of the police. Thus will end the story of Loudun. Laubardemont, Richelieu's clerk, will assign places to possessed women—no longer in onomastic squares, but now in the confinement of cells. State policy now classifies by means of walls—another problem. Meanwhile, the possessed women disturb the operation of religious linguistic identification. The texts often state, "They forget their name." In this fashion they reiterate the enigma of their name by moving into another slot in the dictionary, and—without changing the structure of the demonological system—they alter its functioning by their series of slippages. They neither replace nor destroy this system; they pervert it by constantly compromising the onomastic spots assigned to them. Denomination is never truly defeated, nor is it ever entirely victorious. It becomes akin to a card game in which the queen of spades might be used as the jack of hearts, and where, too, between the king and queen of hearts might slip the unexpected figure of a king of clubs.

Through a softening of figures, or a kind of cinematic lap dissolve, we thus witness a transformation of Leviathan into something else that is named "Aman," or even the eruption of a Souvillon [something of a "sooty pussy"—TR.] or a Dog's Dick between Isacaron and Behemoth. Clearly these metamorphoses and anamorphoses belong to a baroque art; but what matters more is the fact that they indicate disturbances in the code, that they are the mark of a way in which "something else" occurs within demonological discourse.

The List of Proper Names: A "Changed" Toponymy

THE slipping of a king of clubs (from a "Souvillon") into the "classical" list of diabolical names points to a shifting area other than that of "possessed" enunciation: that of the code itself, and at a moment of cultural transition. Beyond the wandering of the "I" over the onomastic grid, instability marks the list everywhere, blurring it with the incertitude that marks religious frames of reference throughout this period. Time and again it is invaded by incongruous remarks and is entirely deformed by the intervention of codifications—medical, political—which progressively impose themselves and short-circuit the whole. Taken as a particular element in this sociohistorical totality, the list is still the witness of this general transformation. Thus in order to clarify its functioning, we must distinguish the theoretical role of proper names in possession and the alterations which the listings at Loudun will undergo.

In opposition to Gardiner, who maintains the insignificance of proper names and who opposes *designation* to *significance*,[11] Lévi-Strauss shows that in societies with finite categories these names "always signify membership of an actual or virtual class, which must be either that of the person named or of the person giving the name."[12] But in proper names he saw the limit of a classificatory enterprise inside a culturally determined system: they "represent the *quanta of signification* below which one does no longer anything but point." If then, "the proper name is always on the side of signification," it is situated at the "passage" marked by a discontinuity between the act of *signifying* and the act of *pointing*.[13]

It is therefore interesting to consider what form this rift between stating and indicating will take in discourse that is specifically concerned with

what cannot be said. The list of demons' names represents in effect one
of the frontiers by which the demonological system is defended and labors to reintegrate what has been taken by "something else." On this
frontier established by nomenclature, this outpost of signification, the
possessed woman steals away from the system. The goal of exorcism is
to secure a passage from the silence of the possessed to the names that
the exorcists provide for her; it transforms the silence of gestures and
inarticulate cries into language.[14] Because the dictionary of diabolical proper
names plays a capital role in this accession or return to language, it can
be assimilated within a pool of signifiers that will fill the lacunae to which
the possessed woman attests. It is situated just on the line of demarcation
between what is unspeakable and what can be signified, always "on the
side of signification."

In traditional societies, reception or confession of the diabolical proper
name has an integrative value, establishing an alliance with the recognized "spirit" (the demon, the ancestor); it officially accounts for what
erupts in a group; sometimes, it thus seals a destiny.[15] In sum, this process is written into the system of communication. Sometimes the proper
name even has the meaning of an answer to signs and voices that the
parents or initiators perceived in the circumstances of birth.[16] In any case,
naming simultaneously posits a linkage and a place. It functions at once
as *participation in a system* and as *access to the symbolic*. Through her own
words, and by virtue of varied procedures, the possessed woman can find
an escape from the silence of her body or her desire by entering into the
network of symbolization that a culture offers her.

At Loudun, things cannot happen just like that, simply because, at the
level at which we are operating, several dictionaries of proper nouns exist:
the demonological, the medical, and the political. As in most cases during
the same period, in this instance possession plays on a plurality of onomastic tables that are stratified and not simultaneous. For the possessed
woman, the capacity for speech is therefore not bound solely to the possibilities that the proper names proposed by demonologists provide for
her. The "stronger" list will win her over, and it is that of the doctors
and politicians. During the first months of Loudun, demonological discourse is set in place and developed in an order of priorities, in the course
of exorcisms inside the convent, but it is already menaced by the systems
with which it competes and which are slowly going to be victorious.

As such, the unabridged dictionary of demons' proper nouns used at
Loudun indeed shows the infiltration of pressures other than those of

demonology. This list bears the mark of internal collapses and colonizations. A population of foreign names has been introduced into the system.

a) In this list of about fifty-five names (plus four pairs), a first category consists of names patented and guaranteed by demonological literature: Asmodeus, Astaroth, Balam, Behemoth, Belzebuth, Berith, Isacaron, etc.[17] To this series can be added other Hebrew names drawn from a more esoteric tradition: Achaph, Agal, Aman (a variant of Amon?), Barberith (composed from Berith), Caleph, Caph, Eazar (or Eazas), Lezear, etc. In this region demoniac nominations are attached to cabalistic workings.

b) Other quite different signifiers originate from Greco-Latin mythology: Caron and Cerberes, Castorin, etc.; or from heresiological Christian nomenclature: Celse, Lucien, Luther, etc.

c) Other terms represent the elevation of common names to the status of proper names: Matchstick of Impurity, Coal of Impurity, Concupiscence, Enemy of the Virgin, Fornication, Lion of Hell, Dog's Dick (there is also Caudacanis, a simple Latin translation), Pollution, Endless, etc. In this French repertoire desire is spelled out clearly.

d) Finally, a last bundle is filled with French proper nouns taken from popular traditions, provincial localizations, and from a regional font of words with double meanings: Buffetison, Carreau, Cédon, Elimy, Grelet or Grelier, Legret, Luret, Luvret, Maron, Penault, Pérou, Rebat, Souvillon, etc.

Without dwelling on the details of these names, which except for category *c* are often to be understood as charades, we can distinguish heterogenous linguistic blocks. Series *a* and *b* belong to the "noble" official dictionary and to a foreign repertoire (Hebrew and Greek) or, in any case, to a "learned" one. They are associated with the nuns of aristocratic families (de Belciel, de Barbezéières, de la Motte-Brasé, de Fougères, de Colombiers, etc.) and with those holding the highest positions in the hierarchy of the convent (prioress, under prioress, "mothers" who are "choir nuns"). Series *c* and *d* pertain to a popular culture, to the French language, and to a repertoire either explicit or equivocal; they are furthermore assigned to commoners (Auffray, Bastad, Blanchard, etc.) or to lay sisters.

The complete dictionary is thus made from the debris of different systems, and it already plays the role of a social description in a hierarchy of cultures and powers. It obeys laws other than those dictating demonological organization. Through these fissures and internal rifts it betrays the law of a political order of which it is the principal metaphor, unbe-knownst to the exorcists. This "place" of signification or classification is already the metaphor of another order; it refers to something other than what it is stating. Nevertheless the dictionary functions as a course of accession to speech, but in the form of a *double play*. Entering into this repertoire is equivalent to discovering a place, but a place that oscillates between ritual and theater; a place that, compromised by the interference between the dictionary of demons and those of families or names of nuns (Jeanne des Anges, Louise de Jésus, etc.), only organizes its own allure. The possessed woman plays with this oscillating language. The silence of the place whence she comes makes her apt to profit from this instable discourse. But finally, the religious equivocation that allows her more easily not to be there without being anywhere else merely signifies ex-tension of "Je est un autre" to an entire group. Lodged in a self-defeating order, this subversion will ultimately be repressed by "state policy," which will assign to an entire society the exact place where, in the name of the king, everyone can speak.

The Falsehood of Interpretation

POSSESSION does not aim at a hidden meaning that must be discov-ered. The content of its discourse is already basically well known; it states little more than the catechisms of the period, even if, thanks to its cast of diabolical characters, it stages them differently. But the new question concerns the enunciation "Je est un autre." Most problematic—and what surreptitiously stirs up an entire semantic organization—is the suspicion that falls upon the locutor of this language, and hence on the status of discourse as a whole. Through this enunciation traditional hermeneutics is inverted. It presupposed an unchanging locus and a stable interlocutor, God, who spoke a language whose secrets were still unknown and had to be deciphered. But here the content is known, and the interlocutor is unknown: texts of possession bear the mark of this ravishing of the subject.

More than its secrets, it is now the *propriety* of language that is ques-tioned. The exorcist is relentless in bringing the interlocutor back to the demons that theological literature identifies as the contrary of God. Through this identification he fiercely attempts to reduce them to the *same*. He reclassifies possessed women within his theological knowledge. He thus defends the propriety of language with respect to God, and he aims not to save the possessed but, through them, to save a theological property —a contract that reserves all possession of language to God.

But it all takes place too late. This operation soon becomes impossible. It functions as a falsehood which once again introduces what has to be eliminated, that is to say, the *elsewhere* of discourse. Possession does not initiate another discourse, as if the alterity it witnessed were being provided with a different and recognizable semantic positivity. It produces a disturbance within demonological discourse.

We have an indication of this disturbance in the manner in which the possessed woman inserts her silence into the system that she "disquiets" and which nevertheless allows her to speak. Her "perversion" is not a matter of her furnishing herself with an interpretation of her difference, but rather in letting the internal relations that had been defining the system now act in another fashion. Therefore she leaves all responsibility for interpretation to others. She hides what moves in her, simply because the only discourse at her disposal is the exorcist's or the scholar's interpretation. She manages to escape because of the explanation that the other provides for her. She is restricted to giving the other what is expected of her. But she fools the other by letting him express her self. In this way, a game develops through which discourse is compromised, a game which can already in part explain the silent distance that she has taken in respect to it. This falsehood affecting demonological discourse is the effect of that which lacks a language of its own. Put in strict terms, there is no discourse of the other, only an alteration of the same. Doubtless this is the "diabolical" implication of what is manifested in cases of possession.

But the historical context for this phenomenon must be provided. The epistemological situation of the period must be given as the frame of reference for the fact that an interrogation of language organizes the discourse of possession at Loudun, and that this interrogation is focused on the point where an interlocutor can appropriate language in its entirely for herself by designating herself as "I."[18] Already in its content the Loudun debate attests to the upheaval of a former assurance that had granted God the ability to assume all possible languages and, in the last resort, to keep the locus of the speaker. This divine appropriation becomes doubtful. The universal speaking subject is effaced from the prose of the world. Lost is the legibility of the cosmos considered as a language spoken by God.[19]

Within this global evolution, I will raise only one point that directly concerns diabolical discourse. Its language changes status. It is not only its relation with a speaker who used to be the "being" and the "truth" of language that comes into question, but also, as a consequence, the entire construction that was founded on this relation and that furnished words—categorized according to a hierarchization of the real—with the function of letting things come into view. This epistemology of transparency referred the *verbum* to a *res*. It is replaced by an epistemology of surface, in which the possibilities of significance are measured by establishing relations among signifiers. Ontological relations (*verbum/res*) are replaced by spatial relations, within whose functioning verbal and pictorial language are defined as one.[20] In the same period there is a general critique of reference to a *suppositum*. With Pascal this is indicated by a vanishing of substance in favor of qualities; with Descartes, by the slippage of the substantive in the direction of the adjective, and so forth. The world is transformed into *space;* knowledge is organized around a *looking-over.* Pascal offers the entire dialectic of distance, or of the "point of view" of the "observer," and Descartes offers the philosophy of the *cogito* performing a labor of discrimination within and in relation to the "Fable of the World."[21]

These few reminders only help in situating what *also* takes place at Loudun when the problem of truth (or of the "adequation between a word and a thing") assumes the form of an unstable *place.* A "truth" becomes doubtful. In the sphere where signifiers are combined we cannot clearly tell if they enter into the category of "truth" or its contrary of "falsehood," if they can be ascribed to reality, or to imagination. Thus a discourse is undone, as the possessed women testify, taking advantage of this play in order to insinuate into it "something else" which "seized" them, and which now writes the question of the subject into the language of illusion.

NOTES

1. Michel de Certeau, *La Possession de Loudun,* 2d. ed. (Paris, Gallimard, 1980); see also my *L'Absent de l'histoire* (Paris: Mame, 1973).

2. Sigmund Freud, "On the History of the Psychoanalytic Movement," in *The Standard Edition of the Complete Psychological Works of Sigmund Freud,* 24 vols., J. Strachey, tr. and ed. (London: Hogarth Press, 1953–1974), 14:41–43. This edition hereafter abbreviated *SE.*

3. [The author plays on "voice-off" (see also chapter 5), where allusion is

made to the disembodied relation of image and sound tracks in film. "Text-*off*" describes a writing originating outside of the frame of optical or rational reference.——TR.]

4. See my *L'Absent de l'histoire*, pp. 41–70 and 153–67.

5. Sigmund Freud, quoting *Faust* (part 1, scene 6), apropos of the witch who is metapsychology, in "Analysis Terminable and Interminable," *SE* 23:225.

6. Letter to Georges Izambard (May 13, 1871), in Arthur Rimbaud, *Oeuvres complètes* (Paris: Gallimard-Pléiade, 1946), p. 252. See also the letter of May 15, 1871, to Paul Demeny: "Je est un autre . . ." (p. 254).

7. Rimbaud, *Oeuvres*, p. 252.

8. Facts are falsified when it is said that the subject *I* is the determination of the verb to think. *Çà* thinks (*es denkt*), but that *çà* can surely be this old and illustrious *I* is, if we cast it in moderate terms, only a hypothesis, an allegation," notes Nietzsche in *Beyond Good and Evil*. [De Certeau's translation from the German.——TR.]

9. In *Letters to a Young Poet*, Rilke says, "The poet is Orpheus, not the 'I' of the 'author.' "

10. Emile Benveniste, "De la subjectivité dans le langage," in *Problèmes de linguistique générale* (Paris: Gallimard, 1966), 1:258–66. [My translation; but see ch. 2, n. 22, for the English edition.——TR.]

11. See Alan Henderson Gardiner, *The Theory of Proper Names: A Controversial Essay*, 2d. ed. (London and New York: Oxford University Press, 1957), and Claude Lévi-Strauss, *La Pensée sauvage* (Paris: Plon, 1962), chs. 6–7; in English, *The Savage Mind* (Chicago: University of Chicago Press, 1967). Cf. also J. R. Searle, "Proper Names," in J. F. Rosenberg and C. Travis, eds., *Readings in the Philosophy of Language* (Englewood Cliffs, N.J.: Prentice-Hall, 1971), pp. 212–18.

12. Lévi-Strauss, *The Savage Mind*, p. 185.

13. *Ibid.*, p. 215.

14. Luc de Heusch, "Possession et chamanisme," in *Pourquoi l'épouser?* (Paris: Gallimard, 1971), p. 236.

15. *Ibid.*, pp. 240–41. See also Nicole Belmont's numerous indications in "Nomen et omen," in *Les Signes de la naissance* (Paris: Plon, 1971).

16. See Maurice Houis, *Les Noms individuels chez les Mossi* (Dakar: Ifan, 1963), pp. 9–23.

17. This "official" list favors the Hebrew names, while, for example, individual names from Byzantine demonology originate especially from former pagan, Greek, or "barbaric" divinities, as A. Delatte and C. Josserant note in "Contribution à l'étude de la démonologie byzantine," *Annuaire de l'IPHO* 2 (1934), *Mélanges Bides*, 2:207–32. Yet in both cases the institution takes its diabolical lexicon from the neighborhood, or family, from which it dissociated itself most aggressively: the labor of denegation and/or exorcism takes place in relation to a disquieting social and genealogical proximity.

18. See Benveniste, *Problèmes de linguistique générale*, 1:262.

19. See for example Michel Foucault's analyses in *Les Mots et les choses* (Paris: Gallimard, 1966), especially in "La Prose du monde," pp. 34–39; in English, "The Prose of the World," pp. 38–44 in *The Order of Things* (New York: Ran-

dom House, 1970); as well as W. S. Howell's "Scholastic Logic: Witchcraft," in *Logic and Rhetoric in England, 1500–1700* (New York: Russell, 1956), pp. 57–63.

20. See Pierre Francastel, *La Figure et le lieu* (Paris: Gallimard, 1968), pp. 312–41.

21. See Sylvie Romanowski, *L'Illusion chez Descartes* (Paris: Klincksieck, 1974), pp. 83–99.

7

A Variant

Hagio-Graphical Edification

O N THE outer edge of historiography, as its temptation and betrayal, there exists another discourse. We can characterize it by a few features which can serve here merely to place it within a context, as a corpus of difference. Basically, this other discourse shows an acquired significance, while claiming only to deal with actions, *Acta, Res gestae.* In his *Vita Sancti Martini,* Sulpicius Severus maintains that the opposition *res, non verba*—things, not words—is fundamental. But in this discourse, "acts" take on instead the character of signifiers in the service of a truth which draws their organizing ground plan, using them to "edify" its own manifestation. *Res* are *verba* out of which discourse creates the cult of a received meaning. It seems that these didactic and epiphanic functions have been thrown out of the orbit of history.

Hagiography is a literary genre that was also called "hagiology" or "the hagiologic" in the seventeenth century. As Hippolyte Delehaye defined it in an epoch-making study, *Les Légendes hagiographiques,* it favors the actors of the sacred realm, "saints," and intends to edify, through "exemplarity." We must, he noted, therefore reserve this name for every written monument inspired by and destined to promote the worship of saints. The rhetoric of this "monument" is saturated with meaning, but with *identical* meaning. It is a tautological tomb.

Certain viewpoints are too narrow. Christian hagiography (the only sort mentioned here) is limited neither to antiquity nor to the Middle Ages, even if, since the seventeenth century onward, it has been viewed too much from the angle of historical criticism and source studies, and thereby classed with legend in the period of an ancient prehistoriography, reserving the privilege of scientific biographies for the modern period. It is also impossible to consider hagiography solely in terms of its "authenticity" or "historical value": this would be equivalent to submitting a literary genre to the laws of another genre—historiography—and to dismantling a proper type of discourse only in order to engage its contrary.

As in *The Life of Saint Martin* (one of hagiography's ancient prototypes), the Life of a Saint is "the literary crystallization of the perceptions of a collective conscience," Jacques Fontaine has said. From a sociological and historical point of view, the stages of this literature must be retraced, its functioning must be analyzed, and its cultural situation will have to be specified. But the hagiographical document is also marked by a textual organization where possibilities implied by the title formerly associated with this kind of tale are deployed: *Acta* or, later, *Acta sanctorum*. From this second point of view, the combination of acts, places, and themes indicates a particular structure that refers not just primarily to "what took place," as does history, but to "what is exemplary." The *res gestae* provide only its lexicon. Every Life of a Saint must indeed be approached as a system which organizes a manifestation, thanks to a topological combination of "virtues" and "miracles."

HISTORY AND SOCIOLOGY

Outlines for a History

ARISING together with liturgical calendars and the commemoration of martyrs by the sites of their tombs, hagiography in its first centuries (from about 150 to 350) is concerned less with the existence than with the death of the witness. A second stage is begun with the *Lives*, those of ascetics in the desert (thus the *Life of Saint Anthony*, by Athanasius) on the one hand, and on the other, of "confessors" and bishops (the *Lives* of Saint Cyprian, dead in 258; of Saint Gregory the Thaumaturge, dead c. 270; of Saint Martin of Tours, by Sulpicius Severus). From this point a great growth of hagiography ensues, in which mystics and founders of religious orders assume growing importance. Now it is the life—and no longer the death—on which they are based. First among the Greeks (Simeon the Metaphraste in the tenth century, for example), then in the medieval West (Jacques Voragine's *Golden Legend* in the thirteenth century is but the most celebrated example), the compilations multiply, more recapitulative and cyclical; ancient titles are attributed to them, whose meanings those texts change: *Menology, Catalogus sanctorum, Sanctilogium, Legendarium,* etc. All through this development the *Life* intended for liturgical offices (the most official and clerical form) is distinguished from the *Life* aimed at the people (a form related to sermons, minstrels' tales, etc.).

In 1643 a turning point is marked by the publication in Anvers of the first volume of the *Acta sanctorum* by the Jesuits Bolland and Henskens (or "Henschenius"). The first dated work among all those that the Bollandists—especially Daniel Papebroch, the most famous member of this erudite "commune"—were to edit, the volume bears the fruit of the project that P. Rosweyde had conceived nearly a half century before. It introduces criticism into hagiography. A systematic research of manuscripts; a categorization of sources; a transformation of texts into documents; a privilege granted to "facts," no matter how minuscule their order; a discreet passage from dogmatic truth to historical truth as an end in itself; a search that is already paradoxically defined, as Ernst Cassirer has said, "not by the discovery of what is true, but of what is false": such principles define the collective work of a team that inscribed itself into the small international brigade of erudition through a network of correspondence and travel, reciprocal channels of information and control. Upon this social infrastructure a *communis eruditorum consensus* is formed. From that point on, in the taxonomy of religious works, "the general and specific lives of saints form a large part of ecclesiastical history" (*Table universelle des auteurs ecclésiastiques,* 1704).

Because erudite selection keeps only what is "sincere" or "truthful" about documents, uncritical hagiography—the most important kind—is cast aside. A rift opens up. On the one hand, the austerity that in liturgical matters both priests and theologians opposed to popular folklorization is now transformed into historical exactitude, a new form of worship through which clerics keep the people in the light of truth. On the other hand, from the rhetoric of sermons on the saints we move to a "devout" literature which cultivates both the affective and the extraordinary. The trench between learned "Biographies" and edifying "Lives" widens. The former are critical, less numerous, and deal with the most ancient saints; that is, those who belong both to a primitive purity of truthfulness and to an elitist privilege of knowledge. The latter, in the form of a thousand popular "Flowers of the Saints," are quite widespread and devoted instead to contemporaries who died "in the odor of sanctity." In the twentieth century, other characters—of political stamp, or of crime, or passion—take the place of "saints," yet between the two series the rift is kept open.

A Sociological Document

THE Life of a Saint is inscribed within the life of a group, either a church or a community. It takes for granted that the group already has an existence. But it conveys its self-consciousness by associating a *figure* with a *place*. An originator (a martyr, a name saint, the founder of an abbey, of an order or a church, etc.) is given to a site (the tomb, the church, the monastery, etc.) which thus becomes a foundation, the product and the sign of an advent. The text also implies a network of supports (oral transmission, manuscripts, or printed works) whose infinite development it stops at a given moment. In the dynamics of social dissemination and proliferation, the text establishes a stopping point. It responds to leaks and "loss"—the price of any diffusion—with the closure of a theatrical scene that circumscribes or rectifies the movement of growing conviction (the progress of devotion, for the first martyrs, or the amplification of, for example, Padro Pio's miracles). In this respect the Saint's Life bears a doubly separative function. It distinguishes both the time and place of a group.

On the one hand, the Life of a Saint connects two apparently contrary movements. It assures a distance with respect to origins (a long-established community is distinguished from its past through the deviation that the very representation of this past constitutes). But furthermore, its return to origins allows unity to be reestablished at a time when the group, through its development, runs the risk of being dispersed. Hence memory, whose construction is linked to the disappearance of beginnings, is combined with the productive "edification" of an image intended to protect the group from dispersion. Thus is expressed that moment in the life of a collectivity when the community is divided between what it loses and what it creates. The collection of the Lives of Pakhôme or of Francis of Assisi is a testimonial at once to the different states and programs appropriate to a distancing with respect to the past, and to the present reaction it is provoking.

On the other hand, the Life of a Saint also points to the relation that the group holds with other groups. Thus the martyrdom tale is predominant wherever the community is very marginal, confronted with the threat of extinction, while the virtue tale represents an established church, as an epiphany of the social order in which it is inscribed. Also revealing from this point of view is the tale of the hero's battles with social figures symbolizing the devil; the character, polemical or paraenetic, of hagiographical discourse; the darkening of the scene against which the saint distinguishes himself through more strongly marked miracles; and the structures of the space, either binary (conflicting, antinomical) or ternary (mediated and "stabilized"), in which the actors are situated.

Also at stake is the hero's historical sociology. Thus the martyr is the dominant figure in the beginnings of the Catholic church (in the *Passions*), of the Protestant church (in the martyrologies of Rabe, of Foxe, of Crespin), or to a lesser degree, of the Camisard church, etc. Then come the confessors (among the Syrians in the fourth century, or in Gaul with Saint Martin) who repeat and ultimately carry on where the martyrs left off: either the hermit who is still a Christian soldier (but in the desert now, fighting the devil) and already a founder, or the pastor (the bishop or abbot restoring a community). We then pass to men of virtue (with members of orders predominating over priests and laymen); women follow, but rather late (in the Merovingian period, if we keep account of those who are canonized) and in small numbers, though there are more of them than of the smallest troop, the children.

A "Vacation" Function

FROM its beginnings in the Christian community, hagiography is entirely separated from another kind of text, the canonical books which essentially constitute the Scriptures. In the fifth-century *Life of Melanie,* we are told that once she was "sated" with canonical books and collections of homilies, "she went through the lives of the Fathers as though she were eating desserts." Tales of the saints' lives bring a festive element to the community. They are situated on the side of relaxation and leisure. They correspond to a free time, a place set aside, a spiritual and contemplative respite; they do not belong in the realm of instruction, pedagogical norms, or dogma. They "divert." Unlike texts that must be practiced or believed, the Saints' Lives oscillate between the believable and the marvelous, advocating what one is at liberty to think or do. From both points of view they create an area of "vacation" and of new conditions outside of everyday time and rule.

The use of hagiography corresponds to its content. Its reading becomes leisure as opposed to work. The Saints' Lives are read during meals, or during monks' times of recreation. In the course of the year the readings intervene on holy days; they are recounted at places of pilgrimage and are heard during free hours.

In these diverse ways the hagiographical account breaks the rigor of daily life by freeing the imagination, introducing once again the repetitive and the cyclic into the linearity of work. By showing through a saint— an exception—how history is opened to the power of God, the Saint's Life creates a locus where *the same* and *leisure* are combined. This exceptional locus gives each reader the possibility of a meaning that is at once an elsewhere and an immutable. The extraordinary and the possible support each other in building up a fiction, placed here in the service of exemplarity. This combination in the form of a story plays the role of a "gratuity," to be found in both the text and in the way in which that text is used. We encounter here a *poetics of meaning* that cannot be reduced to an exactitude of facts or of doctrine without destroying the very genre that conveys it. In the shape of an exception and a deviation—that is, through the metaphor of a specific instance—the discourse creates a freedom in respect to daily, collective, or individual time, but in a non-place.

A Popular Literature?

THE earliest mention of a hagiographer in Christian ecclesiastical literature is a condemnation. The author, a priest, was disgraced for having created apocrypha. Orthodoxy represses fiction. The Gelasian decree (which could be called the first index of the Roman church) gives considerable weight to the prohibition against the tales of martyrs. Thus hagiography enters into ecclesiastical literature only through effraction; in other words, through the back door. It is insinuated into the order of a ministry, but without really forming a part of it. The "passions of martyrs" are introduced into the Roman liturgy only very late, in the eighth century, and with a good deal of reticence. The same will hold for the Greek church, where hagiography develops much faster, however, and as of the ninth century, quite often among the laity. The same reservations can be found in the sixteenth century, at the origins of the Protestant churches, and still more in the eighteenth century, in Catholic church administration, which mobilized against these "legends" and "superstitions" through witch hunts. Later the state will pick up the baton from the ecclesiastical jurisdictions. Thus, to cite one of a thousand examples, in May of 1811 in Paris, ministerial censure attacks a collection of "marvels" taking place at Notre-Dame de Laus: "It is for the benefit of the church," notes the censor, "that we keep inauthentic beliefs from becoming a subject of derision" (Paris, Archives Nationales, f. 18, I 149).

To use the terms that Du Cange used in 1665, "legitimate censors" are constantly put up against the "devotion of the people." In the seventeenth century, as in every epoch, "learned men" are opposed to the "false beliefs" of the people, which are classed with the "barbarity of the past centuries," as A. Godeau writes in 1681. Thus, hagiography would be the field where, localized in the same area and placed under the same condemnation, popular, archaic, and false beliefs proliferate together.

This censure is the task of clerics (when they are not religious, they are political), but it follows different criteria depending on the historical period. The norm in whose name legends are excluded always varies. In the beginning, the concern is especially liturgical. Later it becomes dogmatic. From the seventeenth century onward, censure assumes more of the historian's historical criteria: erudition imposes a new definition of what is "true" or "authentic." In the nineteenth century, censure takes on a more moral allure: to the taste for things extraordinary, which is a loss of meaning and of time, is opposed an order bound to the value of work, to the usefulness of liberal values, to classification according to familial virtues. Censure refers also to a psychological normality—so that now the saint, living in a milieu that must be pathological, ought to distinguish himself by his "equilibrium," which would align him, as an exemplar, with the code established by the new clerics.

Based in each instance upon the rules that characterize the statute of the ecclesiastical society, from the bulk of hagiographical literature clerical censure extracts a portion conforming to a norm of learning. This portion will be canonical and can be canonized. The remainder, which is the principal portion, is judged severely but nonetheless tolerated because of its usefulness among the people. This "heretical" literature is by turns intended for the people by clerics (the authors or the users of so many edifying lives), and challenged in the name of errors that originate in popular ignorance. Thus is born the double-edged problem of a "popular" literature: is it a product of an elite, or an effect of what the elite is eliminating? For more than a century, hagiography is grafted onto folklore; there, it often takes on the privilege of representing a fundamental man, for whom an elite of learned scholars, folklorists, or ethnologists would be the interpreter and consciousness. But is this interpretive work not destined to eliminate what hagiography is supposed to represent, and therefore to lose what it aims to capture?

THE STRUCTURE OF DISCOURSE

The Hero

IN hagiography, individuality counts much less than character. The same features and the same episodes are passed along from one proper name to another; from all of these floating elements, like an array of words and jewels, the combinations make up a given figure and charge it with meaning. The model which results from this bricolage is more important than the proper name; the decoupage that fashions the function and the type is more important than the particular saint's biography.

The construction of the hagiographical figure is elaborated from semantic elements. Thus, in order to indicate the divine origins of the hero's action and the heroism of his virtues, the Saint's Life often confers a noble background upon the character. Blood is a metaphor for grace. Whence the necessity for genealogies. The sanctification of princes and the ennoblement of saints correspond, from text to text: such reciprocal operations turn a religious exemplarity into a social hierarchy, and they sanctify the established order (such is the case with "Saint" Charlemagne or "Saint" Napoleon). But they also adhere to an eschatological schema inverting the political order in order to replace it with a celestial one and turn the impoverished into kings. In fact, a circularity is at work, each order continually leading back to the other. This is the ambiguity of the *Gesta principium et vitae sanctorum:* a reciprocal attraction between the prince and the saint places them together in the proof that "nothing changes" beneath the diversity of human events.

The use of the noble origin, whether known or hidden, is but a symptom of the law which organizes the Saint's Life. While biography aims to posit an evolution—and hence, differences—hagiography postulates that everything is given at the very beginning with a "calling," an "election," or, as in the Lives of antiquity, with an initial *ethos*. Saints' histories are then the progressive epiphany of this given, as if they were also the history of the relations between the generative principle of the text and its surface manifestations. The test or temptation becomes the pathos of this relation, or the fiction of its indecision. Yet the text refers to *itself* by focusing its portrayal of the hero around constancy, the perseverance of the same: "Idem enim constantissime perseverebat qui prius fuerat," is said of Saint Martin in his *Vita*. The end reiterates the beginning. From the adult we go back to the saint's childhood, which already bears the signs of the posthumous effigy. Saints are individuals who lose nothing of what was initially given to them.

The tale is no less dramatic, but the only transformation concerns the progressive manifestation of a destiny. The successive places of the story are essentially divided between a time of trial (solitary struggles) and a time of glorification (public miracles), in a passage from a private to a public sphere. As in Greek tragedy, the outcome is known from the beginning, but with the difference that where the law of Greek destiny implied the fall of the hero, here the glorification of God requires the saint's triumph.

A Discourse of "Virtues"

GENERALLY speaking, hagiography is a discourse of virtues. But the term has only secondarily a moral meaning—and not always. It borders instead on extraordinary and marvelous deeds, but only insofar as they are signs. It designates the exercise of "powers" linked to the *dunameis* of the New Testament and connects the order of appearance to an order of being. "Power" represents the relation between these two levels and upholds their difference. This mediation carries a whole spectrum of representatives, from the martyr, or the miracle, to ascesis, or the accomplishment of state obligations. Every Saint's Life offers a choice and a coherent organization of these virtues. It does so by taking advantage of raw materials that are furnished either by the saint's deeds and doings, or by the episodes pertaining to the common ground of a tradition. "Virtues" constitute the basic units; their rarefaction or multiplication produces effects of recurrence or progress in the story; their combinations allow for the categorization of hagiographies.

These units can be characterized in different ways. Inasmuch as they furnish social models (*exempla*), they are located at a crossroads between the evolution of the individual community in which they are elaborated (this being their diachronic aspect) and the sociocultural conjuncture that this evolution is traversing (their synchronic aspect). Thus the role and the definition of poverty vary in the Middle Ages as, on the one hand, a congregation is either in close or distant proximity to its beginnings and, on the other, as pauperism plays the role of a mobility that has become either a necessity or a threat to order in the overall society. The same holds true in the case, for example, of the contrary virtues of the irreducibility of the confession of faith in respect to a milieu (martyrdom by blood), and integration in the name of social utility (stately duties) or of cultural conformity (psychological equilibrium).

Virtues also pertain to a hierarchy of signs, following their relation to the being they are expressing. In this fashion we can account for an explosion of virtue (*dunameis*) and how virtues become specialized by being separated from "miracles." Both refer to power, but only as a social norm in the former case, and as an exception in the latter. Where it is produced, moralization of virtues appears to be the process that allows signs that conform best to the social rules of a period to be transformed into the most "true" (or most transparent) manifestations of Christian mystery. Elsewhere, the exception (or miracle) is taken to be the eruption of divine power: what is true (what conforms to being) *does not* conform to the social order. Seen in the first perspective, miracles become secondary; they are relativized or effaced, like an indiscreet extra. In the second, virtues offer the figure of preambles and struggles that pave the way for the miraculous unveiling of the essential. Thus we have the life of the saint that goes from ascesis to miracles through progress toward visibility, versus the life that aims—beyond the first prodigies—at common and "hidden" virtues, or "faith in everyday things," marks of true sanctity.

A theology is always invested in hagiographical discourse. It is particularly evident exactly where the Life of a Saint is used to prove a theology, as among the Byzantines especially, or during the sixteenth and nineteenth centuries in the West: the thesis is true, since it was professed by a man who was a saint. More fundamentally, it is a combination of signs which provides the story with meaning. In themselves, the order and table of virtues exhibit a theory of its manifestation, in the fashion of fiction. Thus the organization of a Life depends on diverse types of projections of the systematic table onto the temporal axis. The story can be anthropological, providing through its successive stages philosophical distinctions between "acts," "powers," and "modes of existence," or the tripartition of man into "sensitive," "psychic," and "spiritual"; it can be ethical, classifying its biographical elements according to "catalogues of virtues," or according to the three vows of religion, etc.; or it can be theological, with its chronological expansion following the division into the three theological and four cardinal virtues, and so forth. In modern times, the Eucharist, the basis for the passage from being to appearance, is the object favored by miracle, becoming the doublet and the "proof" of that which makes the narrative of a "manifestation" possible.

Hagiographical Topics

HAGIOGRAPHY offers an immense repertory of themes that historians, ethnologists, and folklorists have often explored. With Günther and many others, we can notice small, tightly structured units whose lingering traits cannot necessarily be explained through influences: thus the apparition of the miraculous crucifix; the body dumped as rubbish and protected from dogs by birds of prey; the statue coming out of the sea; the knight's battle with the dragon; the man carrying his own head, and so on.

There is also an entire bestiary. The Life of a Saint often short-circuits the human element by linking in the miracle the divine power and the animal, which is either a victim or a beneficiary. This vanishing of man in the miracle is the strongest demonstration of a conjunction of polar extremes; it also brings about the return of the fantastic side of desire. Moreover, the animal repertory admits of regions of very different terrain, some stereotypical and symbolic (the pig, the snake, the lion, the eagle, etc.), others more realistic (the chicken, the dog, the horse, etc.). Between them passes the moving barrier separating a received lexicon, whose primitive origins are still quite near, from the language of cultivated nature, the familiar or domesticated animal. Still more important is the language of the body, a topography of holes and valleys: orifices (the mouth, the eye) and internal cavities (the belly, and ultimately the heart), one favored in turn over the other, and written into the dialectics of inside-outside or englobing-englobed, in order to embody a rich spectacle of entries and exits.

In their entirety, these themes refer to systems of representation. One can distinguish a demonic or "agonistic" type that situates the figures of the devil and his metamorphoses within a celestial battle; a historical or scriptural type that reiterates, develops, and illustrates the signs furnished by the Old and the New Testament; an ascetic or moral type that is organized around purity and guilt, and which repeats the representation of health and illness; and so forth.

A GEOGRAPHY OF THE SACRED

HAGIOGRAPHY is marked by a predominance of precise indications of place over those of time. In this way also it differs from biography, following a law of expression that characterizes this basically theophanic genre: discontinuities of time are crushed by the permanence of that which is the beginning, the end, and the foundation. The history of the saint is translated into a course of places and changes of scene; they determine the space of a constancy.

The Circularity of a Closed Time

IN its totality, and from its initial words, the Life of a Saint is subjugated to a time other than that of the hero; its time is that of ritual, of festivity. The liturgical here and now outweighs a past that has to be narrated. The *incipit* confers its own permanent status upon discourse. At stake is not a story, but a "legend," that is, what "must be read" (*legendum*) on that very day. From the first Saints' Calendars up until the *Lives of the Saints for Every Day of the Year* (by J. Caillet, among hundreds of others) and the catalogues of saints following the order of the months, a liturgical frame fixes the place of hagiography within a circularity, that is, within a different time, without duration, already eschatological, a festive time. The order of a calendar is imposed upon the narrative (thus two calendars appear at the origin of the Greek and Latin versions of the *Life of Melanie*). The saint's works are categorized in accord with the calendars in use among communities where their legends are read. This is the order of a cosmos.

This order is also found in the universal catalogues that replace the circularity of the "sanctoral" (the annual cycle of the saints' holy days) with the more inclusive totality of history since the beginnings of the world, as L. Rabe has already done in 1571; this total history is another closed time, because the chronology, introduced in hagiography, still functions as a means for an all-encompassing recapitulation. The liturgical order is merely fragmented when an alphabetical order is imposed. The former still survives surreptitiously (in for example the so-called chronological table which, in Father Jacques-Paul Migne's *Dictionnaire hagiographique* of 1850, follows the calendar). It remains as the hidden norm, the secret support of the space where an elsewhere is enclosed. Does this protection of a place located outside of time do anything more than repeat what the text says in its desire to cover a religious locality with extraordinary feats, or in the apocalyptic and millenarian tendency which it expresses so often?

A Composition of Places

THE Life of a Saint is a composition of places. Primitively, it is born in a founding place (a martyr's tomb, the destination of a pilgrimage, a monastery, a congregation, etc.) that has since become a liturgical site, and the biography ceaselessly returns there through the series of the saint's travels or displacements, as if this place remains its ultimate proof. The aim of the course is to return to this point of departure. The very itinerary of writing leads to the vision of the place: to read is to go and see.

With its hero, the text revolves around the place. It is deictic, always pointing at what it can neither state nor replace. The hero's manifestation is essentially local, visible, and impossible to express. It is missing in the discourse designating, fragmenting, and commenting on it through a succession of scenes. But this "discursiveness," which is a passage from scene to scene, can express the meaning of the irreplaceable, unique, extraordinary, and sacred (*hagios*) place.

The organization of the space through which the saint passes folds and unfolds in order to display a truth which is a place. In a great number of hagiographies both ancient and modern, the life of the hero is divided, as in travel literature, between a departure and a return, but it does not include the description of a foreign society. It goes and then it returns. There is first of all the vocation that exiles the saint from the city, leading him to the desert, the country, or faraway lands—the time of ascesis, closed by the saint's illumination. Then comes the itinerary leading the saint back to the city, or bringing throngs from the cities to him or her—the time of epiphany, of miracles and conversions. This schema allows readers to enter into the movement of the text, producing an itinerant reading, taking charge of the "wicked world" in order, in the first part of the text, to lead it to the named place on the heels of the saint. This is the edifying side of hagiography, either in a paraenetic form or in the mode of a judgment pronounced against the world; the first part is the area set aside for battles with the devil.

And furthermore, these two contrary places, this departure repeated by a return, this outside which is attained by discovery of an inside, designate a *non-place*. A *spiritual* space is marked off through the contrary nature of these movements. The unity of the text lies in the production of a meaning through the juxtaposition of contraries—or, to borrow a phrase used by the mystics, by a "coincidence of opposites." But the meaning is a place which is not a place. It refers readers to a "beyond" that is neither an elsewhere nor even the spot where the saint's life organizes the edification of a community. Here a symbolizing labor is often accomplished. Perhaps the fact that a particular place is made relative through a composition of many places—akin to the effacement of the individual behind a combination of virtues aiming at the manifestation of being—indeed furnishes the "moral" of hagiography: indeed, a pure will to signify, whose non-place is here a discourse of places.

BIBLIOGRAPHY

Aigrain, René. *L'Hagiographie*. Paris: Bloud and Gay, 1953.

De Gaiffier, Baudouin. "Mentalité de l'hagiographe médiéval." *Analecta Bollandiana* (1968), 86:391–99.

Delehaye, Hippolyte. *Les Légendes hagiographiques*. Brussels, 1905. Available in English as *The Legends of the Saints*. Donald Atwater, tr. New York: Fordham University Press, 1962.

Delooz, Father Pierre. *Sociologie et canonisations*. Liège: Faculté de droit, 1969.

Dorn, Erhard. *Der sündige Heilige in der Legend des Mittelalters*. Munich: W. Fink, 1967.

Fontaine, Jacques. Introduction to Sulpice Sévère, *Vie de Saint Martin*. Paris: Editions du Cerf, 1967.

Gilmont, Father Jean-François. *Les Martyrologes protestants du XVIe siècle*. Louvain, 1966).

Graus, František. *Volk, Herrscher, und Heiliger im Reich der Merowinger*. Prague: Nakladatelstri Ceskoslovenské Akademie, 1965.

Gunther, H. *Psychologie de la légende: Introduction à une hagiographie scientifique*. Paris, 1954.

Patlagean, Evelyne. "Ancienne hagiographie et histoire sociale." *Annales E. S. C.* (1968), 23:106–26.

Peeters, Paul. *Orient et Byzance: Le Tréfonds oriental de l'hagiographie byzantine.* Brussels: Société des Bollandistes, 1950.

Wolpers, Theodor. *Die englische Heiligenlegende des Mittelalters.* Tübingen: M. Niemayer, 1964.

IV

Freudian Writing

8

What Freud Makes of History

"A Seventeenth-Century Demonological Neurosis"

W HAT we initially call history is nothing more than a narrative. Everything begins with the shop window of a legend that arranges "curiosities" in an order in which they *must be read*. The legend provides the imaginary dimension that we need so that the elsewhere can reiterate the very here and now. A received meaning is imposed, in a tautological organization expressive only of the present time. When we receive this text, an operation has already been performed: it has eliminated otherness and its dangers in order to retain only those fragments of the past which are locked into the puzzle of a present time, integrated into the stories that an entire society tells during evenings at the fireside.

These signs that are arranged into a legend can be analyzed, however, in another way. Here another history begins. It tends to establish heteronomy ("That's what happened") within the homogeneity of language ("That's what they say," or "That's what we read"). It produces the historical dimension within the element of a text. More strictly speaking, it is tantamount to *making history*.

This study was first published in *Annales E.S.C.* (1970), 25:654–67.

The word "history" vacillates between two poles: the story which is recounted (*Historie*) and what is produced (*Geschichte*). This truism still has the value of designating, between these two meanings, the area of a labor and a change. For historians always begin with the first meaning and then aim toward the second, in order to open within the text of their culture the rift of something that happened elsewhere and otherwise. In this fashion they *generate* history. In the pieces that the imagination of their society has organized beforehand, they effect displacements, add other parts, set up intervals and comparisons among them, discern the trace of something other in these signs; they refer thus to a construct that has vanished. In a word, historians create absences. From these documents —through the twists and turns of the profession, which need not be recalled here—they produce a past that is taken up by but never reduced to their new discourse. Their labor is thus also an event. Because it does not repeat, its effect is one of changing the history-legend into a history-task. An identical operative process transforms historians' relation with the past things that were chatted about, and the internal relations among the documents that designated these things.

It is in this latter sense that the question of history will be put forward here. But my aim is neither to deduce Freud's "conception" of history from a knowledge derivative from his works, nor to measure the results of Freudian interpretation according to current methods of historical investigation. Rather, the goal is to discern what Freud's incursions into the "historical" region of his culture are responding to, and what they result in. How does he deal with this part of his language, where his curiosity meets the taste of so many of his contemporaries? As an analyst, what does he do with history? It may be preferable to study his work in a specific instance. Here we run the risk of opening certain questions without the means of giving them a truly scientific status, and also without our illusory pretension of resolving them.

These remarks are also perhaps a reaction against one way in which psychoanalysis is *used*. In both ethnology and history, certain studies demonstrate that the general use of psychoanalytical concepts runs the risk of blossoming into a new rhetoric. These concepts are thus transformed into figures of style. Recourse to the death of the father, to Oedipus or to transference, can be used for anything and everything. Since these Freudian "concepts" are supposed to explain all human endeavor, we have little difficulty driving them into the most obscure regions of history. Unfortunately, they are nothing other than decorative tools if their only goal amounts to a designation or discreet obfuscation of what the historian does not understand. They circumscribe what cannot be explained, but they do not explain it. They avow an unawareness. They are earmarked for areas where an economic or a sociological explanation forcibly leaves something aside. A literature of ellipsis, an art of expounding on scraps and remnants, or the feeling of a question—yes; but a Freudian analysis—no.

The Historical, a Production of the Freudian Aufklärung

THE study "A Seventeenth-Century Demonological Neurosis" was written in 1922.[1] For all the necessary details of its diagnosis I refer back to the text. The story is well known; it is recounted in a manuscript of the seventeenth and eighteenth centuries (the *Trophaeum Marianocellense* in the National Library of Vienna, ms. 14084) which Freud describes in detail.

Once there lived a Bavarian painter named Christoph Haitzmann. On September 5, 1677, carrying a letter of introduction from the vicar of Pottenbrunn (in lower Austria), he arrived at the monastery of Mariazell (at Zell, in Styria). The letter, written on the first of September, from Leopold Braun to the abbot of the convent, is transcribed in the *Trophaeum*. It recounts that having been in Pottenbrunn for several months, at church on August 29 the painter succumbed to terrible convulsions, and that he showed the same symptoms in the following days. Interrogated by the priest, he confessed to having let himself be seduced by the devil in 1669 and to having then written that he would commit his body and soul to Satan after nine years. Other texts tell us that his "melancholy" was then linked to the death of his father, as the cause for the depression that had preceded his contract with the devil. The expiration of the pact fell on September 24, 1677. The poor soul hoped that the Good Virgin Mary of Zell would save him by obliging the evil one to return this pact written in blood.

According to a story written most probably during September 1677 (also included in the *Trophaeum*), as soon as he arrived in Mariazell, Haitzmann was exorcised for three days and three nights. At about midnight on September 8, the day celebrating the nativity of the Virgin Mary, at the corner of the altar dedicated to her memory he saw the devil appear before him in the form of a winged dragon; tearing himself from the hands of the priests, he jumped toward the altar and took back his pact.

A few days later he returned to Pottenbrunn, then went to Vienna where his married sister was living.

From October 11 until May 1678 he was again afflicted with convulsions, strange visions, and, at one time, with a paralysis of the legs. He began to describe his condition in a diary (also transcribed in the Vienna manuscript) that he kept until January 13, 1678. He also illustrated this diary with paintings representing his visions—especially of the devil, who appeared now and then as an "honorable bourgeois citizen" and as a demon with female breasts. He returned to Mariazell, where he complained of "attacks of the evil spirit." He attributed them to a second pact—now written in ink—that he might have signed with the devil. After the exorcisms were resumed, he recovered this pact on May 9, at about nine o'clock in the evening. Shortly afterward he joined the Hospitaller Brothers, or Brothers of Mercy, and was named Brother Chrysostome. He died on March 14, 1700, at Neustadt, on the Moldava. According to an inquest of 1714, the obituary that the provincial dedicated to him makes mention of a regular life with, from time to time, an evil temptation to renew his pact with the devil; it is true, the report adds, that this occurred when "he had drunk a little too much wine."

The manuscript carefully transcribes the two "syngraphs." One, written in blood, stated: "Christopher Haitzmann. I dedicate myself to this Satan in order to be his own son and to belong to him in body and soul after nine years"; the other, written in ink: "I, Christopher Haitzmann, commit myself in writing with this lord to be his own son after nine years."

Thus we have one case of "possession" among thousand of others in the seventeenth century. This black period of history, this "savage universe of superstitions," arrests and fascinates historians and philosophers alike. Yet no murmur of this marginalized experience figures in our own discourse.

But we discover that for Freud such somber times (*GW* 13:317) have, to the contrary, the appearance of open daylight. What we take to be our night is offered to him, he says, in total clarity (*GW* 13:318). There is enough here to awaken our incredulity or suspicion, since historians, determined by their documentation, grasp sorcery only as a white space in the *margins* of the writing and its text,[2] and philosophers define the diabolical as the *eliminated* term (whose exclusion has more over made it illegible) in a "structure of limits" essential for the establishment of all reason and social activity.[3] But in the text at hand these are not the questions which Freud wants to take up.

Thanks to the Freudian "clarification" cast over the fields of history, do we at least have a scientific model detailing what we call interdisciplinarity? Such a model would allow us to define the conditions of differentiation and confrontation among some related sciences, in this instance between history and psychoanalysis. In this way we might be rid of the "soft" interdisciplinarity that today insinuates itself into the interstices between fields defined by different sciences, that merely takes advantage of their play as if from a vacant, uncertain, and unavowed space between them, or that allows each science the ease of assigning to others what exceeds the limits of its own explanation. Rather, the interdisciplinarity we look toward would attempt to apprehend epistemological constellations as they reciprocally provide themselves with a new delimitation of their objects and a new status for their procedures—but Freud does not understand it in quite this way. He writes for whomever might "believe" (*glauben*) in psychoanalysis (*GW* 13:330). He does so in the name of a science whose "success" overall (*überhaupt*) accords it the imperial right of extending its investigations into new areas (*GW* 13:317) and the assurance of confirming its first conquest. Certain that the walled city of sorcerers will also yield and surrender only to these weapons, Freud sends his arrow in the direction of Troy (*GW* 13:329).

First of all Freud shows a very typical attitude toward the Mariazell manuscript. For if he uses his tools on these still-fallow lands that have yet to be "cultivated" in psychoanalytical terms—that is, on these writings originating in the seventeenth century—it is not because the terrain is foreign, supposedly distant, and set apart as times past. To the contrary, it is because the times are his own. The documents that he reads are part of his own context. They belong to his present time, but that time has not been analyzed—a revealing sign. Here the Mariazell document is a fragment of a whole, factitious but real, that Freud's readings, his knowledge, his interest—in short, that his culture, a flat and entirely contemporary surface—is constituting. Therein a place is given to him before he *authorizes it* for himself. He is *in* this language (that of his clients, his friends, or his readings) before making something of it in the name of science. From this standpoint, the manuscript offers problems not unlike those offered by any of the other fragments of his language. But Freud will specifically turn it into a *historical* document in his own style, and through a scientific operation—his own—that also extends to this element of his culture.

In this locale of words placed, like all other elements, within the cultural geography of a present time (the past is at the start only a modality of the present), the analysis will be given as *depth*. Such is the way Freudian therapeutics proceeds: analysis discerns organizations in the words of patients that "betray" a genesis; it refers them to events that they hide and which become—as *both* absent and present—a past. Interpretation blandly begins with what we can happen upon just about anywhere, Freud tells us, but it also reveals in the present time and in everyday life the most bizarre conclusions (*GW* 13:328). History is a form of this "uncanniness." It is neither an immediate given nor an a priori. It is the *product* of a scientific *act*. Here it results from psychoanalysis. How? By adhering to the Haitzmann case, Freud will demonstrate it through his *Aufklärung* or elucidation (such is the word in the text: *aufklären*, *GW* 13:329). Its general purpose merely needs to be stated: like his others, this analysis will establish the traces of relations between periods of time through relations between words. Through a study of the text, the analysis will transform the surface of verbal elements into a network of interrelations that organize this surface, that articulate words as a function of lost or effaced things, and that turn the text into a deceptive sign of past events.

That a history may be implied by a verbal record and established through Freudian investigation is what I should like to emphasize. The Haitzmann case seems straightforwardly historical: it dates from the seventeenth century—a way of filing it in the drawers of current chronological categories. But in reality the case becomes historical from the time it is inserted within a problematic of history, the very one that Freud cannot fail to make manifest through his interpretive tasks.

Toward a History of the Seventeenth Century

THEREFORE I will not dwell long on the heuristic interest that "A Seventeenth-Century Demonological Neurosis" can hold for both the philosopher and the historian. Having wandered for years along these margins of the history of the seventeenth century, I think that it is very great.[4] From this perspective, the arguments that Ida Macalpine and Richard Hunter use to reject the Freudian hypothesis are too much inspired by an erudition more "scientistic" than scientific,[5] and close to those oriental bazaars which a "philosophy of religions" was proud of resembling for quite some time: heaped together, according to their shapes, are pots of every provenance; all of the devils with female breasts can be found on one shelf, while on another, we can find all of the kinds of moons scattered about the world's civilizations. From the multiplicity of religions, this kind of analysis selects a single "theme," here, for example, the devil sporting female attributes (such as breasts). The analysis isolates an element from the whole to which it belongs, in order to connect it to an *object* fashioned according to the laws of anthology, following analogies founded solely upon the observer's presuppositions. The meaning of an element is, in reality, accessible only through the analysis of its functioning within the historical relations inherent to a society; in other words, only insofar as this element can be taken as a *term* inscribed within the network of a language. Macalpine and Hunter have reason to consider erroneous and insufficient[6] the information that inspires Freud to say that the image of the breasted devil, in Haitzmann's pictures,[7] is unusual (*GW* 13:335). But this point is not crucial to Freud's argumentation, which counters his opponents with their own weapons. Freud means something quite different.

From the perspective of a historiography, interpretation of the Classical Age can retain two points from Freudian analysis which are worthy of being developed along many lines. I mention them only in passing, because they correspond less to the aim of this study than to its repercussions.

First, the importance of the *ambivalence of God and the devil* that Freud emphasizes seems to be confirmed through the multiple shapes of its persistence throughout the seventeenth century. Thus, in taking the place of religious authority, the state (and in theory, "state policy") becomes a substitute (an *ersatz*) for God-the-Father, who was (to use a term from Freud's text) "split up" by the wars of religion. But on the one hand, the initial ambivalence of God-the-Father is still expressed in every church through the vacillation of all religious experience between the divine and the diabolical, while on the other, it resurges as an ambiguity within the movement which then causes this state policy to be read either as "divine right" or as the "policy of Hell."[8] Many other examples could be provided.

And second, in Freud's analysis of the text, Haitzmann's pacts with the devil represent a contract that furnishes the painter, deprived of his dead father, with the *benefit of having another father* in exchange for his life, body, and soul after nine years' time. He will then devote himself in the same fashion to the congregation of the Brothers of Mercy in order to be a faithful son. This interpretation suggests that in the seventeenth century, in the nocturnal discourse of sabbaths just as in the diurnal discourse of civic life, different sociocultural structurings have an analogous genesis. Then, in various forms, one effectively "devotes" oneself in order to enjoy the privilege of being a client, a faithful believer, or a "son." So the problem originates in the fact that *the father* (to whom one can be "devoted") *no longer exists*. Whence the plurality of reinvestments of the role that the king indeed plays for a period of time. This closure of the need to be a son, and to be seen as a son by a father, might be contrasted—but up to what point?—with the current organization of a society in which the desire to exist is established, and is alienated, by encountering the father once again—but as a determining facticity, as a social language and an anonymous *law*.

But we would still do well to linger over two questions, related in a way that seems paradoxical upon cursory glance, but in reality complementary in the way that Freudian procedure interconnects them: one is the legibility of the past; the other involves substitutions of the father.

From the Legible Past to the Hidden Present

DEMONIAC neurosis of the seventeenth century, we are told, is clearly established (*GW* 13:318). Besides, it is assimilated to the neurosis of the child, in whom it can be detected better than in the adult. The seventeenth century—this "age" of humanity that Freud considers "primitive," and that he also calls "medieval"! (see *GW* 13:318 and 332)—discovers with its naked eye (*mit freien Augen, GW* 13:317) the illness that is discovered in the twentieth century only through extended investigation. What is obvious then is what would be obscure today. In sum, the *Aufklärung* of representations proper to these "children" of the seventeenth century is indeed child's play.

Thus, the most ancient element would also be the clearest. This position allows us to interpret the Freudian claim posted at the beginning of his study,[9] of recognizing beneath other words—those of the seventeenth century—the *same* neurotic structures (*GW* 13:317). In no way is the issue one of a submerged, homogenous "reality" such as an "essence" or a *thumos* that would "sub-tend" the discontinutiy of representations. Rather, the professional historian would be inclined to substantiate continuity in the form of a "progress," of a "logic" of which history would be the "expression," or in the form of a "quantified element" whose initial codings establish continuities beforehand, etc. He too quickly takes what is only the coherence of his historiographical discourse to be a reality of history, and what is only the order postulated or advanced through his thinking to be an order governing the succession of facts.

Freud is not speaking here of a permanence of the thing beneath the diversity of its appearances. In his view, the same relation of ambivalence and tension can be repeated and hence discovered again (such as in a "content," he remarks: *Inhalte, GW* 13:317), betrayed through the successive masks that represent it, either in a demonological garb in the seventeenth century, or in the language of organic illnesses in the twentieth century. The constant content is a *relation* among changing terms, one of which is in its turn the diabolical mask of yesterday, and today, the migraine headache, the ulcer, or some organic illness. What is more obvious within the past is the lure itself, for it appears to us then simply as what it is, a lure. The deception through which the repressed conflict is both represented and hidden is therein much "clearer." The "trace" of the devaluation of the father was then far more visible than today. This statement introduces a degree of "historical" distance between readers and the document they are analyzing. This distance can be formulated as "It used to be visible"; yet here, visibility gives its burden to the imperfect tense ("It used to be"); it measures a rift opened between different tenses and times.

Other data in the text are bound to this conception. First, Freud evokes a time anterior to the seventeenth century. Beforehand, an "outset" is posited as an *Anfang* (a beginning, *GW* 13:330) or an *Ursprung* (an origin, p. 331). In this primitive time, the father's duality (the projection of an ambivalent relation with the father) was represented in a single personality that was both the devil and God. In the beginning, the same and the simple prevail. Janus bears in himself alone the conflictual ambiguity. The *Urbild* or primitive prototype was later, we are told, split in two (*GW* 13:331) and fragmented: the duality present in the first infantile image—both a tender submissiveness and hostile defiance—had been made explicit in two opposed personages, God and the devil. Thus progress fragments as it clarifies. If the past, then, is more legible than the present, it is in the name of this "law" (which we can call Freudian without distinguishing yet whether Freud advances it or exhumes it) that furnishes to all forms of explanation, as an originary limit and primary evidence, the simple representation of an unassailable ambiguity.

This is not the place to unravel all the verifications or refutations that anthropology can bring to this view. In any event, Freud never believed that psychoanalysis exempted him from either gathering exact sociohistorical information or from investigating the connection between individual and social features. That an abundant and indeed erudite documentation seemed to him necessary is evinced in his research on the Mariazell manuscripts. Such, too, was the case when he was preparing his studies *A Childhood Memory of Leonardo da Vinci* (1910), "The Moses of Michelangelo" (1914), and so forth; and his attitude is further revealed by his regret, in respect to these works, at having been "obliged to draw vast conclusions from a number of insufficient facts."[10] A specific inventory of phenomena is one of his constant preliminaries. On the other hand, he held *Totem and Taboo* (1912) to be a capital work, as important as *The Interpretation of Dreams* (1900), fulfilling and complementing the earlier work. An analysis of languages, and of the genesis that their structurings can reveal, overcomes the division between "individual psychology" and "collective psychology."[11]

With *Totem and Taboo* Freud selected an objective that would continue to uphold this division. He set forth to "bridge the gap between students of such subjects as social anthropology, philology and folklore on the one hand, and psycho-analysts, on the other." "Cooperation," he said, "could not fail to be of benefit to research," even if it could not "offer to either side what each lacks—to the former an adequate initiation into the new psychological technique or to the latter a sufficient grasp of the material that awaits treatment."[12] With this "lack" he admits that he draws the necessary materials from elsewhere. In the case of Haitzmann, he "owes" everything to Dr. R. Payer-Thurn, member of the Aulic Council and director of what is now the Imperial and Royal Library of the Fideikommis in Vienna, who published his work separately.[13] But also, Freud obtained from Bullitt the documentation on President Wilson, and from Frazer and many others the "facts" concerning totemism, and so on. In reality, this "raw material" is the *product* of researches on which psychoanalysis is based, and is not so much a set of *facts* as a set of *fabrications*. In this light, they are still facts, but *historical* facts, results and signs of related sciences (those of the beginning of the twentieth century). Therefore they play the same role as the "facts" of which any of his clients speak to Freud—remarks or facts that are also elaborated and partially manufactured. When his patients are in question, the analyst quickly seizes upon the "material" of their language as a *product*. Does Freud have the same attitude in respect to the "material" that he obtains from the historian or the anthropologist? That is the question. Contrary to what has been said so often, it therefore matters little if Frazer's knowledge was deficient or has been "superseded." The knowledge of Dora or Little Hans, at the center of the five great *Case Histories,* is still more deficient or superseded. But since the analyst admits his dependency upon a relation to this language (for instance, the language of his client), it is necessary to ask how he deals with it (as a signifier or as reality?) and also how he situates his interpretive labor in relation to this lack.[14] This is an issue of broad implications, but which must not be displaced in the name of concerns foreign to those of Freud's own work.

Concealment, the Task of History

BUT let us now return to Freud's text on the demoniac neurosis, a text that is moreover organized—from the bias of a recourse to the *Urbild* —by the compulsion that in turn inspires other contemporary thinkers to take up the origin of language and the development of plural languages. In any event, the concept introduced by Freud focuses language into a simple picture (a unique *Bild*) that no longer exists (*Ur*, the vanished origin), except as a *multiple outgrowth* buried deeper through the very fact of being fragmented by elucidation, and thus less apparent. The work of history (*Geschichte*) endlessly conceals what had been legible, and through the very gesture that reduces the simple element in order to discover it. Explications effect a deployment of contraries; thus they multiply representations—that is, they break the *Urbild* into a thousand facets when they reiterate it in an "analytic" language. They both decompose *and* camouflage a primitive "clear" conflict, in a single thrust of analysis and effacement. Right where he discerns the labor of explication (whose acceleration in the nineteenth century perhaps made psychoanalysis possible), Freud "recovers" the conflict, no longer as image (*Bild*), but in the name of the law (which is *scientifically* verified) that organizes every new language—that of the patient, of a society, and so on. In the same move, he bestows another object upon science: the signified (the "content"), which one loses through elucidation; the object, which is endlessly being lost through the fact of being analyzed; and finally, the relation between this loss and these explications.

An originary element (*Urbild*) is omnipresent in Freud's study. It is implicated in it, and, more precisely, put forward by it. Yet at stake is neither an "object" existing outside of his research as a pregiven fact, nor the result of a simple tautology by which analytical discourse would make an element of its deployment from its condition of possibility. To the contrary, this science establishes as a law of language, and as its own law, a difference of time periods and a work of time.

Something comparable has been suggested in respect to the totem (the father-animal), an immense ethnological buffoonery taken up by the most serious authors of the period.[15] Freud sees in it the initial term, evident, but necessary, of a *relation* (constitutive of history) which goes from the simple to the complex; that is, from ambivalence figured by the totem to subsequent explicative dissociation. He thus uncovers in the originary "figure" the initial indications of the law that will order the explications, the transformations, and the shatterings of the totemic *Imago*,[16] the "*most ancient [ältersten]* code of humanity." Because ambivalence is more visibly apparent in it, "the taboo is *older [älter]* than the gods and reaches back in time to a period anterior to all religion."[17]

Surely we have before us a conception that would have been unthinkable without the historiographical and scientistic posterity of Hegelianism, that is, without the transpositions of a totalizing vision of history cast in terms of "progress." But within the cultural element of his period, right where he refers to the products fashioned by contemporary anthropology or history and uses them, Freud changes their meaning. He organizes them in terms of another kind of scientific unity or object. He relativizes or even inverts their progress. He poses another set of problems.

In this way the "trace" of the *Urbild*, which remains very "clear" in the seventeenth century, will be buried in the tuff of successive explanations that will conceal it. The process might be compared to what occurs nowadays when a patient is admitted to a psychiatric hospital: legible at the time of his admission, the characters of his neurosis are blurred with his introduction into the medical organization, and are immersed within the law of the hospital society and within the social body of a psychiatric knowledge. They are "driven in" to the rhythm of his enclosure, camouflaged by the therapeutic institution itself.

History would be this progressive initiation into the structures of the asylum, each social discourse in turn effacing the symptoms of what has engendered it. Culture would intercede by *displacing* the representations (for example, we no longer believe in the devil; see *GW* 18:332, note 2). But, while effacing an imaginary (that has become archaic because of these very displacements), culture only believes in working to "take care of," or to suppress, what in reality it takes pride in camouflaging in another way, and better. From this perspective, successive "therapies" would be spread over history as means of "healing"—of taking care of or of progressing—that would always function as means of concealment.

Perhaps we now have signs of the therapeutic "place" that Freud sets up for himself. Psychoanalysis does not institute a new sequence within the progress of a lure that the capacity to demystify, and lucidity itself, are forever expanding. Psychoanalysis would like to establish an *epistemological rupture* within this infinite process. It would be the means of thinking and practicing a new kind of elucidation, worthy (*gültig*) in general, which ultimately intends to account for a double, structural relation that excludes the possibility of closure. This would be, on the one hand, the relation of every analytical process (which fragments the representation while driving deeper what is represented) with what it intends to demonstrate but succeeds in displacing; and on the other hand, the relation of each *Aufklärung* with the elucidations that either precede or are contiguous to it in time, insofar as a clearer focus on what had been represented is at once a scientific necessity, and a new way of being deceived without knowing it.

Substitutions for the Father

FREUD speaks of the father-substitute (*Vaterersatz*) in respect to Haitzmann's devil. The devil is the father's "lieu-tenant."[18] But what Freud calls this ersatz, or, he says, more precisely, this exalted father, or again, this father's copy—in other words, the image that *follows* (*Nach-bild*, *GW* 13:330)—is replaced by still another substitute, the appropriately named congregation of the Brothers of Mercy. This group deprives the painter of pleasure by imposing its law of ascesis upon him (except for an occasional escapade with a bottle of wine). But at this price it offers him a salvation; it answers his abandonment (*Verlassen*, *GW* 13:350) in the course of the desolate winter he spends in Vienna (1667–1678) with his married sister, and which precedes his decision to renounce the world. In both a material and psychological sense, the congregation satisfies the need he has to insure and secure his living (*sein Leben sichern*, *GW* 13:351). For him it represents a life insurance policy. Therein he finds a substitute for the nurturing father.

In a new fashion he is thus fed by angels (*GW* 13:351) who are no longer diabolical, but religious. He pushes his illness a little further (*weiter*, *GW* 13:346), the line between the "pathological" and the "normal" being nothing more than that of a substitution. He merely displaces an unresolved tension, at the same time that he changes the term of the same vow. To be sure, he goes from the single (the devil) to the multiple (the Brothers of the congregation). An imaginary duality (the pact with the devil) is transformed into the law of a society (the community). His prostrated silence—a kind of monoideism that he kept throughout the Viennese winter—is changed into a discourse (an utterance of words), for after May 1678, the painter who never managed to express himself finally finds his words (*GW* 13:350). Yet these are words that state the same thing in reducing and in hiding from him his expression. Hereafter he must still give himself body and soul in order *to receive the privilege of being a son*. It is only the evil inversion (which remains *diabolical* in the very sense that only the story can be) of the intermediary situation that he knew in Vienna after having been delivered from the devil and before entering the congregation. During that winter he was in a state of vacancy and without any protection; for a time he was without work or discipline (without ascesis), and lacking recourse (without a father). The devil had formerly been a mask of which another mask in turn betrays the signified. For Haitzmann, his ascetic discipline as a religious brother exempts him once more from the work or discipline in the world that would consist in securing and insuring himself a living. He wants to practice a common law to which he can *abandon and dedicate himself* in order *not to be abandoned*.

Fundamentally, Freud therefore envisions not so much a set of father-substitutes, as substitutions for the father. By this he does not imply that "displacements" lack any bearing on reality, nor that a "cure" is only a magician's hat trick with a rabbit that was always present, merely hidden elsewhere. More is at stake than mere prestidigitation (*Gaukelspiel, GW* 13:352). From a simple therapeutic standpoint, progress is clear, but in the sense that the manifestations (visions or convulsions) have *disappeared* in Haitzmann's case, or that they are now of a social nature. There remains the conflict which is apparently reabsorbed and still represented in religious form. Elsewhere or in other periods of time, this form will be scientific, political, or of another nature. To speak with Freud's suspicious irony, such a form is called "normal," as it is what one can find everywhere. Such a noble appearance of the "normal," however, modeled according to a law, no longer displays but rather hides the persistence of the most uncanny things.

An opposite type of procedure is evoked in the case of businessmen whose monetary deficits are compensated by pathological symptoms (*GW* 13:352). The same process of substitution is at work, but now according to contrary directions, since Haitzmann is led *from* his neurotic manifestations *to* a profession, his new religious life. "Religion" and "commerce" moreover both refer to a "pact," a sense the two words bear in their etymology.[19] Once our attention is directed to this homologous structure of a pact, this white pebble that puts us on the road to an interpretation, we can wonder what the businessman (*Kaufmann*) is indeed buying from the clientele that feeds him; what analogous assurance he is seeking through the detour of a pathological language; and whether, through these "abnormal" manifestations, he does not reveal the actual profit that he expected from his clientele. The benefit (*Gewinn, GW* 3:352) of the illness would therefore be an *ersatz*. Between the businessman's client and his illness there is an effect of substitution. Under other names an identical tension is found here and there. But where is it revealed more thoroughly? Where is it better hidden? In any event, even the psychoanalyst (when he is simply a dealer in words, dedicated to and through a science, or a follower of a new congregation) obtains thus—through his fidelity to the law of a clientele, of a knowledge, or of a professional society— the means of being nourished by angels.

This suspicion can be extended to all current shapes of knowledge and commerce. Through diverse appearances, a pact guarantees always (by an endlessly repeated lure) an assurance of existence to whomever "applies" a law. Father-substitutes are insinuated within the depths of social or ideological structures. These *ersatz* no longer have the appearance of an archaic night or of an imaginary diabolism, but wear instead the colors of daylight, of "normality" and knowledge. From charming primitive representations, one simply moves to civilized, indeed scientific persistences of the nurturing law that is the object of one's tenderness and challenge, one's recourse against abandonment. That Haitzmann goes to the devil after having lost his father, or to the Brothers after having sent the devil away, is, as Freud notes, easy to explain. But that a thousand current institutional forms fashion from the "normal" a mask of the hidden norms—that is less visible and more difficult to discern.

In one of its essential aspects, history can be considered a series of therapies. Among many distinct modes, in past times there had been devotion to the therapeutic saint or the pact with the devil. Yet the worship of science, the anxious liturgy of business, or analytical practices themselves are also therapeutic. Each step appears to make up a form of "health" or a lucidity replacing the previous forms of the same illness. This process would progressively displace the various manifestations of a single tension; thus sociocultural difference and the diversity of history—the object of historiography—are upheld and founded. But these changes betray and repeat forever the ambivalence posited as patent in the *Urbild*. The "father" does not die. His death is only another legend and an aftereffect of his law. Everything happens as if we were able at any time to kill this dead one, and as if we believed that we have become conscious of him, that we have exorcised him through another power or turned him into an *object* of knowledge (a cadaver); but this simply means that he has been displaced once again, and that now he is precisely where we would never suppose him to be, within this very knowledge and within the "profit" that this knowledge seems to secure.

The Act and the Law

IF history repeats this law that is inaccessible except through its successive manifestations, each one deceptive, which have appeared since the initial *Urbild*; if this law is omnipresent but never given immediately, as such, [20] in an *Aufklärung*—then isn't Freudian science itself a new reincarnation of this law? Isn't it but one more clarification in the movement that better conceals the signified while demystifying one of these representations? This problem is a result of Freudian lucidity, but it turns this lucidity against itself. It is finally tantamount to opposing what history makes of Freud to what Freud makes of history. Besides, isn't it a denial attached, or glued like its shadow, to any science or any philosophy *of* history?

Since the issue cannot be dealt with directly, let us continue to consider the elements of a solution furnished by the particular study of the Haitzmann case. The study is not merely what refers us to a general law, it is the realization of the law. From the standpoint of a praxis, the analysis is both the *application* of Freudian law and Freud's *act*. It interconnects them, thus situating the author in respect to his own science.

Most striking in Freud's praxis is his recourse to a *law*. Within the turning of a clause, a methodological rule operates, in effect proportioning the *postulate* of a research procedure to a law of history. That in it there is an endless movement of concealment is what justifies the eagerness of scientific investigation. Among the elements furnished by the Mariazell manuscript, just as among the successive events in Haitzmann's life, there *must* be some kind of logic. In his study, Freud everywhere implies the a priori of a coherence to be found. Cataloguing both the smaller and greater "indications" that he observes in Haitzmann's case, hence excluding once again all reduction of the analysis to a simple phenomenology, he writes that the "moments"[21] that can be distinguished in the life of the painter are connected (*miteinander verknüpft*) in some simple or complex way (*GW* 13:350). As Lacan might say, they form a "chain of words." Put otherwise, an order exists. There is a possible discursivity, just as there must be some kind of reason (*Motiv, GW* 13:325) behind the painter's actions. In the Freudian *Aufklärung*, what constitutes the rationality of scientific explanation is based upon a hidden law for which Haitzmann's words and disparate actions are *traces*. Some pages back, I suggested that analysis establishes history by virtue of a relation among successive manifestations. Here, analysis appears relative to history; with docility it follows the traces in order to retrieve their relations. A circularity exists between the praxis of investigation and the theory of its "object."

Events do, however, occur within this methodic and scientific praxis: such is the Freudian *act*. The necessary link that has to be discovered does not become—must not become—a law to be "put into practice" or a knowledge to be "upheld"—or anything that would make of a science the equivalent of Haitzmann's devil or congregation.

Between the rationality for which the analysis speaks and the law that history repeats there remains a gap, infinitesimal to be sure, but fundamental. Scientific procedure does not depend only on the law that it exhumes and manifests. A difference—one that by definition can never be localized—separates the discourse that the scientist's *act* initiates from the law that binds science itself to the successive forms of a *need* for protection. The labor by which the subject *authorizes* his own existence is of a kind other than the labor from which he receives the *permission* to exist. The Freudian process attempts to articulate this difference.

More than simply an effect of displacement, history can be construed as the gesture of a new beginning. At least this is what is shown by the form of history that is already constituted by Freudian praxis. Finally, it locates its veritable meaning not in the elucidations with which it replaces former representations, but in the ever-unfinished *act* of elucidation. In every instance this enunciation does not differ from what its states, nor does the act exist anywhere other than within an *Aufklärung*. Moreover, nothing can *guarantee* the difference between these two figures of history or of praxis—the one, which repeats, and the other, which initiates. They bring us back to the ambiguity of the word "history," an unstable word that fluctuates between a "legend" (a received text, a law that must be read, a society's profit) and a "becoming other" (a taking of the risk of self-affirmation, through ourselves assuring our own existences). The analyst himself does not escape this ambivalence. As soon as his science becomes a "deceptive aid"; as soon as he "keeps only the deposit but not the drive";[22] as soon as he turns a teaching, a clientele, even a society into the exalted *ersatz* of the father, into the congregation or the devil of former times, he conceals from himself what he believes he is clarifying.

Freud draws a line of demarcation between these two sides of psychoanalytic practice when he speaks of the protean principle that he will use like a razor to cut through the signifiers on the surface of a discourse or a text. He will express the criterion that saves him from accepting his own science as a nurturing law. And with the wink of an eye he explains to us the imperialism of his diagnoses and, quite a surprise for us, his way of imposing an interpretation by insisting on a patient's word: "There it is." In his practice he establishes the scientist's act as what is *beyond* a necessary knowledge. In effect, a casual ease curiously inhabits the minutiae of his analysis. He legitimizes his work as an author by taking risks. He refers to a stylish "flair" that can be only loosely defined because it is simply his own. From his point of view, analytical practice is always an act of risk. It never eliminates a surprise. It cannot be identified with the accomplishment of a norm. The ambiguity of a set of words could never be brought forward solely by the "application" of a law. Knowledge never guarantees this "benefit." The *Aufklärung* remains an affair of tact—*eine Sache des Takts* (GW 13:330).[23]

Such "divination," the last resort of a "learned ignorance,"[24] probably plays the same role as the bottle that Haitzmann, now Brother Chrysostome, was allowed on certain evenings when he quietly intoxicated himself. At those times the former artist and old man of the world thumbed his nose at his guardian angels, just as he had formerly been sharper than his devil by showing up at the Mariazell pilgrimage in order to take back his pact, or just as he had also tricked the monks of the monastery by playing for them the comedy of two successive pacts (GW 13:345–46). This poor old devil (*armer Teufel*, GW 13:351) was not that crazy. Or at least his madness was perhaps the liberty he took vis-à-vis the law that forced him to depend on a new father. Does Freud mean to say that every scientist plays his own science, as Haitzmann played the law of his congregation? That would have been a drunken joy of tact, a madness of the act. In any case, for the painter's surreptitious freedom, Freud substitutes a decisive and never definitive act. For the rule dodged by binges on the sly, he substitutes the science that in the last instance only the subject authorizes. To a madness that comes before science, in Freud's work there is opposed a madness that expresses science; a science that "allows" is combined with the scientist who "allows himself."

A possible connection can be found here between the psychoanalytical act and psychoanalytical science. But nothing *insures* this act, since the devil of yesterday is replaced by so many other successive nurturing laws, "diabolical" assurances drawn from a knowledge, a clientele, a confinement, and from every other way of being exempted from producing history, thanks to the "privilege of being a son."

NOTES

1. Sigmund Freud, "Eine Teufelsneurose im siebzehnten Jahrhundert," in *Gesammelte Werke*, 18 vols. (London: Imago Press, 1940–1968), 13:315–53. This edition is hereafter abbreviated *GW*. Subsequent citations appear in parentheses in the text of this chapter. "Eine Teufelsneurose" is available in English, as "A Seventeenth-Century Demonological Neurosis," in *The Standard Edition of the Complete Psychological Works of Sigmund Freud*, 24 vols., J. Strachey, tr. and ed. (London: Hogarth Press, 1953–1974), 19:69–105. The *Standard Edition* is hereafter abbreviated *SE*.

2. The information is essentially consituted by documents *on* possession or sorcery (juridical, medical, or religious texts, etc.); it does not originate in sorcerers or the possessed, unless it is taken in the course of interrogations accusing them or provided in narratives judging them.

3. Thus Michel Foucault, in his preface to *Madness and Civilization* (New York: Pantheon, 1965), says in respect to this limit-structure or structure of denial that "history is only possible on the basis of an absence of history" (pp. ix–x); see pp. v–vi in the French, *Histoire de la folie à l'âge classique* (Paris: Plon, 1961). A sketch of the study that Foucault announced on demoniac "experience and the reduction made of it in the sixteenth and seventeenth centuries" (p. 34, n. 1) can be found in his "Médecins, juges, et sorciers au XVIIᵉ siècle," *Médecine de France* (1969), no. 200, pp. 121–28.

4. In addition to Robert Mandrou's already-classic study *Magistrats et sorciers en France au XVIIᵉ siècle* (Paris: Plon, 1968), I should like to refer to the doc-

umentation assembled in Jean-Joseph Surin, *Correspondance*, which I edited (Paris: Desclée de Brouwer, 1966), as well as "La Magistrature devant la sorcellerie du XVIIᵉ siècle," in my *L'Absent de l'histoire* (Paris: Mame, 1973), pp. 13–39.

5. Ida Macalpine and Richard A. Hunter, *Schizophrenia 1677: A Psychiatric Study of an Illustrated Autobiographical Record of Demoniacal Possession* (London: W. Dawson, 1956), which includes reproductions of Haitzmann's paintings.

6. *Ibid.*, p. 103.

7. As both an ethnologist and a psychoanalyst, Géza Roheim adopts a more Freudian perspective when he replaces this element (the female devil) within the organization of indications furnished by Haitzmann. In his *Psychanalyse et anthropologie* (Paris: Gallimard, 1967), pp. 523–25, he accepts the interpretation advanced in "A Seventeenth-Century Demonological Neurosis." Yet he prefers another which would be Freudian in the past conditional tense (what Freud *should have* or *would have* said): "Should Freud have written his article later, I am convinced that he would have interpreted the devil as the superego. The difficulties begin with melancholy, that is, with the superego's violent attacks unleashed against the ego. These occur after the father's death, when the subject feels guilty because of his death wishes. As a painter, he feels inferior (a guilt or inferiority complex) and promises that he will be a good son of the paternal substitute if the latter (the father-substitute or the superego) reduces the pressure it is bringing to bear on him and stops inhibiting the activity of his ego. The *struggle* between the ego and superego *is ended* when the walls of the monastery close around him. From that point on he is secured" (p. 524; my italics). Whatever can be made of the "struggle between the ego and the superego" (which so often resembles a war of the gods), the evocation of this "ending" does not appear to conform with Freud's thinking, which as we shall see hardly tends to end the story as legends end, that is, with a happy reconciliation. Roheim's exegesis avoids the essential problem of "substitutions" or "displacements" (to be discussed later in this chapter) that exclude, as Lacan notes, "the promise of a resolution."

8. See for example Etienne Thuau's study *La Raison d'Etat et pensée politique à l'époque de Richelieu* (Paris: Armand Colin, 1966).

9. Here I envisage only the *theoretical* significance of this position. The fact that Freud attributes the qualities of being clearer and more easily discerned to more distant manifestations (which are also further "isolated" from him), and thus perhaps to disaffected and "dead" traces of the subject, is a point that might be associated with his taste for archeology, and might clarify his own psychology.

10. W. C. Bullitt, preface to Sigmund Freud and W. C. Bullitt, *Thomas Woodrow Wilson, Twenty-Eighth President of the United States: A Psychological Study* (Boston and London: Houghton Mifflin, 1967). Surely Freud was seduced by the abundant and concise documentation which Bullitt assembled. Bullitt observed that for a long time Freud had been intending to write a psychological study of a contemporary about whom thousands of facts had been documented.

11. Sigmund Freud, preface to *Totem and Taboo*, SE 13:xii.

12. *Ibid.*

13. See R. Payer-Thurn, "Faust in Mariazell," in *Chronik des Wiener Goethe-Vereins* (1924), vol. 3.

14. Thus in *Psychanalyse et anthropologie*, pp. 20–21, Géza Roheim too quickly assumes the "primal events" that Freud evokes to be purely mythic and phantasmic. This is equivalent to judging according to an exclusively historiographic viewpoint and not considering well enough their *function* in the Freudian reading of history.

15. On this topic Claude Lévi-Strauss has provided us with a detective story that demystifies the totemism of earlier times, in *Le Totémisme aujourd'hui* (Paris: PUF, 1962); in English, *Totemism* (Boston: Beacon, 1963).

16. Here Freud refers to *Totem and Taboo* (*GW* 13:331; *SE* 19:85). By underscoring the "enigmatic" character of totemism, Freud constantly alludes to the two conceptual schemas of his interpretation: the parallelism between the "primitive" and the child, and the passage from staged ambivalence to its religious usages (see especially chs. 2 and 4, *GW* 9:26–92 and 122–94; *SE* 13:19–74 and 100–61).

17. Sigmund Freud, *Totem and Taboo*, ch. 2, *GW* 9:27. My italics.

18. I am leaving aside Freud's arguments on this topic.

19. ["Religion" is asociated with the Latin *religare*, to bind again, and "commerce" derives from *com* + *mercari*, to negotiate together.——TR.]

20. We do well to recall that in *The Gay Science*, Nietzsche found that the pretension for discovering truth *just like that*, in immediacy, was both "shameless" and "indecent," as well as illusory.

21. In "moments" (*Moments*)—here, depression, inhibition about work, mourning the father, etc., which can be observed during the Viennese period between Haitzmann's first and second pilgrimages to Mariazell—Freud implies factors whose meaning is simultaneously temporal and logical. The term implies a *series* of facts well as a *coherence* of facts.

22. Jacques Lacan, *Ecrits* (Paris: Seuil, 1966), p. 357.

23. Freud uses the word *Takt* on many occasions; see among others *Selbstdarstellung*, section 4 (*GW* 14:66), and *Die Frage der Laienanalyse*, section 5 (*GW* 14:250).

24. Lacan, *Ecrits*, pp. 355 and 362, the pages where one of Freud's astonishing texts, his "Recommendations to Physicians Practising Psychoanalysis" (*SE* 12:111–20), is examined.

The Fiction of History
The Writing of Moses and Monotheism

E RUDITION can easily overwhelm *Moses and Monotheism*, in the wealth of citation employed in its most "serious" passages.[1] But that is not where the text really is. It is a "fantasy,"[2] as Freud notes of these three essays intended to explain the creation of legend (*eine Schöpfung der Sage, GW* 16:103; "a creature of legend," *SE* 23:7). Straight off, his analysis takes a step aside, toward those imaginary productions that a classical usage designated in French as *fantaisie*. Swaying left and right, here is the dancer who is in unstable equilibrium wherever she tips her toes (*GW* 16:160): a fable.

The text initiates a play between religious "legend" (*Sage*) and Freudian "construction" (*Konstruktion*), between the object under study and the discourse performing the analysis. This play takes place in the fuzzy area of an ambivalence, in what gives "fiction" the meaning both of a production (*fingere*, to fashion, to fabricate) and of a disguise or a deceit. Everything is unraveled in the field of relations between the labor that constructs and the ruse that would "make us believe" in the fiction—a mixed terrain of production and lure. What history creates and what narrative dissimulates will meet in that very place. *Moses and Monotheism* is situated at this intersection of history and fiction. But its elucidation does not escape what it is elucidating. In the fashion of a fantasy, it *tells* a story of what *is produced* in a tradition. This theory of fiction is indeed a "theoretical fiction."[3]

It is "my novel," Freud remarks to Arnold Zweig. In order to explain the genesis of the monotheist legend, Freud builds an edifice (*Aufbau*) placed in the proximity of legend. His own relation to writing is the question which endlessly recurs, coming and going in his study of a religion, and making up a text. In this work, Freud's longest planned and his last, born of internal contradictions and doubt, what is ultimately narrated is writing. An autoanalysis of the scriptural construction (or "fiction"), it revolves around the operation that had so often assumed the form of a historiography (a *Geschichtschreibung*), from the *Case Histories* (*Krankengeschichten*) to this last "historical novel." A theory of analytical (or scientific) narrativity is put forward, but once again it takes the shape of historical narration.

Now I must ask: what disturbing uncanniness does Freudian writing trace within the historian's territory, where it enters dancing? Reciprocally, in what fashion will my question, born of an archival and scriptural labor that cultivates this territory, and seduced by the fiction of a psychoanalytical history, be enlightened/distorted through Freud's analysis?

The Discourse of Fragments, or the Body of the Text

IF we omit the very distant precedents for the fascination that the image of Moses holds for Freud, as well as the anonymous publication of "The Moses of Michelangelo" in *Imago* in 1914 (the author's "style of thinking," remarked an editor's note, "offers some analogy with psychoanalytical methods"), the history of the text begins around the years 1933–1934. It begins with questions born of Nazi anti-Semitism, and with the "formula," generative of the text, through which an answer comes to Freud:

> Faced with the new persecutions, one asks oneself again how the Jews have come to be what they are and how they have attracted this undying hatred. I soon discovered the formula: Moses created the Jews. So I gave my work the title: *The Man Moses, a historical novel. . . .* The work fits into three sections. The first is like an interesting novel; the second is laborious and boring; the third is full of content and makes exacting reading. The whole enterprise broke down on this third section, for it involved a theory of reli-

gion—certainly nothing new for me after *Totem and Taboo,* but
something new and fundamental for the uninitiated.[4]

An "Egyptian Moses" is the "starting point" for his analytical work.[5]
As in dreams, a "primal word" (*Urwort*) comes to him expressed in contradictory terms.[6] At the beginning of the genealogy of the text, there is
this "fantasy" which inscribes a violence and a ruse of history into the
question of identity, and it is developed on the triple register of a novel,
an erudite study, and a theory. But in 1934 a Father Schmidt appears,
casting his shadow over the project. From Rome this religious apologist
for primitive monotheism threatens societies of psychoanalysis in Italy
and even in Vienna where, according to Freud, he "decides the policy of
our country!" The phantasm of the "hostile Father," the ghost of Catholic
power, prohibits the publication of *Moses.* In fact, it is above all the "specialists," Kafkaesque guardians of knowledge before the gate of their law,
who arrest Freud. Too great a lack of scholarly credibility keeps him from
publishing the work. Freud needs historical proofs, not in order to be
convinced—he is already convinced enough without them—but in order
to arm the "weakness" of his myth before producing it on foreign ground,
in the field of history.[7] "I was obliged to construct so imposing a statue
upon feet of clay, so that any fool could topple it."[8] As in 1910, Moses
pertains to the sphere of vision; he is a statue. But now Freud is the
Michelangelo, and already he imagines the image and the work broken
by the erudition of others. A paradox. Freud would like to have a seam-
less argumentation to protect this discourse introducing a division within
Moses (the "Egyptian"). But his efforts do not succeed in filling the gap
within the historical verisimilitude. Like its hero, the work remains cloven,
broken, half-history and half-novel.

The text is therefore "repressed." Freud notes, "*Moses,* which has been
laid aside," is left in a silence where "nothing takes its place."[9] This repressed text cannot be obfuscated by substitution, to the contrary of what
happens to the character Moses, excluded by a murder and "replaced" by
a legend. The Freudian study, arrested in an almost messianic position,
must wait in the shadows for its moment to appear (*GW* 16:158).

Yet in 1937 the first part appears in *Imago,* in what for Freud amounts
to a derisory place of publication.[10] The discourse changes its status by
virtue of its staging, which discreetly transforms its seriousness into comedy. At the International Congress of Psychoanalysis held in Paris in August 1938, a fragment of the second part, nothing less than "The Great

Man," is read by Anna Freud. Is the "fantasy" of 1934 reversed into a magisterial academic cloak? Within the institution of knowledge, the fantasy plays the role of the legend of the absent founding father, now told in the voice of the other. Behind this disguise, the author nonetheless continues to keep his distance. When his text reaches the public, the author withdraws. They castle. They are no closer to being in the same place than before. Freud feels neither union nor solidarity with his work (*GW* 16:160); he cannot be identified with it. The entire work is published in 1939, split between the German edition in Amsterdam and the English in London. *Drei Abhandlungen:* "Three Essays." At the threshold of the second, two prefaces contradicting each other. In the middle of the third, an interruption, where a "résumé" of the work is inserted. And soon after this publication, Freud disappears. What remains on the public stage, in likeness to Dubuffet's *Don Coucoubazar,* is a text in pieces, in which the break marked from the beginning by the contradictory formula—making the opposite figures of Moses and the Egyptian coincide—is multiplied. This is not a book, but a discourse of fragments.

But in constructing this history in which the text plays the role of a hero among adversaries, passing through trials to a final disclosure, what am I indeed doing, if not effacing the rupture operative everywhere in the text and taking a chronological continutiy for granted, where the various withdrawals from and returns to the "work" are arranged in order? I am building in turn a "legend" of the text. Through my narrative, I am obliterating the rift which was marked from the beginning, which organizes the form of this text disseminated in small fragments, and which is repeated within its content with the obsessive mention of "lacunae," with the scrutiny of contradictions from which it is developed (*Widerstreit meiner Motive, GW* 16:115; *SE* 23:14), or with the imbroglio into which it sinks further and further as it advances. I am taking this text back to a linearity which betrays it. I am putting the *ersatz* of my history (a connected series of known facts) in the place of this writing which is a novel by dint of its avowed relations with its other. We must therefore return to the text, to its unsure, fissured ground, even at the risk of losing our way there. We must enter into a fiction, which continuously envelops us and disallows mastery, even while it opens paths toward a particular clarification (*Klärung eines Sachverhalts, GW* 16:104; *SE* 23:7).

This cracked surface refers to a movement of what is said. An ambiguity is at work, shaking up these fragments which distort and correspond to each other. Breaks—lacunae—allow some of them to play over the others. Whence the possibilities of meaning that arise or are un-done—the noise and opacity of a body of words. To be sure, everything happens within the field that Freud circumscribes: "the construction and transformation of legends" (*Bildung und Umgestaltung von Sagen, GW* 16:112; *SE* 23:16). But the birth and the transformations of the Mosaic tradition represent only one regime of the analysis. The genesis of the historical figure of the Jew and the genesis of Freudian writing always intervene. The *place* from which Freud writes and the *production of his writing* enter into the text along with the *object* that he is taking up. How does a religious legend take form? How have the Jews become what they are? What is it that builds a writing? The three questions are combined. Thus the text acquires volume, that is, it can be heard better than it can be seen, as if it were increasingly illegible in the process of becoming more and more audible. This complexity would have the ultimate limit of being nothing more than sound. It plays on the rich ambiguity and the ruses of sounds, which the graphic process of writing aims at elim-inating. So at issue here is a vocal text. It oscillates between line (lin-earity) and voice (polysemy).[11] In reading/hearing it, I dream of the fab-ulous representation that Freud gave of Rome one day by supposing an image, coming from nowhere, in which incompatible places would co-incide, "in which nothing that has once come into existence will have passed away and all earlier phases of development continue to exist along-side the latest one." Spatiality forbids such coexistence in the same place. "If we want to represent historical sequence in spatial terms we can only do it by juxtaposition in space."[12] In order to transcribe or paint them, we proceed toward a flattening.

Moses works in the opposite way. Through metaphor, a rhetorical means, and through ambivalence, a theoretical instrument, many things are in play in the same spot, transforming each spatial element into a volume where they intersect, and introducing the movement of a quid pro quo (what comes in place of what?) everywhere. Different histories "subsist" in the same place, as in the Rome Freud had fantasized. They are not localized one *beside* another; the genesis of Mosaic monotheism is not situated in a past which would be "juxta-posed" to the present of Freud-ian writing. The Freudian fiction does not lend itself to this spatial dis-tinction of historiography in which the subject of knowledge is given a place, the "present," separated from the site of his or her object, which in turn would be defined as a "past." Here, past and present are moving within the same polyvalent place. And none of the "levels" of the text is the referent for the others. If there is "meta-phor," it characterizes a system of reciprocal relations. There are no stable elements which arrest this circulation, or which, by assigning one or another of the strata a "truth" value, would bestow upon the others the function of an image, a substitute, or an effect. What is told *at the same time* about Moses, about the Jew, or about Freud cannot be brought back to a single one of the *different* registers on which is analyzed (auto-analyzed and hetero-analyzed) the production of a writing.

This fiction is paid for at a price made noticeable by its structure. It appears to be the text of an old man, burdened and coming apart because of his age,[13] without scholarly assurance and exactness. In the end, in the envoy to the readers (*GW* 16:246; *SE* 23:136–37), it is offered as a gift, in the way that a host contributes a story to conversation with dinner guests. The text is developed in an uncertainty of being received (although in a certainty of being right to the point). From where it is situated, the text would never impose itself as a form of knowledge might, as authorized from elsewhere. To the contrary, the text is constructed as a relation between an analytical method and *doubt* (*Zweifel, GW* 16:130). In the same way as the Bible of which it speaks, the text "contains precious and, indeed, invaluable historical data" (*GW* 16:143; *SE* 23:41). If the Jewish writings betray their "confusion and contradictions and their unmistakable signs of centuries of continuous and tendentious revisions and superimpositions" (*GW* 16:112; *SE* 23:16), the same is true for Freud's "Three Essays." The mark of contradictions, fragmentations, and adjunctions is preserved,[14] before this published plurality can be transformed into a "book" (into a "Bible") through the Freudian tradition.[15] The separation within it is made apparent—through the inner conflict (doubt) or the "in-coherence" of reasoning (interruptions, the fragility of hypotheses, lacunae). Weakness is the ultimate price of this fable. It is the *confession* that causes within the text the stirring of an unknown within the symbolization of its levels, the tumult of a body through the play of its depths.

A "work" (*GW* 16:160; *SE* 23:58), however, is what is at stake: an "analysis," that is, a rigorous practice of delimitation. If Freud's work lets the metaphor of its levels or its quesions spin around, it is not because he denies the breakage. He situates it otherwise. Rupture does not intervene as a separation between regions (the past and the present, the individual and the collective, etc.), but as the very principle of their functioning. Freud's lucidity works quite prudently, obstinately, even craftily at this exact point, on the ground where death is announced to the Jews through the horror of anti-Semitic totalitarianism and through the violence of an "undying hatred."

Traditionally, self-accusation is the price of meaning: it is necessary to accuse oneself so that misfortune may be understood. In the case of Freud, confession is of another sort. Yet his lucidity is affirmed within the continuity of this tradition, as an inherent problem. First of all, his lucidity assumes the form of a witticism that is at once funny and blasphemous: *the Egyptian Moses*.[16] The enigma that Freud opposes to the hatred appears to belong to a rhetoric of dreams. An oxymoron puts together two contradictory poles, the Jew and the Egyptian. But it thus interiorizes the division that until then had been a "distinction" in respect to others. Separation from the Egyptian had been the founding act of the election of the Jews, its doublet being the act that instituted Yahweh as unique and as creator through his separation from the world. For Freud, this break is always internal, cleaving the subject himself. It annihilates the self-identity that had been acquired through the elimination of a "remainder." And since the question is posed in terms of a historical foundation, this annihilation must be inscribed at the origin, namely, in the murder of Moses. Identity is not one, but two. *One and the other*. In the beginning, there is the plural. Such is the principle of writing, of analysis (which is division, decomposition), and of history. We will see that "one and the other" is inverted here, and so is the "un-known," of "neither one nor the other." In any event, this relation cannot be overcome. In the language of an election that is turned into an eliminating hatred, this relation can only be expressed in the style of a *coincidatio oppositorum*, or through a reprise which posits that the relation of opposites—the Jew and the Egyptian—is fundamental. The joke penetrates the stability by re-using its own terms; the joke subverts it. It is a lapsus, the fall of a truth lacking seriousness, or a Rabelaisian fart in a ceremony commemorating history.

Such is the kernal (*Kern*), the content (*Gehalt*), or rather the "piece of truth" (*ein Stück vergessener Wahrheit*, GW 16:239; SE 23:35) which determines the production of legend (and also of writing?). This fragment, a hardened morsel, both breaking and broken, causes the body of the Jewish *Sage* to proliferate, in a tradition repressing the memory without entirely effacing the scar of an initial wound. This body can only be "represented" by a discourse that in turn is wounded—that is analytical and fragmented—while what it narrates as true assumes the form of fiction.

It develops Freud's formula, which argues at once for the *duality* of an initial rupture, the *opposition* of contents that are made to shift together within the same place, and the *deception* belonging to the apparition of each of these contents when it appears without its contrary term. Having been made from these apparitions or figures, history can be narrated as a series of lures. It is no less subject to analysis, as another labor of the same formula: a little piece of truth (*ein Stückchen Wahrheit, GW* 16:239) is endlessly being diffused within history's obscurantist repressions, and repeated in religious obfuscations. This "true" element can be expressed only in illusion, according to a procedure upheld by something akin to an instinct for the lie. Freud notes that it could never be established that the human intellect possesses a particular gift for truth, or the life of the human mind a particular bent for recognizing truth (*GW* 16:237). Supposing that a taste for truth exists would be tantamount to an optimistic and idealist hypothesis. We are led to believe what flatters our desire and our illusions. We all seek fabulations. Therefore there only remains the possibility of working within the elements of representation, of playing the game of "he who loses, wins" with deception. We go from the fictive to fiction when we learn how to play at "You're lying."

Thus the Freudian fable presents itself as "analytical" because it restores or admits the rupture that recurs and shifts; and as "fictional" because it grasps only substitutes for other things and illusory stabilities in relation to the division that makes them castle within the same place. Its own object is the delimitation itself. Freud deals precisely with what historiographers presuppose and place outside of their field of inquiry when they attempt to comprehend various figures (economic, social, mental) established as distinct units. For that very reason Freud is an analyst and not a historian. Yet by working on the terrain of history, Freud inverts the relation between these units and their postulate. He composes the "novel" of history as if, through this chiasmus, he were taking the position of the Marquis de Sade, who thus distinguished these two ways of knowing man, through history and through the novel: "The engraving stylus of history depicts him only when he makes himself seen, but then it is not he; . . . the paintbrush of the novel, to the contrary, seizes his inner nature to the quick . . . takes him when he lets this mask fall."[17]

But where de Sade posits an exclusive disjunction (either one or the other), Freud detects a conjunction (one and the other) giving rise to contrary expressions on the basis of a cleavage. Freud's novel is ultimately constructed in its relation between a zero point and a series, between death and the "quid pro quo." The murder of Moses marks the initial division and represents within the vocabulary of an inherited tradition (man as "he makes himself seen") the event that cannot be written, that has never had and never will have its own place. It is the "inter-dict" lost within the Scripture that betrays it, the invisible bloodstain whence the text is generated. A play on words and a play of appearances in the same spot, the quid pro quo is the means by which the event is repeated by being effaced; it is the process of chronological events, the link between the successive substitutions of the Egyptian and the Jew. Death is something outside of the text; it conditions discursive production. Within the text, the quid pro quo is the effect of the text's functioning as the figure tricking death.

Freud ultimately puts his novel in the place of history, just as he puts the Egyptian Moses in the place of the Jewish Moses—in order to have them shift around the "little piece of truth" that their play represents. Yet this shattering of identity, this discourse of fragments, is still enveloped in historical connotations, just as the character that it takes apart and puts into circulation keeps the name of Moses. The word remains—"history" or "Moses"—but the thing is split, and its fragments come and go in a general rearrangement, reiterating the "de-fection" generating fiction.

Writing in the Language of the Other, or Fiction

ACCORDING to the Marquis de Sade, knowledge that allows accession to "the art of writing novels" is "acquired only through *misfortunes* and through *travel*."[18] Freud's text in effect bears these two marks, which are transformed into *deaths* and *displacements*. I believe that he comes quite near to the preface to de Sade's *Crimes of Love*. "Misfortunes" and "travels" are combined in the text's situation of being a displaced writing, in the same way that we speak of "displaced persons." The novel takes up the question of its own birthplace, that is, the "undying hatred" that compels the Jew to make endless departures. Its contents express this: a founding alteration—an Egyptian Moses—is reiterated in a succession of changed places. The textual construction illustrates the point more clearly: writing ascribes a path for itself in a language that cannot be dissociated from primitive misfortune and perpetual deceit. Freud is not at all "at home" in the language his analysis passes through. A foreignness in regard to his native language is the origin of the relations his writing keeps with the "non-place" of fiction or dreams. Fiction knows none of the stabilities (political, national) taken for granted by historiography. In Freud's case, as in that of Kafka, the fiction supposes that the writer is still "the guest of the German language,"[19] which is nonetheless his native tongue. But he gives its true weight to the fact that he has only been "accepted" when he has been expelled by Nazi anti-Semitism.[20] Right where he might have felt himself at home, the brutal elimination of the Jew forces him to recall that he is only provisionally "tolerated," always in transit.[21] The Nazi event brings back an originary misfortune and leads him back to the inherent structure of the scriptural experience, to *Erinnerung*, which, according to the Hegelian pun, is at once a conscious memory and an *"inwardizing in us"* (*Er-Innerung*).[22] Examination of the Mosaic tradition also concerns writing, insofar as that tradition is articulated within language as if within its other. It amounts to self-analysis. What is said of the unconscious (or of the other) within language, the object of psychoanalytical writing, reveals its inverse with this writing that constitutes the Freudian labor of traveling within another language. It is hardly surprising that this study would put into question the matriarchy of the maternal tongue (German), the mother country (Israel), or the nurturing tradition (the Mosaic Scriptures), and replace these territorial identities with the law of the father that is introduced by the combination of an originary murder ("misfortune") and an endless process of displacements ("travels"). Language is not the "house of being" (Heidegger), but the place of itinerant alteration.

Seen from this angle, the reading of *Moses and Monotheism* leads me, as to a forest clearing for secret rendezvous, back to Kafka's letter on Jewish writers:

> They existed among three impossibilities, which I just happen to call linguistic. It is simplest to call them that. But they might also be called something entirely different. These are: The impossibility of not writing, the impossibility of writing German, the impossibility of writing differently. One might also add a fourth impossibility, the impossibility of writing (since the despair could not be assuaged by writing, was hostile to both life and writing; writing is only an expedient, as for someone who is writing his will shortly before he hangs himeslf, an expedient that may well last a whole life . . .)[23]

In Freud's instance such testamentary writing is not bound to "despair." It plays most cunningly with falsehood. A suspicion moves forward. It follows a prudent and methodical path within the element of the Jewish *Sage* or German *Kultur,* in two maternal languages that are, however, foreign, or "borrowed." To understand it we must return to the "heading"—or "genesis"—of the narrative. The "beginning" of the text does not deal with Moses' origins (instead, this will be a product of the study), but instead deals with the way in which Freud situates himself in present time. Hence the initial sentence of the first essay: "To deprive [*absprechen*] a people of the man whom they take pride in as the greatest of their sons is not a thing to be gladly or carelessly undertaken, least of all by someone who is himself one of them" (*angehört,* belonging to them; *GW* 16:103; *SE* 23:7).

The text is born of the relation between a departure and a debt. What is "theoretical" is the deviation from the avowed institution. Within identity, dispossession and membership create the rift from which writing is produced. This *Zwischenraum,* or interval, is neither adhesion to an established alliance nor the pretension of being "un-bound," "ab-solute" and absolved. It is neither orthodoxy nor liberty. The Freudian "dispute" is still marked by his "solidarity" as a member of B'nai B'rith. It is an exile that is not preserved from genealogical misfortune. It does not imply a lapsus of membership, contrary to what happens in a Freudian "tradition" that betrays his writing by its act of transmission.[24] A lacuna is at work throughout the text (and "fiction" is thus mixed into "history") from the moment when the tacit basis of discourse is no longer a disavowal (*Verleugnung*) of the institution, an obfuscation of belonging to a family, a society, or a people, in other words, no longer a lapse of memory about the debt;[25] and this lacuna operates, inversely, when discourse no longer serves to reiterate a membership and to provide a familial or social "genea-logy" as in the "priestly narrative" which among the Hebrews sought to "establish a continuity between its contemporary period and the remote Mosaic past" by "disavowing" (*verleugnen*) the break between them (*GW* 16:169; *SE* 23:65). This text is authorized from neither a "non-place" nor from the "truth" of a place. It is not ideological, like a so-called asocial discourse, nor is it doctrinal, like priestly discourse which claims to speak forever of the same originary and founding place. In the first case, departure is taken to be a liberation when it denies the debt. In the second, upholding of the proper name (Moses or Jesus, Freud or Lacan) allows only the ellipsis of a death and brings with it the lure of identity.

Freud's narrative has much to do with *suspicion,* which is rupture, doubt;

and with *filiation,* which is both debt and law. Membership is expressed only through distance, through traveling farther and farther away from a ground of identity. A name still obliges, but no longer provides the thing, this nurturing land. Thus Freud must bet his place within writing. He gambles it with his cards on the table—he risks his relation with the real—in the game organized by a loss. The obligation to pay the debt, the refusal to abandon the name and the people ("Jerusalem, I shall not forget thee")[26] and, hence, the impossibility of not writing, are built over the dispossession of all "genea-logical" language. The work has no hereditary soil. It is nomadic. Writing cannot forget the misfortune from which its necessity springs; nor can it count on tacit, rich, and fostering "evidences" that can provide for an "agrarian" speaker his intimacy with a mother tongue. Writing begins with an exodus.[27] It proceeds in foreign languages. Its only recourse is the very elucidation of its travels in the tongue of the other: it is analysis.

Much more than to Exodus, which narrates the Jewish people's acquisition of their own land through the gesture of breaking away from the Egyptian, the Freudian theory of writing refers to the history which inverts the traditional myth: the destruction of the Temple and the loss of the identifying soil. This event was the impossible: a rupture of *being* that had been defined up until then by the relation between *the* land and the election. Hereafter the nation mourns. This experience of defection could not give way to a political legend. Brought back to Egypt, the Jews then make Scripture the substitute for the second Temple (burned in A.D. 70). In the third and fourth centuries, *the* Book (the "Bible" in the singular) is formed, but in Egyptian Greek (the so-called Septuagint Bible), from Hebrew books or scrolls (in the plural) translated by Jews *into* the language of the enemy country in which they find themselves living without any hope of return to Israel.[28] That the loss of the ancestral land is the precondition for the appearance of the "Bible" (a textual and a unique totality); that the book takes the place of lost prophetic speech ("prophetic" writing replacing the oracle, since "there are no more prophets") and of the land given to sight ("O Israel, I shall never see thee again"); that *Scripture is produced in the place and in the language of the other;* finally, that an ability-to-speak-in-the-alienating-element (that is, translation, interpretation, analysis) draws its necessity from the relation between the alteration of identity and the law of the debt: what are all these points, if not "Moses the Egyptian?" The language of the Egyptian—Greek—is riddled with mourning. Inversely, it is in the land that has

become for the Jews the land symptomatic of their death (of the disseminated fatherland) that the text of the law is built. These are Freud's theses.
Everything happens as if he had mistaken one period for another, or as
if he had made one the metaphor of the other. Certainly he speaks of
beginnings. But he narrates in a *novel* about Mosaic origins what the birth
of itinerant Judaism and closed Scripture during the first centuries of our
era had been in *history*.

No matter what, he could never be authorized by the land where he
is writing: neither "his" language, "his" culture, "his" fatherland, nor "his"
scientific competence can authorize the text. These residences all speak
of a familiar foreignness. Freud is the accomplice of the other that speaks
therein, because he is still a foreigner to the opaque intimacy of every
place and even of his own ground. His letters speak of the distance he
takes in respect to the fanaticism of Agoudath Israel; of his resistance to
the German Jews who, with Dr. Neumann's "Union of National Jews,"
for example, felt themselves legitimized by dint of constituting an intelligentsia within German culture; of his reservations about Jewish nationalism attempting to recover an identity in Israel. His works also impugn
the assurance that his proceeding might have been able to draw from an
acquired position. Everywhere his phantasms themselves betray *an uncertainty in respect to place*—the inverse of the certitude invested in a method
(a way of proceeding).

Such is the very question which *Moses and Monotheism* explores. This
"testamentary" work, in Kafka's sense, is dedicated to an analysis of the
relation that writing keeps with a place. Here, the uncertainty of place,
or division, is not what must be eliminated so that discourse can be organized. In the fashion of the Mosaic quid pro quo or of Freudian doubt
(*Zweifel*), it is to the contrary the postulate of the construction (*Konstruction*) and the element within which the discourse is produced. The doubt
and the method imply one another, while they excluded one another in
Descartes. Writing is born of and treats of admitted doubt, of explicit
division; in sum, of the impossibility of its own place. It articulates the
constantly initial fact that the subject is *never authorized* by a place, that
he could never be founded on an inalterable *cogito*, that he is always foreign to himself and forever deprived of an ontological ground, and hence
is always *left over, superfluous*, always the *debtor of a death*, indebted in
respect to the disappearance of a genealogical and territorial "substance,"
and bound to a name lacking property.

This loss and this obligation generate writing. From this genesis, Freud designates the secret, through the "little piece of truth"—the Egyptian Moses—that he extracts from ancient history. But he described it long before in one of his dreams, that is, in that genre of truth which is written in the revealing and deceptive land of dreams, and whose non-place is privileged in every situation in which one lacks a land of one's own. The night after (or before?) the burial of his father, he dreamed that he was facing a storefront where he read the inscription:

PLEASE CLOSE THE EYES

We could interpret: there is no longer either a father or a land to see. But he understood: "One should do one's duties towards the dead."[29] The "notice"—"a printed notice, placard or poster, rather like the notices forbidding one to smoke in railway waiting rooms"[30]—appeared in the dream in the fashion of the Tables of Law come to replace the father, as an "inscription" and as the very statement of the "duty" of writing. "Close the eyes": a gesture of respect and of farewell. A debt and a departure. *Angehören* and *absprechen*. Only in stations do notices post the law of writing, a voyage indissolubly linked to a mourning.

In his study Freud "closes the eyes" of Moses. In the historical sphere, he repeats the gesture that he made in an aesthetic study when he analyzed Michelangelo's *Moses*. "No piece of statuary" he said, "has made a stronger impression on me."[31] But just as "I used to sit down in front of the statue in the expectation that I should now see how it would start up on its raised foot, dash the Tables of the Law to the ground and let fly its wrath . . . nothing of the kind happened."[32] The stone statue does not play ghost. It remains "immobile" and "rigid." Michelangelo's Moses calms himself for the observer in order to avoid letting the Tables slip, fall, and shatter. Moses' passion is extinguished so that the Scripture will remain. By being transformed into a marmoreal monument, he is "holding the Tables."[33] The law is based on a death.

Freud's text *goes away*. But initially made possible through a separation, it does not forget the sorrow that haunts its proceeding. No identity, be it German or Zionist, could ever replace the lost land that endlessly binds the construction of writing to a repetition of that break. There the suspicion works vigilantly in order to save the debt from oblivion, to preserve the labor of analysis in the foreign language, and to uphold the textual staging, or the *Aufklärung,* of alteration. So that writing itself could finally be narrated, necessity doubtless required this scriptural relation of loss and its memory to become the experience of the old Freud, reduced to writing his last testament, and thus finding the "audacity of one who has little or *nothing to lose*" (*GW* 16:156; *SE* 23:54). Now psychoanalysis indeed moves forward over lands that are not its own, in a knowledge of history (as Hebrew once did within the Greek of the Septuagint); it becomes a "novel" within the foreign field of erudition. It is a fragile discourse because its postulate is the non-place of its place. It can only be a "fantasy." Its last ruse involves being no more than a "riddle" without any "answer" (*GW* 16:246; *SE* 23:137) when all is said and done. Here historicity, a relation of transit with the limit, of writing with death, is told in a comic vein, in a "testamentary" fable. Thus every one of Scheherazade's tales won a few hours away from death, which was ceaselessly present all through her thousand and one nights of fabulation. But the fantasy is also the gift, given for nothing, through which there is "nothing to lose" or to gain. It is gratis, no more costly than a joke. The traversing itineracy insinuates suspicion through comedy. The pleasure of "amusing himself," Freud says, is blended with humor which follows in the ancient tradition of the *Aggada,* the game of derision in political and local seriousness. Much more than a history, here we now have a story: this novel written in the foreign language of erudition introduces within historiographical identities the "pleasantry" of their relation to the non-place of a death which obliges.

The Tradition of Death, or Writing

ONE must die in the body before writing can be born. Such is the moral of the story. It is not proven by dint of a system of knowledge. It is merely narrated. The "fantasy" relating it is not authorized by its own place, but is made necessary through the debt that a name signifies. The story is constructed on the basis of a *nothing* (*nichts:* I have nothing to lose) and an *obligation* (I shall not forget thee). No longer being the discourse which provides the thing or which a place upholds, the text becomes fiction. What appears thus on the scene is the analytical discourse, strained by division and capable of articulating the "dia-logical" history of *transference,* in the course of which the analyst is "called by the patient in a place where he is not,"[34] becoming the debtor of this foreign place that he refuses to claim.

Taking on a sense between *absprechen* (renouncing) and *angehören* (belonging), this discourse never comes to the end of its writing, and for this very reason. It succeeds in nothing other than going on with *Entstel-*

lung, displacement, and repeating the division within analysis. When it stops, it is not that it has arrived. Like a fable, it does not conclude. It remains in suspense in the moment of enigma, contradiction, or doubt. Like the beginning of the text, its ending is paradoxical. It concludes like a joke, in which the initial separation is found once again after its symptoms have been displaced. This ending is expressed in a fictive mode, as in comedy, and it calls for the interminable work of writing over and over again, to the point of exhaustion. Unlike tragedy, which moves toward the arrest of a death, this comedy of quid pro quo postulates before it begins, beyond the text, an irreparable division which endlessly recurs in scenic reversals. It never exhausts comic inversions engendered by the unnamable misfortune of which successive historical representations are the successive metaphors.

In this respect writing *is* repetition, the very labor of difference. It is the memory of a forgotten separation. To take up one of Walter Benjamin's remarks concerning Proust, we might say that writing assumes the "form" of memory and not its "contents":[35] it is the endless effect of loss and debt, but it neither preserves nor restores an initial content, as this is forever lost (forgotten) and represented only by substitutes which are inverted and transformed according to the law set up by a founding exclusion. Scriptural practice is itself a work of memory. But all "content" that would claim to assign to it a place or a truth is nothing more than a production of a symptom of that practice—a fiction, including the fantasy of *Moses*. What can be said about this practice is that it is an *analytical* relation within the element of *representation*. In other words, it is a movement that allows the division (essentially sexual) to reappear and thus "explains" the resulting transferences, displacements, or quid pro quos. Erudite history and the analytical novel thus follow opposite procedures. The former claims to bring content back into the text, but in order to save such positivities from oblivion, it is necessary to forget that history obeys the imperative of producing a literary fiction intended to deceive death or to hide the real absence of the figures with which it deals. It plays *as if* it were bent upon constructing verisimilitude and filling the lacunae through which an irreparable loss of presence is betrayed. Yet history is ultimately authorized by its author's present place as a specialist; it aims thus at erasing its own relation to time. It is *discourse*. The Freudian novel is on the other hand *writing*, the labor of spending time without forgetting what organizes it; it narrates its own relation to time both as a bond (a membership) and a dispossession (separation). *Moses and Mon-*

otheism can be seen as this cultivated time made into narrative; or else as the narration in which writing, both the creator and the object of this staging, is analyzed as the tradition of a death.

At this point there intervenes what Maria Torok has called "the aversion that we all feel in sacrilegiously penetrating the intimate nature of mourning."[36] Yet not without the "inner conflict" being marked or doubt being brought "into public notice" (*GW* 16:130; *SE* 23:16), can the Freudian text lead us to this spot where the relation between the murder of Moses and the production of the tradition designates the intimate nature of mourning as an *inscription*. No doubt this is a "sacrilegious" elucidation, since it steals from the sacred (*legere sacrum*) its very essence, presence—if it is true that *mourning this presence* and giving it up as lost is equivalent to writing.

Tradition, a theme central to the three *Moses* essays, first appears bound everywhere to a "historical catastrophe" (*GW* 16:174; *SE* 23:70). From the saga to poetry, the *epos* is not produced without the fall of what it celebrates. As such, the fall is not without traces (*nicht spurlos, GW* 16:174). In the splendor of Minoan-Mycenaean civilization, or in the empire of reason created by Akhenaton and harvested by Moses (*GW* 16:174–75), a mortal wound opens the locus where the Homeric or the biblical poem, a written dream, appears. The fiction is built on the "nothing" of past existence from which nothing (*nichts*) subsists (*GW* 16:175). Great poetry is made from great ruins. In order to mark this connection between two elusive forms, death and poetry—the fact of the *destrudo* and the representation of the *libido*[37]—Freud resorts to a quotation from Schiller. He often punctuates his discourse with poetic intervals (which are not objects of study, but references to authority in crucial moments). Amidst his "analytical" prose he thus inserts the play of his other, in the style of a different and necessary poetic aside, both lacking and generative. "The artist always comes first," remarks Jacques Lacan.[38] One of Schiller's "adages" comes to Freud; it has the form of both a memory and a dream (*erinnern, GW* 16:208; *SE* 23:101):

> All that is to live in endless song
> Must in life-time first be drown'd.[39]

A loss of existence is the condition for immortality in poetry. It is a structure of "sacri-fice," that is, of the production of sacred shapes; Georges Bataille has remarked, "Sacred things are established through a labor of loss."[40] Just as the disappearance of Moses allowed for the appearance of the Mosaic saga, so then, in its many different forms, a lacuna of history makes the production of a *culture* both possible and necessary: a collective epos, a legend, a tradition. In his own way, James Joyce expresses the same law when he tells of the end of a youthful love. A presence, as it vanishes, founds the obligation of writing: "In the indecisive fog of former notes a weak shaft of light flickers: the speech of the soul will be heard. Youth here has end: here is the end. Never will it ever occur. That you already know. And after? Write it, goddamn, write it! What else can you do?"[41]

The "speech of the soul" is the foreign speech of the old Dutch composer Jan Pieterszoon Sweelinck, whose aria contains the words "Youth here has end." It is the occasion, in the elsewhere of a song, for what in finishing "does not occur" in history but only in poetry. "After" comes the imperative of the inscription: "Write it." The trace "flickers" when no specific end can be found for what is being lost. With the trace the law of writing, debt, and memory surges forth. The imperative to "write it" is connected with the loss of voice and the absence of place. It is the obligation to be passing away and to pass away endlessly. What is necessary is what writes endlessly.[42] The debt must be traced relentlessly. Writing is what remains to be done in an "interminable" proceeding in which the event that never takes place (or never took place) is always repeated.

But with Freud the tradition is specific in not being relative only to loss; it must also be understood within the strategies of a *will to lose*. It reiterates what exists in the begining—a murder. The act which turns into a trace through writing is the rejection of the founding father. In the text it is multiplied with the movement of refusal (*versagen*), of scorn, (*verschmähen*), of abjuring (*abschwören*), or of contesting (*absprechen*) that intervenes at every decisive moment in the narrative, from Ikhnaton's erasure of the religion and the name of his father or the Egyptian people's contempt for Ikhnaton's monotheism, all the way up to the murder of Christ. The "initial" event is basically nothing more than the name given to a series begun long before the narrative, in Egypt, a series that will end in the text, long after the story narrated in Freud's "contestatory" gesture. Such is the movement followed during periods of latency, within the tradition that "would like to forget" and that, in laboring to efface the memory of the initial murder, betrays (reveals) what it is hiding. A wish not to know: the tactic of repression is exactly what, through the production of something "forgotten" (unknown), forms the *knowledge* of "the murder of the primal father."[43] Within the tradition, a "will to lose" (the father) is repeated by a "will to lose" (the truth) of the initial event that it silences in order to become a substitute in its place. The tradition would therefore be no more faithful to what it reproduces if it were to abstain from hiding it. What is *known* therein functions as what is *silenced*. This way of obliterating memory by repeating the repressive gesture defines the traditional legend as "memory," which is a loss of "content" and a reproduction of "form." It is what must be said if something else is to be understood.

But doesn't the same also hold for the primal event which Freud reconstructs? Rather than to the category of "facts" or historical "truths," the event has to be assigned to the novel, among the effects of a writing that in turn must be repression (therefore "true" in this way) *and* a staging intended to hide what it is doing. It would take up again this very tradition that it is supposed to explain. The content—Moses assassinated—brings us back to the text which produces it. A repression also seems to be the "truth" repeated throughout the Freudian fiction; it would be hidden by an erudite argumentation, the disguise of a fable, and then betrayed by the lacunae of chronological reconstruction; in other words, by what is missing in historical verisimilitude. But what rupture is the Freudian text creating in respect to tradition if it functions as tradition does, even while elucidating it? These two questions—whether the construction of the novel "wants to make us forget" a repressed element, and how, in this case, the psychoanalytical labor differs from the legend—turn the analysis back toward its own discourse. We are thus led back to the connection of theory with fiction, in play within that space between history and the novel, and developed on the level of the visible text within the relation between demonstration (historiographical "verisimilitude") and its lacunae (an analytical "truth").

In other words, for Freud the lacuna is not the absence of a stone in the finished building, but the trace and return of what the text has to "replace." In *Moses and Monotheism*, two expressions return obsessively as a refrain. One is "taking the place" of the other (*die Stelle einnehmen*) or "settling in its place" (*an seine Stelle setzen*), and the other is "filling the lacunae" (*die Lücken ausfüllen*) or "covering one's traces" (*die Spuren verwischen*). The concealing (*Beseitigung*) of traces, which concerns the perpetration of a crime (*GW* 16:144; *SE* 23:43), gives their true significance to the lacunae of the textual staging that occupies the place of the dead. Who then is the dead one? According to David Bakan, Freud "renounces" Moses; he takes his place by initiating a "Jewish science" as a substitute for religious rabbinism; but at the same time that he "desires" Moses' assassination (by the Jew or by Jews), he "remits the guilt" and wipes parricide clean, since it is a question of the death of a foreigner.[44] For Marthe Robert, Freud's *Moses* is "a last gasp of revolt before the inexorable fatality of filiation," "an obstinate refusal of blood bonds," a rejection of his father, Jakob Freud, in order to take his place as a "son of no one" and a "son of his works."[45] This is a Freudian ambition beyond all doubt, and is declared as such: the hero always revolts against his father and, in one fashion or another, ultimately kills him (*GW* 16:193). Yet Otto Rank perceived the ambivalence somewhat more correctly when he described the "founding father" of psychoanalysis as a "rebellious son who defends paternal authority."[46]

These interpretations hint at a relation between the traditional gesture of repressing (or replacing) and the break that it creates in respect to tradition. But they determine a "truth" within the text (for example, the founding of "modern" Judaism—Moses as "Egyptian"—according to David Bakan; the enigma of the psychological identity—Freud the man in front of the "man" Moses—for Marthe Robert), and they take for granted that it can be *translated* into a referential language. That, I believe, is exactly what the text prohibits, and that is the way in which it is to be distinguished from tradition. The text provides for a plurality of possible interpretations. What it "means" can only be *silenced*, infinitely *repressed*, forever remaining *to be expressed*. In its form, the text upholds the terms of a contradiction that, while playing on several levels (the biography of Moses, the history of Judaism, autobiography, etc.), aims at the blind spot of an *I don't know* reiterated in respect to every one of its objects.[47] *That* has no proper place within discourse. Therefore the text teaches the reader, *You won't know anything*. As Freud writes of Aten's religion, "Care has however been taken that none too much information . . . should reach us" (*GW* 16:162; *SE* 23:59), to which we can add, if the information were somewhere written, "that would be known." Fiction has the characteristic power of *having us understand* what it does *not express*.

More than content, form conveys what will be understood: the relation of a statement with a repressed. But form does not exactly reinstate contradiction even if, as for Lévi-Strauss, "*Conter* (to tell a story) is always *conte redire* (to retell a story), which can also be written *contredire* (to contradict)," repeating the ancient legend in contradicting it.[48] Rather, a structure of *trial* is in question here, at play (within content) in terms of crime and traces that must be covered. Hence the argumentation is *avowedly* lacunary (*lückenhaft, GW* 16:189) and defends itself as such. The author accuses his own work, but rebels against "unjustified reproaches." His hero is at once a "renegade" and a victim; he betrays and is assassinated. Every element is the site of that internal trial which for Freud assumes the figure of doubt. Accusation and justification win out over affirmation and negation (which themselves have the value of pretension and denial). A conflict determines the contraries upon the always-shifting ground of an aggression and a counterattack. On every occasion, a break reappears on the site of a new state of war. Repressions are expressed through writing, but writing responds through a labor (an elucidation) aimed against death.

Such is the situation of the text. It does not escape the trial that it analyzes. It goes on with this trial and remains unable to find a sure, overlooking view protected from "doubt." It is not exempted from the struggle needed to "take the place," nor is it protected from the law that makes the eliminated element return. The violence of the construction is not expressed without its weakness (*schwache Seite, GW* 16:151; *SE* 23:50). Nor is the "inner conflict" of the subject foreign to his text: the "author" cannot be rid of death by letting his book take charge of the task (my works pass, but I remain in a stable place), nor take death on himself by providing immortality for the literary monument (I die, but my book will not perish). As much as Moses, literature is assassinated and is murderous, involved in a sacrilegious conflict that transforms Scripture into writings. There are battles, but not immortality: Freud does not believe in it any more than did the Jews, who "renounced" immortality, he said, while the Egyptians "denied" death (*GW* 16:117; *SE* 23:26).

In this way Freud departs from Schiller. No immortal poem will assume the place of the gods who are dead. There exists no stable and immortal place, even scriptural, nor a revelation that fills this immense gap and creates a sure space. What is written in texts—and in Freud's novel—is their mourning, since the labor of closing the eyes of the father also heralds the law of his return. Without believing in the utopian possibility of outwitting death, Freudian writing conveys both its tradition and its betrayal. This writing steals something—time to inscribe/take this place—in or from the secret/sacred it reveals. In this way it is "sacrilege." But the writing accomplishes this in the style of a joke that will repeat the law of the enigma. It has the appearance of a parody.

The Quid Pro Quo, or the Comedy of the "Proper"

"REMOVE yourself so that I can take your place" ["Ote-toi que je m'y mette"]: written in French in the Freudian text, the remark is the law of the dream. "You have got what you deserve now that you have left your place for me [*den Platz räumen*]; why did you want to throw me out of there [*vom Platze verdrängen*]?"[49] Such is the law of history, individual or collective. The murdered soul surges up exactly where he was killed. Like Hamlet's father,[50] so returns the "ghost not laid" of Moses.[51] On the very scene of the crime, this "revenant" will forever return: the victim who, yesterday, was a threat. In the seventh chapter of part three, entitled "The Return of the Repressed," Freud affirms at the same time that the religion of the founding father returns in the Jewish religion which had "chased it away," and that the father "scorned" (*geringgeschätzt*, GW 16:168; SE 28:126) by Goethe reappears in the character of the old poet—a way for Freud, who identifies with the "great Goethe," to see himself in his last days also dispossessed of the very place that he had made for himself by repressing his father Jakob.[52] It is impossible to kill this dead one. He comes back right where the conservation of his name—"Moses" or "Freud"—conceals the will to eliminate him. The name's identity is the scene for the play where repression (*Verdrängung*) identifies displacement (*Verschiebung*), such that beneath the disguise of the "proper," only the quid pro quo of the proper is known.

In *Moses and Monotheism*, the old man Freud has become will gather all of his essential theses around the idea of repression, which had been, as he wrote to Romain Rolland in 1936, "the true point of departure for our extended study of psycho-pathology."[53] In sum, he entirely recomposes *the* place that he had made for himself—psychoanalysis, "born just after the death of Jakob Freud and really indeed, thanks to it"[54]—in its relation with an exclusion, represented here by the murder of Moses. But when he collects all of the furniture around him that proves the establishment of his own place, the other returns, in the inevitability of an effacement; that is, of filiation and of death. When Freud makes his inventory of acquired goods, he is really packing his bags. His own "construction" brings him the very message announcing the return of the repressed—not by chance, but on the ground of a law that Freud analyzes methodically through this "Egyptian Moses." In the same period of time he evokes the king Boabdil learning of the fall of his city Alhama, the sign of the end of his reign: "He does not wish to know [Er will es nicht 'wahr haben'] and decides to treat the message as if it had never reached him"; he burns the letters and kills the messenger.[55] On the contrary, Freud "wishes to know" the news, and in the very language of the place he occupies. His own place, which the repressing of his father made possible for the "rebellious son," now reverts into a ghost's message.

Finally, *who* wins? The son who transformed all established and "proper" knowledge within a place altered by the return of an excluded party? Or the father who, as always, after a "latency period" (*Inkubationszeit*) or "latency" (*Latenz, GW* 16:171; *SE* 23:75), returns from afar? Who is "un-done"? Who is where, and in whose place? These questions have no answer. "It must remain uncertain" (*dahingestellt, GW* 16:245; *SE* 23:135). The violence of the conflict is matched by the victor's *dissimulation,* but it is a structural dissimulation that renders impossible any homogeneity of the self with what appears to be part of it. There is a "de-fection" from the place. Therein the other is always a "rightful claimant." How can it be written except within a discourse which impugns the historiographical postulate of "subjects" who can be identified with places, and which makes *fiction* the very motive of its construction? If the subject is a quid pro quo, then his story can only be the turning of the quid pro quo into a narrative; in other words, a comedy of identity.

Of particular interest to me in this study of Freudian writing is that the novel happens to be a *practice,* conforming to what it is saying. If it posits, as content, the absence of a place or of an identifying "substance," the novel itself can only be a function of the quid pro quo. Hence the genesis of the text, and not only the statement of ideas, is the deployment (or the "analysis") of the "truth" it is designating. *The practice producing the text is the theory.* The literary construction (legible in terms of rhetorical procedures organizing the work, or semiotic "structures" generating the textual "manifestation") is the very praxis of "taking the place" (*die Stelle einnehmen*). As in Marivaux's theater, *Moses* is developed through "substitutions," "disguises," "disfigurements" and "deformations," "eclipses" and "ellipses," "reversals" of situations—that is, in a play of "light" and "shadow," of "vanishings," and of "reappearances." All of this Freudian vocabulary indicates a *stage technique* that is not only in the service of the "subject" under treatment. It also establishes the very writing itself as a process of repression/return. *Producing the text* amounts to *making a theory.* In this respect, it is indeed a theoretical fiction. Theory, invested entirely within the operation of being written, is the task of the subject who is produced only insofar as he can *be inscribed,* analytically, as a quid pro quo.

If, for Freud, a "know-how" may be exposition itself; if the procedures that make discourse into narrative constitute theoretical practice: these are questions I should like to study in terms of the way some fragments of *Moses* function. I shall select several strategic points of reference: the family romance, and the duality of Yahweh and of Moses. These examples will specify the relation that Freudian *fiction* holds with this effective *history* that turns out to be a way of "making the text."[56] Here the status of theory can also be clarified. Far from being a science (defined by the establishment of a field proper and a univocal language), theory, for Freud, is exercised both from and within fiction (dreams, legends); its work traces within the foreign language of these fantasies a "knowledge" that is inseparable from them but which becomes increasingly capable of articulating them *historically,* that is, through a practice of inversions and displacements. The quid pro quo is at once the statement and operation of theory.

The "child's family romance" (*Familienroman*) takes up only a few pages in the *Moses* (*GW* 16:106–12; *SE* 23:11–15), but it plays a decisive role. It also figures in the dossier of Freud's relation with Otto Rank.[57] Favoring the Egyptian origins of Moses, it represents Freud's personal investment. After having "adopted" as his own Breasted's arguments on the Egyptian origins of the name "Mosche,"[58] Freud "takes back" from Rank the thesis that the latter had published in 1901 "at my suggestion" when "then still working under my influence."[59] In the two cases of Breasted and Rank, Freud puts himself in the place of the other. In matters of birth, the Freudian narrative begins with two citations. The first is an extract from Rank's *Der Mythus von der Beburt des Helden:* the stereotypical myth includes two families; one of them is a noble family, and the true one, that rejects the hero; the other family is modest, and adopts the hero before he takes vengeance upon his father and takes the father's place. The second text cited is the autobiography of Sargon d'Agode (2,800 B.C.), the witness who is the "most remote of the historical personages to whom this myth attaches." The first text Freud cites provides a general "schema," a "legend type" (*Durchschnittssage, GW* 16:107; *SE* 23:14); the second, a primitive image (*Urbild*) or a prototype. Therefore we have both a literary *structure* and a historical *beginning.*

These two cards are in fact two variants of the same hand, but with the nuance that Freud supposes that the structure is more legible in the *Urbild* than in the "formula" (*Bild; GW* 16:107; *SE* 23:14) obtained from a series. By way of this doubling which brings him back from Rank's "model" to Sargon's "original," he takes up once more the mastery of the subject. In its serial form, the quotation procures a site for *his* labor, on the very terrain where he is host and whose language he utilizes. A framing of the quotation (set aside and placed between quotation marks) creates a virtual play within this space where technical procedure will generate the Freudian text, but it gives to the text no place other than that of quotation. In this respect, it hardly resembles the delimitation which initiates historiography by distinguishing it from "chronicles" or "documents" (see the subsection of chapter 2 above entitled "Split Constructions") and which establishes a priori that the discourse of historical knowledge is not in the same circumstances and is not subject to the same unawareness as are its documents. To the contrary, analysis postulates that it obeys the same law as documents and that it is no better situated than they, although its success consists in clarifying them: the document *silences* what it *knows;* it hides what it organizes; it reveals only through its *form* what it effaces from its *contents.*

The quotation therefore functions in a specific way within the Freudian text. The quotation does not authorize that text any more than the text is authorized by its relation to a nonknowledge. The quotation is the place crisscrossed by a labor that puts contents into play and deploys (or "ana-lyzes") their ambivalences, therefore their displacements and virtualities. Into the quotation as into the word, analysis inserts plurality in the place of univocality. Far from being based upon "comprehension" or "judgment" pronounced from a different standpoint, exempted from nonknowledge and "ambi-guity," thus "noble" and distinguished, at every juncture the quotation restores a movement in which it participates— precisely because it admits its own relation with a nonknowledge, its debt in respect to the other, and its inner conflicts.

The "family romance" is therefore the occasion of a treatment which displaces, reduces, or inverts contents in order to discern the variants of an identical formal functioning, whether in the general or originary model (*Bild*) of the "myth of the hero's birth," or in its inversion with the unique case of the Moses legend. This functioning is a relation between one and two which is marked as the conflict between two characters (the father and the son, or the parents and the children) within a single family. *Two in the same place.* Elsewhere, for example in *The Ego and the Id* (1923), this tension is elucidated as the very question of the "I": the subject is fashioned through his experience of being both inseparable from and foiled by the other; he is divided by the prohibition that establishes the very transgression, and which institutes pleasure within a vital relation to lack and difference; he has no place of his own. But here everything takes place on the family scene. In such a unity of place, the son must—but never truly can—dislodge the father.

In the common presentation and in the Jewish exception, Freud marks the adjunction of a second place ("invented") within the history ("real," *GW* 16:111; *SE* 23:15) of the conflict. Legend inverts history through this creation, since there are hereafter *two* places (two families) for *one* character (the hero). The operation yields a profit. It saves the identity of place where the legend is produced. Through his exile in a second family, the foreigner from within leaves his place of origin intact and simple. The enemy is merely something outside; the inside is washed clean of difference. The return of the prodigal or contested son becomes thus the return of the same. Everything amounts to the same and evinces the original "nobility" of the place, after the split and the transitional adoption into a "modest" family. In sum, the legend is the genealogical discourse of the place. *Apologia pro domo sua.* It expresses the law of the land, a place, or a milieu that must be "noble" from beginning to end. There is no possible equivocation: what is noble is *over here* and what is modest is *over there*. Everything is set in place. Yet the space arranged by an order is intersected by the unique time of the narrative and the hero. The *uniqueness of the trajectory* contrasts with the *duality of places*. In every meaning of the term, it is the *trace* of what topography has eliminated. Legend repeats in its dynamics what it has excluded from its description. Narrativity states the inverse of what is founded by spatial structure. Through the unity of character, narrativity maintains as a movement of history the coincidence of opposites. Under the same name, there are two places. Legend thus betrays the "fictive" character (see figure 9.1) of its first sequence (A), which is supposed to stabilize a place of reference; and through the relation of the sequences (B) and (C), it designates the eruption of an "upstart coming from nowhere" (*ein hergelaufener Abenteurer, GW* 16:110; *SE* 23:13) in the sacred place. An uncanniness is part of familiarity. An endless conflict moves into the heart of the "family."

The Jewish legend of Moses' birth diverges from "all the others of its kind" (*GW* 16:112; *SE* 16:15); it "occupies a special position and, indeed, in one essential point contradicts the rest" (*GW* 16:109; *SE* 16:12).

Moses is born of a modest family (of Levites), and he is adopted by a noble family (of the Pharaoh). In fact, this detail is secondary in respect to the fact that, because it is produced in a Jewish place, the legend establishes *the same* (the Jewish place) *as an origin:* the Jewish birth functions here as a noble origin, and it legitimizes the place by classifying foreignness in the (apparently) noble exteriority, where the hero *of the family* was provisionally adopted (see figure 9.2).

In reality the inversion is only a variant. The *law of the same* (place) prevails in both cases, but in the more common model it plays the role of the law of a social and political milieu, while in Jewish legend, it intervenes as the law of the family (the law of blood), relativizing a foreign "nobility" destined for humility.

Freud slips into this legend as the thief of a legitimacy. He is sacrilegious; he pilfers the sacred place. With his "Egyptian Moses," he initiates a "dis-order" in the very place protected by the legend: the foreigner, the man of lower extraction who lacks any avowed origin (*hergelaufener*), the adventurer (*Abenteurer*), in a word the Egyptian, is inside the place. An uncanny familiarity. The same holds for each signifier where, beneath all clarity—one single meaning for each word—a contrary uncertainty is restored, marked by a usage which is in motion. There is always an "obscene" figure, an upstart in the noble place.

But Freud also provides his own version of the "family romance." The child, he notes, first of all overestimates his father, then breaks away and becomes critical of him: "The humble and noble families of the myth are two images reflecting [*Spiegelungen*] the same family as it appears to the

FIGURE 9.1

The Myth of the Hero's Birth

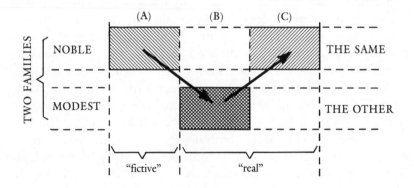

child at successive periods in his life." They are thus mixed together (*zu-sammenfallen*), reunited locally, and separated only by time (*zeitlich, GW* 16:109). Freud distributes into various moments what the legend divides into various places.[60] Where it spatializes, he chronologizes. Just as in his vision of Rome, he replaces juxtaposition (which localizes objects *next to* one another: *neben*) with succession (which stacks them up in the place where they appear one *after* the other: *nach;* see above, "The Discourse of Fragments," and especially note 12). What advantage is to be gained from this difference within the process of making into narrative the relation between the father and the son—that is, between the humble and the strong, or the intruder and the owner? If it were simply a question of the same edifying category, constitutive of proper places, but working according to another code, the advantage would be practically nil. In fact, the difference holds to the nature of Freudian time. No matter what it reveals or conceals, such a time loses nothing. It deploys a play of psychic stratifications. Through successive displacements it brings forth the returns of an initiating division. It is *memory,* a movement of what is repeated through changes of content. In this fashion, Freudian time contradicts the illusory stabilities of space. Freud is suspicious of places. He mistrusts what it is to "take root" (*Bodenständigkeit*).[61] He leads us back to a *march* of time based upon a *lost* origin (or land).

The aspect of fiction that the Freudian representation nevertheless conserves, however, is the linearity of time, successivity itself. For what *follows* is in reality *inside*. The character's alter ego is concealed within. A "double" always lurks within him at every moment and in every place. The

FIGURE 9.2

The Jewish Legend of the Birth of Moses

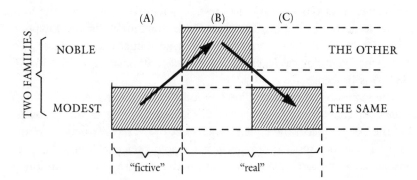

same holds true both *through* and *in* Freud's "temporal" exposition (*Darstellung*). By demystifying the legalization of the place and by showing its effects on the construction of a staging, this analysis made out of the language of time is still based upon what is hidden and therefore functions as a fiction. A second fragment of the *Moses* allows it to proceed, since it posits the necessity of a rejection: something *must* be repressed for movement to go forward. And also, *fiction* is needed for the progress (interminable) of *analysis*. Far from being the occult element that must be suppressed, or the lacuna to be filled (what, moreover, would this gesture be if not a new rejection?), the repressed is the very principle of displacement. No longer is there "life" where nothing conceals itself. Through its content and its movement, Freudian *Aufklärung* is diametrically opposed to a philosophy of clarity or of Enlightenment. It "defends" something that can only be removed or *silenced*.

In the second essay, "a purely historical study" (Freud emphasizes the point: *GW* 16:154, 161, etc; *SE* 23:59, 66), the fourth and fifth paragraphs (*GW* 16:130–41; *SE* 23:31–41) are the pivot of the argument, which he takes up again in his conclusion (*GW* 16:154–55; *SE* 23:59–60), concerning *duality*—of Yahweh, Moses, the people, etc. They have much to do with the *name*, whereas the family romance dealt with an originary *place*. On first view it appears curious that after having reduced the two (places) to a single one when examining the hero's childhood, now Freud introduces two (characters) where the Jewish saga only provides one. In fact, he reestablishes the conflictual structure of *two in the same place*, whether it be the legend that creates a second place in which his second character can be lodged, or the legend that eliminates the second character because only one name exists. Thus, in the two cases, the law that holds for Freud now returns; it prohibits him both from occupying a proper place, liberated from indebtedness in respect to the other's name, and from a loyalty incontestably identifying him with the Jewish or scientific institution. In other words, for him as for the Egyptian Moses, a *proper place* or a *proper name* can no longer exist. In these two ways, the "genealogical legend" (*die genealogische Sage, GW* 16:134; *SE* 23:38) is broken.

The same textual practice allows Freud to *force the return of the effaced double* (of Yahweh or Moses) here and to *knock down the decorative doublet* (of the unique place) there. The procedures of his reconstruction are the same. I shall not insist on this point; I would prefer to follow his path insofar as it indicates the need for something repressed (a tradition is defined by what it silences) and organizes itself as repression, but in such a way that the *two elements move forward together* within the same text. In Freudian terms, they "merge" (*verschmelzen, verlöten, zusammentreten,* etc.) in the same name—"fiction" (see above, note 3)—while remaining foreign to each other. In effect, Freudian analysis appears to maintain the same type of relation with the legend that the Egyptian Moses keeps with the Midianite Moses: stirred by the movement that makes them return now and again, sometimes as "dream," sometimes as "psychoanalysis" on the surface of the text, they evince the same conflict (two in the same place), but either to the degree that it is *dictated* (the law of the "father") or to the degree that it is *known* (the conquest of the "son").

At this point, behind (or "after") the "universal god" of Ikhnaton's monotheism, the analysis exhumes a Yahweh or "god of the volcanoes," an uncanny (*unheimlicher*), bloodthirsty demon who walks by night and shuns the light of day (*GW* 16:133), a local god (*Lokalgott*), avaricious and savage (*engherziger, roher, GW* 16:151), who contrasts with the ideology of the Egyptian *Aufklärung*. Such is the "barbarous god of volcanoes and wildernesses," writes Freud, "whom I grew to dislike very much in my studies on Moses and who was quite alien to my Jewish conscience."[62] Of Arabic origins, this god of the Sinai and Horeb was *adopted* by the Jews and was accredited by them with "deliverance," which in fact was the work of the Egyptian Moses. Moses is the usurper. Yet, because derision and savagery serve in the hands of reason, the shadow (*Schatten*) of the god whose place he had taken became stronger than he was; at the end of the historical development, there arose beyond his being that of the forgotten Mosaic god (*GW* 16:152), in the same way that the "tradition," having originated in Egypt, had gradually grown in the darkness (*GW* 16:153). The Egyptian god (Aton) returns, but in the name of the other—"Yahweh"—that is, under an *adopted* name.

Inversely, another character is erected "behind" the Egyptian Moses: equally a foreigner, one who has become Jethro's son-in-law, this "irascible and violent" Midianite is the man of the vision on Sinai and the witness of Yahweh. He is associated with the Jewish resistance that brought about the assassination of the Egyptian. But *he has no name*. He only triumphs with an alias (the Egyptian one of "Moses"), and his success is followed by the return of what he had helped to eliminate, Aton's religion passed on to Israel in the name of Moses.

Such is the beginning of the imbroglio that Freud "spins"[63] with an old man's wily subtlety, with a visible pleasure, but also with the always-disquieting worry of having to please "qualified" researchers and of "contradicting the authentic findings of historical research" (*GW* 16:136; *SE* 23:37). Before becoming extremely complex, the game begins with four places (two gods and two leaders) and only three names (Aton, Yahweh, Moses), since one of the characters is nameless. Freud's scenic montage works in two phases, after which it will be repeated, although with new contents.

The "primal" phase posits stable relations between a being (*Wesen*) and a name (*Name*). On the one hand, there is the "popular" (Egyptian) or "primitive" (Hebraic) being of the former religion; it is designated by the name of "Amenhotep" in Egypt or by "Yahweh" in Israel. If *Wesen* is indicated by the capital letter A and *Name* by a in lower case, we have the stable relation Aa. Then a second term intervenes: B. It takes its place after a struggle, just as the son occupied the place of the father. It is Aton's monotheist religion upheld by Ikhnaton. It effaces at once the being (*Wesen*) and the name (*Name*) of the paternal religion, before succumbing in turn to the return of the former being and former names. Egyptian history is presented as a series of reversals whose every moment nonetheless maintains adequation between the name and the thing: $Aa \rightarrow Bb \rightarrow Aa$.

The second phase is begun with the exile of Egyptian monotheist religion among the Jews. Hereafter everything works by dint of a *break between the name and the thing*. Exteriority of development in respect to the original place perverts the alliance of *Wesen* with the *Name* and constantly inverts their relation. A problem of exodus: hereafter in Israel *Wesen* will always be distanced from the name. In this *adoptive* place (where Moses, Aton's "son," is first of all adopted), the name can no longer match the thing. B (monotheism) is accepted in the name of a (Yahweh); then, following Moses' assassination, A (primitive religion) wins over but in the name of b (as "Mosaic"), before this repression returns, but under the name of Yahweh. In Israel, also punctuated with violent breaks, we have the series $Ba \rightarrow Ab \rightarrow Ba$.

Wounded at the juncture of its connection with a ground, this story moves forward limping. Names (language) are no longer in the same spot as things (history). Surely, from the time of the initial rupture or "separations" (*Trennungen*) that reiterate it, "fusions" (*Verschmelzungen*) are produced in one same ("national") name; but "restorations" (*Wiederherstellungen*) forcibly bring this break to the surface and prohibit the people from letting themselves be taken in by the illusion of unity. The suture

(*Verlötung*) only conceals the break (*Zerfall, GW* 16:138). Here Freud agrees with the Marxist analysis of class conflict: national unity, the illusion of the common name, conceals the division of labor within history.[64]

Put to use in a hundred ways throughout the whole "novel" (for example, Moses, the Egyptian among the Jews, "stammers" and practices with hesitation or doubt a language which is foreign to him), a constant trait characterizes the endless weave of the plot: lacking a place, a homeland, or a native and proper language, *speech no longer prevails*. Presence (*Wesen*) is no longer given in the signifier (*Name*). The body is the other of language. The exodus has made *voice* impossible. There remains only the possibility of writing, which is a quid pro quo between language and reality, or a fiction, since it expresses something other than the thing it names. This is the end of a presence that can be named. Vanished are the voice of the earth and the speech of the body. There are no more prophets, but only writers, who practice scriptural displacement and in every instance produce fictions.

In *Moses,* two signs attest to this elimination of voice. On the one hand, all of the elements in this text move and castle according to the play of the quid pro quo, *except for one*. A "confirmation" (a certificate and document, or *Zeugnis, GW* 16:139) lasts through the ups and downs of relations among signifiers and realities: circumcision. At one time, Freud notes, it was practiced solely in Egypt; it was something of its own, a particularity, but it was inert, valued as being one detail among others. By contrast, it becomes a law (*Gebot, GW* 16:126, 139, etc.) when it passes among the Jews as the sign of the lost origin and the lost homeland. Only at that time does it become a law and acquire meaning. In effect it signifies both as a *mark* of a loss, and by the *act* of losing. Unlike a relic, which is kept, or stigmata, which are added, circumcision signifies being removed. And furthermore, it is no longer a name, but now the gesture which *enacts* on the individual body what it says about the social body. A primitive (*uralt*) custom (*Sitte, GW* 16:128) existing outside of the event that makes it meaningful, created as a deed long before becoming a document, it acquires—by dint of being deported and deprived of its context—the change of status which transforms it from a *sign* of Egyptian identity into the *law* of Jewish identity. It becomes the trace of Moses' passage into foreign lands, and hence of the privation of place, by tracing privation at the center of the body, at the sex, and by making a shard of the very place of power. Circumcision is "troublesome" (*beschwerliche, GW* 16:126; *SE* 23:27) to be sure, very strange (*sehr befrem-*

dlich, GW 16:128; *SE* 23:29); "those who do not practice [*üben*] it are
a little horrified [*grausen*]" (*GW* 16:128; *SE* 23:29). This loss causes
anguish. But those who have "adopted" (*annehmen*) it, since it has come
from further afar than they, since it is a mark received as one's own because of its foreign appeal, are indeed "proud" of it. They fancy themselves "elevated" (*erholt*) and as if exalted (*geadelt, GW* 16:128; *SE* 23:28)
despite their "modest" or unknown origin, believing impure those in whom
this wound of an absence is lacking.

Circumcision is therefore an *inscription*, a sculpture or an engraving of
law upon the body—in other words, that which produces meaning by
taking away (unlike painting, which adds), a practice which deprives and,
by virtue of this fact, is productive of meaning. It is writing. *Leitfossil*,
remarks Freud (*GW* 16:139): an inaugurating fossil, an inducing document. Reproduced all through this story, no matter what may be the
relations between language and reality, circumcision is the gesture that
does not deceive, since it is on the track (*leiten*) toward castration. The
relation of the name to the thing ceases being one of quid pro quo, since
a *practice* generating meaning is at stake. And, too, this "document"
(*Zeugnis*) is precisely the "little piece of truth" (*ein Stückchen Warhheit*)
that Freud claims to exhume from the legend. Moses the Egyptian—here
is what the inscription produces by signifying him. It is a theoretical practice where fiction no longer remains.

A second sign, the reciprocal of the first, is provided through the
text—insofar as the text, itself a practice of circumcision, subtracts in
order to signify. This sign is never lacking (which would be a contradiction of terms); it is marked in the Freudian novel as what is *removed*
from it, or *silenced,* so that it can be a "tradition." In the language of
rhetoric, it is an ellipsis; or in Freudian language, a repression. This labor
of retraction could be analyzed in many forms. I will mark off only one,
simply because it deals with the name. Jacques Lacan has noted that Freud
"elides" a "fundamental speech, which is the following: 'I am . . . I am
that I am, that is, a God who is put forward as essentially concealed.' "[65]
Whatever Freud's intentions may be, his textual practice effectively offers
the "deforming tendencies" (*entstellenden Tendenzen*) that in the course
of these very pages he notes throughout the legend. He cuts or adds
material, as an "assassin" of the legend, if indeed "in its implications the
distortion [*Entstellung*] of a text resembles a murder [*Mord*]" (*GW* 16:144;
SE 23:43). The practice of *Entstellung*, a "de-formation" and displacement, is constant with Freud. It bears as much upon what the biblical

texts express as upon what they keep silent. While they speak abundantly about Moses' vision of the burning bush on Mount Horeb, the Freudian narrative says nothing of the inspired Midianite that Freud has distinguished from the "aristocratic Egyptian"; nothing of Horeb or of the burning bush, a burned and burning sign; nothing of the word given by the God who disappears. Freud mentions only "the prohibition upon a god's name," a "taboo of primaeval age" (*GW* 16:139; *SE* 23:40). This law, which in fact is hardly observed, has a very minor place in *Moses;* it is indeed nothing more than a detail, exactly as circumcision had been among the Egyptians before exodus made it a law of inscription.

In this instance Freudian *elision* has a technical value: it suppresses *voice* (the vowel) *which is not spoken,* the mute *e,* which is only *written. Ehyeh,* says the verse of the Book of Exodus, in an unfinished tense, the durative future: "I shall be that I shall be."[66] An end of nonreception. The name "Yahweh" says that nothing can be spoken other than through the orders "Draw not nigh hither" (stay away) and "Go" (go away).[67] Likewise, the tetragrammaton YHWH, "Yahweh," inscribes what is *being* withdrawn. It is not the sacrament of a being who is there, nor does it signify something else which might be hidden behind it, but it is the trace of an evanescence. It *is not pronounced.* It is the *written figure* of a loss, the very operation of being erased. It cannot be voice (a sign of the body that comes and speaks), but solely a *graph.* The abstention of the speaking presence and of the divine *Wesen* creates the travail of writing. "Write it, goddamn, write it!" What else can you do?

The voice, in being muted, moves to unutterable writing. Why then is it this silent voice that Freud is eliding? Exactly why this particular rejection? For lack of information? Doubtless so, but such a neat and easy explanation refers the question to the tradition which Freud is "reiterating." Something quite fundamental is at stake in this graph of the exodus. Freud replaces the "Yahweh" of Mount Horeb with the Judeo-Egyptian *circumcision.* The two *inscriptions* play the same decisive role of being connected with the "real," and there, because it is no longer a matter of *words,* it can be neither quid pro quo nor "two in the same place." Then why the substitution? I believe it concerns what circumcision marks but does not express in Freud's text.

Freud is Jewish, and I am not. Then what can I ultimately "understand" about this *other* without whom I could not be a Christian, and who evades me by being, "behind," the necessary figure who stays inaccessible, the repressed who returns? Everything takes place as if Moses the Egyptian whom the Jew has become (with one more reversal in the quid pro quo, since he is a native Jew of "Egyptian" origins) corresponds to the Jewish Egyptian that I am (my upbringing owing what it is to the other which it has rejected and which returns in my language). No longer does the text state the quid pro quo and the comedy of my name; through the practice of its reading I discover the relation—the Egyptian Moses—which includes *us* and is inverted in passing from one to the other.

It appears to me that, between these two inscriptions, a difference is silenced, that this silenced difference is reiterated by two traditions, and is thus traced/hidden: *circumcision* marks the *body;* the *graph* "Yahweh" marks *language,* the linguistic body. The one takes its "auto-nomy" from the unspeaking opacity of a "real," lived as a continuity of blood; the other thwarts the transparency of being through *meaning.* One is anterior to all language; it strikes the *"in-fans,"* just as the exodus precedes the tradition that it organizes from the beginning ("Weil ich Jude war," writes Freud, to explain how his story has been constructed.)[68] The Yahwist graph in itself designates in advance the impossibility of an "obedience to the truth of being."[69]

The Novel of History

I HAVE taken the risk of approaching the Freudian text with a historian's question. Freud's text speaks a language with which I am acquainted, which with a modest irony, he attributes to "qualified researchers," or historians. In fact, he adopts this language. He practices it with a foreign accent, as a man "from abroad." This gap between the language (the place) and the proceeding indicates the dancer's entry. *Displaced* right where he is, in transit, this "Egyptian Moses" also displaces my questions. He does not fill the lacunae that I could not help presuming I should be capable of filling by reading this text. He creates other ones. They are fundamental, inasmuch as they put into question *the place that legitimizes historiography,* the territory whose textual product historiography becomes.

As such, fed by a philosophy that it no longer admits, our historiography, remarks Emmanuel Levinas, conceives in turn the "relation with others as if it were at play within the destiny of sedentary populations, owners, and builders of land." According to this *logos* of a revelation of being, transformed into a comprehension of "historical facts," "possession is the form par excellence by which the Other becomes the same by becoming mine."[70] But these productions that "obey" the logic of places and names, instituted as a knowledge by being rooted in a soil,[71] are submitted here to Freudian deformation (*Entstellung*). The labor of difference changes the scientific and didactic discourse of history into a "displaced" writing (displaced both in itself and in respect to the "discipline"), that is, into a novel, a text constructed in a somewhere else that is made possible by "misfortunes and travels." Yet for Freud, this operation does not create another place; it does not locate the novel within a field other than history; it does not obey the law of specialization which drives alterity outside, aside (*neben*), or elsewhere, in a "fictive" place other than that which is already occupied. Freud reintroduces the *other within the same place*.[72] It is "Moses the Egyptian." It is also the "historical novel," since the fiction (*Fiktion*) bears the "privilege" of being able, like the public with the actor, to "recall" (*hervorrufen*) onstage or to "repress" (*hemmen*) the "feeling of uncanniness."[73]

To be sure, historiography is "familiar" with the question of the other, dealing especially with the relation which the present holds with the past. But its discipline must create proper places for each, by pigeonholing the past into an area other than the present, or else by supposing a continuity of genealogical filiation (by way of a homeland, a nation, a milieu, etc.; it is always the same topic of history). Technically, it endlessly presupposes homogeneous unities (century, country, class, economic or social strata, etc.) and cannot give way to the vertigo that critical examination of these fragile boundaries might bring about: historiography does not want to know this. In all of its labors, based on these classifications, historiography takes it for granted that the place where it is itself produced has the capacity to provide meaning, since the current institutional demarcations of the discipline uphold the divisions of time and space in the last resort. In this respect, historical discourse, which is political in essence, takes the *law of place* for granted. It legitimizes a place, that of its production, by "including" others in a relation of filiation or of exteriority. It is authorized by this place which allows it to explain whatever is different as "foreign," and whatever is inside as unique. In other words, historiography simplifies the problem of authority by stating that, as in the Egyptian history of the Freudian model, the "father" is in the very place that keeps his name (and that he authorizes); or that, driven away, past and dead, he no longer can be found in the place where we would have ceased being "sons" by taking another name.

The problematic of Freud's quid pro quo and the fiction which formulates his discourse can allow us, no doubt, to reflect on the uncanniness that both contradicts this simplicity and is already marked in every truthful history, be it with the notion of *survivals* (which ought not to be there and which, more often than not, are edited in a present tense in the fashion of an already past or "outcast" foreign body) or with that of *stratifications* of levels at play with each other in the same place. The ways in which these questions asked and marked by history might be dealt with through an "application" of psychoanalysis, as Freud puts it, cannot be entertained here. But on three essential points in the *Moses*—religion, history, and fiction—I should like to conclude by at least pointing out the perspective in view.

For Freud the problem of religion cannot be dissociated from his tradition. The former even embodies the specificity of the tradition. "Just think, this strip of our motherland [*Muttererde*]," he writes to Zweig of Palestine, "with no other progress, no discovery or invention . . . has never produced anything but religions, sacred frenzies. . . . And we hail from there . . . and it is impossible to say what heritage from this land we have taken over into our blood and nerves."[74] The "nothing" of progress, or capitalized knowledge, corresponds to a proliferation of the saga; what heritage remains for the sons, unless it is "nothing," an exodus? For they have "come out," from afar. They move forward, they "write," bound between debt and dispute, if it is true that travel and writing are a form of "treading upon the body of mother earth [*Mutter Erde*]."[75] Received by Freud as an expression "of the relation between the child and the father,"[76] tradition appears to the "child," now a "natural atheist," the adoptive son of another time and another society, in the form of an *uncanny familiarity* whose "ghost" is Moses[77]—or even this Yahweh, the uncanny God (*unheimlicher, GW* 16:133) toward whom Freud feels only antipathy. This "uncanniness" (*das Unheimliche*) is, in my view, the very heritage that was expressed in biblical fiction, and that is reiterated otherwise within the *Case Histories,* the *Krankengeschichte* or the "novels" of Freud. Moreover, this heritage was exhumed at once by the entire psychoanalytical school. In 1919 Theodor Reik saw in Moses something "half-animal and half-God," God's assassin: "The son overturns the father and takes his place," he wrote, "but the father returns as the law when Moses is presented as the mediator."[78] In 1920, in a lecture given at Vienna, the relations between the "uncanny God" and "*our* own god" provided Reik with the terms for an exposition on "uncanny familiarity," the site of analysis.[79]

I wonder if the religious "tradition," the home that today has been abandoned by a society that no longer lives in it, the home that is no longer even there, cannot be seen historically from the basis of two propositions that can be drawn from Freudian analysis. The first was already expressed by Agathon, the hero of Wassermann's premonitory novel: "Neither am I a Jew any more nor am I a Christian":[80] *neither one nor the other*—a statement of "dispute," of exodus, of historical break. The second is the contrary: *one and the other,* but in the fashion of the quid pro quo and of the straw man—a statement of "debt," of "return," and of bizarre "deformations" which bring the repressed religious elements back in the form of *fictions.* This "displaced" ghost haunts the new dwelling. It remains the rightful heir in the spot that we occupy in his place: such is a current problematic of religious history.

This return is exactly the object of the pages Freud dedicates to "historical truth" (*die historischer Wahrheit, GW* 16:236–40; *SE* 23:127–32). That "element of grandeur" (*etwas grossartiges, GW* 16:236; *SE* 23:128) which is attached to religion is related to "a small fragment of truth" (*ein Stückchen Wahrheit, GW* 16:239; *SE* 23:130) in a problematic of "memory" (*Erinnerung*) which is indeed distorted (*entstellte*) yet justified (*berechtigte, GW* 16:238; *SE* 23:130), or "displaced" but nonetheless "in its rightful place." Such is the relation of fiction to history. *Fiction* because man has neither taste (*Witterung*) nor inclination (*Geneigtheit*) to receive truth. Truth is what man silences through the very practice of language. Communication is always the metaphor of what it hides. Yet *truth* because, having the right to occupy this very place, something infantile (*infantil, GW* 16:236; "familiar to all children," *SE* 23:132) "remains" there: the "*in-fans*" document, the excluded figure, the originator of communicated language (tradition), "the kernal of historical truth" (*Kern von historischer Wahrheit, GW* 16:112; *SE* 23:16), a written and illegible mark, an imprint. In Freud's work it appears as circumcision (*Zeugnis*), an inscription which is verbally transcribed in the paradox of the "Egyptian Moses," or of the *Aufdruck,* the "impression" of uncanniness, the *Gefühl* (the tactile feeling of what is affected) bound to the *Zweifel,* "the imprint" of the division. Written breaks, mute impressions: an engraved law which can only remain silent.[81] That the excluded figure produces the fiction which relates it in a comic or tragic "manner of speaking"—that is the "truth" of the history.

This truth radically contradicts the power that didactic discourses of historiography attribute to themselves on the grounds of their occupying this place of truth. These discourses only provide its representations, the "verisimilitude," the "semblance." More to the point, historiography (*Geschichtsschreibung*) has taken the place of tradition (*an die Stelle der Tradition getreten*, GW 16:175): it is a cannibalistic history. It assimilates traditions in order to speak in their place, in the name of a site (of *progress*) authorizing it to know better than do these traditions exactly what they are saying. But that is tantamount to taking for granted that traditions *say* what they *know*; and, too, that what they know does not "come back" within the discourse that is held far from them, at a distance, and which is satisfied with "citing" them (as before a court). In fact, historiography is neither more nor less truthful than they are. It is not true that this discipline is fooled (that it *errs*), as if the question were one of better revealing what there might be "beneath" all appearances. Freud is a stranger to the issues of "revealing" or to the Greek ("Egyptian") conception of truth, which presupposes the adequate relation between a *Wesen* and a *Name*. Like Nietzsche, he "abolishes this world of appearances" created through the Platonic break between appearance and reality, between opinion and science.[82]

The lure exists because historical discourses are *themselves* deceived by failing to admit the fundamental debt that they owe, over distance, in respect to what, now *silenced*, was known in the traditions (and which remains within them). The gap on which history is constructed may never be denied without a fall into doctrine and "genealogical legend"; yet this gap, an exodus of the "son" and the means of his victory in the place of the father, can also never impede the return (under a different name) of the repressed—of the "uncanny familiarity" *in the very place* of a scientific rationality and production. There are many indications of this. Thus, to select one of the most glaring signs, we see that in remaining a narrative, historiography retains this "element of grandeur" that once characterized religion. In effect, narrative means impossible totalization. It takes charge of the relation of "science" with its repressed. A "reason" (a form of coherence, the delimitation of a field of study) is endlessly conjoined to the "rubbish" that it creates by being established as such. *One and the other* —the occupant and the ghost—are put in play *within the same* text; present theory meets that unassimilable element returning from the past as an exteriority placed within *one* text. By virtue of this fact, the latter can only be a narrative—a "history" that one tells. This novelistic effect expresses the relation of two opponents in the same position, in a fashion that is still one of "juxta-position" (*neben*) but already also that of "chronologizing" (*nach*). It is the historiographical equivalent of the Egyptian Moses: science-fiction is the law of history.

Freud's novel is the *theory* of science-fiction. He goes from myth to novel by virtue of the interest that he invests in "the man Moses": *Der Mann Moses* says the German title. From the myth, whose force it possesses, to the novel, there has been travel, from the moment when the subject could no longer be thought of as the world but as the individual, and when, as Georges Dumézil demonstrates in respect to the Hadingus Saga, we moved from the social to the psychological.[83] The novel is the psychologizing of myth; it interiorizes conflict among the gods. Rather than "an extenuation of myth,"[84] it is born of its fragmentation and of its reduction into miniature. But it reiterates the "primal scene" on the individual space created by a point of no return within history. With Freud, as with Defoe or Kafka, myth returns in the psychological figure that has taken its place, with a labor of difference (of death, but we must speak with discretion about what we do not know), with the illegible inscription (the "familiar uncanniness") of doubt (*Zweifel*) and of the impression (*Aufdruck*), the "unanalyzable" fragment of truth.[85]

As for me, I doubt whether I have understood this "knowledge." Thus I have left, marked within the space of a study which "takes the place" of Freud's, but which could never recount it, the foreign footprints— German—left by the dancing lady. But in this place that I occupy, the uncanny familiarity reminds me of the words of another, of Jean Cavaillès, who considered the progress of science a "perpetual revision of contents through deepening and erasure."[86]

NOTES

1. Sigmund Freud, *Der Mann Moses und die Monotheistische Religion*, in *Gesammelte Werke*, 18 vols. (London: Imago Press, 1940–1968), 16:101-246; hereafter abbreviated *GW*. Available in English in *The Standard Edition of the Complete Psychological Works of Sigmund Freud*, 24 vols., J. Strachey, tr. and ed. (London: Hogarth Press, 1953–1974), 23:1-137; hereafter abbreviated *SE*. Subsequent citations appear in parentheses in the text of this chapter. *Moses and Monotheism* was first published in full in 1939 in Amsterdam (in German) and in London and New York (in English). The French translation by Anne Berman (Paris: Gallimard, 1948; Idées, 1967) often transforms (textual) "truth" into fable: an illustration of the Freudian thesis.

2. Sigmund Freud to Arnold Zweig, February 21, 1936, in *The Letters of*

Sigmund Freud and Arnold Zweig, Ernst L. Freud, ed. (New York: New York University Press, 1987), p. 122. Freud takes up his theme of writing as *a freely wandering or fantastic thinking* (*GW* 13:440).

3. In respect to Freud's text, I will use the words "fiction," "fable," or "novel," as distinguished from "fictive," "fabulation," or "legend," which characterize a tale of denial. In fact, these two sets of terms are unstable and crisscross each other. The same genre can undergo different practices. In order to speak of his discourse, Freud himself says: *Darstellung* (exposition), *Konstruktion* or *Rekonstruktion, Aufbau* (edifice), *Aufstellung* (thesis). In order to designate religious legend, he uses *Sage, Mythus* (myth), *Tradition, Dichtung* or *fromme Dichtung* (poetry or pious poetry), *Erfindung* (invention), *Phantastieche* (fantastic), but also *Darstellung* or *Konstruktion*—that is, the words which qualify his own production. Other terms are equally worthy of his "historical novel" and of the Jewish tradition: *Bericht* (tale), *Geschichte* (history), *Erzählung* (relation); they concern narrativity, a type of ambivalent discourse which can function as a "theory" or as a "disavowal." Except as noted otherwise, the terms cited in the text (in quotation marks when translated, in italics when in German) are Freud's.

4. Freud to Zweig, Sept. 30, 1934, in *Letters of Freud and Zweig*, p. 92.

5. Freud to Zweig, Dec. 16, 1934, *ibid.*, p. 98.

6. See Freud's "The Antithetical Meaning of Primal Words," *SE* 11:153–62. ("Uber den Gegensinn der Urworte," *GW* 8:213–21), published in 1910.

7. Freud to Zweig, Sept. 30, 1934, in *Letters of Freud and Zweig*, pp. 90–93.

8. Freud to Zweig, Dec. 16, 1934, *ibid.*, p. 98.

9. Freud to Zweig, June 13, 1935, *ibid.*, p. 107.

10. "So only a few short papers have been usable for the Almanack or *Imago*," notes Freud to Pfister; see *Psychoanalysis and Faith: The Letters of Sigmund Freud and Oscar Pfister*, Heinrich Meng and Ernst L. Freud, eds. (New York: Basic Books, 1963), p. 144. In respect to the thesis of Karl Abraham (which Freud will later take up as his own, despite having ridiculed it), in 1912 Freud writes that it is "worthy of *Imago*, just good enough for *Imago*." See Jacques Trilling, "Freud, Abraham, et le Pharaon," *Etudes freudiennes* (1969), nos. 1–2, pp. 219–26. [See also note 59 below.——TR.]

11. Sound can be written as well (in sonographs), but precisely through a *plurality* of lines representing the differences of pitch that sound energy follows and mixes, in harmonics, into a *single sound*. See for example Louis-Jacques Rondeleux, "La Mécanique verbale," *La Recherche* (September 1974), no. 48, pp. 734–43.

12. Sigmund Freud, *Civilization and Its Discontents*, seventh paragraph (*GW* 14:427–28; *SE* 22:70). See also Conrad Stein, "Rome imaginaire," *L'Inconscient* (1967), 1:1–30. Freud's idea-image, which is incompatible with iconic flattening, is grounded on the interaction of stratified structures within the same area: a *diachrony within synchrony*. It anticipates the concept of the city that is sought in works suggesting archeological spatial organizations in motion within the spatial structure manifest today, or heightened by an analysis. See A. Van Eyck, *Meaning in Architecture* (New Haven: Yale University Press, 1960).

13. In the letters sent to his friends during his last years (to Pfister, Zweig, etc.), Freud tells how, under his very eyes, his body falls apart piece by piece. The body appears to be like a writing that is disaggregated. A continuity between the body and the text involves writing in the process of aging, while pictorial or musical expression escapes this fate better; among many painters and composers, a reverse process is evident.

14. The most patent instance is that of the two contradictory prefaces kept at the threshold of the third essay (*GW* 16:156–60; *SE* 23:54–58).

15. As one detail among many others, Freud leaves the trace of the successive publications that the complete *Moses* text assembles. Thus, the second essay begins: "In an earlier contribution to this periodical [*Imago*] . . ." (*GW* 16:114; *SE* 23:17). The French tranlation loses this trace ("dans le premier *chapitre* de ce *livre*"). It hides the break. The fragmented text thus receives the appearance of a scholarly and continuous discourse, of a "book." These transformations are not without analogy to the mutation of "intertestamentary writings" in the Bible in the course of the second century. See André Paul, *L'Impertinence biblique* (Paris: Desclée de Brouwer, 1974), 57ff.

16. In this expression, the structure of the Aggada may be found—as is the case everywhere in the Freudian text. See Dan Amos, *Narrative Forms of Haggadah* (Indianapolis: 1969). See also below, the end of the section "Writing in the Language of the Other, or Fiction."

17. D. A. F. Sade, "Idée sur les romans," preface to *Les Crimes de l'amour,* in *Oeuvres complètes du Marquis de Sade* (Paris: Cercle du Livre Précieux, 1966), 10:16. Sade responds to "the perpetual objection" of those who ask "what good are novels": "For you, hypocrites and perverts . . . they are worthy in depicting you as you are." In respect to the novel—to its contents, its evolution, or its relation with historiography—Sade reasons according to the schema of "either/ or." For Freud, the alternative pertains to representation.

18. Sade, "Idée sur les romans," p. 16. The emphasis is Sade's.

19. Max Brod, *Franz Kafkas Glauben und Lehre* (Winterthur: Mondial-Verlag 1948), quoted by Marthe Robert in Franz Kafka, *Journal* (Paris: Grasset, 1954), p. xvii.

20. No doubt it is within this perspective that we have to understand Freud's desire to be "accepted" as a professor; on this last point, see Carl E. Schorske, "Politique et parricide dans *L'Interprétation des rêves* de Freud," *Annales E. S. C.* (1973), 28:309–28.

21. "In Vienna-Grinzing," notes Freud to Zweig (letter of February 21, 1936, in *Letters of Freud and Zweig,* p. 122). Nazi excommunication thus surprises him, just as it does the Jewish members of the German intelligentsia when, all of a sudden, they are treated as foreigners. Yet he is not duped by this establishment, any more than he is seduced by an installation in Israel, even if he writes to Zweig, who tries the experiment, "Everywhere else you would be a scarcely tolerated alien" (*ibid.*). For Freud, "foreignness" is figured in the relation between the Austrian *home* ("Vienna-Grinzing") and the *fantasy* ("about Moses"), between the place and writing.

22. See Hegel, *The Phenomenology of Mind* (New York: Harper and Row, 1967), pp. 754 and 807–08.

23. Franz Kafka to Max Brod, June 1921, in Franz Kafka, *Letters to Friends, Family, and Editors* (New York: Schocken Books, 1977), p. 289.

24. It must be noted that *gehören* is the term Freud uses to characterize his relation with the Jews in his May 6, 1926 Allocution to the Members of the B'nai B'rith Association (*GW* 17:53; *SE* 20:273).

25. Even the psychoanalytical history of psychoanalysis practices this "lapse of memory." One example can suffice, simply because it deals with the remarkable "Contribution à l'étude de l'histoire du mouvement psychanalytique," *Scilicet* (1973), 4:323–43. The study is faithful to the discipline of the French Freudian school, in the site of its publication (*Scilicet* is the organ of the Freudian school), in the anonymity of the author (as in the "priestly tradition" of which Freud speaks, the review knows only the proper name of the founding father), etc. Even more, this "contribution" that aims at Lacan everywhere in its study of Freud does respect the linguistic taboo. "Blasphemy" (which would transgress the prohibition against uttering a proper name—Lacan's) is replaced here by the "euphemy" of historical apologue: the name is never pronounced. By means of this strict observance of the laws of the society, the text can declare, "Psychoanalysis is fundamentally asocial, and to speak of a psychoanalytical society is a contradiction in terms" (*ibid.,* p. 341). This discourse *expresses* the contrary of what it *does*. Such is the "legend" of a school: what *must* be said, *then and there*. The conditions of its production are not inserted within the text as rifts and lacunae of such a pretty "doctrine."

26. See Freud's preface to the Hebrew translation of *Totem and Taboo* (1920) in *SE* 13:xv.

27. How can we fail to apply this to the Freudian text itself, when it states of its object, "The Exodus . . . from Egypt remains our starting point" (*GW* 16:137; *SE* 23:37)? Departure (*Auszug*) from the land is the beginning (*Ausgangspunkt*) of writing.

28. See for example André Paul, "De la mort de la langue (terre et culture) à l'appariton d'une Torah biblique," in *L'Impertinence biblique*, pp. 74–84; or Ernest Gugenheim, "Le Judaïsme après la révolte de Bar-Kokheba," in *Histoire des religions* (Paris: Gallimard-Pléiade), 2:697–748: "Hereafter, the *Torah* will be the site of their homeland." On several occasions Freud himself refers to Rabbi Jochanan ben Sakkaï's foundation of the school of Jabneh after the destruction of the Temple of Jerusalem, especially at the time of the emigration of the Psychoanalytical Society from Vienna to London: "We are going to do the same. We are, after all, used to persecution by our history, tradition and some of us by personal experience," he remarked, as quoted by Ernest Jones in *The Life and Work of Sigmund Freud*, 3 vols., (London: Hogarth Press, 1957), 3:236. To depart for London is tantamount to going to Jabneh, to pursue Scripture in a foreign land. This work is more essential than the reconstitution of a homeland. An old axiom said, "One must interrupt the teaching of a school, even for the reconstruction of the Temple"; quoted in Marcel Simon, *Verus Israel* (Paris: Boccard, 1948), p. 30.

29. Sigmund Freud, *The Birth of the Psychoanalytical Movement* (New York: Basic Books, 1954), p. 171; letter to Wilhelm Fliess, November 2, 1896, on the dream "during the night after the burial." In *The Interpretation of Dreams* (1900; *SE* 6:317–18), Freud once again describes this dream that came upon him "during the night before my father's funeral," when he emphasizes the ambiguity of the expression "close the eyes," meaning to bury the father and to be indulgent. See also Marthe Robert, *D'Oedipe à Moïse* (Paris: Calmann-Lévy, 1974), pp. 143–217: "On est prié de fermer les yeux."

30. Freud, *The Interpretation of Dreams, SE* 6:317.

31. Sigmund Freud, "The Moses of Michelangelo" (1914), *SE* 13:213.

32. *Ibid.*, p. 220.

33. *Ibid.*, pp. 233 and 235.

34. Conrad Stein, *L'Enfant imaginaire* (Paris: Denoël, 1971), p. 34.

35. Walter Benjamin, *Mythe et violence* (Paris: Denoël, 1971), p. 316. In the Proustian "labor of memorization," the author adds, "memory is packing its bags, while oblivion is content." [See "The Image of Proust," in *Illuminations* (New York: Schocken, 1969), pp. 201–15.——TR.]

36. Maria Torok, "Maladie du deuil et fantasme du cadavre exquis," *Revue française de psychanalyse* (1968), vol. 23, no. 4. Cf. J. Trilling, "Freud, Abraham, et le Pharaon," p. 220.

37. We know that for some time Freud thought of naming "destrudo" what he later called the "death drive." He thus was thinking of opposing it more directly to the libido.

38. Jacques Lacan, "Hommage à Marguerite Duras, du ravissement de Lol V. Stein," in *Marguerite Duras* (Paris: Editions Albatros, 1980), p. 95. ["We must recall that for Freud in his field the artist always comes first and that he does not play at being a psychologist wherever the artist leads the way."——TR.]

39. These are the last lines of the second poem, "The Gods of Greece" ("Die Griechenlands," 1800), on the death of the gods:

> Was unsterblich im Gesang soll leben
> Muss im Leben untergehen.

[English translation by E. A. Bowring in Sigmund Freud, *Moses and Monotheism* (New York: Vintage, 1939), p. 130——TR.]

40. Georges Bataille, "La Notion de dépense," in *La Part maudite* (Paris: Seuil-Points, 1971), p. 28.

41. James Joyce, *Giacomo Joyce* (Paris: Gallimard, 1973), p. 16. [De Certeau alludes to Jan Pieterzoon Sweelinck's "Mein junges Leben hat ein End," which Joyce quotes in *Ulysses* (New York: Random House, 1961), p. 663.——TR.]

42. See Jacques Lacan, *Le Séminaire,* book 20, *Encore* (Paris: Seuil, 1975), pp. 86–87 and 99.

43. "Men have always known"—but (Freud adds in parenthesis)—*in this special way,*" that is, through the work of repression, "that they once possessed a primal father and killed him" (*GW* 16:208; *SE* 28:101). Here I leave aside the

textual indications about the *topography* of this knowledge. In order to define where (by whom) this knowledge has been kept and in what form its tradition persists, Freud refers to a "people's unconscious": he establishes, but merely in passing, a fundamental place for the efficacy of the tradition.

44. David Bakan, "Le Thème de Moïse dans la pensée de Freud," in *Freud et la tradition mystique juive* (Paris: Payot, 1964), pp. 107–52.

45. Marthe Robert, "Le Dernier Roman," in *D'Oedipe à Moïse*, pp. 219–78. According to her interpretation, comparison with Kafka's "Brief an den Vater" (1919) is necessary. See Franz Kafka, *Dearest Father: Stories and Other Writings* (New York: Schocken Books, 1954).

46. "Psychoanalysis is as conservative as it seems to be revolutionary, for its founder is a rebellious son who defends paternal authority, a revolutionary who, through fear of his own revolt as a son, took refuge in the security of the paternal role, which however had already been, from an ideological standpoint, disinte-grated," notes Otto Rank in *Modern Education* (New York: Knopf-Vintage, 1932); quoted by Michèle Bouraux-Harteman, "Du fils," *Topique* (1974), no. 14, pp. 63–64.

47. Thus, finally, "The original form of that tradition is unknown to us" (*GW* 16:132; *SE* 23:33).

48. Claude Lévi-Strauss, *The Naked Man* (New York: Harper and Row, 1981), p. 644.

49. Freud, *The Interpretation of Dreams*, GW 23:488.

50. The role that Shakespeare's *Hamlet* plays in Freud's work is well known. It is one of the texts that he quotes most often; see *GW* 5:19; 6:10, 43–44; 10:432; 14:314.

51. Freud thus names Moses. See his letter of April 28, 1938, quoted in Ernest Jones, *Sigmund Freud*, 3:240.

52. See Marthe Robert, *D'Oedipe à Moïse*, p. 276.

53. "A Disturbance of Memory on the Acropolis. Letter to Romain Rolland" (1936), *GW* 16:255 and *SE* 22:246. Once again we can note the founding re-lation that the Freudian *earth*, his edifice (*Aufbau*), upholds with an exclusion, a "contestation," an *exodus*.

54. See Marthe Robert, *D'Oedipe à Moïse,*, p. 36, n. 3.

55. "A Disturbance of Memory on the Acropolis," quoting the complaint of the Spanish Moor: *Ay de mi Alhama* (*GW* 16:255 and *SE* 22:246).

56. [The author is playing on what in *The Practice of Everyday Life* (Berkeley and Los Angeles: University of California Press, 1984) he entitles *arts de faire*, or the "arts of making," doing, or producing, as a practice that is intransitive and always ongoing (pp. 29–44). To analyze perpetually is an act—an art—of doing which marks a positive intellectual activity, not unlike that of the artist who changes the shape and form of objects making up the decor of everyday life.——TR.]

57. Freud took up the subject on several occasions (*GW* 8:74; 10:104, etc.) after he had first dealt with it in 1909 in "Family Romances," *SE* 9 (*Der Fam-ilienroman der Neurotiker, GW* 7:227–31. This study, which had been intended for inclusion in Rank's *Myth of the Birth of the Hero* (1909), was published only

in 1924 (see Jones, *Sigmund Freud,* 2:273 and 372). Freud shows how the "detachment" (*Ablösung*) that follows children's "overestimation" of their parents can lead them to feel themselves "adopted" by the family in which they live, hence born elsewhere, issued from a family of higher status. In the "romance," the sense of being the son from another bed (*Stiefkind*) puts a "noble" father in the place of an overly common father (*pater semper incertus est*) and often attributes sexual infidelities to the mother (*certissima*).

58. See James Henry Breasted, *The Dawn of Conscience* (London and New York: Scribner's, 1934).

59. Freud adds in a footnote, "It is far from being my intention to belittle the value of Rank's independent contributions to this work" (*GW* 16:106, n. 2; *SE* 23:10). Here there is a conflict (of two names) over the same thesis (or place). Yet Freud still names and quotes Rank, while he completely covers over Karl Abraham's name and work in taking up once again—almost verbatim—his thoughts on Ikhnaton (moreover, these are also based on Breasted and Rank). "The first important man in the spiritual realm of which the history of humanities informs us," Abraham notes, Ikhnaton "refuses paternal authority" and "the *Tradition* transmitted by the father" in "the desire to be self-conceived, to be his own father"; for a founding father, he adds, there is the neurosis of the son's erasing the father's footsteps. See "Amenhotep IV. Psycho-analytical Contributions Towards the Understanding of His Personality and the Monotheistic Cult of Aton," in Karl Abraham, *Clinical Papers and Essays on Psycho-analysis* (London: The Hogarth Press, 1955), pp. 262–90. See also the letters between Freud and Abraham on the same topic, from January to June 1912, in *A Psycho-analytic Dialogue: The Letters of Sigmund Freud and Karl Abraham,* H. C. Abraham and E. L. Freud, eds. (London: Hogarth Press, 1965). Has the disciple (who died in 1925) been effaced because he touched on the repression of the father by the founding father? See also Trilling, "Freud, Abraham, et le Pharaon."

60. In his study of 1909 (see note 57), Freud distinguished three moments in the father's life: the *overesteemed* father, the *rejected* father, and the father *replaced* by the son. These three moments correspond to the three places through which the hero of the myth circulates.

61. A "call to take root" (*behaupten . . . seine Bodenstandigkeit, GW* 16:147) —to claim to reattach oneself to the soil and sustain oneself through alliance with the favored ground—that is the illusion.

62. Freud to Zweig, February 13, 1935, in *Letters of Freud and Zweig,* p. 102.

63. "Unsere Fäden weiter zu spinnen": in order to weave our (spider's) web and to thicken our plot. Mentioned on several occasions, this objective justifies recourse to the "hypotheses" and "ideas" that Freud amasses from all sides insofar as they provide him with what he needs to fuel the action of his detective novel.

64. See *GW* 16:137–38, in respect to the *Judah* and *Israel,* these "quite different elements" which "have been placed together for the edification [*Aufbau*] of the Jewish people." Thus *national unity* appears everywhere as a lure of the name and as a source of illusion (see also *GW* 16:103, 110, 137, 138, and 142 etc).

65. Jacques Lacan, *L'Ethique de la psychanalyse,* unpublished seminar of 1959–60; his lecture of March 16, 1960.

66. Exodus 3:14. See for example Michel Allard, "Note sur la formule 'Ehyeh ašer ehyeh,'" *Recherches de science religieuse* (1957), 44:79–86.

67. Exodus 3:5 and 16.

68. Because I was a Jew . . ."; Allocution to the Members of B'nai B'rith, May 6, 1926 (*GW* 13:52).

69. In respect to Heidegger and "Western history," see Emmanuel Levinas, *Totalité et infini* (The Hague: Nijhoff, 1971), p. 17.

70. *Ibid.,* p. 17.

71. On this postulate of "place" in the construction of historiography, see chapters 2 and 5 above.

72. See *Der Familienroman der Neurotiker* (1909), *GW* 7:229.

73. "The Uncanny," *SE* 17:219 ("Das Unheimliche," *GW* 12:266).

74. Freud to Zweig, May 8, 1932, in *Letters of Freud and Zweig,* p. 40.

75. [De Certeau is quoting "Inhibitions, Symptoms, and Anxiety," *SE* 20:90. See chapter 5, n. 62 above.——TR.]

76. Freud, quoted in Jones, *Sigmund Freud,* 3:308ff.

77. *Ibid.*

78. Theodor Reik, "The Moses of Michelangelo and the Scene of the Sinai," in *Ritual: Psycho-analytic Studies* (New York: Farrar, Straus and Giroux, 1946), pp. 305–62. In his preface to the French edition (Paris: Denoël, 1974), Jacques Hassoun finds in Reik an "echo of his own expression, recognized as inspired by this familiar other" (p. 14).

79. Theodor Reik, "The Foreign God and Our Own God," abstract of the proceedings of the Sixth International Psycho-Analytical Congress, in *The International Journal of Psycho-Analysis* (London, 1920), 1:350.

80. Jakob Wassermann, *Les Juifs de Zirndorf* (Pierre-Jean Oswald, 1973), p. 227.

81. On the relation of the "imprint" and the "graph," see my *L'Absent de l'histoire* (Paris: Mame, 1973), pp. 177–80, where I deal with the other modern myth, of Robinson Crusoe.

82. Frederic Nietzsche, *Twilight of the Idols,* in W. Kauffmann, ed., *The Portable Nietzsche* (New York: Viking, 1954), p. 492ff. See also Philippe Lacoue-Labarthe, "La Fable (littérature et philosophie)," *Poétique,* (1970), no. 1, pp. 51–63.

83. Georges Dumézil, *Du mythe au roman* (Paris: PUF, 1970), pp. 122–23.

84. Claude Lévi-Strauss, *The Origin of Table Manners* (New York: Harper and Row, 1979), p. 131.

85. Hélène Cixous, "La Fiction et ses fantômes: Une lecture de l'*Unheimliche* de Freud," in *Prénoms de personne* (Paris: Seuil, 1973).

86. Jean Cavaillès, *Sur la logique et la théorie de la science* (Paris: PUF, 1960), p. 78.

Index

Absence, past as, 85
Abstract objects of knowledge, 73
Abstraction, structural, 75–76
Academies, seventeenth-century, 135, 145n32
Act, Freudian, 305–5
Acta sanctorum, Bolland and Henskens, 271
Action: history-producing, 30; socialization of, 160–61
Administrative apparatus, eighteenth-century church, 189
Allegory, x–xi, 134–35, 136, 145n34
Almanacs, 191
Alterity, xviii–xix, 85, 134, 209; of diabolic possession, 247; discourse of, 250–51; and heresy, 151; language and, 224; marvels, 227; medieval, 150; narrative movement, 220–23; in primitive society, 219
Ambivalence: of God and the devil, 293; of *Moses and Monotheism,* 312
Amenhotep, 338
America: allegory of, xxv; dissimilarities of, 218–29; sanctuary in, 199n72
American historians, 110n82

Analysis, 69; contemporary, 75–76; Freudian, 292; historical, 31
Animism, xii
Anti-intellectualism, 143n9, 184
Anti-Semitism, Freud and, 309–10, 314, 317, 349n21
Apologetics, seventeenth-century, 151–52
The Archaeology of Knowledge, Foucault, 60
Archeology, 8, 12, 14; and religious history, 19; and sociological model of religion, 25
Archives, 74–77, 107n54
Argenson, René d', 169
Ariès, Philippe, 100
Aristotle, 93, 236
Aron, Raymond, 30, 58, 59–60
Associations, seventeenth-century, 135
Athanasius, *Life of Saint Anthony,* 270
Atheism, 135, 193n23; seventeenth-century, 153–54; and state, 202n108
Aton, 337, 338
Authorial "we," 63–64
Auxiliary science, 69

Bach, Johann Sebastian, 184, 203n121
Bachelard, Gaston, 28

European Perspectives

A Series of Columbia University Press